Essential Works of Chinese Communism

ESSENTIAL WORKS OF CHINESE COMMUNISM

Edited
and with an
Introduction by
WINBERG CHAI

PICA PRESS
New York City

Published in the United States of America in 1970
by PICA PRESS
Distributed by Universe Books
381 Park Avenue South, New York City 10016

Copyright © 1969 by Bantam Books, Inc.

Library of Congress Catalog Card Number: LC 75-99755
SBN 87663-703-9

ACKNOWLEDGMENTS

"First Manifesto of the CCP on the Current Situation" and
"Manifesto of the Second National Congress of the CCP" are
reprinted with permission from A Documentary History of
Chinese Communism *by Conrad Brandt, Benjamin Schwartz and John K.
Fairbank, Harvard University Press, Cambridge, Mass., and George
Allen & Unwin Ltd., London.*

*"On the Intra-Party Struggle" by Liu Shao-chi is reprinted with
permission from* Mao's China: Party Reform Documents *by Boyd
Compton, University of Washington Press, Seattle.*

Printed in the United States of America

This book is humbly dedicated to my parents,
Dr. and Mrs. Ch'u Chai,
in gratitude for their love, encouragement and
unfailing interest.

Preface

THIS BOOK includes a comprehensive collection of thirty-one major works of Chinese Communism from the "First Manifesto" of the Party Central Committee on the situation in China in 1922, through the major works of Mao Tse-tung, Liu Shao-chi, Lin Piao and P'eng Chen, to a July, 1968, Chinese newspaper editorial.

This book is intended as an introduction to the study of Chinese Communism. As such, it is not a complete history of the growth of Communism in China, although the works are arranged chronologically. For the non-specialists on China, the editor has written an introduction describing the development of Chinese Communism since 1921. He has written additional notes preceding each document.

In preparation of this work, the editor is most indebted to his father and co-worker for many years, Dr. Ch'u Chai, without whose guidance and contributions this project could never have been completed. He also wishes to acknowledge valuable assistance freely rendered to him by his colleagues. Thanks are due also to authors and publishers who have graciously given permission to reprint materials in this volume.

The editor is also most appreciative to the publishers, especially Miss Jean Highland, and to the Haynes Foundation of Los Angeles for a research grant during the summer of 1968 to make the writing of this work possible. My acknowledgments would indeed be incomplete if I did not record the personal debt I owe to my wife, Carolyn, not only for her patience and support, but also for reading and commenting on many parts of the manuscript.

Winberg Chai

Redlands, California
December, 1968

Contents

Chronology of the Growth
of Chinese Communism: 1921–1968

1921   Chinese Communist Party founded in Shanghai

1922   Central Committee of CCP issues its "First Manifesto"

1923   Kuomintang-Comintern collaboration

1924   Beginning of "Northern Expedition" to unify China

1925   Sun Yat-sen dies; May 30th Movement

1926   Canton coup, first break between Chiang Kai-shek and Chinese Communists

1927   Mao Tse-tung leads peasant insurrection in Hunan; CCP expelled from KMT

1928   Mao Tse-tung and Chu Teh establish guerrilla base in Kiangsi

1929   Li Li-san line begins

1930   Chiang Kai-shek begins "extermination campaigns" against Communists

1931   Chinese Soviet Republic formed in Kiangsi

1932   Communists declare war on Japan

1933   Chiang Kai-shek continues "extermination campaigns"

1934   Communists' "Long March" begins

1935   Mao Tse-tung wins control of CCP

1936   Sian Incident, Chiang Kai-shek kidnapped

1937   Second "united front" between KMT and CCP; Sino-Japanese War begins

1938   Clashes between KMT and CCP resume; Japan occupies large areas of China

1939   Wang Ching-wei sets up puppet regime in Japanese-occupied Nanking

1940   War resistance against Japan continues

1941   KMT attacks Communist "New Fourth Route Army"

1942   *"Cheng-feng"* Movement (rectification) within CCP

1943   Cairo Declaration restores Taiwan to China

1944   Communists attend "Constitutional Convention" in Chungking sponsored by KMT

1945   Japan surrenders; Marshall mission sent to China to form a "coalition government" of CCP and KMT

1946   Full-scale civil war erupts between CCP and KMT

1947   KMT troops occupy Yenan; Communists consolidate control over Manchuria under the protection of Soviet troops

1948   Communists begin major offensive in China

1949   Chiang abdicates to pave way for peace talks; Communists establish People's Republic in Peking on October 1; United States publishes White Paper on China; KMT re-establishes its government in Taiwan

1950   Sino-Soviet Treaty of Friendship and Alliance concluded; Communist China enters Korean War

1951   Thought reform movement launched in China

1952   Land reform program completed

1953   Inauguration of First Five Year Plan; Korean armistice concluded

1954   New Constitution of the People's Republic of China proclaimed; Geneva Conference begins on Indochina

1955   First major purge begins with Kao Kang expelled from Party; China attends Bandung Conference

1956   Khrushchev denounces Stalin in the Twentieth Party Congress of the CPSU; China begins "Hundred Flowers" movement; Eighth Party Congress of CCP convenes in Peking

1957   Anti-rightist movement begins in China; Mao visits Moscow

1958   Great Leap Forward begins; people's communes established

1959   China suppresses Tibetan revolt; second major purge with resignation of Defense Minister P'eng Teh-huai; Liu Shaochi succeeds Mao as Chairman of Republic

1960   Sino-Soviet disputes in an "open stage"; Soviet technicians withdraw from China; China in deep economic crisis

1961   Chou En-lai arrives in Moscow for Twenty-second Party Congress; Sino-Soviet relations worsen

1962   Sino-Indian border clashes; CCP publicly attacks Soviet "revisionism"; China begins "socialist education" campaigns

1963   Test-Ban Treaty concluded; China refuses to sign

1964   CCP rejects Soviet call for world conference of Communist parties; Gulf of Tonkin resolution adopted by United States; Khrushchev falls and China explodes first atomic bomb

1965 Major changes within CCP; Chinese army ranks abolished; Lin Piao publishes important article on "people's wars"

1966 Third major purge begins within CCP; Mayor of Peking P'eng Chen is dismissed; Central Committee meets in Eleventh Plenary Session and adopts resolution on "Great Proletarian Cultural Revolution"; Red Guards formed in Chinese universities and secondary schools; mass demonstrations supporting Chairman Mao against Chairman of Republic Liu Shao-chi begin

1967 Cultural Revolution continues in Communist China; Liu Shao-chi is denounced as China's Khrushchev; major purges within CCP continue

1968 Cultural Revolution continues; "Revolutionary Committees" formed on local level to replace Party organizations; reorganization of Chinese Communist Party contemplated; Liu Shao-chi was expelled from the Party by the "Enlarged 12th Plenary Session of the 8th Central Committee of the Communist Party of China" on Oct. 31, 1968

Introduction: Historical Setting

THE PERIOD from the end of the 19th century to the establishment of the People's Republic of China in 1949 was an age of great social disturbance, political instability and intellectual anarchy. The age tended toward skepticism and destructiveness. All established institutions—marriage, the family, society, the state, the law—came in for destructive criticism. The general character of Chinese thought in this half century (1898–1949) was intimately connected with political, social and moral events of the time. Christianity had acquired a firm foothold in China, and with it came Western science and philosophy. The pragmatic theories of John Dewey[1] and the dynamic doctrines of Karl Marx[2] exerted a tremendous influence on Chinese intellectuals. Meanwhile, translations from the works of eminent Western writers such as Tolstoy, Ibsen, Maupassant, Shelley, Emerson, and Marx and Engels were extensively undertaken.

Intellectuals revolted against age-old traditions which they thought were detrimental to the new forces of progress. This intellectual revolt started with the Reform Movement of 1898

---

[1]Hu Shih introduced pragmatism, especially that of John Dewey, his former teacher, to China. During his sojourn in China from 1919 to 1921 Dewey spoke at universities in eleven provinces, explaining his ideas, especially on the subject of education.

[2] Ch'en Tu-hsiu, founder of the Chinese Communist Party, and Li Ta-ch'ao were the first exponents of Marxist theses in China.

1

(June 11 to September 16) and reached its climax in the New Culture Movement (1917–1921).

The Reform Movement was led by K'ang Yu-wei, who wanted a constitutional monarchy supported by officials of a new type, similar to those of the Meiji era in Japan. But the Reform Movement aroused a storm of opposition from those who by conviction or interest were wedded to the old order. After the failure of the Reform Movement, K'ang went abroad and continued to write and raise funds in behalf of the movement. However, he no longer played any important part in Chinese politics and his place was soon taken over by Sun Yat-sen, who turned the Reform Movement into a revolution.

Sun Yat-sen's revolutionary ideas might be traced back to 1885, when China was defeated by France. He then believed that a revolutionary movement might replace the decadent Manchu dynasty and its imperial system with a republican government. Despite many reverses and persecutions Sun's revolution broke out in October, 1911, and succeeded in overthrowing the Manchu dynasty.

However, China continued to face economic difficulties, ideological conflicts and political chaos. Political power very soon passed into the hands of Yüan Shih-k'ai, a political opportunist and militarist. As a result, China was torn by civil wars among the warlords for thirteen years. Meanwhile, the Armistice of 1918 and promulgation of Wilson's Fourteen Points brought to a new high point the faith of the Chinese people in the liberal democracy of the West. Now the Chinese leaders hoped that foreign domination, especially Japan's seizure of Shantung of 1914 and its twenty-one demands of 1915, would come to an end. But when the bitter news of the defeat at the Paris peace table of the Chinese attempt to restore full Chinese sovereignty reached China, shortly before May 4, 1919, the reaction was immediate: some five thousand students from Peking University and other institutions staged a demonstration against the Versailles settlement. The May 4th Movement has been regarded by the Communists as the basis for the founding of the Chinese Communist Party.[3] Within a year after the May 4th Move-

---

[3] In his "On New Democracy" (Selection 12), Mao Tse-tung called the year 1919 the turning point at which the "capitalist cultural revolution of the world bourgeoisie" became "part of the socialist cultural revolution of the world proletariat."

ment many "Marxist Study Groups" had been organized in major cities. The Charter members and early leaders of the Chinese Communist Party were young intellectuals rather than people from the ranks of industrial labor, the armed forces or the peasantry. Had it not been for the intervention of the Moscow leaders, through the Communist International (Comintern), the Communist movement in China might have remained academic and theoretical. The Chinese Communist Party was in fact a creation of the Comintern and was closely controlled by Moscow from the very beginning. Nevertheless, it is best to attempt to trace its history in order to assess the forces and factors which contributed to the triumph of Communism on the mainland of China.

Communist historians divide the years from 1921 to 1949 into four periods: the founding of the Party and the First Revolutionary Civil War (1921–1927); the Second Revolutionary Civil War (1927–1937); the War of Resistance Against Japanese Aggression (1937–1945); and the Third Revolutionary Civil War (1945–1949).

I. The First Revolutionary Civil War (1921–1927)

1. *Birth of the CCP:* The founding of the Chinese Communist Party (CCP) can be traced to the formation of a society for the study of Marxism by Ch'en Tu-hsiu and Li Ta-ch'ao in 1918, and various other Marxist study groups after the May 4th Movement. For example, there was the Enlightenment Society in Tientsin led by Chou En-lai and Teng Yin-chao and the Benefit Book Club in Hupei organized by Yun Tai-ying. These study groups were not purely Marxist, however. In fact many groups were directed by two agents of the Third International—Gregory Voitinsky and an overseas Chinese, Yang Ming-chai. With their assistance, Communist groups were brought into existence in Shanghai in May, in Peking and Changsha in September, and in Canton at the end of 1920. Before long, Chinan, Hangchow, Wuhan, Tokyo and Paris had Chinese Communist groups. In addition, Ch'en Tu-hsiu initiated the socialist youth corps in August,

and Ch'en's example was followed by Mao Tse-tung in Changsha (Hunan).

These groups were small in number.[4] For example, the Shanghai group had seven members, but later four left it; the Peking group had, in addition to Li Ta-ch'ao and Chang Kuo-t'ao, eight anarchists; the Canton group, organized by Ch'en Tu-hsiu during his visit, included T'an Ping-shan, Ch'en Kung-po and several anarchists, and later all the anarchists withdrew. Finally, Ch'en Tu-hsiu began a reorganization campaign with the establishment of a socialist youth corps at Peking University with fifty-five members. This Peking group ran workers' evening classes and published *Labor's Voice*. The Shanghai group also ran evening classes and published a workers' tabloid, *Labor World*, and the Canton group followed the same pattern by setting up workers' schools and publishing *Labor's Echo*.

Certainly Moscow was keeping a watchful eye on developments in China. In order to transfer the Communist movement in China from the intellectuals to the workers, the Comintern dispatched an important agent, G. Maring (also known as Henricus Sneevliet) to attend the formal organization meeting of the Chinese Communist Party. For the purpose of subterfuge, the delegates to the First Congress of the CCP gathered at the Po-ai Girls' School in the French Concession of Shanghai on July 1, 1921. Later, to avoid police harassment, the Congress was moved to the South Lake of Chiahsing. The twelve delegates—Chang Kuo-t'ao, Ch'en Kung-po, Ch'en Tan-chiu, Chou Fo-hai, Ho Shu-heng, Li Han-chun, Li Ta, Liu Jen-ching, Mao Tse-tung, Teng En-ming, Tung Pi-wu and Wang Ching-mei—representing only fifty-seven members, opened a new chapter in Chinese history and grew to the largest Communist party in the world with effective control over 700 million people.

Much of the records for the First Congress have been lost. It is known however that the delegates adopted a Party Constitution and elected a Central Committee, which consisted of Ch'en Tu-hsiu as party secretary (he was in Canton during the Congress meeting in Shanghai); Chang Kuo-t'ao as head of the organization department; Li Ta as head of the propaganda department; and three alternate members, Chou Fo-hai, Li Han-chun and Liu Jen-ching. Mao Tse-tung was

---

[4] For a detailed study of the Chinese Communist Party see Jerome Ch'en, *Mao and the Chinese Revolution*, New York: Oxford University Press, 1965.

sent back to his native province, Hunan, as the secretary of the Hunan branch of the CCP. His tasks included the re-education of the members of the former socialist youth corps so as to induct them into the Chinese Communist Party. In addition, the labor movement began in earnest after the First Congress and strikes were held in many parts of China. It is of course true that the success of the Communists was due in no small measure to the fact that industrial labor in China was already ripe for organization. In fact, China at this time had no organized labor, and working conditions were most deplorable and no effective remedy was ever made on the workers' behalf.

The Second Congress, which was held in June and July, 1922 in Hangchow,[5] adopted two important documents: the First Manifesto (Selection 1) and the Manifesto of the Second National Congress (Selection 2). In the First Manifesto, the Party had urged the calling of a conference "to be participated in by the revolutionary elements of the Kuomintang (KMT) and revolutionary socialists, to discuss the question of creating a united front for struggle against the warlords of the feudal type and against all relics of feudalism."[6] In the July Manifesto, it made clear that support for the Kuomintang was temporary and did not imply surrender to the capitalists. In addition, the Second Party Congress made a formal decision to join the Comintern and set up a Political Bureau within the Party. Ch'en Tu-hsiu was re-elected Secretary-General and Chairman of the Political Bureau.

In August, 1922, Maring, the Comintern representative, proposed to a special plenum of the CCP Central Committee that a Communist bloc be formed inside, instead of alongside, the KMT, so as to make the KMT "the central force of the national revolution," as instructed by the Comintern. The Party leaders, including Ch'en Tu-hsiu, opposed this plan on the ground that it would cost the Party its class independence. Maring countered this objection by declaring that the KMT was, in fact, a multi-class Party. This view, as advanced by Maring, was "clearly in conflict with the Marxist concept of parties as organs of single, individual class interest."[7] As a re-

---

[5] The official Communist record says Shanghai.
[6] See the First Manifesto of the CCP on the Current Situation (Selection 1).
[7] See Conrad Brandt *et al.*, *A Documentary History of Chinese Communism*, Cambridge, Mass.: Harvard University Press, 1959, p. 52.

sult, Maring invoked the Party discipline of the Comintern to force adoption of his plan.

2. *The First KMT–CCP Alliance:* After the overthrow of the Manchu dynasty, China was in a state of almost complete political disintegration. Leaders of regional military organizations and cliques, known as "warlords," with the encouragement of foreign powers, fought among themselves for power and control of the central government, which had become merely a pawn of the warlords.

After the establishment of the Republic, Sun Yat-sen was forced to pass his power to Yüan Shih-k'ai, who fought against the revolutionaries. With the promise of the Presidency of the new Republic from Sun, Yüan helped to bring about the end of the throne. In 1916, Yüan proclaimed himself the new Emperor of China. Upon his death, Chinese politics was dominated by the struggles of warlords. Among these there was the Manchurian warlord, Chang Tso-lin, an ex-bandit who had risen as Japan's ally against Russia. Others included Wu P'ei-fu, who ruled central China, and Feng Yü-hsiang, the "Christian general" who fought and destroyed the power of the Peiyang warlords.

During these years of trouble Sun Yat-sen continued his work, though ignored by the Western powers. In 1912, his T'ung-meng Hui was reorganized, together with other political groups, into the Kuomintang (Nationalist Party), as an open political party with the purpose of implanting the foundation of the Three People's Principles into the minds and lives of the people.

Sun Yat-sen was greatly influenced by the success of the Bolshevik Revolution in Russia. To the Comintern, Sun's revolutionary movement seemed to have the greatest potential for mass appeal, and offered an instrument for armed struggle against the warlords then in control of the rest of China. By allying themselves with this movement under the leadership of Sun, the Chinese Communists would be able to utilize the prestige of the Kuomintang and operate openly in KMT-controlled areas, thereby broadening their contacts with the masses and strengthening their own power. At the same time, by influencing the policies adopted by the KMT, they would lay the foundation for "a socialist revolution," once they had gained the hegemony they sought.

To carry out the plan as initiated by Maring, the Soviet

representative Adolf Joffe came to China and built up relations with Sun. On January 26, 1923, they issued a joint
statement, which was in fact a strictly limited arrangement.
It stated that "Dr. Sun is of the opinion that, because of the
non-existence of conditions favorable to their successful application in China, it is not possible to carry out either Communism or even the Soviet system in China"; that "M. Joffe
agrees with this view; he is further of the opinion that
China's most important and pressing problems are the completion of national unification and the attainment of full national independence." Sun now sought and accepted Comintern aid, which Joffe assured Sun of "the Russian people's
willingness to lend."

However, the Sun-Joffe Manifesto only marked the open-
ing of the negotiations which were to end with the conclusion
a year later of the KMT–CCP Alliance at the First KMT
Congress in January, 1924. These negotiations were continued
during the summer of 1923 between Joffe and Liao Chung-
kai,[8] a vigorous leader of the KMT Left wing. On the basis
of these negotiations, Sun agreed to adopt the Soviet system
of party organization and government. He also agreed to allow Communists to join the KMT as individuals and to participate in the cause of the national revolution simply because their anti-imperialist aims coincided with those of the
KMT. This policy, which came to be known in the KMT
circles as *yung-kung* (let the Communists join as individuals),
did not, however, imply co-operation between the KMT and
the CCP as equals (known as *lien-kung*).

In the fall of 1923, a Soviet mission headed by Michael
Borodin came to Canton with military supplies and then began reorganization of the KMT and its armies after the
Soviet pattern. Meanwhile, Chiang Kai-shek was sent to Moscow to study the Red Army. Upon his return, Chiang was
named by Sun Yat-sen as President of the Whampoa Military
Academy for the training of Nationalist officers. From the
time of this appointment, Chiang played a decisive role in
the KMT and in the Nationalist government.

In June, 1923, the CCP held its Third Congress in Canton,
attended by thirty members, twenty-seven of whom were delegates, representing 432 members. After heated debates at the
Congress on the question of the united front with KMT as

---

[8] Liao was suddenly and mysteriously assassinated on August 20, 1925.

proposed by the Comintern agent, it passed a resolution that Party members might join the KMT as individuals, but that the Party political and organizational independence should be preserved. The Communist strategy was to build up Party strength within the KMT and ultimately capture the KMT machinery, thereby seizing total power in China.

At this congress Mao Tse-tung was elected to the Party Central Committee.

In 1924, the Chinese Communists received instructions from the Party to join the KMT as individuals. Accordingly, many important Communists, such as Mao Tse-tung, Lin Tsu-han, Li Ta-ch'ao, Chang Kuo-t'ao, Ch'ü Ch'iu-pai and T'an P'ing-shan, who joined the KMT, worked either as commissars in the army or as cadres in central and local Party headquarters. Under the protection of the KMT, the Chinese Communists embarked on a period of rapid expansion in size and influence within the KMT. In January, 1924, the Fourth Congress of the CCP, held in Shanghai, reported 950 members, but within a year after this congress membership had soared to over 10,000.

Meanwhile Sun reorganized the KMT and set up the Whampoa Military Academy for the training of an officer corps. Sun also recast his Three Principles of the People (the principle of Nationalism, the principle of democracy and the principle of people's livelihood), and in a new version of his book with this title he showed a friendly attitude toward Soviet Russia, and for the first time, announced the oft-quoted formula that "essentially there is no difference between the Principle of People's Livelihood[9] and Communism."

At this point the Chinese Communists began to create incidents, organize a federation of trade unions, and widen Communist influence among the masses and thus provide a basis for the future hegemony of the proletariat. On May 30, 1925, a nation-wide anti-imperialist patriotic movement consisting of demonstrations, strikes and boycotts broke out in Shanghai.

More significant, in view of the later KMT–CCP rupture, is the Communists' attempt to install themselves in key positions within the KMT organization. At the First Congress of

---

[9] The definition of Sun's third principle of the people (a variety of socialism adapted to Chinese conditions) is rather vague; its essential ingredients, however, are equal distribution of land and government control of capital.

the reorganized KMT in 1924, seven Communists who had only recently joined the KMT on an individual basis were elected to its Central Executive Committee.[10] And Communist influence was further extended at the Second Congress of the KMT, held at Canton early in January, 1926. At this congress, one-fourth of the places on the Executive Committee fell to the Communists.[11] It is understandable that the rise of Communist influence within the KMT stirred apprehension and opposition elsewhere in the Party, and particularly among its senior members.

Sun steadfastly discouraged anti-Communist feeling within the KMT and suppressed any open expression of it. In his own mind, what he needed most for the national revolution was Soviet aid and support. He believed, though naively, that it was the KMT and not the CCP the Russians wanted to support. In fact, he wrote early in 1924: "If Russia wants to cooperate with China, it must cooperate with our Party and not with Ch'en Tu-hsiu. If Ch'en disobeys our Party, he will be ousted."[12]

After the death of Sun on March 12, 1925, there followed a time of tension between the Right and Left wings of KMT over the question of collaborating with the CCP. However, the three strong men in Canton after Sun's departure to Peking—Borodin, Chiang Kai-shek and Wang Ching-wei—were all determined, for various reasons, to prevent any break in the KMT–CCP Alliance at this time.

While this alliance was still in force, the National Revolutionary Army under the supreme command of Chiang Kai-shek set out on July 9, 1926, on the famous Northern Expedition from Canton to central China. The purpose of this important military campaign, long planned by Sun Yat-sen before his death on March 12, 1925, was to destroy the northern warlords and unify China. It was also aimed at rising above local conflicts at Canton and expanding the revenue area of the Nationalist government. Under the supreme command of Chiang Kai-shek there were six main armies, mostly reorganized warlord forces. Preceded by its newly trained

---

[10] Li Ta-ch'ao and T'an P'ing-san were named regular members, while five others were made alternate members, including Ch'ü Ch'iu-pai, Chang Kuo-t'ao and Mao Tse-tung.

[11] Of the 36 regular members of Central Executive Committee, 7 were now Communists, as were 7 of the 24 alternate members—Mao Tse-tung remaining as one of the latter.

[12] See "Sun Yat-sen's Comments on an Accusation Against the CCP" in Brandt *et al., op. cit.*, p. 73.

propagandists, the Expedition forces advanced rapidly against opposition, they showed respect for the people and were welcomed by them. They overtook some thirty-four warlord armies by the time they reached the Yangtze River valley.

By the spring of 1927, the KMT and the CCP had each achieved the primary objective of their alliance: a position attained with the help of the other from which it could claim the conquest of power in China. With the support of the Communists, the KMT had built up a party apparatus and a party army to defeat the warlords. Under the protection of the KMT, the CCP had expanded its membership and extended its sway over the masses. Thus each had won a lever with which to strive against the other.

II. *The Second Revolutionary Civil War (1927–1937)*

1. *Rupture of the Alliance:* The Northern Expedition continued its success, although the KMT faced internal political crisis. The KMT Left, now more fearful of Chiang Kaishek's military power, moved the National government from Canton to Wuhan where it was supported by the Communists. And the Communists devoted their energies to the peasant-and-labor movements. Communist-led labor unions in Shanghai and Hankow carried out major strikes. In Shanghai, they even tried to prevent Chiang Kai-shek's army from occupying the city; in Hunan the peasant movement carried out a bloody agrarian revolt in which hundreds of landlords and rich peasants lost their lives.

To meet this challenge to his own position, Chiang had to make a decision: Should he continue to support the KMT Left and co-operate with the Communists and Soviet advisers? Or should he turn to the KMT Right, which was allied with the capitalists, to oust all the Communists and end the two-party alliance? At the siege of Shanghai in 1927, Chiang and his closest colleagues, now established in headquarters at Nanchang in Kiangsi, decided on the second alternative. Shanghai came into Chiang's hands with the aid of the capitalists without a fight on March 22, 1927. Moreover, capital of the Shanghai financiers and industrialists was placed at his disposal, so that he could finance his troops and administration independently of the KMT Left. Assured of financial resources, Chiang made a clear break with the Communists and set up a new regime in Nanking on April 5, 1927.

Although the KMT Left and the Communists had moved the Canton government to Wuhan, they controlled only two provinces, lacked internal unity and depended on armies of dubious loyalty. Moreover, the Comintern had no real intention of upholding the KMT Left under the leadership of Wang Ching-wei, who had returned from abroad. In contrast, Chiang's Nanking government now controlled rich eastern coastal provinces and had large, loyal, unified armies. Assured of the support of the KMT Right and of the Western powers, Chiang began a bloody purge of the Communists on the morning of April 12, 1927, which lasted four days. This purge has since been denounced by the Communists as "the April 12th Massacre."

To counteract Chiang's estrangement from the Communists, the Chinese Communist Party held its Fifth Congress in Hankow in late April and early May, 1927, at which it was reported that the membership had increased to 57,968. The question discussed was how to settle accounts with the Kuomintang and thereby to reorientate "the revolutionary movement." Ch'en Tu-hsiu came in for vigorous criticism and attack, though he was re-elected as Secretary-General of the Party.[13] In accordance with the Comintern's directive, the Communists, while maintaining the alliance with the KMT Left, was to work out a program of its own for taking over the leadership from the "bourgeois elements" within the Wuhan KMT. Meanwhile, Stalin, who had gained control of the Soviet government, issued a set of instructions, among which were the following:

(1) combat peasant excesses by means of the peasant unions rather than by KMT troops and form a new huge army of peasants and workers under the CCP's control;
(2) call for the purge of "reliable" KMT generals and reshuffle the KMT Central Executive Committee;

---

[13] Mao Tse-tung attended the Congress but was deprived of the right to vote by Ch'en's group. His report on the Hunan peasant movement (Selection 3) was suppressed.

(3) reorganize the Wuhan government, headed by Wang Ching-wei, in order to strengthen the leadership of the CCP.

In order to achieve this collaboration, M. N. Roy, the Indian Comintern delegate then in Wuhan, showed these instructions directly to Wang on June 1, 1927. In this manner, Wang learned of the conspiracy by which the CCP was to take over the "leading role" in the KMT. He therefore took steps leading to the suppression of the Communist-led mass movement and the expulsion of the Communists from the Wuhan KMT (June–July, 1927). After these suppression campaigns, the CCP was smashed,[14] and the united front was destroyed. Thus the period from 1924 to 1927, called the "First Revolutionary Civil War," ended in the rupture between the two parties.

Something more may be said about the unrealistic and misleading Comintern directives. After the death of Lenin in 1924, the CCP became subject to the influence of Stalin and the internecine Kremlin intra-Party struggle. It was required to obey Comintern directives issued to help Stalin in his struggle with Trotsky. As far as we know, Stalin and Bukharin at that time were on the same side, and their policy was one of co-operating with the KMT, representing the bourgeoisie. But Trotsky, joined by Zinoviev, warned that the CCP would be the victim of this misleading policy. After the Wuhan disaster, the CCP should have left the KMT. In fact, the CCP had been cast out of the KMT. However, in the intra-Party struggle, Stalin needed the alleged KMT–CCP alliance as a shield to hide the facts that belied his infallibility. It is therefore understandable that the Comintern ordered the CCP to remain in the KMT in name, in order to "reorganize the KMT and make it a genuine mass organization."[15]

2. *The Rise of Mao Tse-tung:* On August 7, 1927, the CCP held an emergency meeting to meet the new situation which marked its transition from a legal party to an outlawed party. This is now known as the "August 7th Conference"; it was attended by twenty-two delegates. Ch'en Tu-hsiu was condemned for his "rightist opportunism," which was said to be responsible for the total failure of the Party. Ch'ü Ch'iu-pai, a Russian-trained Communist, replaced him

---

[14] After these suppression campaigns, the CCP membership dropped from almost 58,000 to 10,000.

[15] See Brandt *et al., op. cit.,* p. 122.

as Party Secretary-General. Meanwhile, the old Comintern delegation had been recalled and replaced by a new group under the leadership of Besso Lominadze. This was to show that the Comintern would tighten its control over the CCP. In fact, the Congress was convened by telegraphic order of the Comintern and was under the guidance of the Comintern delegates.

The CCP at this juncture had been expelled from the Wuhan KMT and outlawed by the Nanking KMT. Hence the Communists had no other means of survival than conspiracy and rebellion. It is no wonder that the August 7th Conference adopted a new policy of armed uprisings. On August 1, 1927, Communist-led troops staged an uprising in Nanchang. But by August 8, the city was recaptured by the KMT Army and the rebel troops were dispersed. A series of peasant uprisings followed the decision of the August 7th Conference. The most significant of these revolts was the so-called August Harvest Insurrection, led by Mao Tse-tung on September 8, but this peasant revolt also ended in a bitter defeat. In these abortive uprisings, many Communists lost their lives and many cities suffered looting. The Chinese Communist Party became badly demoralized and disorganized.

In November, 1927, the Central Committee of the CCP called an enlarged meeting of the provisional Political Bureau set up at the August 7th Conference. This meeting, presided over by Chü Ch'iu-pai and dominated by Moscow-trained Communists, adopted a new policy of "emphasizing the leadership in the cities." This policy, which later was denounced as "left Putschism," caused heavy losses to the Party. The CCP could not hold its conference in China, and, accordingly, the leaders went to Moscow, where the Sixth Congress was held from July to September, 1928. Under the auspices of Bukharin, the Congress, after reviewing the events of the Chinese Revolution since the Fifth Congress of April–May, 1927, passed four important resolutions on the political question, propaganda work, the land question and peasants' movements. These four resolutions are hailed by Communist historians as comprising a theoretically sound policy which overcame Ch'en Tu-hsiu's "right opportunist mistakes," as well as Chü Ch'iu-pai's "left Putschist errors."[16]

---

[16] The Congress attacked Ch'en for his conciliatory policy toward the Wuhan KMT and reprimanded Chü for his "ill-prepared, ill-directed Putschism."

The Congress also adopted the Ten Policies (also known as the Ten Great Demands of the Chinese Revolution) and a Party Constitution of fifteen chapters and fifty-three articles.[17] What was significant in the Congress was that it failed "to make a proper estimate of the importance of the revolutionary bases in the countryside, of the protracted nature of the democratic revolution, and of the characteristics of the national bourgeoisie in China."[18] As a result, the Congress still emphasized "leadership in the cities" and elected Hsiang Chungfa,[19] a former boatman, as Secretary-General, replacing Chü Ch'iu-pai. Because of the intellectual incompetence of the new Secretary-General, actual power fell to Li Li-san, also a Moscow-trained Communist, who dominated the Central Committee and followed Moscow directives to carry on the city uprisings that led the CCP to collapse.[20]

It is worth noting that Mao's feat in carrying out the peasant movement in Hunan did not win him any key position in the Party leadership; on the contrary, as Mao proceeded to organize the "Autumn Harvest Insurrection" in Hunan,[21] he was several times reprimanded by the Central Committee for "deviations," and once dismissed from his position as an alternate member of the Provisional Politburo of the CCP. While the Communist leaders continued to direct the policy of urban uprisings as prescribed by Moscow, Mao, after the failure of the peasant uprising in Hunan, led the remnants of his forces to the Ching-kang-san area on the Kiangsi-Hunan border, where, later joined by Chu Teh, he established the first peasant revolutionary base for the development of a disciplined, trained and equipped Red Army, as well as for the organization of a soviet government.

---

[17] This Constitution was later revised at the Seventh Congress in April, 1945.

[18] See "From the First to the Seventh National Congress of the CCP," *People's China* (No. 18), September 16, 1956.

[19] Hsiang was later executed by the Nanking government.

[20] Li Li-san, who insisted on following the Comintern's directives, directed Party affairs from 1928 to 1930, when he was purged for "leftist deviationism" and recalled to Moscow where he stayed until the end of World War II. Then the Central Committee of the Party fell under the sway of the so-called "twenty-eight quasi-Bolsheviks," who were known to be versed in Marxist theory and who were brought back from Moscow by the Comintern agent Pavel Mif. The group was headed by Wang Mong (Ch'en Shao-yü), and included Wang Chia-chiang, Chinese Communist ambassador to Moscow, Ch'en Wen-tien and Liu Shao-chi. They continued to advocate an urban proletarian revolution and gave orders for general strikes and armed uprisings, which were all crushed by the KMT troops.

[21] At the August 7th Conference, Mao was sent to Hunan to lead the "Autumn Harvest Insurrection."

The road that led Mao to unchallenged predominance in the CCP was a long and tortuous one.[22] Before 1927 Mao's role in the CCP is not clearly known. On the basis of his report on the peasant movement in Hunan (Selection 3), we may assume that Mao remained inwardly opposed to the policy of urban proletarian revolution pursued by the Communist leadership. The essence of his line was a rural strategy based on the peasantry. By making the peasantry the main force of the revolution, Mao diverged from the dogma of the Marxist-Leninist school. It was only after the total failure of the armed uprisings in cities that Mao separated the CCP from its urban base and established the theory that a Communist Party might function on a base of peasant and army support. This shift in the theory and framework of the CCP operations made it possible for the CCP to emphasize a program of agrarian reform. Everywhere it went, Mao's group organized the landless peasants, and set up village soviets (councils). After 1928 Mao's influence increased, the Red Army gained strength and the soviet area grew in size.

After 1929 a string of Chinese soviets spread eastward through Kiangsi to Fukien. At first these soviets were essentially local in character. It was not until 1931, when the Japanese invasion of Manchuria on September 18, 1931, diverted the attention of the Nanking government, that Mao succeeded in organizing a nation-wide soviet in the Kiangsi-Hunan border region. On November 7, 1931, the First National Congress of the Soviets was convoked in Juichin, the capital of Mao's Kiangsi soviet. A Chinese Soviet Republic, embracing all the soviet areas under Communist control,[23] was formally established. Over 600 delegates attended this congress and adopted a Draft Constitution, a land law, a

---

[22] As Mao said to Edgar Snow, before he rose to power in the Party he had been expelled three times from the Central Committee and received eight warnings. Read Edgar Snow, *Red Star over China*, New York: Random House, 1944. Indeed, during much of this period Mao found himself at odds with many of his colleagues at home and with Comintern policy. It was only after elimination of rival Communist officers and the purge of Party political leaders that Mao emerged as the main leader of this rural Communist base.

[23] At the time of this First Congress of Soviets, the territorial bases of the CCP comprised about 300 counties, scattered through eleven of the eighteen provinces of China, making up about one-sixth of the area of China proper. The total population of soviet areas, according to Communist estimates, was over 60 million. Of these areas, the most important was the Central Soviet Area, with a total population of 15 million and a territorial extent of 45 to 50 counties, scattering over Kiangsi, Fukien, Kwangtung and Hunan provinces.

labor law, and resolutions on economic policies and other matters. They elected a sixty-four member Central Executive Committee (CEC), including Mao, Chu Teh, Liu Shao-chi, Chou En-lai and Ch'en Shao-yü, who still remained the Secretary-General of the CCP. On November 27, the CEC of the Republic in turn elected Mao Tse-tung Chairman and Hsiang Ying and Chang Kuo-t'ao Vice-Chairmen.

The battle lines were thus drawn between the KMT under Chiang Kai-shek and the CCP under Mao Tse-tung. In November, 1930, the KMT forces began the first of the six "extermination campaigns" designed to destroy the Chinese soviets, the Red Army, and the Chinese Communists. However, these campaigns, extending over a period of four years, failed to dislodge the Communist-held bases. Finally, the Nationalists changed their tactics and began to circle the Communist bases with fortresses. They then applied a blockade of supplies and forced the Communists to retreat.

The Communist forces under the command of Mao Tse-tung, Chu Teh, Lin Piao and P'eng Teh-huai made a breakthrough in October, 1934, and set out on the "Long March" (1934–1935) to the borderlands of northwest China. The Long March took the Communist armies over a distance of more than six thousand miles in one year's time through the whole of west China. The soldiers marched by foot and covered the territory of twelve different provinces, passed over eighteen high mountain ranges and went through the forbidding areas of Chinese Tibetan borderland. And the march greatly weakened the Communists. Over 90,000 men had left the Soviet area of southern Kiangsi at the beginning of the Long March, but only 20,000 men including new recruits reached the final destination in northwest Kiangsi.

However, the Long March marked the rise of Mao Tse-tung as the leader of the Chinese Communist Party. Mao had been Chairman of the Soviet Republic in Kiangsi but now became the undisputed leader of the whole Party. Mao obtained formal control over the CCP in January, 1935, when an Enlarged Session of the Central Politburo was held at Tsungyi, Kweichow, to remove the Moscow-directed group from the central leadership of the Party. In October, 1935, the Central Red Army arrived in northern Shensi, where it established its new headquarters. But after the seizure of the city of Yenan, the Communists transferred their headquarters to that city in December, 1936, and made it their capital early in 1937.

3. *The United Front Policy:* During the earlier years, Mao Tse-tung's basic strategy was one of a united front with the "national bourgeoisie." Speaking in December, 1935, Mao ascribed the severe setbacks which the CCP suffered between 1927 and 1934 to "the advocates of closed-door tactics."[24] By 1935 Mao became convinced that the strategy of forming a united anti-Japanese front would afford the Chinese Communists the possibilities of winning the wide support of the people. Mao's strategy paralleled that of the Comintern, which proposed at its Seventh Congress in 1935 the "formation of an Anti-Fascist Popular Front" in order to support the isolated USSR.

However, it would be wrong to assume that the strategy of the united front was entirely "channeled to the CCP from a Comintern source." On the contrary, it "grew as a response to national conditions."[25] As early as 1932, following the Japanese invasion of Manchuria in 1931, the CCP announced its willingness to conclude an agreement with all anti-Japanese groups, but no agreement with the KMT was intended at this time. Technically, this was still a "united front from below," or a united front formed for the overthrow of the KMT regime. In July, 1934, a similar proposal was made without eliciting any response from the KMT. As late as August, 1936, the CCP presented to the KMT a formal "proposal of a united anti-Japanese front." This proposal remained unanswered. In carrying out his anti-Communist campaign, Chiang Kai-shek refused to listen to arguments for a united front. His program was to placate the Japanese so long as they did not take Peking and to "wipe out" the Communists and their weak northwestern base.

However, as the threat of Japanese invasion became more serious toward the end of 1936, anti-Japanese sentiment enveloped the whole country, punctuated by popular demands for resistance. Meanwhile, the National Salvation Association was organized to promote a resistance movement

---

[24] See Mao's report, "On Tactics of Fighting Japanese Imperialism," at a conference of Party activists on December 27, 1935 (Selection 5).

[25] See Boyd Compton, *Mao's China: Party Reform Documents, 1942–1944* Seattle and London: University of Washington Press (Washington Paperbacks), 1966, pp. xxi–xxii.

against Japanese aggression.[26] The Association made demands which were meant to embarrass Chiang and also strengthened Communist efforts for a united anti-Japanese front. Chiang's stubborn refusal to yield to demands for war against Japan led to his strange kidnapping in Sian in December, 1936.

This act was the work of Chang Hsüeh-liang, former warlord of Manchuria, whose troops were garrisoned at Sian, capital and strategic key city of south central Shensi. In 1936 he was one of Chiang's deputies and commander in chief of the Bandit (Communist) Suppression Campaign in the Northwest. His Manchurian troops, cut off from their homeland, were especially susceptible to the Communist demand for the united front against Japan and became increasingly bitter about Chiang's anti-Communist campaign. In December, 1936, when Chiang flew to Sian to urge Chang and his troops to move against the Communists, they mutinied, "kidnapped" Chiang, and held him prisoner. It appeared at first to be certain that Chiang's arrest would end in his execution.

At this point, Moscow interceded by sending agents to participate with Chou En-lai in negotiations which eventually led to Chiang's release, effected on the condition that the anti-Communist campaign was to be terminated and a new truce between the KMT and the CCP worked out. This marked a decisive turning point in the history of the CCP.[27]

III. The War of Resistance Against Japanese Aggression (1937–1945)

1. *The War and United Front Against Japan:* The war to resist Japanese aggression was decided upon at the time of Chiang's release at Sian, and broke out in July, 1937. The United Anti-Japanese Front, consisting of the KMT, the CCP and other parties, was soon formed as a symbol of national unity. In September, 1937, the Central Committee of the CCP

---

[26] Its members included Shen Chun-yü, now Chief Justice of the Supreme Court of the People's Government, and Shih Liang, now the Minister of Justice.

[27] Details of the political negotiations carried on in Sian still remain unknown.

issued a manifesto, "The United Front for the National Emergency." In it the Communists agreed to accept the Three People's Principles of the KMT as "the paramount need of China today," to abandon their policy of overthrowing the KMT by force, and to discontinue their policy of forcible confiscation of land. They promised also to abolish the soviet government and to incorporate the Red Army into the National Revolutionary Army under Chiang's supreme command. While negotiations went on concerning incorporation of the Communist forces, the Red Army under the command of Chu Teh and P'eng Teh-huai was officially reorganized as the Eighth Army, consisting of three divisions and assigned to the Second War Zone in northern Shansi. By the end of 1937, the New Fourth Army, made up of the old Red Army units under the command of Yeh T'ing and Hsiang Ying, was constituted and assigned to the Third War Zone in the area south of the Yangtze.

This united front agreement was more a tactical truce than a peaceful settlement, and was agreeable to each side for different reasons. In the course of its first year, certain measures were taken on each side which appeared to meet the terms of the agreement. From the end of 1937 until the fall of 1938 there seemed to exist a common war strategy under which Communist forces co-ordinated their moves and attacks with those of the KMT troops. KMT–CCP relations began to deteriorate in 1939–1940 as the Japanese pressure on China lessened and the war became an endurance contest. It also became apparent that the Communists had no intention of submitting to real direction and control by the KMT government; instead, they insisted after 1937 on retaining control of their own territorial bases and maintaining their own armed forces. On the other hand, the KMT became increasingly fearful that under the guise of anti-Japanese activity the CCP would arouse a mass revolutionary movement, which to the KMT was almost as unhappy a prospect as Japanese victory.[28]

The first major clash between the KMT and CCP forces broke out in January, 1941, on the lower Yangtze River, where the New Fourth Army had successfully established its guerrilla bases. In the ensuing clash the commander of the Red Army, Yeh T'ing, was captured and his deputy Hsiang

---

[28] For instance, in August, 1938, the KMT government, still in Hankow, outlawed the Communist mass organizations.

Ying was killed in action. This clash marked the end of the
new KMT–CCP Alliance. From then on, hostilities and
clashes continued intermittently.

These clashes certainly weakened China's war efforts against
the Japanese. It is true that from the end of 1941 until the
early part of 1944 the KMT massed its forces to blockade the
Red base in the northwest, with Sian as key fortress. And yet
it is also true that the CCP devoted its main efforts to develop
its military strength and expand its controlled areas. These
years, therefore, were marked by the steady collapse of the
KMT–CCP united front.

When the United States, Great Britain and other Western
powers entered the Pacific War at the end of 1941, they were
interested in seeing China united against Japan. The United
States, in particular, was disposed to build up a united and
powerful China to become a balance wheel in postwar Far
Eastern politics. Toward this end, American envoys were sent
to China, trying to bring about reconciliation between the
KMT and the CCP.[29] However, the KMT–CCP cleavage was
too far advanced for their efforts to succeed.[30] When the
Japanese surrendered in August, 1945, China was hopelessly
divided. The glory of victory was overshadowed by the
KMT–CCP struggle for control of the Japanese-occupied
areas.

2. *Growth of Communist Power:* During the war years,
the Chinese Communists under the leadership of Mao Tse-
tung not only gained territory and organizational strength,
but also built up a very powerful Red Army and a highly
disciplined Party. Before the war the Chinese Communists
had been considered outlaws and bandits, but during the war
their status was legalized; they were regarded as patriots.
Many young men left Szechuan and Yunnan to join them.
And they were no longer contained, as they had been, in
Kiangsi; on the contrary, they now had free access to large
areas in north China, where they could send their military

---

[29] The most important of these missions were those of Henry Wallace,
then Vice-President of the United States, in May, 1944, and of General
Patrick Hurley, personal representative of President Roosevelt, in June, 1944.

[30] However, on August 22, 1945, General Hurley brought Mao Tse-tung
from Yenan to Chungking, which was a great accomplishment in terms of
diplomacy. The great achievement of his mission lay in his success in
bringing the KMT and CCP to a consultative conference, later known as the
Political Consultative Conference, which became the foundation for General
Marshall's work of mediation.

forces into Manchuria and establish contact with Soviet Russia.[31]

The Long March had left the CCP with only 20,000 men, but eight years later, by the end of 1943, the Communists claimed to have a People's Liberation Army of 470,000 men,[32] including the Eighth Route Army, the New Fourth Army and other anti-Japanese people's troops, with a militia force of two million men. They also claimed to control 90 million people in the nineteen Liberated Areas, which extended across the north China plain from Shensi to Shantung, thus cutting off central China from overland access to Peking and Manchuria.

Moreover, the Party grew from 40,000 members in 1937 to about 1,200,000 in 1945. This great expansion of Party membership made the Chinese Party the world's second largest Communist Party at the end of the war. The increase in the number of Party members and in the "Liberated Areas" made it all the more essential that the Party should be welded together into a well-disciplined and well-indoctrinated body. For the purpose of indoctrination, the Communist leaders in 1941 inaugurated a study campaign (consisting of group discussion, criticism and self-criticism), and from 1942 to 1944 carried on a thoroughgoing *"cheng-feng"* or Party Rectification Movement in which rightist and leftist "deviationists" within the Party were purged or brought into line.[33]

When the Seventh Party Congress convened at Yenan on April 23, 1945, Mao had established himself as the undisputed leader of a greatly strengthened Communist Party. He was re-elected Party Chairman, and a Politburo of his loyal "comrades" was also designated. The Party Constitution adopted by the Congress provided the basis of a disciplined Party organization. Before the war was over, in sum, the balance of military and political power had shifted to the side of the CCP.

---

[31] This situation was further strengthened by the Yalta Pact—concluded between the United States and Soviet Russia with China's cognizance—which brought the Russians into Manchuria against the Japanese and consequently enabled the Chinese Communists to move in and arm themselves with equipment surrendered by the withdrawing Japanese army.

[32] According to the report at the Seventh National Congress at Yenan on April 23, 1945, the People's Liberation Army numbered 910,000 men.

[33] "Cheng-Feng thus had two major characteristics," said Compton (*op. cit.,* p. xxxix). "A group of high leaders fell from power; to this extent it was a purge. On the other hand, its principal importance to the entire Party was intensive indoctrination and education in the principles of Mao Tse-tung's communism."

IV. The Third Revolutionary Civil War (1945-1949)

1. *The KMT–CCP Peace Negotiations:* The end of the Anti-Japanese War in August, 1945, found the Kuomintang government exhausted by the long struggle and opposed by the Chinese Communist Party which had grown in military and territorial strength. The KMT found it difficult to undertake the two main tasks which now confronted it—to deal with the Communists and to restore the economy of China. Although the KMT had been weakened by years of protracted war, the CCP was not yet strong enough to engulf the whole country. Thus the Communist demand for a coalition government was merely an extension of their classical strategy of the united front: it would give them a chance to compete for support from outside the government while infiltrating it from within.

Under the circumstances, in spite of their military clashes for control of the territory evacuated by the Japanese, the KMT and the CCP still sought a negotiated settlement through the mediation of the United States. Bringing the KMT and CCP into a coalition government became, for a time after 1945, the chief aim of United States diplomacy in China. Through the mediation of Patrick Hurley, Mao came to Chungking on August 28, 1945, and entered into negotiations with Chiang. On October 10, the two sides signed an agreement—the so-called Double Tenth Agreement—announcing that "civil war must be averted at all costs," and calling for a Political Consultative Conference to discuss fundamental plans for the peaceful reconstruction of the country.

While these negotiations were in progress, armed clashes between KMT and CCP forces in the areas evacuated by the Japanese armies became more serious. At this stage, on December 15, 1945, President Truman announced a new American policy and appointed a special envoy, General George Marshall, to carry it out. The policy statement of December 15 subscribed to two conflicting objectives of American policy: (1) "the United States recognizes and con-

tinues to recognize the National Government of China"; and
(2) "it is the firm belief of this Government that a strong,
united and democratic China is of the utmost importance to
the success of the United Nations organization and for
world peace."

General Marshall came to China on December 19, 1945,
and he urged the cessation of hostilities between KMT and
CCP forces, and the calling of a political conference which
would decide the questions of army integration, coalition
government and a new constitution. In the early stages of
Marshall's mission the outlook appeared very promising because, through his mediation, an order for the cessation of
hostilities was issued on January 10, 1946, the Political
Consultative Conference was opened on January 11,[34] and
an agreement, dependent upon the political settlement as discussed in the Political Consultative Conference, was reached
for the reorganization of the Chinese Army, both KMT and
CCP.

On January 31, 1946, the Political Consultative Conference
passed unanimous resolutions on major issues, including (1)
reorganization of the national government, (2) nationalization of the armed forces and (3) establishment of a reviewing committee to prepare a draft constitution. Hopes
were raised that peace might come to China through these
resolutions. In fact, however, the Political Consultative Conference had solved nothing. It reached no final settlement on
the legal status of the Communist armies and on the administrative structures in the Communist-controlled areas. Despite
the tireless efforts of General Marshall to reconcile the KMT
and the CCP, no effective truce was reached. The KMT
saw no possibility of an acceptable solution without complete
elimination of Communist military strength. The CCP, knowing the KMT military strength, might have accepted a minority status in a coalition government, but was never prepared
to consider any formula which would deprive it of its own
armed forces. And this ruled out, of course, any meaningful
unification of China.

Meanwhile, both sides were stepping up their preparations

---

[34] The conference was attended by thirty-eight delegates—eight from
the KMT, seven from the CCP, four from the Youth Party, two from the
Democratic League, two from the Democratic-Socialist Party, two from the
National Salvation Association, and one each from the Vocational Education Society, the Rural Reconstruction Society and the Third Party. Nine
members had no party affiliations.

for an impending clash. The KMT intensified its efforts to stamp out the Communist rebellion, and the CCP, continuing its aggrandizement during the truce talks, worked to expand the territories under its control. Under these circumstances, the January rapprochement was completely vitiated. As the year drew to an end, hostilities broke out in full force. Marshall concluded that no useful purpose could be served by his remaining in China. He left China on January 8, 1947. With the expulsion of the Communist delegation from Nanking on February 21, 1947, China was once more in the throes of a full-scale civil war.

2. *Outbreak of the Civil War:* The civil war of 1947–1949 brought final victory to the Communists. At the outset the KMT, relying on its numerical superiority and magnificent equipment, adopted the strategy of an all-out offensive, frantically attacking and seizing cities and territories in the hope of quickly destroying the Communists. This offensive started in June, 1946, and reached its peak when the KMT troops captured the Communist capital of Yenan in March, 1947. From July to September 1947, the Communists went on the offensive on a nation-wide scale and shifted the major battle fronts to the KMT-controlled areas. It was a turning point in the civil war.

In the spring and summer of 1948, the Communists successively attacked and captured a large number of heavily fortified and strongly defended cities and towns. After September, 1948, the Communists launched the three major campaigns of Liaohsi-Shenyang, Huai-Hai and Peking-Tientsin, extending from Changchuan and Mukden in Manchuria to Hsuchow and Nanking in the lower Yangtze region. In each of the campaigns, huge KMT armies defected to the Communists either after they were outflanked or after their supplies were cut by enemy forces in control of the countryside. The three campaigns cost the KMT Army the greater part of its main force and enabled the CCP to win a decisive military victory.[35]

Because of his military failure, Chiang Kai-shek retired

---

[35] According to Communist figures, between July, 1946, and June, 1950, the Communist Army put out of action more than 8,070,000 men of the KMT forces, captured more than 54,400 artillery pieces, 319,000 machine-guns, 1,000 tanks and armored cars, 20,000 motor vehicles and large quantities of other arms and equipment. See Chien Po-tsan *et al., Concise History of China*, Peking: Foreign Language Press, 1964, p. 245.

from the presidency in January, 1949. Vice-President Li Tsung-jen became acting President. While peace negotiations were in progress, the Communists renewed their attack in April, crossing the Yangtze and occupying Nanking. Then they advanced southward to Canton and westward into Szechwan where the last refuge of the KMT on the mainland was abandoned in December, 1949. With complete control of the mainland virtually assured, the CCP inaugurated the People's Republic of China in Peking on October 1, 1949.

To speak of the Communist triumph over the KMT on the mainland as a "popular revolution" is to misinterpret the Communist movement in China. As historical records indicate, the primary purpose of the CCP throughout the war years was the pursuit of power in China. Its strategy of a "united front" with the KMT, the limited nature of its military operations against the Japanese forces, its posture toward the United States and the Western allies, its moderate land-reform program in the areas it controlled, and its proclaimed program for political, economic and cultural development under a "new-democratic regime"[36] were all geared to the overriding tactical objective. And, by the close of the Sino-Japanese War, the CCP had succeeded in laying the foundation for later achievement of its objective.

Many explanations have been offered for the victory of the CCP and its army in 1948–1949. Some attribute the victory of the CCP to superior military organization and strategy. This explanation may be taken as the immediate cause of the Communist victory, but it is not the basic reason why the Communists succeeded, where the KMT failed, in coordinating its military organization with political and social institutions capable of mobilizing and controlling the mass of the people. An examination of changes in 20th-century China will make two points clear: first, the old foundations of Chinese society had been gradually eaten away. Secondly, the traditional concept of a social norm had been gradually collapsing. From the Reform Movement of 1898 to the advocacy of complete Westernization in the 1920's, the old value system had been steadily deteriorating and the old order proceeding toward disintegration. Sun Yat-sen, founder of the KMT, was the first in China's history to introduce a new political order as a substitute for the old order. But

---

[36] See Mao Tse-tung's "On New Democracy" (Selection 12).

the KMT and its regime persisted in pursuing its military campaign against the Communists, without implementing the program of Sun Yat-sen in political, economic and social reforms. This failure could be easily exploited by the new dogmatism—Communism. In this sense, the fall of the KMT was not merely a military collapse, but a failure in ideology and its application to politics.

V. The People's Republic (1949–   )

With the whole of China in his palm, Mao Tse-tung began to implement the basic strategies he had formulated earlier. First, he convened the Chinese People's Political Consultative Conference in September, 1949, in the ancient capital of China, Peking. Three basic documents were formally promulgated which contained much of Mao's ideas about New Democracy: the Common Program of the Chinese People's Political Consultative Conference, the Organic Law of the Central People's Government of the People's Republic of China and the Organic Law of the Chinese People's Political Consultative Conference.[37] This paved the way for the proclamation of the establishment of the People's Republic of China on October 1, 1949.

The "Common Program" is perhaps the most important of all. It is in fact an "interim constitution" because, according to Mao, the Chinese society was not yet ready for the establishment of a socialist society. Under this program, however, economic reforms were made;[38] a strong centralized government was organized; and a host of mass organizations were formed to transmit the orders of the government directly to the people. The Chinese Communist Party also expanded its membership from three million in 1949 to over five million by the end of 1953.

One of the "comic" events during the formative years of the Chinese Communist regime was the introduction of the Marriage Law of 1950. It required some 95.5% of Chinese

---

[37] For these documents, see Theodore H. E. Chen, *The Chinese Communist Regime*, New York: Frederick A. Praeger, 1967.

[38] For a detailed study of Chinese economy, see Yuan-li Wu, *The Economy of Communist China*, New York: Frederick A. Praeger, 1965.

married peasants to seek divorces and then remarry the same partner. This was the first civil code introduced by the Communists after they took over the Chinese mainland. The complete statute is divided into eight chapters, with twenty-seven articles. By the new marriage law, the Communists wanted to build up a "new democratic marriage, which is based on free choice of partners, on monogamy, on equal rights for both sexes, and on protection of the lawful interests of women and children" (Article 1). Provisions were made for the prohibition of "polygamy, concubinage, child betrothal, interference with the remarriage of widows, and the exaction of money or gifts in connection with marriage" (Article 2). These provisions are not revolutionary in Western terms, nor are they radically different from the civil code of the Nationalist government. However, the enforcement of the new marriage law has been much more revolutionary and destructive than its provisions indicate.

For example, Article 3 of the Marriage Law states that marriage shall be the voluntary union of individuals, and economic production and building a new society are among the duties of husband and wife. In other words, personal sentiments of love and mutual attachment must be subordinated to loyalty to the Communist Party and the state. Armed with the ideology of Engels and Lenin, the Chinese Communists believe that love is not a personal but a social affair, and hence cannot be separated from politics. Only in this sense can one understand the tremendous emphasis placed on the registration of marriage and divorce as required in Articles 16 and 17.

1. *Totalitarianism and Socialism:* After having successfully completed the initial stage of political consolidation and economic rehabilitation, the regime announced in October, 1953, the beginning of a new policy, defined as "general line of the state during the period of transition to socialism." The new line was inaugurated by nation-wide election of delegates to the National People's Congress, which adopted the present Constitution in 1954.

The 1954 Constitution was designed to bring the policy and operation of the new government into close collaboration with the social and economic development of China. Its provisions for highly centralized direction and control of all kinds of state and local affairs gave the new government a free hand to bring about "socialist industrialization and socialist transformation." It proposed a policy of "voluntary . . . co-operation" or collectivization of farms, together with the restriction and gradual elimination of "rich peasants" as a class. For example, the "national capitalists" had previously been assured of protection because of their "usefulness"; now the state would "use, restrict and transform them." Thus the socialization (another name for nationalization) of all private business became more or less imminent.

The structure of the "command economy" was further consolidated through the adoption of the First Five Year Plan (1953–1957), which called for roughly doubling the value of gross industrial output, increasing gross agricultural output by close to one-quarter, and increasing by about one-half the gross commodity output of agriculture and industry combined. The specific target figures were 98.3 percent, 23.3 percent and 51.1 percent. To achieve these goals, the plan demanded such average annual increases in production as 14.7 percent in industry, 4.3 percent in agriculture and 8.6 percent in gross commodity output.

By the end of the First Five Year Plan, Peking claimed that the value of gross industrial output had increased by close to 120 percent, gross agricultural output by almost 25 percent and gross commodity output of industry and agriculture by more than 60 percent. Moreover, Communist China had surpassed its investment target for the Plan period and had invested over $20 billion, instead of the $18 billion planned, on "capital construction." It also asserted that over 800 "above-norm" industrial projects had been completed.

A general atmosphere of success prevailed at the Party's Eighth National Congress held in September, 1956. At the Congress the Party leaders further strengthened the leadership machinery and adopted a revised Party Constitution to guide the new phase of policy operation.

The success of the First Five Year Plan led the Communist leaders to seek an unusually ambitious expansion of production in the Second Five Year Plan, as they moved into "the line of socialist construction." The Party leaders, relying on the political enthusiasm of the Party cadres, demanded "greater, faster, better and more economic results." Thus, in 1958, the agricultural co-operatives were replaced by the communes and the "Great Leap Forward" started.

A commune is much bigger than a collective. The average

commune as of the end of the year 1958 held five thousand farm households, while the collectives contained only a few dozen, at most a few hundred. A commune generally corresponds to a township. If a township is too small, then several townships may be combined to form a commune. And again, being large, the commune can undertake more fields of operation and extend its activities to a wider sphere than the collective. The Communists assert that it is a basic social unit of the society and is the best form of organization for accelerating socialist construction and the transition to Communism. Unlike the collective, where members were allowed to own their own plots of land, the commune is the owner of all lands and other assets. It retains the traditional wage and supply systems; however, it is at the beginning of the transition to the stage of "from each according to his ability, to each according to his needs."

Together with the establishment of the people's communes, the Chinese Communists embarked upon a startling program to build small "factories" for the production of pig iron, steel and many other commodities throughout rural China. The Great Leap Forward met tremendous resistance from the peasants, and the situation was aggravated by two successive years of drought and flood. It is impossible to assess accurately the economic progress the Communists may have made since the First Five Year Plan. However, there has been more emphasis on moderate economic growth and growth of agriculture rather than the development of heavy industry in recent years. The communes have been preserved in form, although actual practice since the 1960–1962 economic crisis has reverted to conditions predating the collective farms, i.e., allowing private plots (discontinued during the 1966–1967 Cultural Revolution). The failure of the Great Leap Forward led to serious questioning by various prominent Party figures of the efficiency of Mao Tse-tung's leadership, as well as the reliability of "Maoism."

2. *Maoism and Revisionism:* The real driving force behind the People's Government in China until 1966 was the seven-man Standing Committee of the Party Politburo of the Central Committee which developed, formulated and co-ordinated China's domestic, foreign and military policies. The seven are Mao Tse-tung, Chairman of the Party; Liu Shao-chi, Chairman of the Republic; Chou En-lai, Premier of the State

Council of the Republic; Chu Teh, Chairman of the Standing Committee of the National People's Congress; Teng Hsiao-p'ing, Secretary-General of the Party; Chen Yun, Vice-Premier of the State Council; and Lin Piao, Defense Minister. These are men who are widely experienced in party, state and military affairs, men who have laid the foundations of new power with remarkable success.

But there are many unsolved problems and dilemmas confronting them. From the founding of the People's Republic in 1949 to the present day, a series of fundamental disputes, both doctrinal and tactical, on how China should be governed as a Communist nation have split the leadership right to the peak of the hierarchy. For example, the open rifts of Kao Kang and Jao Shu-shih with other Chinese Communist leaders, especially Liu Shao-chi, Teng Hsiao-p'ing and Chou En-lai, began in 1950 over the question of following Soviet models or a "Maoist" line. This was when the influence of the Soviet Union upon China was at its peak.

Kao Kang, Chairman of the Northeast (Manchuria) People's Government, wanted to adopt a complete Soviet system, especially in the field of industrial management. His opponents, on the other hand, suggested a Mao-approved method of "collective leadership" plan under the guidance of Party committees. Under the facade of the ideological debate, a power struggle was emerging. Kao allied himself with Jao Shu-shih, the powerful Chairman of the East China Military and Administrative Committee, and demanded the resignation of Liu Shao-chi, Teng Hsiao-p'ing and Chou En-lai. Meanwhile, Liu, Teng and Chou had anticipated this move and by enlisting the strong support of Peng Chen, Mayor of Peking, expelled Kao and Jao at the 1954 Party Central Committee meeting.

Disputes in China seldom involve the military, for Mao Tse-tung has always kept the military establishment under his own command. Marshal P'eng Teh-huai, the Minister of Defense and noted revolutionary war hero, and General Huang Ke-ch'eng, Chief of Staff of the Army and P'eng's senior Vice-Minister, were denounced as "right-wing opportunists" and replaced. The full resolution adopted by the Party to purge P'eng and Huang was not published for the public until 1967 during the Cultural Revolution when the attack upon Peng Teh-huai continued.

Meanwhile, discontent spread among non-Party intellectuals and Party members. Not only did they criticize the Party, the Great Leap Forward, the commune system and the vaunted "Three Red Banners," but they also resisted the ideological remolding campaigns. The communique issued by the Tenth Plenary Session of the Chinese Communist Party Central Committee in September, 1962, made it clear that the CCP would "sharpen its vigilance and wage a struggle on two fronts—against revisionism and against dogmatism," in order to safeguard the "Party line" and strengthen "the unity of the Party." In this session, Mao Tse-tung renewed the call for "class struggle" against "Khrushchev-style modern revisionism," to be followed by nation-wide new socialist-education and other related campaigns.

The domestic difficulties China encountered were further complicated by the Sino-Soviet rift which began as early as 1957. Communist China attributes the origin and development of differences with the Soviet Union to[39] "revisionism" of the leadership of the CPSU (Communist Party of the Soviet Union); negation of Stalin; Khrushchev's theory of "peaceful transition" from capitalism to socialism, especially through "the parliamentary road"; great-power chauvinism (regarding Sino-Polish relations) and policy of capitulation regarding Hungary's revolution and the Cuban missile crisis; recall of economic experts from China in 1960 and political and economic pressure including border conflicts with the Soviet Union and other countries such as India. In recent years China has begun to concentrate on the charge that the Soviet Union and the United States are collaborating to contain China—in the United Nations, in nuclear discussions, and in the efforts to end the Vietnam War. Charges concerning Vietnam have become more pronounced as relations between China and the Soviet Union deteriorated. Some of the major subthemes noted were: (1) the Soviet Union reversed itself and accepted the United States version of the Test-Ban Treaty, contrary to the interests of the Soviet people and the people of the world; (2) the Soviet Union assisted counter-revolutionary forces by discussing a United Nations force; (3) the Soviet Union generally joined with the United States to fend off uprisings of people in underdeveloped areas; and (4) the Soviet Union has specifically assisted the United States in efforts to defeat the Vietnamese people. When Premier Aleksei Kosygin recently met with

---

[39] *Peking Review*, September 13, 1963.

President Johnson at Glassboro, New Jersey, discussing the 1967 Middle East crisis, China's immediate reaction was: "Big Betrayal at Hollybush."[40]

Since 1964, an intensive campaign for the study of Mao's works and the application of Mao's thinking in every activity has been vigorously propagated in the rural areas, and then extended to the Army and the intellectuals. Whatever its success in the Army and in the rural areas, it is clear that in the cultural community the campaign has encountered stiff and stubborn resistance. As Mao expressed dismay with the obstinacy of the intellectuals, a series of purges were launched in the 1964–1965 "rectification" campaign against highly placed intellectuals, including many eminent novelists and playwrights. This campaign was intensified at a meeting of the CCP Central Committee in September, 1965, when Mao "pointed to the need to subject reactionary bourgeois ideology to criticism." The signal for an intensive rectification campaign against the "reactionary bourgeoisie" was given by Yao Wen-yuan's article, "On the New Historical Drama *The Dismissal at Hai Jui* [written by Wu Han, a historian and Vice-Mayor of Peking],"[41] carried by the Shanghai *Wen Hui Daily* on November 10, 1965, "which raised the curtain on the current upsurge of the great cultural revolution."

Between the publication of Yao Wen-yuan's article in November, 1965, and April, 1966, the rectification campaign revolved mainly around criticism and exposure of "Wu Han's anti-Party and anti-socialist crimes." The purge was later extended to Teng T'o, a leading journalist and close aide of P'eng Chen, the powerful First Secretary of the Peking Municipal Party Committee and close associate, in turn, of China's chief of state, Liu Shao-chi. Teng T'o was accused of being the leader of an organized and deliberate attack on Mao, on the Party leadership and on the principal policies of the regime in recent years. During May and early June, his writings and those of his associates were publicly analyzed almost daily in the press and in broadcasts throughout China.

From April to June, 1966, a great number of articles deifying Mao as an all-wise sage whose thought is the "uni-

---

[40] *Peking Review*, July 7, 1967.
[41] The play tells the story of a legendary Ming dynasty official who brought exploiters of the people to justice only to be cashiered for his efforts through court intrigue. It was written and produced in 1960–1961. Yao Wen-yuan alleged that the play had employed the tactic of using "the past to ridicule the present."

versal truth that guides the world revolution" were published
in most of the newspapers and periodicals of the mainland.
These articles have developed the "Great Proletarian Cultural
Revolution," a vigorous mass movement, to "eliminate
bourgeois ideology and promote Mao Tse-tung's thought in a
thoroughgoing way." The Red Guard movement, which
has no historical parallel in scale, sweep, strength or momentum, soon spread throughout the country.

By November, 1966, this "revolutionary movement" was
in full cry, and tens of millions of Chinese youths swarmed
across China and congregated in the main cities to attack
anti-Mao leaders, shake up the bureaucracy, and enshrine
the "thought of Mao Tse-tung." Among the Party leaders
purged during the Cultural Revolution were P'eng Chen
(Mayor of Peking), Lu Ting-yi and Chou Yang (top Party
propaganda officials), Lo Jui-ch'ing (Chief of Staff of the
Army), Teng Hsiao-p'ing, (Party Secretary-General) and
Lui Shao-chi (China's chief of state).[42]

Mao has also changed the control apparatus of the Chinese
Communist Party into a "troika" system during the Cultural
Revolution. The troika consists of the Military Committee of
the Central Committee, the Cultural Revolution Committee
and the State Council. The policymaking power was taken
away from the Central Committee of the Chinese Communist Party and placed in the hands of the Military Committee
after reorganization of that committee in 1966 (although
policy pronouncements were still issued in the name of the
disintegrated Central Committee). The decisions made by the
Military Committee are to be carried out by the newly formed
Cultural Revolutionary Committee and the State Council, bypassing Party functional departments.

On the provincial and local level, the changes made by
Mao have been slow and, at times, difficult and bloody.
Since the Constitution was adopted in 1954, China has been
divided administratively into twenty-two provinces, five autonomous regions, and two cities directly under the central
government. Below these divisions are more than two
thousand counties and cities, which in turn are subdivided
into people's communes (towns and villages). Under the

---

[42] The purging of Liu Shao-chi and Teng Hsiao-p'ing has not been officially
announced due to their many supporters within the Party. Liu is identified
as the leader of the anti-Mao group in China. The pro-Mao group within
the Party is under the leadership of Lin Piao and Chou En-lai.

new program envisioned by Mao, all these local areas are to be taken over by the newly organized "revolutionary committees," "preparatory groups" and "military committees."

Just how these "revolutionary committees" differ from the existing Party organizations in provinces and cities may be seen from the tentative programs of the "Tientsin Revolutionary Committee" promulgated in December, 1967:

(1) place the creative study and application of Chairman Mao's works above everything;

(2) establish the concept of confidence in and reliance on the masses and master the work method of "from the masses, to the masses";

(3) conscientiously implement the Party's policy of democratic centralism;

(4) establish the style of self-criticism;

(5) strengthen unity between old and new cadres with "fight self-interest, repudiate revisionism" as the guide;

(6) persevere in the practice of cadres taking part in collective productive labor;

(7) be models in publicizing and implementing the Party's principles and policies, maintain high revolutionary enthusiasm, step up investigation and study and improve work efficiency;

(8) always retain the characteristics of an ordinary laborer.

Although conclusive answers on the success of the new programs are unavailable, the programs strongly reflect Mao's desire to press forward his own prescriptions for the China of tomorrow.

Chapter One

The Birth of the Chinese Communist Party

Twelve men, representing the fifty-seven members of various Marxist study groups in China, opened the First Congress of the Chinese Communist Party in the French Concession of Shanghai on July 1, 1921. The Congress had to move from place to place during its first session to avoid police harassment. But it firmly established a Chinese Communist Party and opened a new chapter in modern Chinese history.

The original small group of founders, predominantly intellectuals, would have liked to turn the Party into an "academic institution where intellectuals might study Marxism," if it had not been for the persuasion of a Comintern agent. They finally adopted the Bolshevik rules and regulations including its iron discipline, compulsory subscriptions, obligatory attendance at Party meetings, and the practice of self-criticism.[1]

The records of the First Congress have long been lost; and the earliest statements of the CCP issued are the "First Manifesto on the Current Situation" (June 10, 1922; Selection 1) adopted by the Party Central Committee, and the "Manifesto of the Second National Congress" (July 22,

---

[1] Jerome Ch'en, *Mao and the Chinese Revolution*, New York: Oxford University Press, 1965, p. 80.

1922; Selection 2). From the "First Manifesto," we learn that the Party founders had fully accepted the Moscow-directed line that the Party, "as the vanguard of the proletariat, struggles for working-class liberation and for the proletarian revolution."

In its analysis of the political situation of 1922, the "First Manifesto" expressed a friendly attitude toward the KMT (Kuomintang), admitting that the KMT could be characterized as a revolutionary party, and lauding its Canton government for a liberal labor policy. It chided the KMT for its inclination "for a rapprochement . . . with the 'Pei-yang' [Northern] military clique."

At the Second Congress, held in July, 1922, the subject discussed was the basic problem of the Chinese Revolution. The Party Manifesto drawn up by the Congress declared that the ultimate task of the Party was "to organize the proletariat and to struggle for (the establishment of) the dictatorship of the workers and peasants, the abolition of private property, and the gradual attainment of a Communist society."

Significant in these two manifestos is their call for "a conference, to be participated in by the revolutionary elements of the KMT and revolutionary socialists, to discuss the question of creating a united front for struggle against warlords," and "a democratic united front of workers, poor peasants, and petty bourgeoisie."

Heated debates arose on the question of the united front when Comintern delegate G. Maring proposed that a Communist bloc be formed inside, instead of alongside, the KMT, so as to make the KMT "the central force of national revolution, as instructed by the Comintern." This proposal, in terms of traditional Communist doctrine, was a theoretical monstrosity and was opposed by the Trotskyists in Russia and also was hard for the Chinese Communists to accept. Ch'en Tu-hsiu and his group were reluctant to accept the Moscow-forced co-operation. Maring, therefore, had to invoke the discipline of the Comintern to force adoption of his plan. Such divergence later led to two basically different lines within the Party—the Stalinist line, represented by Mao Tse-tung and his group, and the Trotskyist line, represented by Ch'en Tu-hsiu and his group.[2]

---

[2] Mao's line is also characterized as Bolshevism, and Ch'en's line as Menshevism. See Ho Kan-chih, *A History of the Modern Chinese Revolution*, Peking: Foreign Language Press, 1959, p. 70.

1. Central Committee of the Chinese Communist Party: First Manifesto of the CCP on the Current Situation (June, 1922)*

For thousands of years China has endured feudal economic conditions. Agriculture has been the basis of China's economy. Hence, China has been socially disunited and has lacked organizational strength and (so has lacked) interest in the country's political life. Not until the second half of the nineteenth century did the development of world capitalist production raise before the capitalist governments the problem how to use the boundless (extent of) China as a market. China, which had previously been inaccessible to alien influence for thousands of years, was now subjected to oppression by other states. During the period when the annexationist aspirations of capitalist states were asserting themselves, China's masses attempted to resist the conqueror by direct action. After the popular revolt was crushed, China began to feel the yoke of foreign enslavement more than ever and to discover at the same time the mercenary and sinful nature of her own government.

In the process of the struggle the Chinese popular masses learned the truth that the country's defence from foreign enslavement was impossible without a decisive change of the entire political system of the country. The struggle headed by K'ang Yu-wei [leader of the Reform Movement of 1898] was one of the manifestations of the aroused self-consciousness of China. But the 1911 revolution, which offered the popular masses an opportunity to participate directly in the political reconstruction of the country, was the most significant event in the period of struggle against the old régime. Under the conditions of China's political and economic oppression by foreign states, the popular masses of China, in their political development and in the growth of their power

* From Conrad Brandt, Benjamin I. Schwartz, and John K. Fairbank, *A Documentary History of Chinese Communism*, Cambridge, Mass.: Harvard University Press, 1959, pp. 54–63.

to organize, had to go beyond the phase of minor reform for the correction and improvement of the state administration and reach the point of revolution, which launched slogans and demands for democratic power. The revolution [of 1911] cast aside China's traditional monarchy, which had existed for thousands of years, and opened a new era in China's political history.

The revolution of 1911 had two historical tasks: first, the overthrow of the Manchu dynasty and, second, the liberation of China from foreign oppression and the transformation of China into an independent state. In this second objective the 1911 revolution aimed to create, within a framework of racial and national independence, favourable conditions for the industrial development of China. The 1911 revolution expressed the transition from the political system of feudalism to a democratic régime, from manual labour and an artisan economy to capitalist production.

The revolution in China—under the definite conditions of its historical environment—did not consummate a victory. The democratic party [presumably, the Kuomintang, or KMT], which expressed the demands of liberal social strata, resorted to a compromise with the counter-revolutionary class of feudal lords. The first error of the democratic party was its reconciliation with Yüan Shih-k'ai [military leader and president of the Chinese Republic, 1912–16] in spite of the fact that in view of the forced "abdication" of the dynasty under exceptionally unfavourable financial conditions, the position of the head of the reactionary classes was extremely difficult. The leaders of the revolutionary government issued an order to the revolutionary troops to quarter themselves in Nanking instead of ordering them to cross the Yangtze for a further offensive against North China.

The revolutionary government handed the reins to Yüan Shih-k'ai, the organizer of the "Pei-yang" military party, which united all the feudal lords, the counter-revolutionary warlords, and military commanders.

After Yüan Shih-k'ai's unsuccessful attempt [in 1915–16] to restore the monarchy in China, authority passed momentarily into the hands of the democratic party, which was (however) incapable of holding it and turned it over to the reactionary Tuan Ch'i-jui, the new head of the "Pei-yang" military party. For a second time the conciliatory policy of the democratic party led it to defeat.

Under present conditions, when Hsü Shih-ch'ang, the President of the Peking (government) [September 1918–June 1922], has left the capital and power is in the reactionary hands of Ts'ao K'un and Wu P'ei-fu—the present leaders of "Pei-yang" military party—a third democratic party defeat can be averted only if the democratic elements of the country renounce completely the policy of conciliation and compromise, and take the path of revolutionary struggle. Democratic power can triumph in China only through revolutionary seizure of power.

The result of the revolution's defeat has been a strengthening of the world imperialist yoke in China and of the reactionary régime of her own militarists. The so-called republican rule is in the hands of militarists who, under conditions of a semi-feudal economy, use it to join their own actions with those of the world imperialists, who are concluding an agreement with the Chinese military clique regarding loans for their military needs and for the state's self-preservation. The foreign states are making use of the opportunity to invest their capital in China, thus acquiring, by means of a system of financial enslavement, "spheres of influence" in China and special rights and privileges.

But the maintenance of civil war in China is of first importance to the world imperialists, for it delays China's progress, prevents China from developing her own industry, saturates the Chinese market with goods of their own foreign manufacture, and also prevents the Chinese bourgeoisie from utilizing the country in the interests of domestic exploitation. Under these historical conditions the development of Chinese industry is hindered by unequal competition on Chinese territory between Chinese and foreign capital, which has insured its own dominance through measures of economic pressure (a tariff system, etc.), by the civil war, by local disturbances, by the looting of the population by the officials, and by every type and form of oppression.

The socio-economic conditions in China affect the middle, intermediary classes with particular force. The owners of small enterprises are being deprived of property; artisans fill the ranks of the army of the unemployed; peasants sell their land to landlords for absurd sums of money because they are unable to conduct their own economy, owing to the continuously rising cost of living.

These conditions will remain unchanged so long as power

remains in the hands of the feudal-lord government, in the hands of militarists; so long as power is not seized from their hands; and so long as a democratic government is not established. Democratic government means a democratic party government. We have in mind the creation of power on the basis of a total reorganization of the entire political system of administration. Basically, this demand entails the overthrow of the authority of the reactionary, counter-revolutionary elements and groups by revolutionary methods, by a democratic party, or by a bloc of democratic groupings which will organize power to conform to the historical requirements of their own country and with consideration for the realities of the new international environment.

As a result of the compromise achieved [in February 1912] by Yüan Shih-k'ai on the one hand and Sun Yat-sen and Sung Chiao-jen [the KMT leaders] on the other (both men were leaders of the KMT), a cabinet was formed composed of members of the KMT party, headed by Chao Ping-chün, Yüan Shih-k'ai's puppet, in the role of Prime Minister. What were the results of the activities of this so-called Kuomintang Cabinet? During the second year of the republic (1913), Sung Chiao-jen, who wanted to form a cabinet composed exclusively of KMT party members, was assassinated. Even if Sung Chiao-jen had not been assassinated, he would have suffered the same fate as that suffered by the entire movement against Yüan Shih-k'ai. The assassination of Sung Chiao-jen and the dismissal from Kiangsi province of General Li Lieh-chün [a KMT member, then commanding the expeditionary forces against North China] were caused by that movement. Both these occurrences were practical evidence of the impossibility of a coalition between the KMT and Yüan Shih-k'ai.

After the rout of the KMT, "power was seized" [sic] by the party of "progressives" [presumably the Progressive party, or Chin-pu-tang, first organized by Liang Ch'i-ch'ao] and Hsiung Hsi-ling was commissioned to form a cabinet. The party of "progressives" served as a tool in the hands of Yüan Shih-k'ai. Its participation in the government merely discredited the party to the very limit.

After Yüan Shih-k'ai's fall [d. June 6, 1916], the struggle against the counter-revolutionary government ended in the restoration of constitutionalism, the election of Li Yüan-hung [vice-president, 1913] to the presidency, and the convening of the parliament. All this was, however, not accompanied by actually removing the power of Yüan Shih-k'ai's adherents and friends, who were firmly installed in their seats. The leaders of the democratic party were proud of the victories they had won and of the fact that the republic was restored.

After the collapse of Chang Hsün's plans [July 1917] for returning the Manchu dynasty to the throne, the democratic elements entered the government along with the reactionary military, with General Feng Kuo-chang as President and Marshal Tuan Ch'i-jui as Prime Minister (leader of the Anfu clique). All this was called a "republic".

The postulate must be clear to everyone that the political struggle is not a struggle between individuals for power, but a manifestation and expression of class struggle—the social struggle of the proletariat against the bourgeoisie in the period of revolution and, in the period of bourgeois revolution, the struggle of the bourgeoisie against the feudal lords and the system of feudal economy. The postulate must also be clear that only such freedom is precious as is achieved in the process of hard struggle and at the price of human blood, in distinction from those methods of struggle which are used by our class enemies.

The struggle for democracy is a struggle of one class, a struggle which aims to overthrow the dominance of another class; it is the replacement of one system by another, and in no event can it be regarded as a struggle of one individual or one group for the overthrow of another individual or group.

A real democratic party must possess two characteristic elements: (1) its principles must be correlated with the concepts of democracy; and (2) its actions must consist in an active struggle against feudalism in the form of the military. Of all the political parties existing in China, only the KMT can be characterized as a revolutionary party, yet it possesses only a relative amount of democratic and revolutionary spirit. The programme of this party has not yet been fully elaborated. But its three principles, "of the people, for the people, and by the people" [evidently an oblique reference to Sun Yat-sen's Three People's Principles], in conjunction with plans for the industrial development of China [cp. Sun's *International Development of China*, 1922 (1919)] reflect the democratic spirit of the KMT. In addition to this party's participation in the revolutionary struggle through its parliamentary members, the KMT has offered a number of other proofs of its democratic spirit, namely: the Canton government [headed by Sun Yat-sen, 1921–2] has not been restricting the labour movement; it has abolished police regulations in regard to "public order and national security"; and it has abolished the law by which workers were deprived of the right to strike. Not infrequently, however, this party's actions have been contradictory in nature. On occasion the KMT manifests a friendly attitude even with respect to . . . [periods as in original] monarchists, and an inclination for a rapprochement "for tactical reasons" with the "Pei-yang" military clique. If the KMT, as a party, wishes to play a definite role in the revolutionary struggle for the consolidation of democracy in China, it must renounce once and for all every policy of vacillation, compromise, and endless zigzags.

With respect to the present situation, the view is very popular that the convening of the old parliament [at Peking] and the restoration of Li Yüan-hung as President [June 1922] are cardinal events which assure the solution of the political problems confronting China. This point of view cannot stand criticism and is in complete contradiction to the facts. Is there any basis for asserting that parliament will be able to realize its "legal power" when there is a dominance of a feudal power of the "Pei-yang" party type, a power which pursues the idea of a monopolistic military control over the government and appraises itself as a group of "relatives" who fell heir to the "Pei-yang" military clique? The account of past experience has testified plainly that Li Yüan-hung during his presidency in the recent past (1915–17) [this should be 1916–17] did not manage to resolve a single political task or any problem as a whole. What reasons are there for asserting that Li Yüan-hung will be able to organize a democratic government when—in the face of all the unfavourable historical circumstances—Li Yüan-hung's term of office, as such, has already expired? So long as the military dominates in China and over China, the organized struggle against democracy will not end, nor will the struggle end among the militarists themselves.

This thought can be illustrated by examples: the war between Fengtien and Chihli (Fengtien—the military party of the Mukden satrap, Chang Tso-lin; Chihli—the military party with its actual leader General Wu P'ei-fu and its nominal

head, Marshal Ts'ao K'un) can by no means be regarded
as concluded: it will flare up again. If Chang Tso-lin is victorious, then struggle will inevitably go on within the ranks
of the Fengtien party. Chang Tso-lin will fight against his
own colleague and "co-partisan", General Sun Lieh-chen,
the present military governor of Kirin province in Manchuria;
and the latter in turn will battle with General Wu Chun-sheng,
the present governor of Heilungkiang province in Manchuria. If the Chihli party is victorious, then wars will be
inevitable between the members of this party—between Wu
P'ei-fu and Ts'ao K'un or Feng Yü-hsiang, the present military governor of Honan province, known as "the Christian
general". If the [rival] Anfu party wins and manages to take
power away from the Chihli party, a clash between the
Fengtien and Anfu parties will be inevitable. And within the
Anfu party itself, "Little Hsü" [General Hsü Shu-cheng], the
soul of the Anfu party, a pro-Japanese, will immediately
after victory over the Chang Tso-lin party declare war upon
his worst enemy, General Lu Yung-hsiang, commander
of the troops of Chekiang province. Besides the aforemen-
tioned eventualities guaranteeing and conditioning [*sic*] military developments in China, the struggle for the positions of
military governor (*tu-chün*) and military command posts in
the provinces of Shensi, Szechwan, Hunan, and elsewhere will
not cease.

The military is the cause of civil war in China. So long as
the military exists and rules, the creation of a so-called "good
government" will be out of the question. In the present circumstances no government in China can be stable and firm,
and the life and property of Chinese citizens are subject to
destruction every time the militarists clash.

You kind advocates of good government, after the appearance of the first issue of your magazine *Endeavor* [pre-
sumably *Nu-li*]—the weekly organ of the liberal professorial
staff of Peking National University—and as soon as the helpless and powerless Hsü Shih-ch'ang (Peking president, who
was seated at the helm by the Anfuists and resigned under
Wu P'ei-fu's pressure) was exiled from Peking [June 1922],
you found it possible to feel satisfied and reconciled, and
addressed a wire to the South proposing that the offensive
against the North be discontinued. This bourgeois pacifism,
this opportunist policy, this broken line of compromises is
indeed an obstacle to giving life to your own lofty slogans

and cries of "struggle", "endeavour", "combat the sons of evil". Considering the conditions prevailing in Tientsin and Paoting [in Chihli province], nominally the staff headquarters of the Chihli party's Marshal Ts'ao K'un, do you really believe that a "good government" can be organized under existing conditions? Do you count on carrying out your three principles and the six concrete aims of your programme under military dictatorship? (The programme of the Peking professors has been announced in the group's declaration and published in the first issue of *Endeavor*.) After the fall of the Manchu dynasty, Chang Ping-lin [a scholar-revolutionist] tried his best to reach a compromise with Marshal Tuan Ch'i-jui, head of the Anfu clique. All these efforts and honourable intentions ended in the triumph of reaction. Aren't you also proceeding along the same path and don't you think that you will fall heir to the inglorious reputation of your predecessors?

Members of the KMT! You were originally revolutionary fighters for the triumph of democracy. You should also conduct a revolutionary struggle now for democracy and prefer to perish in this struggle than to vanish from the socio-political arena in consequence of a policy of compromise. During the first year of the existence of the Chinese Republic [1912] you were deceived by Yüan Shih-k'ai, who tried his best to demonstrate his loyalty to the republic. You were cruelly deceived also by Tuan Ch'i-jui, when he proposed the restoration of parliament and of the constitution [1916–17]. Do not let yourselves be deceived now by all this talk about restoring parliament, abolishing the *tu-chün* system, demobilizing provincial troops, for the sake of concluding another compromise with the military of North China. Does the present constitutional parliament differ in any way from the parliament of the fifth and the sixth year of the Republic [1916–17]? Aren't the hopes for abolishing the *tu-chün* system and for demobilization merely hopes that the tiger may shed its own skin? Does the title of "troop commander" as distinct from or other than *tu-chün*—a phenomenon which can be observed in the provinces of Yunnan, Szechwan, and Hunan—differ essentially from the *tu-chün* institution and the conditions which existed prior to the nominal abolition of the *tu-chün*?

Is there any hope whatever for a troop demobilization at a time when war between militarists is at its height? "Little Hsü

(General Hsü Shu-cheng, an active Anfuist) said: "I am an advocate of disarmament, but wait until my soldiers are adequately trained and equipped, so that I may disarm the soldiers of my adversaries." General Chang Shao-cheng said: "War is raging now in Shansi province. The situation is extremely critical in Fengtien and Honan provinces. It is imperative that someone control affairs in the provinces. If Generals Wu P'ei-fu and Ts'ao K'un should actually put the demobilization scheme into effect, imagine what would become of the provinces."

The military's incapacity for disarming itself is most convincingly expressed in these cited views of two ranking militarists. All that is left for you to do is to fulfill completely your historical mission of struggle for the triumph of the democratic revolution and watch out that you are not deceived again by political charlatans.

Workers, peasants, students, soldiers, policemen, and merchants! So long as the authority of the military is not overthrown, there will be no hope of disarming the provincial armies and abolishing the *tu-chün* system. So long as the authority of the military is not overthrown, there will be no hope of reducing the demands for national funds, which are used to cover war expenses and further to disrupt the entire national and local financial system. So long as the authority of the military is not overthrown, all conditions will be present to allow the military to secure new loans from foreigners and thus bring about an intensification of foreign influence in China. So long as the authority of the military is not overthrown, there will be no hope that the military will cease imposing heavy imposts on the citizens of China; there will be no hope that looting may cease, no hope that order may be restored in all regions of China. So long as the authority of the military is not overthrown, there will be no hope of a broad development of education in China and of industrial progress in our country. So long as the authority of the military is not overthrown, there will be no hope that the struggle among militarists for the expansion of their own spheres of influence may cease. Peasants and merchants are always war victims. These wars will be inevitable and endless if they are not stopped by the people themselves.

For all of us, the only way by which we can liberate ourselves from the hard yoke of the military is to join the democratic struggle against the relics of the past—a struggle for freedom and peace. The government opposition game, played by the bourgeoisie, the intelligentsia, and the politicians, cannot be trusted. We all want peace, but real peace rather than false peace. We welcome a war to achieve the triumph of democracy, to overthrow the military and the militarists and to liberate the Chinese people.

The CCP, as the vanguard of the proletariat, struggles for working-class liberation and for the proletarian revolution. Until such time as the Chinese proletariat is able to seize power in its own hands, considering the present political and economic conditions of China's development and all the historical processes now going on in China, the proletariat's urgent task is to act jointly with the democratic party to establish a united front of democratic revolution to struggle for the overthrow of the military and for the organization of a real democratic government.

The concrete aims of the present political struggle cannot be limited to a fight for the publication of data on government finances or for surveillance over the activity of the parliament or of local organs of administration.

Our most immediate aims are as follows:

(1) Revision of the system of tariffs forcibly imposed on China by world capitalism; abolition of consular jurisdiction [extra-territoriality] and of the entire system of privileges for foreigners; the estimation of railway subsidies made to China by foreign capital and the immediate transfer of all railways to the hands of the state.

(2) Abolition of the régime of the military and of the mercenary bureaucrats; confiscation of the property of the militarists and distribution of their large landholdings among the poorest peasants.

(3) General suffrage.

(4) Freedom of assembly, speech, and press; annulment of laws for the safeguarding of "public order" by police; freedom to strike.

(5) Restricted taxation on land.

(6) Compulsory education.

(7) Prohibition of child and woman labour; laws pertaining to sanitary conditions in factories and shops; laws on workers' insurance.

(8) Abolition of all tariff surtaxes and of the *likin* system [provincial transit taxes on domestic trade].

(9) Revision of the entire Law Code with immediate abolition of the death penalty and physical torture.

Equality of the rights of men and women.

Introduction of a progressive income tax.

Under the rule of feudal militarists, none of this minimum programme can be carried out by the methods of compromise, petition, or requests. The CCP takes the initiative in calling a conference, to be participated in by the revolutionary elements of the KMT and revolutionary socialists, to discuss the question of creating a united front for struggle against warlords of the feudal type and against all relics of feudalism. This struggle along a broad united front is a war to liberate the Chinese people from a dual yoke—the yoke of foreigners and the yoke of powerful militarists in our country—a war which is just as urgently needed as it is inevitable.

2. Second National Congress of the Chinese Communist Party: Manifesto (July, 1922)*

The proletariat's support of the democratic revolution is not (equivalent to) its surrender to the capitalists. Not to prolong the life of the feudal system is absolutely necessary in order to raise the power of the proletariat. This is the proletariat's own class interest. It would be no liberation for the proletariat if a successful democratic revolution brought it only some minor liberties and rights. The successful democratic revolution develops the capitalist class, at present in its infancy—capitalist opposition to the proletariat being left to the future. When that stage is reached, the proletariat must launch the struggle of the second phase: (the struggle) for the dictatorship of the proletariat allied to the poor peasants against the bourgeoisie. If the organization and fighting power of the proletariat has been [sufficiently] strengthened, the struggle of this second phase will carry the victory of the democratic revolution to its completion.

* From Conrad Brandt, Benjamin I. Schwartz and John K. Fairbank, *A Documentary History of Chinese Communism*, Cambridge, Mass.: Harvard University Press, 1959, pp. 63–65. (Résumé.)

The CCP is the party of the proletariat. Its aims are to organize the proletariat and to struggle for (the establishment of) the dictatorship of the workers and peasants, the abolition of private property, and the gradual attainment of a Communist society. At present the CCP must, in the interest of the workers and poor peasants, lead the workers to support the democratic revolution and forge a democratic united front of workers, poor peasants, and petty bourgeoisie. In the interest of the workers, the CCP struggles to secure, within this united front, the following objectives:

(1) The quelling of internal disorders, the overthrow of military cliques, and the establishment of internal peace.

(2) The removal of oppression by international imperialism and the complete independence of the Chinese nation.

(3) The unification of China proper (including Manchuria) into a genuine democratic republic.

(4) The achievement of a genuine democratic republic by the liberation of Mongolia, Tibet, and Sinkiang.

(5) The establishment of a Chinese Federated Republic by the unification of China proper, Mongolia, Tibet, and Sinkiang into a free federation.

(6) The unlimited right to vote for (all) workers and peasants, regardless of sex, in all assemblies and municipal assemblies, and absolute freedom of speech, assembly, publication, association, and strike.

(7) Legislation for workers, peasants, and women (as follows):

(*a*) Better treatment of workers. Abolition of the contracting system. The eight-hour working day. Provision of employees' clinics and sanitary installations in factories. Factory insurance. Protection for female and child labour. Protection for the unemployed.

(*b*) Abolition of heavy poll and transport taxes. Establishment of a national—municiple and village—land-tax.

(*c*) Abolition of *likin* and all extraordinary taxes. Establishment of a progressive income tax.

(*d*) Passing of legislation limiting land-rents.

(*e*) Abolition of all legislation restricting women.

(*f*) Improvement of the educational system.

The above seven items are all in the interest of the workers, peasants, and petty bourgeoisie and are prerequisites for their liberation from their present oppression. If we ourselves put up a concerted struggle for liberation, the workers and poor peasants will flock to the banner of (our) Party and the petty bourgeoisie will also link up with us. However, the workers must not become the appendage of the petty bourgeoisie within this democratic united front, but must fight for their own class interests. Therefore it is imperative that the workers be organized in the Party as well as in labour unions. Ever mindful of their class independence, the workers must develop the strength of their fighting organization (in order to) prepare for the establishment of soviets in conjunction with the poor peasantry and in order to achieve (the goal of) complete liberation. The CCP is a section of the CI. The Party calls the Chinese workers and peasants to rush to its banner for the (coming) struggle: it asks the oppressed masses of all China to fight in common with the workers and poor peasants under the Party banner; and it hopes that the revolutionary masses of the whole world will march forward shoulder-to-shoulder. Only an alliance of the world proletariat and the oppressed peoples can lead to the liberation of the world.

Chapter Two

The Rise of Mao Tse-tung

THE PERIOD from 1927 to 1937 marked the rise of Mao Tse-tung as the leader of the Party. He attained the position in 1935 during the retreat from the Kiangsi-Fukien border area on the so-called "Long March" to the new "base area" located at Yenan in the northwest. Born in 1893 in Hunan, he came from a peasant family. At the end of World War I, he went to Peking to work as a librarian at Peking University, where the May 4th Movement originated. Mao, though a graduate of a normal school, is well versed in Chinese classics and history, as well as in Marxist-Leninist doctrine. He was one of the founding members of the Party, and had participated in the Northern Expedition. But Mao was a realist, as well as strategist—a man who consistently drew his own lessons of operation from his early experiences in labor and peasant organizations. With these qualities, he led the Party to power in 1949.

However, the road that led Mao and his Party to power was a long and tortuous one. In the Introduction, we summarized Mao's revolutionary career. We cannot follow it here in all its twists and turns. What concerns us is not the history of the Party, but Mao's views and thoughts, or "Maoism," as reflected in his writings of this period. Authorities disagree about the originality of Mao's contribution to Communist theory, but "Maoism" usually claims credit for three innovations: first, the peasant base on which Mao relied for the support of the Party (Selection 3); secondly, the creation of a guerrilla force drawn from the peasants with a "base area" in the countryside (Selection 4); thirdly, the strategy of the four-class and two-stage revolution (Selection 5).

3. Mao Tse-tung: Report on an Investigation of the Peasant Movement in Hunan (March, 1927)*

This report is a revolutionary classic, written in February, 1927. Though it cannot be taken as a complete expression of Mao's political outlook, it expresses the essence of Mao's line—his rural strategy based on the peasantry. In the report, Mao allotted the peasants seven out of ten points in the accomplishments of the "bourgeois-democratic revolution."[1] By making the poor peasantry the "revolutionary vanguard," he diverged from the orthodox Marxist-Leninist doctrine, which maintained that the "revolutionary vanguard" should be the urban proletariat. Mao never eschewed orthodox Communism, but the almost total destruction of the Party's urban base which followed the 1927 debacle led him, on the contrary, to urge the peasant revolution, instead of the "proletarian revolution," to fit conditions of China. The significance of this report lies in his recognition of the importance of peasant support which became highly important for the Party's conquest of all China. His prediction of the rising of "several hundred million peasants" might be full of exaggerations. In spite of the importance of the poor peasantry, Mao failed in his report to say anything about land expropriation, in order not to offend some of the Kuomintang leaders and to threaten the co-operation between the Kuomintang and the Communists.

---

* From *Selected Works of Mao Tse-tung*, Peking: Foreign Language Press, 1965, I, 23–34. (The last section, on "Fourteen Great Achievements," and most footnotes omitted.)

[1] In rewriting the Hunan report in 1951, Mao made significant changes bearing directly on the role of the various classes in the revolution, but prime importance is still attached to the peasantry.

Communist exploitation of peasant discontent for the seizure of power was nothing new. Lenin had used the land hunger of the Russian peasant in the Russian proletarian revolution. In this sense Mao "is a Leninist in the best tradition; and his *Report* is a classic of Chinese Leninism."[2] But we wish to point out that Lenin, in spite of his reliance on the support of the peasants, regarded the peasantry as only an auxiliary force in the proletarian revolution, and that Mao, by giving the peasant the main role, diverged from Lenin and made a new contribution. It is true that Mao's strategy eventually won the full approval of Stalin. On the other hand, there is ample evidence of Moscow's full support to Li Li-san's strategy based on the urban proletariat and the conquest of the cities.[3]

THE IMPROVEMENT OF THE PEASANT PROBLEM[†]

During my recent visit to Hunan I made a first-hand investigation of conditions in the five counties of Hsiangtan, Hsianghsiang, Hengshan, Liling and Changsha. In the thirty-two days from January 4 to February 5, I called together fact-finding conferences in villages and county towns, which were attended by experienced peasants and by comrades working in the peasant movement, and I listened attentively to their reports and collected a great deal of material. Many of the hows and whys of the peasant movement were the exact opposite of what the gentry in Hankow and Changsha are

[2] Conrad Brandt *et al., A Documentary History of Chinese Communism,* Cambridge, Mass.: Harvard University Press, 1959, p. 79.

[3] In his *Power Relations Within the Chinese Communist Movement, 1930–1934: A Study of Documents,* Seattle and London: University of Washington Press, 1961, Hsiao Tso-liang holds that Moscow disagreed with Li Li-san (the Party's leader) and Mao's line was essentially that of Moscow. His theory, however, has not been conclusively established.

[†] This article was written as a reply to the carping criticisms both inside and outside the Party then being levelled at the peasants' revolutionary struggle. Comrade Mao Tse-tung spent thirty-two days in Hunan Province making an investigation and wrote this report in order to answer these criticisms. The Right opportunists in the Party, headed by Chen Tu-hsiu, would not accept his views and stuck to their own wrong ideas. Their chief error was that, frightened by the reactionary trend in the Kuomintang, they dared not support the great revolutionary struggles of the peasants which had erupted or were erupting. To appease the Kuomintang, they preferred to desert the peasantry, the chief ally in the revolution, and thus left the working class and the Communist Party isolated and without help. It was mainly because it was able to exploit this weakness within the Communist Party that the Kuomintang dared to betray the revolution, launch its "party purge" and make war on the people in the summer of 1927.

saying. I saw and heard of many strange things of which I had hitherto been unaware. I believe the same is true of many other places, too. All talk directed against the peasant movement must be speedily set right. All the wrong measures taken by the revolutionary authorities concerning the peasant movement must be speedily changed. Only thus can the future of the revolution be benefited. For the present upsurge of the peasant movement is a colossal event. In a very short time, in China's central, southern and northern provinces, several hundred million peasants will rise like a mighty storm, like a hurricane, a force so swift and violent that no power, however great, will be able to hold it back. They will smash all the trammels that bind them and rush forward along the road to liberation. They will sweep all the imperialists, warlords, corrupt officials, local tyrants and evil gentry into their graves. Every revolutionary party and every revolutionary comrade will be put to the test, to be accepted or rejected as they decide. There are three alternatives. To march at their head and lead them? To trail behind them, gesticulating and criticizing? Or to stand in their way and oppose them? Every Chinese is free to choose, but events will force you to make the choice quickly.

GET ORGANIZED!

The development of the peasant movement in Hunan may be divided roughly into two periods with respect to the counties in the province's central and southern parts where the movement has already made much headway. The first, from January to September of last year, was one of organization. In this period, January to June was a time of underground activity, and July to September, when the revolutionary army was driving out Chao Heng-ti, one of open activity. During this period, the membership of the peasant associations did not exceed 300,000-400,000, the masses directly under their leadership numbered little more than a million, there was as yet hardly any struggle in the rural areas, and consequently there was very little criticism of the associations in other circles. Since its members served as guides, scouts and carriers of the Northern Expeditionary Army, even some of the officers had a good word to say for the peasant associations. The second period, from last October to January of this year, was one of revolutionary action. The membership of the associations jumped to two million and the masses directly under their leadership increased to ten million. Since the peasants generally enter only one name for the whole family on joining a peasant association, a membership of two million means a mass following of about ten million. Almost half the peasants in Hunan are now organized. In counties like Hsiangtan, Hsianghsiang, Liuyang, Changsha, Liling, Ninghsiang, Pingkiang, Hsiangyin, Hengshan, Hengyang, Leiyang, Chenhsien and Anhua, nearly all the peasants have combined in the peasant associations or have come under their leadership. It was on the strength of their extensive organization that the peasants went into action and within four months brought about a great revolution in the countryside, a revolution without parallel in history.

DOWN WITH THE LOCAL TYRANTS AND EVIL GENTRY! ALL POWER TO THE PEASANT ASSOCIATIONS!

The main targets of attack by the peasants are the local tyrants, the evil gentry and the lawless landlords, but in passing they also hit out against patriarchal ideas and institutions, against the corrupt officials in the cities and against bad practices and customs in the rural areas. In force and momentum the attack is tempestuous; those who bow before it survive and those who resist perish. As a result, the privileges which the feudal landlords enjoyed for thousands of years are being shattered to pieces. Every bit of the dignity and prestige built up by the landlords is being swept into the dust. With the collapse of the power of the landlords, the peasant associations have now become the sole organs of authority and the popular slogan "All power to the peasant associations" has become a reality. Even trifles such as a quarrel between husband and wife are brought to the peasant association. Nothing can be settled unless someone from the peasant association is present. The association actually dictates all rural affairs, and, quite literally, "whatever it says, goes". Those who are outside the associations can only speak well of them and cannot say anything against them. The local tyrants, evil gentry and lawless landlords have been deprived of all right to speak, and none of them dares even mutter dissent. In the face of the peasant associations' power and pressure, the top local tyrants and evil gentry have fled to Shanghai, those of the second rank to Hankow, those of the third to Changsha and those of the fourth to the county towns, while the fifth rank and the still lesser fry surrender to the peasant associations in the villages.

"Here's ten yuan. Please let me join the peasant association," one of the smaller of the evil gentry will say.

"Ugh! Who wants your filthy money?" the peasants reply.

Many middle and small landlords and rich peasants and even some middle peasants, who were all formerly opposed to the peasant associations, are now vainly seeking admission. Visiting various places, I often came across such people who pleaded with me, "Mr. Committeeman from the provincial capital, please be my sponsor!"

In the Ching Dynasty, the household census compiled by the local authorities consisted of a regular register and "the other" register, the former for honest people and the latter for burglars, bandits and similar undesirables. In some places the peasants now use this method to scare those who formerly opposed the associations. They say, "Put their names down in the other register!"

Afraid of being entered in the other register, such people try various devices to gain admission into the peasant associations, on which their minds are so set that they do not feel safe until their names are entered. But more often than not they are turned down flat, and so they are always on tenterhooks; with the doors of the association barred to them, they are like tramps without a home or, in rural parlance, "mere trash". In short, what was looked down upon four months ago as a "gang of peasants" has now become a most honourable institution. Those who formerly prostrated themselves before the power of the gentry now bow before the power of the peasants. No matter what their identity, all admit that the world since last October is a different one.

"It's Terrible!" or "It's Fine!"

The peasants' revolt disturbed the gentry's sweet dreams When the news from the countryside reached the cities, it caused immediate uproar among the gentry. Soon after my arrival in Changsha, I met all sorts of people and picked up a good deal of gossip. From the middle social strata upwards to the Kuomintang right-wingers, there was not a single person who did not sum up the whole business in the phrase, "It's terrible!" Under the impact of the views of the "It's terrible!" school then flooding the city, even quite revolutionary-minded people became down-hearted as they pictured the events in the countryside in their mind's eye; and they were unable to deny the word "terrible". Even quite progressive people said, "Though terrible, it is inevitable in a revolution." In short, nobody could altogether deny the word "terrible". But, as already mentioned, the fact is that the great peasant masses have risen to fulfil their historic mission and that the forces of rural democracy have risen to overthrow the forces of rural feudalism. The patriarchal-feudal class of local tyrants, evil gentry and lawless landlords has formed the basis of autocratic government for thousands of years and is the cornerstone of imperialism, warlordism and corrupt officialdom. To overthrow these feudal forces is the real objective of the national revolution. In a few months the peasants have accomplished what Dr. Sun Yat-sen wanted, but failed, to accomplish in the forty years he devoted to the national revolution. This is a marvellous feat never before achieved, not just in forty, but in thousands of years. It's fine. It is not "terrible" at all. It is anything but "terrible". "It's terrible!" is obviously a theory for combating the rise of the peasants in the interests of the landlords; it is obviously a theory of the landlord class for preserving the old order of feudalism and obstructing the establishment of the new order of democracy, it is obviously a counter-revolutionary theory. No revolutionary comrade should echo this nonsense. If your revolutionary viewpoint is firmly established and if you have been to the villages and looked around, you will undoubtedly feel thrilled as never before. Countless thousands of the enslaved—the peasants—are striking down the enemies who battened on their flesh. What the peasants are doing is absolutely right; what they are doing is fine! "It's fine!" is the theory of the peasants and of all other revolutionaries. Every revolutionary comrade should know that the national revolution requires a great change in the countryside. The Revolution of 1911 did not bring about this change, hence its failure. This change is now taking place, and it is an important factor for the completion of the revolution. Every revolutionary comrade must support it, or he will be taking the stand of counter-revolution.

THE QUESTION OF "GOING TOO FAR"

Then there is another section of people who say, "Yes, peasant associations are necessary, but they are going rather too far." This is the opinion of the middle-of-the-roaders. But what is the actual situation? True, the peasants are in a sense "unruly" in the countryside. Supreme in authority, the peasant association allows the landlord no say and sweeps away his prestige. This amounts to striking the landlord down to the dust and keeping him there. The peasants threaten, "We will put you in the other register!" They fine the local tyrants and evil gentry, they demand contributions from them, and they smash their sedan-chairs. People swarm into the houses of local tyrants and evil gentry who are against the peasant association, slaughter their pigs and consume their grain. They even loll for a minute or two on the ivory-inlaid beds belonging to the young ladies in the households of the local tyrants and evil gentry. At the slightest provocation they make arrests, crown the arrested with tall paper-hats, and parade them through the villages, saying, "You dirty·landlords, now you know who we are!" Doing whatever they like and turning everything upside down, they have created a kind of terror in the countryside. This is what some people call "going too far", or "exceeding the proper limits in righting a wrong", or "really too much". Such talk may seem plausible, but in fact it is wrong. First, the local tyrants, evil gentry and lawless landlords have themselves driven the peasants to this. For ages they have used their power to tyrannize over the peasants and trample them underfoot; that is why the peasants have reacted so strongly. The most violent revolts and the most serious disorders have invariably occurred in places where the local tyrants, evil gentry and lawless landlords perpetrated the worst outrages. The peasants are clear-sighted. Who is bad and who is not, who is the worst and who is not quite so vicious, who deserves severe punishment and who deserves to be let off lightly—the peasants keep clear accounts, and very seldom has the punishment exceeded the crime. Secondly, a revolution is not a dinner party, or writing an essay, or painting a picture, or doing embroidery; it cannot be so refined, so leisurely and gentle, so temperate, kind, courteous, restrained and magnanimous. A revolution is an insurrection, an act of violence by which one class overthrows another. A rural revolution is a revolution by which the peasantry overthrows the power of the feudal landlord class. Without using the greatest force, the peasants cannot possibly overthrow the deep-rooted authority of the landlords which has lasted for thousands of years. The rural areas need a mighty revolutionary upsurge, for it alone can rouse the people in their millions to become a powerful force. All the actions mentioned here which have been labelled as "going too far" flow from the power of the peasants, which has been called forth by the mighty revolutionary upsurge in the countryside. It was highly necessary for such things to be done in the second period of the peasant movement, the period of revolutionary action. In this period it was necessary to establish the absolute authority of the peasants. It was necessary to forbid malicious criticism of the peasant associations. It was necessary to overthrow the whole authority of the gentry, to strike them to the ground and keep them there. There is revolutionary significance in all the actions which were labelled as "going too far" in this period. To put it bluntly, it is necessary to create terror for a while in every rural area, or otherwise it would be impossible to suppress the activities of the counter-revolutionaries in the countryside or overthrow the authority of the gentry. Proper limits have to be exceeded in order to right a wrong, or else the wrong cannot be righted. Those who talk about the peasants "going too far" seem at first sight to be different from those who say "It's terrible!" as mentioned earlier, but in essence they proceed from the same standpoint and likewise voice a landlord theory that upholds the interests of the privileged classes. Since this theory impedes the rise of the peasant movement and so disrupts the revolution, we must firmly oppose it.

The "Movement of the Riffraff"

The right-wing of the Kuomintang says, "The peasant movement is a movement of the riffraff, of the lazy peasants." This view is current in Changsha. When I was in the countryside, I heard the gentry say, "It is all right to set up peasant associations, but the people now running them are no good. They ought to be replaced!" This opinion comes to the same thing as what the right-wingers are saying; according to both it is all right to have a peasant movement (the movement is already in being and no one dare say otherwise), but they say that the people running it are no good and they particularly hate those in charge of the associations at the lower levels, calling them "riffraff". In short, all those whom the gentry had despised, those whom they had trodden into the dirt, people with no place in society, people with no right to speak, have now audaciously lifted up their heads. They have not only lifted up their heads but taken power into their hands. They are now running the township peasant associations (at the lowest level), which they have turned into something fierce and formidable. They have raised their rough, work-soiled hands and laid them on the gentry. They tether the evil gentry with ropes, crown them with tall paper-hats and parade them through the villages. (In Hsiangtan and Hsianghsiang they call this "parading through the township" and in Liling "parading through the fields".) Not a day passes but they drum some harsh, pitiless words of denunciation into these gentry's ears. They are issuing orders and are running everything. Those who used to rank lowest now rank above everybody else; and so this is called "turning things upside down".

VANGUARDS OF THE REVOLUTION

Where there are two opposite approaches to things and people, two opposite views emerge. "It's terrible!" and "It's fine!", "riffraff" and "vanguards of the revolution"—here are apt examples.

We said above that the peasants have accomplished a revolutionary task which had been left unaccomplished for many years and have done an important job for the national revolution. But has this great revolutionary task, this important revolutionary work, been performed by all the peasants? No. There are three kinds of peasants, the rich, the middle and the poor peasants. The three live in different circumstances and so have different views about the revolution. In the first period, what appealed to the rich peasants was the talk about the Northern Expeditionary Army's sustaining a crushing defeat in Kiangsi, about Chiang Kai-shek's being wounded in the leg and flying back to Kwangtung, and about Wu Pei-fu's recapturing Yuehchow. The peasant associations would certainly not last and the Three People's Principles could never prevail, because they had never been heard of before. Thus an official of the township peasant association (generally one of the "riffraff" type) would walk into the house of a rich peasant, register in hand, and say, "Will you please join the peasant association?" How would the rich peasant answer? A tolerably well-behaved one would say, "Peasant association? I have lived here for decades, tilling my land. I never heard of such a thing before, yet I've managed to live all right. I advise you to give it up!" A really vicious rich peasant would say, "Peasant association! Nonsense! Association for getting your head chopped off! Don't get people into trouble!" Yet, surprisingly enough, the peasant associations have now been established several months, and have even dared to stand up to the gentry. The gentry of the neighbourhood who refused to surrender their opium pipes were arrested by the associations and paraded through the villages. In the county towns, moreover, some big landlords were put to death, like Yen Jung-chiu of Hsiangtan and Yang Chih-tse of Ninghsiang. On the anniversary of the October Revolution, at the time of the anti-British rally and of the great celebrations of the victory of the Northern Expedition, tens of thousands of peasants in every township, holding high their banners, big and small, along with their carrying-poles and hoes, demonstrated in massive, streaming columns. It was only then that the rich peasants began to get perplexed and alarmed. During the great victory celebrations of the Northern Expedition, they learned that Kiukiang had been taken, that Chiang Kai-shek had not been wounded in the leg and that Wu Pei-fu had been defeated after all. What is more, they saw such slogans as "Long live the Three People's Principles!" "Long live the peasant associations!" and "Long live the peasants!" clearly written on the "red and green proclamations". "What?" wondered the rich peasants, greatly perplexed and alarmed, " 'Long live the peasants!' Are these people now to be regarded as emperors?" So the peasant associations are putting on grand airs. People from the associations say to the rich peasants, "We'll enter you in the other register," or, "In another month, the admission fee will be ten yuan a head!" Only under the impact

of all this are the rich peasants tardily joining the associations, some paying fifty cents or a yuan for admission (the
regular fee being a mere ten coppers), some securing admission only after asking other people to put in a good word
for them. But there are quite a number of die-hards who
have not joined to this day. When the rich peasants join the
associations, they generally enter the name of some sixty or
seventy year-old member of the family, for they are in constant dread of "conscription". After joining, the rich peasants
are not keen on doing any work for the associations. They
remain inactive throughout.

How about the middle peasants? Theirs is a vacillating attitude. They think that the revolution will not bring them
much good. They have rice cooking in their pots and no credi-
tors knocking on their doors at midnight. They, too, judging
a thing by whether it ever existed before, knit their brows
and think to themselves, "Can the peasant association really
last?" "Can the Three People's Principles prevail?" Their conclusion is, "Afraid not!" They imagine it all depends on the
will of Heaven and think, "A peasant association? Who knows
if Heaven wills it or not?" In the first period, people from
the association would call on a middle peasant, register in
hand, and say, "Will you please join the peasant association?" The middle peasant would reply, "There's no hurry!"
It was not until the second period, when the peasant associations were already exercising great power, that the middle
peasants came in. They show up better in the associations
than the rich peasants but are not as yet very enthusiastic;
they still want to wait and see. It is essential for the peasant
associations to get the middle peasants to join and to do a good
deal more explanatory work among them.

The poor peasants have always been the main force in the
bitter fight in the countryside. They ·have fought militantly
through the two periods of underground work and of open
activity. They are the most responsive to Communist Party
leadership. They are deadly enemies of the camp of the
local tyrants and evil gentry and attack it without the slightest
hesitation. "We joined the peasant association long ago," they
say to the rich peasants, "why are you still hesitating?" The
rich peasants answer mockingly, "What is there to keep you
from joining? You people have neither a tile over your heads
nor a speck of land under your feet!" It is true the poor

peasants are not afraid of losing anything. Many of them really have "neither a tile over their heads nor a speck of land under their feet". What, indeed, is there to keep them from joining the associations? According to the survey of Changsha County, the poor peasants comprise 70 per cent, the middle peasants 20 per cent, and the landlords and the rich peasants 10 per cent of the population in the rural areas. The 70 per cent, the poor peasants, may be sub-divided into two categories, the utterly destitute and the less destitute. The utterly destitute, comprising 20 per cent, are the completely dispossessed, that is, people who have neither land nor money, are without any means of livelihood, and are forced to leave home and become mercenaries or hired labourers or wandering beggars. The less destitute, the other 50 per cent, are the partially dispossessed, that is, people with just a little land or a little money who eat up more than they earn and live in toil and distress the year round, such as the handicraftsmen, the tenant-peasants (not including the rich tenant-peasants) and the semi-owner-peasants. This great mass of poor peasants, or altogether 70 per cent of the rural population, are the backbone of the peasant associations, the vanguard in the overthrow of the feudal forces and the heroes who have performed the great revolutionary task which for long years was left undone. Without the poor peasant class (the "riffraff", as the gentry call them), it would have been impossible to bring about the present revolutionary situation in the countryside, or to overthrow the local tyrants and evil gentry and complete the democratic revolution. The poor peasants, being the most revolutionary group, have gained the leadership of the peasant associations. In both the first and second periods almost all the chairmen and committee members in the peasant associations at the lowest level were poor peasants (of the officials in the township associations in Hengshan County the utterly destitute comprise 50 per cent, the less destitute 40 per cent, and poverty-stricken intellectuals 10 per cent). Leadership by the poor peasants is absolutely necessary. Without the poor peasants there would be no revolution. To deny their role is to deny the revolution. To attack them is to attack the revolution. They have never been wrong on the general direction of the revolution. They have discredited the local tyrants and evil gentry. They have beaten down the local tyrants and evil gentry, big and small, and kept them underfoot. Many of their deeds in the period of revolutionary action, which were labelled as "going too far", were in fact the very things the revolution required. Some county governments, county head-quarters of the Kuomintang and county peasant associations in Hunan have already made a number of mistakes; some have even sent soldiers to arrest officials of the lower-level associations at the landlords' request. A good many chairmen and committee members of township associations in Hengshan and Hsianghsiang Counties have been thrown in jail. This mistake is very serious and feeds the arrogance of the reactionaries. To judge whether or not it is a mistake, you have only to see how joyful the lawless landlords become and how reactionary sentiments grow, wherever the chairmen or committee members of local peasant associations are arrested. We must combat the counter-revolutionary talk of a "movement of riffraff" and a "movement of lazy peasants" and must be especially careful not to commit the error of helping the local tyrants and evil gentry in their attacks on the poor peasant class. Though a few of the poor peasant leaders undoubtedly did have shortcomings, most of them have changed by now. They themselves are energetically prohibiting gambling and suppressing banditry. Where the peasant association is powerful, gambling has stopped altogether and banditry has vanished. In some places it is literally true that people do not take any articles left by the wayside and that doors are not bolted at night. According to the Hengshan survey, 85 per cent of the poor peasant leaders have made great progress and have proved themselves capable and hard-working. Only 15 per cent retain some bad habits. The most one can call these is "an unhealthy minority", and we must not echo the local tyrants and evil gentry in undiscriminatingly condemning them as "riffraff". This problem of the "unhealthy minority" can be tackled only under the peasant associations' own slogan of "strengthen discipline", by carrying on propaganda among the masses, by educating the "unhealthy minority", and by tightening the associations' discipline; in no circumstances should soldiers be arbitrarily sent to make such arrests as would damage the prestige of the poor peasants and feed the arrogance of the local tyrants and evil gentry. This point requires particular attention.

4. Mao Tse-tung: The Struggle in the Chingkang Mountains (November, 1928)*

This is a report submitted to the Central Committee of the Party in November, 1928, summing up the experiences in the war against the Kuomintang. It analyses the nature and situation of the "bourgeois-democratic revolution" at that time so as to lay down the Party's policies, tasks and tactics for struggle.

As noted in the Introduction, after the failure of the "Autumn-Harvest Uprising" in Hunan in September, 1927, Mao retreated with his remaining forces into the Chingkang Mountains on the Hunan-Kiangsi border. There he founded the revolutionary rural base and consolidated the Red Army to turn away a series of "extermination campaigns" directed against them by the Kuomintang troops. Afterward, the Red Army became well known for guerrilla warfare. In this report, Mao stressed his policy of transferring "the revolutionary forces to the countryside where they could set up revolutionary bases, and muster and develop their strength in order to surround, and eventually capture, cities." Implementation of this policy, as Mao pointed out in his report, took two major lines: the development of a disciplined, trained and equipped Red Army able to withstand the attacks of the Kuomintang troops with their bases in the cities; and the organization of state power in the areas under Communist control, in the form of a soviet following the example of the Russian Revolution. This latter organization was implemented with the hope that eventually all the soviets could be brought together into a central government for all China, supported and defended by the united Red Army. In this way, central government control would be able to reach the masses. This policy was, in fact, a further

---

* From *Selected Works of Mao Tse-tung*, Peking: Foreign Language Press, 1965, I, 73–78. (The second part of the report, dealing with "The Current Situation in the Area Under the Independent Regime," and footnotes omitted.)

development of "Maoism" for the support of the peasantry. It was this policy that led Mao to the prime leadership of the Party and to the conquest of the mainland.

This text, like the preceding Hunan report, has undergone extensive modifications in the current edition. The text in the original form is not available.

THE INDEPENDENT REGIME IN THE HUNAN-KIANGSI BORDER AREA AND THE AUGUST DEFEAT

China is the only country in the world today where one or more small areas under Red political power have emerged in the midst of a White regime which encircles them. We find on analysis that one reason for this phenomenon lies in the incessant splits and wars within China's comprador and landlord classes. So long as these splits and wars continue, it is possible for an armed independent regime of workers and peasants to survive and grow. In addition, its survival and growth require the following conditions: (1) a sound mass base, (2) a sound Party organization, (3) a fairly strong Red Army, (4) terrain favourable to military operations, and (5) economic resources sufficient for sustenance.

An independent regime must vary its strategy against the encircling ruling classes, adopting one strategy when the ruling class regime is temporarily stable and another when it is split up. In a period when the ruling classes are split up, as during the wars between Li Tsung-jen and Tang Sheng-chih in Hunan and Hupeh Provinces and between Chang Fa-kuei and Li Chi-shen in Kwangtung Province, our strategy can be comparatively adventurous and the area carved out by military operations can be comparatively large. However, we must take care to lay a solid foundation in the central districts so that we shall have something secure to rely on when the White terror strikes. In a period when the regime of the ruling classes is comparatively stable, as it was in the southern provinces after April this year, our strategy must be one of gradual advance. In such a period, the worst thing in military affairs is to divide our forces for an adventurous advance, and the worst thing in local work (distributing land, establishing political power, expanding the Party and organizing local armed forces) is to scatter our personnel and neglect to lay a solid foundation in the central districts. The defeats which many small Red areas have suffered have been due either to the absence of the requisite objective conditions or to subjective mistakes in tactics. Mistakes in tactics have been made solely because of failure to distinguish clearly between the two kinds of period, that in which the regime of the ruling classes is temporarily stable and that in which it is split up. In a period of temporary stability, some comrades advocated dividing our forces for an adventurous advance and even proposed leaving the defence of extensive areas to the Red Guards alone, as though oblivious of the fact that the enemy could attack not merely with the landlords' levies but even in concentrated operations with regular troops. In local work, they utterly neglected to lay a solid foundation in the central districts and attempted unrestricted expansion regardless of whether it was within our capacity. If anyone advocated a policy of gradual advance in military operations or a policy of concentrating our effort in local work on laying a solid foundation in the central districts so as to secure an invincible position, they dubbed him a "conservative". Their wrong ideas were the root cause of the defeats sustained last August by the Hunan-Kiangsi border area and by the Fourth Red Army in southern Hunan.

Our work in the Hunan-Kiangsi border area began in October last year. At the start, all our Party organizations in the counties were defunct. The local armed forces consisted only of the two units under Yuan Wen-tsai and Wang Tso in the vicinity of the Chingkang Mountains, each unit having sixty rifles in bad repair, while the peasant self-defence corps in the counties of Yunghsin, Lienhua, Chaling and Linghsien had been totally disarmed by the landlord class and the revolutionary ardour of the masses had been stifled. By February this year Ningkang, Yunghsin, Chaling and Suichuan had county Party committees, Linghsien had a special district Party committee, and in Lienhua a Party organization was beginning to function and establish connections with the Wanan County Committee. All the counties except Linghsien had a few local armed units. In Ningkang, Chaling, Suichuan and Yunghsin, and especially in the two latter counties, there were a good many guerrilla uprisings against the landlords which aroused the masses, and all were fairly successful. In that period the agrarian revolution had not yet been carried very far. The organs of political power were called governments of the workers, peasants and soldiers. Soldiers' committees were set up in the army. When units went on separate missions, action committees were set up to direct them. The leading body of the Party there was the Front Committee (with Mao Tse-tung as secretary), which had been appointed by the Hunan Provincial Committee during the Autumn Harvest Uprising. In early March, upon the request of the Southern Hunan Special Committee, the Front Committee was abolished and reorganized as the Divisional Party Committee (with Ho Ting-ying as secretary), which thus became a body in charge of Party organizations in the army only and without authority over the local Party organizations. Meanwhile, Mao Tse-tung's forces were dispatched to southern Hunan upon the request of the Special Committee there, and consequently the Hunan-Kiangsi border area was occupied by the enemy for more than a month. At the end of March came the defeat in southern Hunan, and in April the forces under Chu Teh and those under Mao Tse-tung, together with the peasant army of southern Hunan, withdrew to Ningkang and began to re-establish the independent regime in the border area.

From April onward the independent regime in the Hunan-Kiangsi border area was confronted with a temporarily stable ruling power in the south, and Hunan and Kiangsi would dispatch at least eight or nine regiments of reactionary forces to "suppress" us and sometimes as many as eighteen. Yet with a force of less than four regiments we fought the enemy for four long months, daily enlarging the territory under our independent regime, deepening the agrarian revolution, extending the people's political power and expanding the Red Army and the Red Guards. This was possible because the policies of the Party organizations (local and army) in the border area were correct. The policies of the Border Area Special Committee (with Mao Tse-tung as secretary) and the Army Committee (with Chen Yi as secretary) of the Party were then as follows:

> Struggle resolutely against the enemy, set up political power in the middle section of the Lohsiao mountain range, and oppose flightism.
> Deepen the agrarian revolution in areas under the independent regime.
> Promote the development of the local Party organization with the

help of the army Party organization and promote the development of the local armed forces with the help of the regular army.

Be on the defensive against Hunan with its comparatively strong ruling power, and take the offensive against Kiangsi with its comparatively weak ruling power.

Devote great efforts to the development of Yunghsin, set up an independent regime of the people there and prepare for a prolonged struggle.

Concentrate the Red Army units in order to fight the enemy confronting them when the time is opportune, and oppose the division of forces so as to avoid being destroyed one by one.

Adopt the policy of advancing in a series of waves to expand the area under the independent regime, and oppose the policy of expansion by adventurist advance.

Thanks to these proper tactics, to the terrain of the border area which favoured our struggle, and to the inadequate co-ordination between the troops invading from Hunan and those invading from Kiangsi, we were able to win a number of military victories and expand the people's independent regime in the four months from April to July. Although several times stronger than we, the enemy was unable to prevent the expansion of our regime, let alone to destroy it. Our regime tended to exert an ever-growing influence on Hunan and Kiangsi. The sole reason for the August defeat was that, failing to realize that the period was one of temporary stability for the ruling classes, some comrades adopted a policy suited to a period of splits within the ruling classes and divided our forces for an adventurous advance on southern Hunan, thus causing defeat both in the border area and in southern Hunan. Tu Hsiu-ching, the representative of the Hunan Provincial Committee, and Yang Kai-ming, the secretary of the Border Area Special Committee who had been appointed by the Provincial Committee, failed to grasp the actual situation and, taking advantage of the fact that Mao Tse-tung, Wan Hsi-hsien and other strongly dissenting comrades were far away in Yunghsin, they disregarded the resolutions of the joint meeting of the Army Committee, the Special Committee and the Yunghsin County Committee of the Party, which disapproved of the views of the Hunan Provincial Committee. They just mechanically enforced the order of the Hunan Provincial Committee to march to southern Hunan and fell in with the desire of the Red Army's 29th Regiment (composed of peasants from Yichang) to evade struggle and return home, thus causing defeat both in the border area and in southern Hunan.

Originally, in mid-July, the Eighth Army from Hunan, under Wu Shang, had invaded Ningkang, penetrated to Yunghsin, sought battle with us in vain (our men tried to attack them from a side road but missed them) and then, being afraid of the masses who supported us, hurriedly retreated to Chaling via Lienhua. In the meantime, the major detachment of the Red Army, which was advancing from Ningkang to attack Linghsien and Chaling, changed its plans on reaching Linghsien and turned towards southern Hunan, while the enemy forces from Kiangsi, consisting of 5 regiments of the Third Army under Wang Chun and Chin Han-ting and 6 regiments of the Sixth Army under Hu Wen-tou, launched a joint assault on Yunghsin. At that point we had only 1 regiment in Yunghsin which, under the cover provided by the broad masses of the people, pinned down these 11 regiments within a radius of thirty *li* of Yunghsin county town for as long as twenty-five days by means of guerrilla attacks from every direction. In the end we lost Yunghsin because of the enemy's fierce assault, and also lost Lienhua and Ningkang shortly afterwards. At that moment internal dissensions suddenly flared up among the Kiangsi enemy forces; the Sixth Army under Hu Wen-tou withdrew in haste and presently engaged Wang Chun's Third Army at Changshu. The other 5 Kiangsi regiments then hastily withdrew to the county town of Yunghsin. Had our major detachment not moved to southern Hunan, it would have been entirely possible to rout this enemy force and extend the area of the independent regime to include Kian, Anfu and Pinghsiang and to link it up with Pingkiang and Liuyang. But as the major detachment was away and the one remaining regiment was much too exhausted, it was decided that some men should remain to defend the Chingkang Mountains in co-operation with the two units under Yuan Wen-tsai and Wang Tso, and that I should take the rest to Kueitung to meet the major detachment and to invite it back. By that time the major detachment was retreating from southern Hunan to Kueitung, and on August 23 we joined forces there.

When the major detachment of the Red Army had arrived in Linghsien in mid-July, the officers and men of the 29th Regiment, who were wavering politically and wanted to return to their homes in southern Hunan, refused to obey orders, while the 28th Regiment was against going to southern Hunan and wanted to go to southern Kiangsi, but in any case did not want to return to Yunghsin. As Tu Hsiu-ching encouraged the 29th Regiment in their mistaken ideas and the Army Committee failed to dissuade them, the major detachment set out from Linghsien for Chenchow on July 17. In an engagement with the enemy forces under Fan Shih-sheng in Chenchow on July 24, it was initially successful but was later defeated and withdrew from the battle. Thereupon, acting on its own, the 29th Regiment hurried homeward to Yichang with the result that one section was annihilated at Lochang by Hu Feng-chang's bandits, another scattered in the Chenchow-Yichang area and has never been heard of since, and no more than a hundred men were mustered again that day. Fortunately, the 28th Regiment, which was the main force, had not suffered great losses and on August 18 it occupied Kueitung. On August 23 the regiment was joined by the troops from the Chingkang Mountains, to which it was decided that the combined forces should return by way of Chungyi and Shangyu. When we reached Chungyi, battalion commander Yuan Chung-chuan defected with an infantry company and an artillery company, and though the two companies were brought back, our regimental commander Wang Erh-cho lost his life in this action. When our men were returning but had not yet reached their destination, enemy units from Hunan and Kiangsi seized the opportunity to attack the Chingkang Mountains on August 30. Using their points of vantage, the defending troops, numbering less than one battalion, fought back, routed the enemy and saved the base.

The causes of our August defeat were as follows: (1) some officers and men, who were wavering and homesick, lost their fighting capacity, while others, who were unwilling to go to southern Hunan, were lacking in enthusiasm; (2) our men were exhausted by long marches in the sweltering summer heat; (3) having ventured several hundred *li* away from Linghsien, our men lost contact with the border area and became isolated; (4) as the masses in southern Hunan had not yet been aroused, the expedition proved to be pure military adventurism; (5) we were uninformed about the enemy situation; and (6) the preparations were inadequate, and officers and men did not understand the purpose of the operation.

5.   Mao Tse-tung: On Tactics of Fighting Japanese Imperialism (December, 1935)*

This report was delivered at a conference of the Party activists at Wayaopao, northern Shensi, in December, 1935. It followed a resolution passed by the Political Bureau of the Central Committee on the tactics of building a national united front against Japanese aggression.[1] In this report, Mao dealt fully with the possibility and importance of re-establishing a national united front with the "national bourgeoisie" against Japanese aggression. He emphasized the leading role the Party should play in that front. He also criticized narrow, "closed-door" sectarianism for its excommunication of the bourgeoisie and revolutionary impetuosity for its insistence on the "proletarian hegemony"— the two extremes which had prevailed in the Party for a long time.

As a matter of fact, the main thesis in his writings on this subject, beginning with this report in 1935, and culminating in "On People's Democratic Dictatorship" in 1949 (Selection 18), is that of the "four-class bloc," composed of workers, peasants, petty bourgeoisie and national bourgeoisie, and the two-stage revolution—"bourgeois-democratic" and socialist. Indeed, Mao's report of December, 1935, marked a turning point for the Party, over which Mao obtained control in January, 1935. He then moved toward broad collaboration with the bourgeoisie. Since Chiang Kai-shek's coup of April, 1927, the Party, in accordance with the instructions of the Comintern, had dropped the bourgeoisie from the revolutionary bloc. Opinions are divided as to the originality of the strategy of

---

* From *Selected Works of Mao Tse-tung,* Peking: Foreign Language Press, 1965, I, 162–171. (The first part, dealing with "The Characteristics of the Present Political Situation," and footnotes omitted.)

[1] In August, 1935, when the Seventh Congress of the Comintern passed a resolution for the "Formation of an Anti-Fascist Popular Front," the Party leaders inaugurated their historic policy of an anti-Japanese national united front. In the official proclamation, they urged all social forces to unite against Japan. These developments might reflect the simultaneous implementation of a policy previously agreed upon by the Moscow leadership.

the relation with the bourgeoisie. It has been generally accepted that although Mao may not have made any strikingly original contributions to this strategy, he may, nevertheless, be considered a type of innovator, for he constantly avoided the tactic of sectarianism and subordination to the bourgeoisie.

There is a further point worthy of mention, namely Mao's attitude toward Chiang Kai-shek. Although urging the necessity of collaboration with the bourgeoisie against Japanese aggression, he had not yet suggested the possibility of an understanding with the Kuomintang, still less with Chiang Kai-shek. On the contrary, in his report, he still treated Chiang as the representative of the landlords and compradores, and not of the national bourgeoisie. Even in 1936, when the Central Committee wrote to the Kuomintang calling for a "united democratic Chinese republic," Mao was not enthusiastic for collaboration with Chiang until after the Sian incident of December, 1936. Indeed, his attitude toward Chiang at that time was much more hostile than that of Moscow.

THE NATIONAL UNITED FRONT

Having surveyed the situation with regard to both the counter-revolution and the revolution, we shall find it easy to define the Party's tactical tasks.

What is the basic tactical task of the Party? It is none other than to form a broad revolutionary national united front.

When the revolutionary situation changes, revolutionary tactics and methods of leadership must change accordingly. The task of the Japanese imperialists, the collaborators and the traitors is to turn China into a colony, while our task is to turn China into a free and independent country with full territorial integrity.

To win independence and freedom for China is a great task. It demands that we fight against foreign imperialism and the domestic counter-revolutionary forces. Japanese imperialism is determined to bludgeon its way deep into China. As yet the domestic counter-revolutionary forces of the big landlord and comprador classes are stronger than the people's revolutionary forces. The overthrow of Japanese imperialism and the counter-revolutionary forces in China cannot be accomplished in a day, and we must be prepared to devote a long time to it; it cannot be accomplished by small forces, and we must therefore accumulate great forces. In China, as in the world as a whole, the counter-revolutionary forces are weaker than before and the revolutionary forces stronger. This estimate is correct, representing one aspect of the matter. At the same time, it must be pointed out that the counter-revolutionary forces in China and in the world as a whole are stronger than the revolutionary forces for the time being. This estimate is also correct, representing another aspect of the matter. The uneven political and economic development of China gives rise to the uneven development of her revolution. As a rule, revolution starts, grows and triumphs first in those places in which the counter-revolutionary forces are comparatively weak, while it has yet to start or grows very slowly in those places in which they are strong. Such has long been the situation for the Chinese revolution. It can be predicted that the general revolutionary situation will grow further at certain stages in the future but that the unevenness will remain. The transformation of this unevenness into a general evenness will require a very long time, very great efforts, and the Party's application of a correct line. Seeing that the revolutionary war led by the Communist Party of the Soviet Union took three years to conclude, we must be prepared to devote to the already protracted revolutionary war led by the Chinese Communist Party the longer time necessary to dispose of the domestic and foreign counter-revolutionary forces finally and thoroughly. The kind of impatience that was formerly displayed will never do. Moreover, sound revolutionary tactics must be worked out; we will never achieve great things if we keep on milling around within narrow confines. This does not mean that in China things have to be done slowly; no, they must be done boldly, because the danger of national subjugation does not allow us to slacken for a moment. From now on the revolution will certainly develop much faster than before, for both China and the world are approaching a new period of war and revolution. For all that, China's revolutionary war will remain a protracted one; this follows from the strength of imperialism and the uneven development of the revolution. We say that the present situation is one in which a new high tide in the national revolution is imminent and in which China is on the eve of a great new nation-wide revolution; this is one characteristic of the present revolutionary situation. This is a fact, and it represents one aspect of the matter. But we must also say that imperialism is still a force to be earnestly reckoned with, that the unevenness in the development of the revolutionary forces is a serious weakness, and that to defeat our enemies we must be prepared to fight a protracted war; this is another characteristic of the present revolutionary situation. This, too, is a fact, and represents another aspect of the matter. Both characteristics, both facts, teach and urge us to revise our tactics and change our ways of disposing our forces and carrying on the struggle to suit the situation. The present situation demands that we boldly discard all closed-doorism, form a broad united front and guard against adventurism. We must not plunge into decisive battles until the time is ripe and unless we have the necessary strength.

Here I shall not discuss the relation of adventurism to closed-doorism, or the possible dangers of adventurism as events unfold on a larger scale; that can be left for later. For the moment I shall confine myself to explaining that united front tactics and closed-door tactics are diametrically opposed.

The former requires the recruiting of large forces for the purpose of surrounding and annihilating the enemy.

The latter means fighting single-handed in desperate combat against a formidable enemy.

The advocates of united front tactics say, if we are to make a proper estimate of the possibility of forming a broad revolutionary national united front, a proper estimate must be made of the changes that may occur in the alignment of revolutionary and counter-revolutionary forces in China resulting from the attempt of Japanese imperialism to turn China into a colony. Without a proper estimate of the strong and weak points of the Japanese and Chinese counter-revolutionary forces and of the Chinese revolutionary forces, we shall be unable fully to understand the necessity of organizing a broad revolutionary national united front, or to take firm measures to break down closed-doorism, or to use the united front as a means of organizing and rallying millions of people and all the armies that are potentially friendly to the revolution for the purpose of advancing to strike at our main target, namely, Japanese imperialism and its running dogs, the Chinese traitors, or to use this tactical weapon of ours to strike at the main target before us, but instead we shall aim at a vari-

ety of targets so that our bullets will hit not the principal
enemy but our lesser enemies or even our allies. This would
mean failure to single out the principal enemy and waste of
ammunition. It would mean inability to close in and isolate
him. It would mean inability to draw to our side all those in
the enemy camp and on the enemy front who have joined
them under compulsion, and those who were our enemies
yesterday but may become our friends today. It would in fact
mean helping the enemy, holding back, isolating and con-
stricting the revolution, and bringing it to a low ebb and even
to defeat.

The advocates of closed-door tactics say the above arguments are all wrong. The forces of the revolution must be
pure, absolutely pure, and the road of the revolution must be
straight, absolutely straight. Nothing is correct except what
is literally recorded in Holy Writ. The national bourgeoisie is
entirely and eternally counter-revolutionary. Not an inch must
be conceded to the rich peasants. The yellow trade unions
must be fought tooth and nail. If we shake hands with Tsai
Ting-kai, we must call him a counter-revolutionary at the
same moment. Was there ever a cat that did not love fish or
a warlord who was not a counter-revolutionary? Intellectuals
are three-day revolutionaries whom it is dangerous to recruit.
It follows therefore that closed-doorism is the sole wonder-
working magic, while the united front is an opportunist tactic.

Comrades, which is right, the united front or closed-
doorism? Which indeed is approved by Marxism-Leninism?
I answer without the slightest hesitation—the united front
and not closed-doorism. Three-year-olds have many ideas
which are right, but they cannot be entrusted with serious
national or world affairs because they do not understand them
yet. Marxism-Leninism is opposed to the "infantile disorder" found in the revolutionary ranks. This infantile disorder is just what the confirmed exponents of closed-doorism
advocate. Like every other activity in the world, revolution
always follows a tortuous road and never a straight one. The
alignment of forces in the revolutionary and counter-revolutionary camps can change, just as everything else in the world
changes. The Party's new tactics of a broad united front
start from the two fundamental facts that Japanese imperialism is bent on reducing all China to a colony and that China's
revolutionary forces still have serious weaknesses. In order to
attack the forces of the counter-revolution, what the revolu-

tionary forces need today is to organize millions upon millions of the masses and move a mighty revolutionary army into action. The plain truth is that only a force of such magnitude can crush the Japanese imperialists and the traitors and collaborators. Therefore, united front tactics are the only Marxist-Leninist tactics. The tactics of closed-doorism are, on the contrary, the tactics of the regal isolationist. Closed-doorism just "drives the fish into deep waters and the sparrows into the thickets", and it will drive the millions upon millions of the masses, this mighty army, over to the enemy's side, which will certainly win his acclaim. In practice, closed-doorism is the faithful servant of the Japanese imperialists and the traitors and collaborators. Its adherents' talk of the "pure" and the "straight" will be condemned by Marxist-Leninists and commended by the Japanese imperialists. We definitely want no closed-doorism; what we want is the revolutionary national united front, which will spell death to the Japanese imperialists and the traitors and collaborators.

THE PEOPLE'S REPUBLIC

If our government has hitherto been based on the alliance of the workers, the peasants and the urban petty bourgeoisie, from now on it must be so transformed as to include also the members of all other classes who are willing to take part in the national revolution.

At the present time the basic task of such a government should be to oppose the annexation of China by Japanese imperialism. It will have a broader representation so that it may include those who are interested only in the national revolution and not in the agrarian revolution, and even, if they so desire, those who may oppose Japanese imperialism and its running dogs, though they are not opposed to the European and U.S. imperialists because of their close ties with the latter. Therefore, as a matter of principle, the programme of such a government should be in keeping with the basic task of fighting Japanese imperialism and its lackeys, and we should modify our past policies accordingly.

The special feature on the revolutionary side at present is the existence of a well-steeled Communist Party and Red Army. This is of crucial importance. Great difficulties would arise if they did not exist. Why? Because the traitors and collaborators in China are numerous and powerful and are sure to devise every possible means to wreck the united front; they will sow dissension by means of intimidation and bribery and by manoeuvring among various groupings, and will employ their armies to oppress and crush, one by one, all those weaker than themselves who want to part company with them and join us in fighting Japan. All this would hardly be avoidable if the anti-Japanese government and army were to lack this vital factor, *i.e.*, the Communist Party and the Red Army. The revolution failed in 1927 chiefly because, with the opportunist line then prevailing in the Communist Party, no effort was made to expand our own ranks (the workers' and peasants' movement and the armed forces led by the Communist Party), and exclusive reliance was placed on a temporary ally, the Kuomintang. The result was that when imperialism ordered its lackeys, the landlord and comprador classes, to spread their numerous tentacles and draw over first Chiang Kai-shek and then Wang Ching-wei, the revolution suffered defeat. In those days the revolutionary united front had no mainstay, no strong revolutionary armed forces, and so when the defections came thick and fast, the Communist Party was forced to fight single-handed and was powerless to foil the tactics of crushing their opponents one by one which were adopted by the imperialists and the Chinese counter-revolutionaries. True, we had the troops under Ho Lung and Yeh Ting, but they were not yet politically consolidated, and the Party was not very skilled in leading them, so that they were finally defeated. The lesson we paid for with our blood was that the lack of a hard core of revolutionary forces brings the revolution to defeat. Today things are quite different. Now we have a strong Communist Party and a strong Red Army, and we also have the base areas of the Red Army. Not only are the Communist Party and the Red Army serving as the initiator of a national united front against Japan today, but in the future too they will inevitably become the powerful mainstay of China's anti-Japanese government and army, capable of preventing the Japanese imperialists and Chiang Kai-shek from carrying through their policy of disrupting this united front. However, we must be very vigilant because the Japanese imperialists and Chiang Kai-shek will undoubtedly resort to every possible form of intimidation and bribery and of manoeuvring among the various groupings.

Naturally we cannot expect every section of the broad national united front against Japan to be as firm as the Communist Party and the Red Army. In the course of their activities some bad elements may withdraw from the united front under the influence of the enemy. However, we need not fear the loss of such people. While bad elements may drop out under the enemy's influence, good people will come in under ours. The national united front will live and grow as long as the Communist Party and the Red Army live and grow. Such is the leading role of the Communist Party and the Red Army in the national united front. The Communists are no longer political infants and are able to take care of themselves and to handle relations with their allies. If the Japanese imperialists and Chiang Kai-shek can manoeuvre in relation to the revolutionary forces, the Communist Party can do the same in relation to the counter-revolutionary forces. If they can draw bad elements in our ranks over to their side, we can equally well draw their "bad elements" (good ones from our point of view) over to our side. If we can draw a larger number over to our side, this will deplete the enemy's ranks and strengthen ours. In short, two basic forces are now locked in struggle, and in the nature of things all the forces in between will have to line up on one side or the other. The Japanese imperialists' policy of subjugating China and Chiang Kai-shek's policy of betraying China will inevitably drive many people over to our side—either directly into joining the ranks of the Communist Party and the Red Army or into forming a united front with us. This will come about unless we pursue closed-door tactics.

Why change the "workers' and peasants' republic" into a "people's republic"?

Our government represents not only the workers and peasants but the whole nation. This has been implicit in our slogan of a workers' and peasants' democratic republic, because the workers and peasants constitute 80 to 90 per cent of the population. The Ten-Point Programme adopted by the Sixth National Congress of our Party embodies the interests of the whole nation and not of the workers and peasants alone. But the present situation requires us to change our slogan, to change it into one of a people's republic. The reason is that Japanese invasion has altered class relations in China, and it is now possible not only for the petty bourgeoisie but even for the national bourgeoisie to join the anti-Japanese struggle.

The people's republic will definitely not represent the interests of the enemy classes. On the contrary, it will stand in direct opposition to the landlord and comprador classes, the lackeys of imperialism, and will not count them among the people. In the same way, Chiang Kai-shek's "National Government of the Republic of China" represents only the wealthiest, but not the common people whom it does not count as part of the nation. As 80 to 90 per cent of China's population is made up of workers and peasants, the people's republic ought to represent their interests first and foremost. However, by throwing off imperialist oppression to make China free and independent and by throwing off landlord oppression to free China from semi-feudalism, the people's republic will benefit not only the workers and peasants but other sections of the people too. The sum total of the interests of the workers, peasants and the rest of the people constitutes the interests of the whole Chinese nation. The comprador and the landlord classes also live on Chinese soil, but as they have no regard for the national interests, their interests clash with those of the majority. This small minority are the only ones that we break with and are clashing with, and we therefore have the right to call ourselves the representatives of the whole nation.

There is, of course, a clash of interests between the working class and the national bourgeoisie. We shall not be able to extend the national revolution successfully unless the working class, the vanguard of the national revolution, is accorded political and economic rights and is enabled to direct its strength against imperialism and its running dogs, the traitors. However if the national bourgeoisie joins the anti-imperialist united front, the working class and the national bourgeoisie will have interests in common. In the period of the bourgeois-democratic revolution, the people's republic will not expropriate private property other than imperialist and feudal private property, and so far from confiscating the national bourgeoisie's industrial and commercial enterprises, it will encourage their development. We shall protect every national capitalist who does not support the imperialists or the Chinese traitors. In the stage of democratic revolution there are limits to the struggle between labour and capital. The labour laws of the people's republic will protect the interests of the workers, but will not prevent the national bourgeoisie from making profits or developing their industrial and commercial enterprises, because such development is bad for imperialism and good for the Chinese people. Thus it is clear that the people's republic will represent the interests of all strata opposed to imperialism and the feudal forces. The government of the people's republic will be based primarily on the workers and peasants, but will also include representatives of the other classes which are opposed to imperialism and the feudal forces.

But is it not dangerous to let the representatives of such classes join the government of the people's republic? No. The workers and peasants are the basic masses of the republic. In giving the urban petty bourgeoisie, the intellectuals and other sections of the population who support the anti-imperialist and anti-feudal programme the right to have a voice in the government of the people's republic and to work in it, the right to vote and stand for election, we must not allow the interests of the workers and peasants, the basic masses, to be violated. The essential part of our programme must be the protection of their interests. With their representatives comprising the majority in this government and with the Communist Party exercising leadership and working within it, there is a guarantee that the participation of other classes will present no danger. It is perfectly obvious that the Chinese revolution at the present stage is still a bourgeois-democratic and not a proletarian socialist revolution in nature. Only the counter-revolutionary Trotskyites talk such nonsense as that China has already completed her bourgeois-democratic revolution and that any further revolution can only be socialist. The revolution of 1924–27 was a bourgeois-democratic revolution, which was not carried to completion but failed. The agrarian revolution which we have led since 1927 is also a bourgeois-democratic revolution, because it is directed not against capitalism, but against imperialism and feudalism. This will remain true of our revolution for quite a long time to come.

Basically, the workers, the peasants and the urban petty bourgeoisie are still the motive forces of the revolution, but now there may be the national bourgeoisie as well.

The change in the revolution will come later. In the future the democratic revolution will inevitably be transformed into a socialist revolution. As to when the transition will take place, that will depend on the presence of the necessary conditions, and it may take quite a long time. We should not hold forth about transition until all the necessary political and economic conditions are present and until it is advantageous and not detrimental to the overwhelming majority of the people throughout China. It is wrong to have any doubts on this matter and expect the transition to take place soon, as some of our comrades did when they maintained that the transition in the revolution would begin the moment the democratic revolution began to triumph in key provinces. They did so because they failed to understand what kind of country China is politically and economically and to realize that, compared with Russia, China will find it more difficult, and require much more time and effort, to complete her democratic revolution politically and economically.

INTERNATIONAL SUPPORT

Finally, a word is necessary about the relation between the Chinese and the world revolution.

Ever since the monster of imperialism came into being, the affairs of the world have become so closely interwoven that it is impossible to separate them. We Chinese have the spirit to fight the enemy to the last drop of our blood, the determination to recover our lost territory by our own efforts, and the ability to stand on our own feet in the family of nations. But this does not mean that we can dispense with international support; no, today international support is necessary for the revolutionary struggle of any nation or country. There is the old adage, "In the Spring and Autumn Era there were no righteous wars." This is even truer of imperialism today, for it is only the oppressed nations and the oppressed classes that can wage just wars. All wars anywhere in the world in which the people rise up to fight their oppressors are just struggles. The February and October Revolutions in Russia were just wars. The revolutions of the people in various European countries after World War I were just struggles. In China, the Anti-Opium War, the War of the Taiping Heavenly Kingdom, the Yi Ho Tuan War, the Revolutionary War of 1911, the Northern Expedition of 1926–27, the Agrarian Revolutionary War from 1927 to the present, and the present resistance to Japan and punitive actions against traitors—these are all just wars. Now, in the mounting tide of nation-wide struggle against Japan and of world-wide struggle against fascism, just wars will spread all over China and the globe. All just wars support each other, while all unjust wars should be turned into just wars—this is the Leninist line. Our war against Japan needs the support of the people of the whole world and, above all, the support of the people of the Soviet Union, which they will certainly give us because they and we are bound together in a common cause. In the past, the Chinese revolutionary forces were temporarily cut off from the world revolutionary forces by Chiang Kai-shek, and in this sense we were isolated. Now the situation has changed, and changed to our advantage. Henceforth it will continue to change to our advantage. We can no longer be isolated. This provides a necessary condition for China's victory in the war against Japan and for victory in the Chinese revolution.

6. Mao Tse-tung: On Practice (July, 1937)*

"Without revolutionary theory, without historical knowledge and an understanding of the concrete movement, it is impossible to lead a great revolutionary movement to victory."[1] This is the lesson which Mao learned from Lenin; it also indicates the great importance which Mao attached to the theory and practice of Chinese Communism. In the late 1930's, during the Yenan period, Mao devoted himself to the study of Marxist philosophy, more particularly to current Soviet writings on the subject. He assumed the role of the leading Marxist theoretician among the Communist leaders, a necessary prerequisite for dictatorial authority. Whether Mao's theoretical writings contribute any new concepts is frequently debated. But these writings established him as the accepted interpreter of Marxist-Leninist doctrine and strategy in China.

The two basic theoretical works by Mao, "On Practice" and "On Contradiction," were written from lectures delivered at the Anti-Japanese Military and Political College at

* From *Selected Works of Mao Tse-tung*, Peking: Foreign Language Press, 1965, I, 295–308. (Footnotes omitted.)
[1] See Mao's "On the New Stage," a report to the Sixth Plenum of the Sixth Central Committee in October, 1938. Also cf. Lenin's statement: "Without a revolutionary theory, there can be no revolutionary movement."

Yenan in 1937, although the latter was not published until 1952.

In "On Practice," Mao perpetuates dialectical materialism and the neo-Confucian school of idealism. Mao stressed in this work that the process of knowledge has three stages: perception, conception and verification. Mao also emphasized the relevancy of ideology to action; that is, the unity of theory and practice. On the basis of this analysis, Mao is said to have discovered "the criterion of scientific truth" which can be applied to the criticism of opposing policies as well as to the maintenance of leadership infallibility.

Before Marx, materialism examined the problem of knowledge apart from the social nature of man and apart from his historical development, and was therefore incapable of understanding the dependence of knowledge on social practice, that is, the dependence of knowledge on production and the class struggle.

Above all, Marxists regard man's activity in production as the most fundamental practical activity, the determinant of all his other activities. Man's knowledge depends mainly on his activity in material production, through which he comes gradually to understand the phenomena, the properties and the laws of nature, and the relations between himself and nature; and through his activity in production he also gradually comes to understand, in varying degrees, certain relations that exist between man and man. None of this knowledge can be acquired apart from activity in production. In a classless society every person, as a member of society, joins in common effort with the other members, enters into definite relations of production with them and engages in production to meet man's material needs. In all class societies, the members of the different social classes also enter, in different ways, into definite relations of production and engage in production to meet their material needs. This is the primary source from which human knowledge develops.

Man's social practice is not confined to activity in production, but takes many other forms—class struggle, political life, scientific and artistic pursuits; in short, as a social being, man participates in all spheres of the practical life of society. Thus man, in varying degrees, comes to know the different relations between man and man, not only through his material life but also through his political and cultural life (both of which are intimately bound up with material life). Of these other types of social practice, class struggle in particular, in all its various forms, exerts a profound influence on the development of man's knowledge. In class society everyone lives as a member of a particular class, and every kind of thinking, without exception, is stamped with the brand of a class.

Marxists hold that in human society activity in production develops step by step from a lower to a higher level and that consequently man's knowledge, whether of nature or of society, also develops step by step from a lower to a higher level, that is, from the shallower to the deeper, from the one-sided to the many-sided. For a very long period in history, men were necessarily confined to a one-sided understanding of the history of society because, for one thing, the bias of the exploiting classes always distorted history and, for another, the small scale of production limited man's outlook. It was not until the modern proletariat emerged along with immense forces of production (large-scale industry) that man was able to acquire a comprehensive, historical understanding of the development of society and turn this knowledge into a science, the science of Marxism.

Marxists hold that man's social practice alone is the criterion of the truth of his knowledge of the external world. What actually happens is that man's knowledge is verified only when he achieves the anticipated results in the process of social practice (material production, class struggle or scientific experiment). If a man wants to succeed in his work, that is, to achieve the anticipated results, he must bring his ideas into correspondence with the laws of the objective external world; if they do not correspond, he will fail in his practice. After he fails, he draws his lessons, corrects his ideas to make them correspond to the laws of the external world, and can thus turn failure into success; this is what is meant by "failure is the mother of success" and "a fall into the pit, a gain in your wit". The dialectical-materialist theory of knowledge places practice in the primary position, holding that human knowledge can in no way be separated from practice and repudiating all the erroneous theories which deny the importance of practice or separate knowledge from practice. Thus Lenin said, *"Practice is higher than (theoretical) knowledge, for it has not only the dignity of universality, but also of immediate actuality."* The Marxist philosophy of dialectical materialism has two outstanding characteristics. One is its class nature: it openly avows that dialectical materialism is in the service of the proletariat. The other is its practicality: it emphasizes the dependence of theory on practice, emphasizes that theory is based on practice and in turn serves practice. The truth of any knowledge or theory is determined not by subjective feelings, but by objective results in social practice. Only social practice can be the criterion of truth. The standpoint of practice is the primary and basic standpoint in the dialectical-materialist theory of knowledge.

But how then does human knowledge arise from practice and in turn serve practice? This will become clear if we look at the process of development of knowledge.

In the process of practice, man at first sees only the phenomenal side, the separate aspects, the external relations of things. For instance, some people from outside come to Yenan on a tour of observation. In the first day or two, they see its topography, streets and houses; they meet many people, attend banquets, evening parties and mass meetings, hear talk of various kinds and read various documents, all these being the phenomena, the separate aspects and the external relations of things. This is called the perceptual stage of cognition, namely, the stage of sense-perceptions and impressions. That is, these particular things in Yenan act on the sense organs of the members of the observation group, evoke sense perceptions and give rise in their brains to many impressions together with a rough sketch of the external relations among these impressions: this is the first stage of cognition. At this stage, man cannot as yet form concepts, which are deeper, or draw logical conclusions.

As social practice continues, things that give rise to man's sense perceptions and impressions in the course of his practice are repeated many times; then a sudden change (leap) takes place in the brain in the process of cognition, and concepts are formed. Concepts are no longer the phenomena, the separate aspects and the external relations of things; they grasp the essence, the totality and the internal relations of things. Between concepts and sense perceptions there is not only a quantitative but also a qualitative difference. Proceeding further, by means of judgement and inference one is able to draw logical conclusions. The expression in *San Kuo Yen Yi*, "knit the brows and a stratagem comes to mind", or in everyday language, "let me think it over", refers to man's use of concepts in the brain to form judgements and inferences. This is the second stage of cognition. When the members of the observation group have collected various data and, what is more, have "thought them over", they are able to arrive at the judgement that "the Communist Party's policy of the National United Front Against Japan is thorough, sincere and genuine". Having made this judgement, they can, if they too are genuine about uniting to save the nation, go a step further and draw the following conclusion, "The National United Front Against Japan can succeed." This stage of conception, judgement and inference is the more important stage in the entire process of knowing a thing; it is the stage of rational knowledge. The real task of knowing is, through perception, to arrive at thought, to arrive step by step at the comprehension of the internal contradictions of objective things, of their laws and of the internal relations between one process and another, that is, to arrive at logical knowledge. To repeat, logical knowledge differs from perceptual knowledge in that perceptual knowledge pertains to the separate aspects, the phenomena and the external relations of things, whereas logical knowledge takes a big stride forward to reach the totality, the essence and the internal relations of things and discloses the inner contradictions in the surrounding world. Therefore, logical knowledge is capable of grasping the development of the surrounding world in its totality, in the internal relations of all its aspects.

This dialectical-materialist theory of the process of development of knowledge, basing itself on practice and proceeding from the shallower to the deeper, was never worked out by anybody before the rise of Marxism. Marxist materialism solved this problem correctly for the first time, pointing out both materialistically and dialectically the deepening movement of cognition, the movement by which man in society progresses from perceptual knowledge to logical knowledge in his complex, constantly recurring practice of production and class struggle. Lenin said, "The abstraction of *matter*, of a *law* of nature, the abstraction of *value*, etc., in short, *all* scientific (correct, serious, not absurd) abstractions reflect nature more deeply, truly and *completely*." Marxism-Leninism holds that each of the two stages in the process of cognition has its own characteristics, with knowledge manifesting itself as perceptual at the lower stage and logical at the higher stage, but that both are stages in an integrated process of cognition. The perceptual and the rational are qualitatively different, but are not divorced from each other; they are unified on the basis of practice. Our practice proves that what is perceived cannot at once be comprehended and that only what is comprehended can be more deeply perceived. Perception only solves the problem of phenomena; theory alone can solve the problem of essence. The solving of both these problems is not separable in the slightest degree from practice. Whoever wants to know a thing has no way of doing so except by coming into contact with it, that is, by living (practising) in its environment. In feudal society it was impossible to know the laws of capitalist society in advance because capitalism had not yet emerged, the relevant practice was lacking. Marxism could be the product only of capitalist society. Marx, in the era of laissez-faire capitalism, could not concretely know certain laws peculiar to the era of imperialism beforehand, because imperialism, the last stage of capitalism, had not yet emerged and the relevant practice was lacking; only Lenin and Stalin could undertake this task. Leaving aside their genius, the reason why Marx, Engels, Lenin and Stalin could work out their theories was mainly that they personally took part in the practice of the class struggle and the scientific experimentation of their time; lacking this condition, no genius could have succeeded. The saying, "without stepping outside his gate the scholar knows all the wide world's affairs", was mere empty talk in past times when technology was undeveloped. Even though this saying can be valid in the present age of developed technology, the people with real personal knowledge are those engaged in practice the wide world over. And it is only when these people have come to "know" through their practice and when their knowledge has reached him through writing and technical media that the "scholar" can indirectly "know all the wide world's affairs". If you want to know a certain thing or a certain class of things directly, you must personally participate in the practical struggle to change reality, to change that thing or class of things, for only thus can you come into contact with them as phenomena; only through personal participation in the practical struggle to change reality can you uncover the essence of that thing or class of things and comprehend them. This is the path to knowledge which every man actually travels, though some people, deliberately distorting matters, argue to the contrary. The most ridiculous person in the world is the "know-all" who picks up a smattering of hearsay knowledge and proclaims himself "the world's Number One authority"; this merely shows that he has not taken a proper measure of himself. Knowledge is a matter of science, and no dishonesty or conceit whatsoever is permissible. What is required is definitely the reverse—honesty and modesty. If you want knowledge, you must take part in the practice of changing reality. If you want to know the taste of a pear, you must change the pear by eating it yourself. If you want to know the structure and properties of the atom, you must make physical and chemical experiments to change the state of the atom. If you want to know the theory and methods of revolution, you must take part in revolution. All genuine knowledge originates in direct experience. But one cannot have direct experience of everything; as a matter of fact, most of our knowledge comes from indirect experience, for example, all knowledge from past times and foreign lands. To our ancestors and to foreigners, such knowledge was—or is—a matter of direct experience, and this knowledge is reliable if in the course of their direct experience the requirement of "scientific abstraction", spoken of by Lenin, was—or is—fulfilled and objective reality scientifically reflected, otherwise it is not reliable. Hence a man's knowledge consists only of two parts, that which comes from direct experience and that which comes from indirect experience. Moreover, what is indirect experience for me is direct experience for other people. Consequently, considered as a whole, knowledge of any kind is inseparable from direct experience. All knowledge originates in perception of the objective external world through man's physical sense organs. Anyone who denies such perception, denies direct experience, or denies personal participation in the practice that changes reality, is not a materialist. That is why the "know-all" is ridiculous. There is an old Chinese saying, "How can you catch tiger cubs without entering the tiger's lair?" This saying holds true for man's practice and it also holds true for the theory of knowledge. There can be no knowledge apart from practice.

Thus it can be seen that the first step in the process of cognition is contact with the objects of the external world; this belongs to the stage of perception. The second step is to synthesize the data of perception by arranging and reconstructing them; this belongs to the stage of conception, judgement and inference. It is only when the data of perception are very rich (not fragmentary) and correspond to reality (are not illusory) that they can be the basis for forming correct concepts and theories.

Here two important points must be emphasized. The first, which has been stated before but should be repeated here, is the dependence of rational knowledge upon perceptual knowledge. Anyone who thinks that rational knowledge need not be derived from perceptual knowledge is an idealist. In the history of philosophy there is the "rationalist" school that admits the reality only of reason and not of experience, believing that reason alone is reliable while perceptual experience is not; this school errs by turning things upside down. The rational is reliable precisely because it has its source in sense perceptions, otherwise it would be like water without a source, a tree without roots, subjective, self-engendered and unreliable. As to the sequence in the process of cognition, perceptual experience comes first; we stress the significance of social practice in the process of cognition precisely because social practice alone can give rise to human knowledge and it alone can start man on the acquisition of perceptual experience from the objective world. For a person who shuts his eyes, stops his ears and totally cuts himself off from the objective world there can be no such thing as knowledge. Knowledge begins with experience—this is the materialism of the theory of knowledge.

The second point is that knowledge needs to be deepened, that the perceptual stage of knowledge needs to be developed to the rational stage—this is the dialectics of the theory of knowledge. To think that knowledge can stop at the lower, perceptual stage and that perceptual knowledge alone is reliable while rational knowledge is not, would be to repeat the historical error of "empiricism". This theory errs in failing to understand that, although the data of perception reflect certain realities in the objective world (I am not speaking here of idealist empiricism which confines experience to so-called introspection), they are merely one-sided and superficial, reflecting things incompletely and not reflecting their essence. Fully to reflect a thing in its totality, to reflect its essence, to reflect its inherent laws, it is necessary through the exercise of thought to reconstruct the rich data of sense perception, discarding the dross and selecting the essential, eliminating the false and retaining the true, proceeding from the one to the other and from the outside to the inside, in order to form a system of concepts and theories—it is necessary to make a leap from perceptual to rational knowledge. Such reconstructed knowledge is not more empty or more unreliable; on the contrary, whatever has been scientifically reconstructed in the process of cognition, on the basis of practice, reflects objective reality, as Lenin said, more deeply, more truly, more fully. As against this, vulgar "practical men" respect experience but despise theory, and therefore cannot have a comprehensive view of an entire objective process, lack clear direction and long-range perspective, and are complacent over occasional successes and glimpses of the truth. If such persons direct a revolution, they will lead it up a blind alley.

Rational knowledge depends upon perceptual knowledge and perceptual knowledge remains to be developed into rational knowledge—this is the dialectical-materialist theory of knowledge. In philosophy, neither "rationalism" nor "empiricism" understands the historical or the dialectical nature of knowledge, and although each of these schools contains one aspect of the truth (here I am referring to materialist, not to idealist, rationalism and empiricism), both are wrong on the theory of knowledge as a whole. The dialectical-materialist movement of knowledge from the perceptual to the rational holds true for a minor process of cognition (for instance, knowing a single thing or task) as well as for a major process of cognition (for instance, knowing a whole society or a revolution).

But the movement of knowledge does not end here. If the dialectical-materialist movement of knowledge were to stop at rational knowledge, only half the problem would be dealt with. And as far as Marxist philosophy is concerned, only the less important half at that. Marxist philosophy holds that the most important problem does not lie in understanding the laws of the objective world and thus being able to explain it, but in applying the knowledge of these laws actively to change the world. From the Marxist viewpoint, theory is important, and its importance is fully expressed in Lenin's statement, "Without revolutionary theory there can be no revolutionary movement." But Marxism emphasizes the importance of theory precisely and only because it can guide action. If we have a correct theory but merely prate about it, pigeonhole it and do not put it into practice, then that theory, however good, is of no significance. Knowledge begins with practice, and theoretical knowledge is acquired through practice and must then return to practice. The active function of knowledge manifests itself not only in the active leap from perceptual to rational knowledge, but—and this is more important—it must manifest itself in the leap from rational knowledge to revolutionary practice. The knowledge which grasps the laws of the world, must be redirected to the practice of changing the world, must be applied anew in the practice of production, in the practice of revolutionary class struggle and revolutionary national struggle and in the practice of scientific experiment. This is the process of testing and developing theory, the continuation of the whole process of cognition. The problem of whether theory corresponds to objective reality is not, and cannot be, completely solved in the movement of knowledge from the perceptual to the rational, mentioned above. The only way to solve this problem completely is to redirect rational knowledge to social practice, apply theory to practice and see whether it can achieve the objectives one has in mind. Many theories of natural science are held to be true not only because they were so considered when natural scientists originated them, but because they have been verified in subsequent scientific practice. Similarly, Marxism-Leninism is held to be true not only because it was so considered when it was scientifically formulated by Marx, Engels, Lenin and Stalin but because it has been verified in the subsequent practice of revolutionary class struggle and revolutionary national struggle. Dialectical materialism is universally true because it is impossible for anyone to escape from its domain in his practice. The history of human knowledge tells us that the truth of many theories is incomplete and that this incompleteness is remedied through the test of practice. Many theories are erroneous and it is through the test of practice that their errors are corrected. That is why practice is the criterion of truth and why "the standpoint of life, of practice, should be first and fundamental in the theory of knowledge". Stalin has well said, "Theory becomes purposeless if it is not connected with revolutionary practice, just as practice gropes in the dark if its path is not illumined by revolutionary theory."

When we get to this point, is the movement of knowledge completed? Our answer is: it is and yet it is not. When men in society throw themselves into the practice of changing a certain objective process (whether natural or social) at a certain stage of its development, they can, as a result of the reflection of the objective process in their brains and the exercise of their subjective activity, advance their knowledge from the perceptual to the rational, and create ideas, theories, plans or programmes which correspond in general to the laws of that objective process. They then apply these ideas, theories, plans or programmes in practice in the same objective process. And if they can realize the aims they have in mind, that is, if in that same process of practice they can translate, or on the whole translate, those previously formulated ideas, theories, plans or programmes into fact, then the movement of knowledge may be considered completed with regard to this particular process. In the process of changing nature, take for example the fulfilment of an engineering plan, the verification of a scientific hypothesis, the manufacture of an implement or the reaping of a crop; or in the process of changing society, take for example the victory of a strike, victory in a war or the fulfilment of an educational plan. All these may be considered the realization of aims one has in mind. But generally speaking, whether in the practice of changing nature or of changing society, men's original ideas, theories, plans or programmes are seldom realized without any alteration. This is because people engaged in changing reality are usually subject to numerous limitations; they are limited not only by existing scientific and technological conditions but also by the development of the objective process itself and the degree to which this process has become manifest (the aspects and the essence of the objective process have not yet been fully revealed). In such a situation, ideas, theories, plans or programmes are usually altered partially and sometimes even wholly, because of the discovery of unforeseen circumstances in the course of practice. That is to say, it does happen that the original ideas, theories, plans or programmes fail to correspond with reality either in whole or in part and are wholly or partially incorrect. In many instances, failures have to be repeated many times before errors in knowledge can be corrected and correspondence with the laws of the objective process achieved, and consequently before the subjective can be transformed into the objective, or in other words, before the anticipated results can be achieved in practice. But when that point is reached, no matter how, the movement of human knowledge regarding a certain objective process at a certain stage of its development may be considered completed.

However, so far as the progression of the process is concerned, the movement of human knowledge is not completed. Every process, whether in the realm of nature or of society, progresses and develops by reason of its internal contradiction and struggle, and the movement of human knowledge should also progress and develop along with it. As far as social movements are concerned, true revolutionary leaders must not only be good at correcting their ideas, theories, plans or programmes when errors are discovered, as has been indicated above; but when a certain objective process has already progressed and changed from one stage of development to another, they must also be good at making themselves and all their fellow-revolutionaries progress and change in their subjective knowledge along with it, that is to say, they must ensure that the proposed new revolutionary tasks and new working programmes correspond to the new changes in the situation. In a revolutionary period the situation changes very rapidly; if the knowledge of revolutionaries does not change rapidly in accordance with the changed situation, they will be unable to lead the revolution to victory.

It often happens, however, that thinking lags behind reality; this is because man's cognition is limited by numerous social conditions. We are opposed to die-hards in the revolutionary ranks whose thinking fails to advance with changing objective circumstances and has manifested itself historically as Right opportunism. These people fail to see that the struggle of opposites has already pushed the objective process forward while their knowledge has stopped at the old stage. This is characteristic of the thinking of all die-hards. Their thinking is divorced from social practice, and they cannot march ahead to guide the chariot of society; they simply trail behind, grumbling that it goes too fast and trying to drag it back or turn it in the opposite direction.

We are also opposed to "Left" phrase-mongering. The thinking of "Leftists" outstrips a given stage of development of the objective process; some regard their fantasies as truth, while others strain to realize in the present an ideal which can only be realized in the future. They alienate themselves from the current practice of the majority of the people and from the realities of the day, and show themselves adventurist in their actions.

Idealism and mechanical materialism, opportunism and adventurism, are all characterized by the breach between the subjective and the objective, by the separation of knowledge from practice. The Marxist-Leninist theory of knowledge, characterized as it is by scientific social practice, cannot but resolutely oppose these wrong ideologies. Marxists recognize that in the absolute and general process of development of the universe, the development of each particular process is relative, and that hence, in the endless flow of absolute truth, man's knowledge of a particular process at any given stage of development is only relative truth. The sum total of innumerable relative truths constitutes absolute truth. The development of an objective process is full of contradictions and struggles, and so is the development of the movement of human knowledge. All the dialectical movements of the objective world can sooner or later be reflected in human knowledge. In social practice, the process of coming into being, developing and passing away is infinite, and so is the process of coming into being, developing and passing away in human knowledge. As man's practice which changes objective reality in accordance with given ideas, theories, plans or programmes, advances further and further, his knowledge of objective reality likewise becomes deeper and deeper. The movement of change in the world of objective reality is never-ending and so is man's cognition of truth through practice. Marxism-Leninism has in no way exhausted truth but ceaselessly opens up roads to the knowledge of truth in the course of practice. Our conclusion is the concrete, historical unity of the subjective and the objective, of theory and practice, of knowing and doing, and we are opposed to all erroneous ideologies, whether "Left" or Right, which depart from concrete history.

In the present epoch of the development of society, the responsibility of correctly knowing and changing the world has been placed by history upon the shoulders of the proletariat and its party. This process, the practice of changing the world, which is determined in accordance with scientific knowledge, has already reached a historic moment in the world and in China, a great moment unprecedented in human history, that is, the moment for completely banishing darkness from the world and from China and for changing the world into a world of light such as never previously existed. The struggle of the proletariat and the revolutionary people to change the world comprises the fulfilment of the following tasks: to change the objective world and, at the same time, their own subjective world—to change their cognitive ability and change the relations between the subjective and the objective world. Such a change has already come about in one part of the globe, in the Soviet Union. There the people are pushing forward this process of change. The people of China and the rest of the world either are going through, or will go through, such a process. And the objective world which is to be changed also includes all the opponents of change, who, in order to be changed, must go through a stage of compulsion before they can enter the stage of voluntary, conscious change. The epoch of world communism will be reached when all mankind voluntarily and consciously changes itself and the world.

Discover the truth through practice, and again through practice verify and develop the truth. Start from perceptual knowledge and actively develop it into rational knowledge; then start from rational knowledge and actively guide revolutionary practice to change both the subjective and the objective world. Practice, knowledge, again practice, and again knowledge. This form repeats itself in endless cycles, and with each cycle the content of practice and knowledge rises to a higher level. Such is the whole of the dialectical-materialist theory of knowledge, and such is the dialectical-materialist theory of the unity of knowing and doing.

7.   Mao Tse-tung: On Contradiction (August, 1937)*

This philosophical essay is a companion piece to "On Practice," with the same object of "combating doctrinairism which was a serious problem to the Party." This essay was published in 1952, but is claimed to have been written for inner Party use in 1937. Taking the Marxist-Leninist doctrine as a base, Mao insisted that contradictions are inherent in human relations and, therefore, govern politics. His ideas on this subject were given an incisive and definitive formulation in "On Contradiction," stressing on the one hand the

---

* From *Selected Works of Mao Tse-tung*, Peking: Foreign Language Press, 1965, I, 311–346. (Footnotes omitted.)

universality of contradictions, and on the other their particularity as determined by the needs of time and place. Since its publication, the theory of contradictions has played a prominent part in the official ideology of the Chinese Communists. This essay, as we shall note later, became supremely important in Chinese Communist ideology after Mao's speech "On the Correct Handling of Contradictions Among the People" (Selection 22) was published in 1957.

Mao's reasons in writing this essay related to the real contradictions which the Communists faced during the early years of their "national united front" policy—contradictions between the radical revolutionary aims and actions of the Party and the need for the "four-class bloc" alliance against the Japanese. However, Mao stressed that contradictions are universal, absolute, existing "in the process of development of all things," and "from beginning to end" in the process of development of each thing. Not only has Mao stressed the day-to-day programs of orderly "resolution of contradictions," but he also has launched periodical large-scale movements to tighten discipline in the Party and to strengthen his personal leadership. Hence the theory of contradictions has been elevated to the level of supreme dogma in Communist China.

The law of contradiction in things, that is, the law of the unity of opposites, is the basic law of materialist dialectics. Lenin said, "Dialectics in the proper sense is the study of contradiction *in the very essence of objects*." Lenin often called this law the essence of dialectics; he also called it the kernel of dialectics. In studying this law, therefore, we cannot but touch upon a variety of questions, upon a number of philosophical problems. If we can become clear on all these problems, we shall arrive at a fundamental understanding of materialist dialectics. The problems are: the two world outlooks, the universality of contradiction, the particularity of contradiction, the principal contradiction and the principal aspect of a contradiction, the identity and struggle of the aspects of a contradiction, and the place of antagonism in contradiction.

The criticism to which the idealism of the Deborin school has been subjected in Soviet philosophical circles in recent years has aroused great interest among us. Deborin's idealism has exerted a very bad influence in the Chinese Communist Party, and it cannot be said that the dogmatist thinking in our Party is unrelated to the approach of that school. Our present study of philosophy should therefore have the eradication of dogmatist thinking as its main objective.

I. The Two World Outlooks

Throughout the history of human knowledge, there have been two conceptions concerning the law of development of the universe, the metaphysical conception and the dialectical conception, which form two opposing world outlooks. Lenin said:

> The two basic (or two possible? or two historically observable?) conceptions of development (evolution) are: development as decrease and increase, as repetition, *and* development as a unity of opposites (the division of a unity into mutually exclusive opposites and their reciprocal relation).

Here Lenin was referring to these two different world outlooks.

The dialetical world outlook emerged in ancient times both in China and in Europe. Ancient dialectics, however, had a somewhat spontaneous and naive character; in the social and historical conditions then prevailing, it was not yet able to form a theoretical system, hence it could not fully explain the world and was supplanted by metaphysics. The famous German philosopher Hegel, who lived in the late 18th and early 19th centuries, made most important contributions to dialectics, but his dialectics was idealist. It was not until Marx and Engels, the great protagonists of the proletarian movement, had synthesized the positive achievements in the history of human knowledge and, in particular, critically absorbed the rational elements of Hegelian dialectics and created the great theory of dialectical and historical materialism that an unprecedented revolution occurred in the history of human knowledge. This theory was further developed by Lenin and Stalin. As soon as it spread to China, it wrought tremendous changes in the world of Chinese thought.

This dialectical world outlook teaches us primarily how to observe and analyse the movement of opposites in different things and, on the basis of such analysis, to indicate the methods for resolving contradictions. It is therefore most important for us to understand the law of contradiction in things in a concrete way.

II. THE UNIVERSALITY OF CONTRADICTION

For convenience of exposition, I shall deal first with the universality of contradiction and then proceed to the particularity of contradiction. The reason is that the universality of contradiction can be explained more briefly, for it has been widely recognized ever since the materialist-dialectical world outlook was discovered and materialist dialectics applied with outstanding success to analysing many aspects of human history and natural history and to changing many aspects of society and nature (as in the Soviet Union) by the great creators and continuers of Marxism—Marx, Engels, Lenin and Stalin; whereas the particularity of contradiction is still not clearly understood by many comrades, and especially by the dogmatists. They do not understand that it is precisely in the particularity of contradiction that the universality of contradiction resides. Nor do they understand how important is the study of the particularity of contradiction in the concrete things confronting us for guiding the course of revolutionary practice. Therefore, it is necessary to stress the study of the particularity of contradiction and to explain it at adequate length. For this reason, in our analysis of the law of contradiction in things, we shall first analyse the universality of contradiction, then place special stress on analysing the particularity of contradiction, and finally return to the universality of contradiction.

The universality or absoluteness of contradiction has a twofold meaning. One is that contradiction exists in the process of development of all things, and the other is that in the process of development of each thing a movement of opposites exists from beginning to end.

In war, offence and defence, advance and retreat, victory and defeat are all mutually contradictory phenomena. One cannot exist without the other. The two aspects are at once in conflict and in interdependence, and this constitutes the totality of a war, pushes its development forward and solves its problems.

Every difference in men's concepts should be regarded as reflecting an objective contradiction. Objective contradictions are reflected in subjective thinking, and this process constitutes the contradictory movement of concepts, pushes forward the development of thought, and ceaselessly solves problems in man's thinking.

Opposition and struggle between ideas of different kinds constantly occur within the Party; this is a reflection within the Party of contradictions between classes and between the new and the old in society. If there were no contradictions in the Party and no ideological struggles to resolve them, the Party's life would come to an end.

Thus it is already clear that contradiction exists universally and in all processes, whether in the simple or in the complex forms of motion, whether in objective phenomena or ideological phenomena.

III. The Particularity of Contradiction

Contradiction is present in the process of development of all things; it permeates the process of development of each thing from beginning to end. This is the universality and absoluteness of contradiction which we have discussed above. Now let us discuss the particularity and relativity of contradiction.

This problem should be studied on several levels.

First, the contradiction in each form of motion of matter has its particularity. Man's knowledge of matter is knowledge of its forms of motion, because there is nothing in this world except matter in motion and this motion must assume certain forms. In considering each form of motion of matter, we must observe the points which it has in common with other forms of motion. But what is especially important and necessary, constituting as it does the foundation of our knowledge of a thing, is to observe what is particular to this form of motion of matter, namely, to observe the qualitative difference between this form of motion and other forms. Only when we have done so can we distinguish between things. Every form of motion contains within itself its own particular contradiction. This particular contradiction constitutes the particular essence which distinguishes one thing from another. It is the internal cause or, as it may be called, the basis for the immense variety of things in the world. There are many forms of motion in nature, mechanical motion, sound, light, heat, electricity, dissociation, combination, and so on. All these forms are interdependent, but in its essence each is different from the others. The particular essence of each form of motion is determined by its own particular contradiction. This holds true not only for nature but also for social and ideological phenomena. Every form of society, every form of ideology, has its own particular contradiction and particular essence.

It is necessary not only to study the particular contradiction and the essence determined thereby of every great system of the forms of motion of matter, but also to study the particular contradiction and the essence of each process in the long course of development of each form of motion of matter. In every form of motion, each process of development which is real (and not imaginary) is qualitatively different. Our study must emphasize and start from this point.

Qualitatively different contradictions can only be resolved by qualitatively different methods. For instance, the contradiction between the proletariat and the bourgeoisie is resolved by the method of socialist revolution; the contradiction between the great masses of the people and the feudal system is resolved by the method of democratic revolution; the contradiction between the colonies and imperialism is resolved by the method of national revolutionary war; the contradiction between the working class and the peasant class in socialist society is resolved by the method of collectivization and mechanization in agriculture; contradiction within the Communist Party is resolved by the method of criticism and self-criticism; the contradiction between society and nature is resolved by the method of developing the productive forces. Processes change, old processes and old contradictions disappear, new processes and new contradictions emerge, and the methods of resolving contradictions differ accordingly. In Russia, there was a fundamental difference between the contradiction resolved by the February Revolution and the contradiction resolved by the October Revolution, as well as between the methods used to resolve them. The principle of using different methods to resolve different contradictions is one which Marxist-Leninists must strictly observe. The dogmatists do not observe this principle; they do not understand that conditions differ in different kinds of revolution and so do not understand that different methods should be used to resolve different contradictions; on the contrary, they invariably adopt what they imagine to be an unalterable formula and arbitrarily apply it everywhere, which only causes setbacks to the revolution or makes a sorry mess of what was originally well done.

In order to reveal the particularity of the contradictions in any process in the development of a thing, in their totality or interconnections, that is, in order to reveal the essence of the process, it is necessary to reveal the particularity of the two aspects of each of the contradictions in that process; otherwise it will be impossible to discover the essence of the process. This likewise requires the utmost attention in our study.

There are many contradictions in the course of development of any major thing. For instance, in the course of China's bourgeois-democratic revolution, where the conditions are exceedingly complex, there exist the contradiction between all the oppressed classes in Chinese society and imperialism, the contradiction between the great masses of the people and feudalism, the contradiction between the proletariat and the bourgeoisie, the contradiction between the peasantry and the urban petty bourgeoisie on the one hand and the bourgeoisie on the other, the contradiction between the various reactionary ruling groups, and so on. These contradictions cannot be treated in the same way since each has its own particularity; moreover, the two aspects of each contradiction cannot be treated in the same way since each aspect has its own characteristics. We who are engaged in the Chinese revolution should not only understand the particularity of these contradictions in their totality, that is, in their interconnections, but should also study the two aspects of each contradiction as the only means of understanding the totality. When we speak of understanding each aspect of a contradiction, we mean understanding what specific position each aspect occupies, what concrete forms it assumes in its interdependence and in its contradiction with its opposite, and what concrete methods are employed in the struggle with its opposite, when the two are both interdependent and in contradiction, and also after the interdependence breaks down. It is of great importance to study these problems. Lenin meant just this when he said that the most essential thing in Marxism, the living soul of Marxism, is the concrete analysis of concrete conditions. Our dogmatists have violated Lenin's teachings; they never use their brains to analyse anything concretely, and in their writings and speeches they always use stereotypes devoid of content, thereby creating a very bad style of work in our Party.

Not only does the whole process of the movement of opposites in the development of a thing, both in their interconnections and in each of the aspects, have particular features to which we must give attention, but each stage in the process has its particular features to which we must give attention too.

The fundamental contradiction in the process of development of a thing and the essence of the process determined by this fundamental contradiction will not disappear until the process is completed; but in a lengthy process the conditions usually differ at each stage. The reason is that, although the nature of the fundamental contradiction in the process of development of a thing and the essence of the process remain unchanged, the fundamental contradiction becomes more and more intensified as it passes from one stage to another in the lengthy process. In addition, among the numerous major and minor contradictions which are determined or influenced by the fundamental contradiction, some become intensified, some are temporarily or partially resolved or mitigated, and some new ones emerge; hence the process is marked by stages. If people do not pay attention to the stages in the process of development of a thing, they cannot deal with its contradictions properly.

It can thus be seen that in studying the particularity of any kind of contradiction—the contradiction in each form of motion of matter, the contradiction in each of its processes of development, the two aspects of the contradiction in each process, the contradiction at each stage of a process, and the two aspects of the contradiction at each stage—in studying the particularity of all these contradictions, we must not be subjective and arbitrary but must analyse it concretely. Without concrete analysis there can be no knowledge of the particularity of any contradiction. We must always remember Lenin's words, the concrete analysis of concrete conditions.

Marx and Engels were the first to provide us with excellent models of such concrete analysis.

When Marx and Engels applied the law of contradiction in things to the study of the socio-historical process, they discovered the contradiction between the productive forces and the relations of production, they discovered the contradiction between the exploiting and exploited classes and also the resultant contradiction between the economic base and its superstructure (politics, ideology, etc.), and they discovered how these contradictions inevitably lead to different kinds of social revolution in different kinds of class society.

When Marx applied this law to the study of the economic structure of capitalist society, he discovered that the basic contradiction of this society is the contradiction between the social character of production and the private character of ownership. This contradiction manifests itself in the contradiction between the organized character of production in individual enterprises and the anarchic character of production in society as a whole. In terms of class relations, it manifests itself in the contradiction between the bourgeoisie and the proletariat.

Because the range of things is vast and there is no limit to their development, what is universal in one context becomes particular in another. Conversely, what is particular in one context becomes universal in another. The contradiction in the capitalist system between the social character of production and the private ownership of the means of production is common to all countries where capitalism exists and develops; as far as capitalism is concerned, this constitutes the universality of contradiction. But this contradiction of capitalism belongs only to a certain historical stage in the general development of class society; as far as the contradiction between the productive forces and the relations of production in class society as a whole is concerned, it constitutes the particularity of contradiction. However, in the course of dissecting the particularity of all these contradictions in capitalist society, Marx gave a still more profound, more adequate and more complete elucidation of the universality of the contradiction between the productive forces and the relations of production in class society in general.

Since the particular is united with the universal and since the universality as well as the particularity of contradiction is inherent in everything, universality residing in particularity, we should, when studying an object, try to discover both the particular and the universal and their interconnection, to discover both particularity and universality and also their interconnection within the object itself, and to discover the interconnections of this object with the many objects outside it. When Stalin explained the historical roots of Leninism in his famous work, *The Foundations of Leninism*, he analysed the international situation in which Leninism arose, analysed those contradictions of capitalism which reached their culmination under imperialism, and showed how these contradictions made proletarian revolution a matter for immediate action and created favourable conditions for a direct onslaught on capitalism. What is more, he analysed the reasons why Russia became the cradle of Leninism, why tsarist Russia became the focus of all the contradictions of imperialism, and why it was possible for the Russian proletariat to become the vanguard of the international revolutionary proletariat. Thus, Stalin analysed the universality of contradiction in imperialism, showing why Leninism is the Marxism of the era of imperialism and proletarian revolution, and at the same time analysed the particularity of tsarist Russian imperialism within this general contradiction, showing why Russia became the birthplace of the theory and tactics of proletarian revolution and how the universality of contradiction is contained in this particularity. Stalin's analysis provides us with a model for understanding the particularity and the universality of contradiction and their interconnection.

On the question of using dialectics in the study of objective phenomena, Marx and Engels, and likewise Lenin and Stalin, always enjoin people not to be in any way subjective and arbitrary but, from the concrete conditions in the actual objective movement of these phenomena, to discover their concrete contradictions, the concrete position of each aspect of every contradiction and the concrete interrelations of the contradictions. Our dogmatists do not have this attitude in study and therefore can never get anything right. We must take warning from their failure and learn to acquire this attitude, which is the only correct one in study.

The relationship between the universality and the particularity of contradiction is the relationship between the general character and the individual character of contradiction. By the former we mean that contradiction exists in and runs through all processes from beginning to end; motion, things, processes, thinking—all are contradictions. To deny contradiction is to deny everything. This is a universal truth for all times and all countries, which admits of no exception. Hence the general character, the absoluteness of contradiction. But this general character is contained in every individual character; without individual character there can be no general character. If all individual character were removed, what general character would remain? It is because each contradiction is particular that individual character arises. All individual character exists conditionally and temporarily, and hence is relative.

This truth concerning general and individual character, concerning absoluteness and relativity, is the quintessence of the problem of contradiction in things; failure to understand it is tantamount to abandoning dialectics.

IV. The Principal Contradiction and the Principal Aspect of a Contradiction

There are still two points in the problem of the particularity of contradiction which must be singled out for analysis, namely, the principal contradiction and the principal aspect of a contradiction.

There are many contradictions in the process of development of a complex thing, and one of them is necessarily the principal contradiction whose existence and development determine or influence the existence and development of the other contradictions.

For instance, in capitalist society the two forces in contradiction, the proletariat and the bourgeoisie, form the principal contradiction. The other contradictions, such as those between the remnant feudal class and the bourgeoisie, between the peasant petty bourgeoisie and the bourgeoisie, between the proletariat and the peasant petty bourgeoisie, between the non-monopoly capitalists and the monopoly capitalists, between bourgeois democracy and bourgeois fascism, among the capitalist countries and between imperialism and the colonies, are all determined or influenced by this principal contradiction.

Hence, if in any process there are a number of contradictions, one of them must be the principal contradiction playing the leading and decisive role, while the rest occupy a secondary and subordinate position. Therefore, in studying any complex process in which there are two or more contradictions, we must devote every effort to finding its principal contradiction. Once this principal contradiction is grasped, all problems can be readily solved. This is the method Marx taught us in his study of capitalist society. Likewise Lenin and Stalin taught us this method when they studied imperialism and the general crisis of capitalism and when they studied the Soviet economy. There are thousands of scholars and men of action who do not understand it, and the result is that, lost in a fog, they are unable to get to the heart of a problem and naturally cannot find a way to resolve its contradictions.

As we have said, one must not treat all the contradictions in a process as being equal but must distinguish between the principal and the secondary contradictions, and pay special attention to grasping the principal one. But, in any given contradiction, whether principal or secondary, should the two contradictory aspects be treated as equal? Again, no. In any contradiction the development of the contradictory aspects is uneven. Sometimes they seem to be in equilibrium, which is however only temporary and relative, while unevenness is basic. Of the two contradictory aspects, one must be principal and the other secondary. The principal aspect is the one playing the leading role in the contradiction. The nature of a thing is determined mainly by the principal aspect of a contradiction, the aspect which has gained the dominant position.

But this situation is not static; the principal and the nonprincipal aspects of a contradiction transform themselves into each other and the nature of the thing changes accordingly. In a given process or at a given stage in the development of a contradiction, A is the principal aspect and B is the nonprincipal aspect; at another stage or in another process the roles are reversed—a change determined by the extent of the increase or decrease in the force of each aspect in its struggle against the other in the course of the development of a thing.

We often speak of "the new superseding the old". The supersession of the old by the new is a general, eternal and inviolable law of the universe. The transformation of one thing into another, through leaps of different forms in accordance with its essence and external conditions—this is the process of the new superseding the old. In each thing there is contradiction between its new and its old aspects, and this gives rise to a series of struggles with many twists and turns. As a result of these struggles, the new aspect changes from being minor to being major and rises to predominance, while the old aspect changes from being major to being minor and gradually dies out. And the moment the new aspect gains dominance over the old, the old thing changes qualitatively into a new thing. It can thus be seen that the nature of a thing is mainly determined by the principal aspect of the contradiction, the aspect which has gained predominance. When the principal aspect which has gained predominance changes, the nature of a thing changes accordingly.

Some people think that this is not true of certain contradictions. For instance, in the contradiction between the productive forces and the relations of production, the productive forces are the principal aspect; in the contradiction between theory and practice, practice is the principal aspect; in the contradiction between the economic base and the superstructure, the economic base is the principal aspect; and there is no change in their respective positions. This is the mechanical materialist conception, not the dialectical materialist conception. True, the productive forces, practice and the economic base generally play the principal and decisive role; whoever denies this is not a materialist. But it must also be admitted that in certain conditions, such aspects as the relations of production, theory and the superstructure in turn manifest themselves in the principal and decisive role. When it is impossible for the productive forces to develop without a change in the relations of production, then the change in the relations of production plays the principal and decisive role. The creation and advocacy of revolutionary theory plays the principal and decisive role in those times of which Lenin said, "Without revolutionary theory there can be no revolutionary movement." When a task, no matter which, has to be performed, but there is as yet no guiding line, method, plan or policy, the principal and decisive thing is to decide on a guiding line, method, plan or policy. When the superstructure (politics, culture, etc.) obstructs the development of the economic base, political and cultural changes become principal and decisive. Are we going against materialism when we say this? No. The reason is that while we recognize that in the general development of history the material determines the mental and social being determines social consciousness, we also— and indeed must—recognize the reaction of mental on material things, of social consciousness on social being and of the superstructure on the economic base. This does not go against materialism; on the contrary, it avoids mechanical materialism and firmly upholds dialectical materialism.

In studying the particularity of contradiction, unless we examine these two facets—the principal and the non-principal contradictions in a process, and the principal and the non-principal aspects of a contradiction—that is, unless we examine the distinctive character of these two facets of contradiction, we shall get bogged down in abstractions, be unable to understand contradiction concretely and consequently be unable to find the correct method of resolving it. The distinctive character or particularity of these two facets of contradiction represents the unevenness of the forces that are in contradiction. Nothing in this world develops absolutely evenly; we must oppose the theory of even development or the theory of equilibrium. Moreover, it is these concrete features of a contradiction and the changes in the principal and non-principal aspects of a contradiction in the course of its development that manifest the force of the new superseding the old. The study of the various states of unevenness in contradictions, of the principal and non-principal contradictions and of the principal and the non-principal aspects of a contradiction constitutes an essential method by which a revolutionary political party correctly determines its strategic and tactical policies both in political and in military affairs. All Communists must give it attention.

V. THE IDENTITY AND STRUGGLE OF THE ASPECTS OF A CONTRADICTION

When we understand the universality and the particularity of contradiction, we must proceed to study the problem of the identity and struggle of the aspects of a contradiction.

Identity, unity, coincidence, interpenetration, interpermeation, interdependence (or mutual dependence for existence), interconnection or mutual co-operation—all these different terms mean the same thing and refer to the following two points: first, the existence of each of the two aspects of a contradiction in the process of the development of a thing presupposes the existence of the other aspect, and both aspects coexist in a single entity; second, in given conditions, each of the two contradictory aspects transforms itself into its opposite. This is the meaning of identity.

Lenin said:

> *Dialectics* is the teaching which shows how *opposites* can be and how they happen to be (how they become) *identical*—under what conditions they are identical, transforming themselves into one another,—why the human mind should take these opposites not as dead, rigid, but as living, conditional, mobile, transforming themselves into one another.

What does this passage mean?

The contradictory aspects in every process exclude each other, struggle with each other and are in opposition to each other. Without exception, they are contained in the process of development of all things and in all human thought. A simple process contains only a single pair of opposites, while a complex process contains more. And in turn, the pairs of opposites are in contradiction to one another. That is how all things in the objective world and all human thought are constituted and how they are set in motion.

Our agrarian revolution has been a process in which the landlord class owning the land is transformed into a class that has lost its land, while the peasants who once lost their land are transformed into small holders who have acquired land, and it will be such a process once again. In given conditions having and not having, acquiring and losing, are interconnected; there is identity of the two sides. Under socialism, private peasant ownership is transformed into the public ownership of socialist agriculture; this has already taken place in the Soviet Union, as it will take place everywhere else. There is a bridge leading from private property to public property, which in philosophy is called identity, or transformation into each other, or interpenetration.

To consolidate the dictatorship of the proletariat or the dictatorship of the people is in fact to prepare the conditions for abolishing this dictatorship and advancing to the higher stage when all state systems are eliminated. To establish and build the Communist Party is in fact to prepare the conditions for the elimination of the Communist Party and all political parties. To build a revolutionary army under the leadership of the Communist Party and to carry on revolutionary war is in fact to prepare the conditions for the permanent elimination of war. These opposites are at the same time complementary.

Such is the problem of identity. What then is struggle? And what is the relation between identity and struggle?

Lenin said:

> The unity (coincidence, identity, equal action) of opposites is conditional, temporary, transitory, relative. The struggle of mutually exclusive opposites is absolute, just as development and motion are absolute.

What does this passage mean?

All processes have a beginning and an end, all processes transform themselves into their opposites. The constancy of all processes is relative, but the mutability manifested in the transformation of one process into another is absolute.

There are two states of motion in all things, that of relative rest and that of conspicuous change. Both are caused by the struggle between the two contradictory elements contained in a thing. When the thing is in the first state of motion, it is undergoing only quantitative and not qualitative change and consequently presents the outward appearance of being at rest. When the thing is in the second state of motion, the quantitative change of the first state has already reached a culminating point and gives rise to the dissolution of the thing as an entity and thereupon a qualitative change ensues, hence the appearance of a conspicuous change. Such unity, solidarity, combination, harmony, balance, stalemate, deadlock, rest, constancy, equilibrium, solidity, attraction, etc., as we see in daily life, are all the appearances of things in the state of quantitative change. On the other hand, the dissolution of unity, that is, the destruction of this solidarity, combination, harmony, balance, stalemate, deadlock, rest, constancy, equilibrium, solidity and attraction, and the change of each into its opposite are all the appearances of things in the state of qualitative change, the transformation of one process into another. Things are constantly transforming themselves from the first into the second state of motion; the struggle of opposites goes on in both states but the contradiction is resolved through the second state. That is why we say that the unity of opposites is conditional, temporary and relative, while the struggle of mutually exclusive opposites is absolute.

When we said above that two opposite things can coexist in a single entity and can transform themselves into each other because there is identity between them, we were speaking of conditionality, that is to say, in given conditions two contradictory things can be united and can transform themselves into each other, but in the absence of these conditions, they cannot constitute a contradiction, cannot coexist in the same entity and cannot transform themselves into one another. It is because the identity of opposites obtains only in given conditions that we have said identity is conditional and relative. We may add that the struggle between opposites permeates a process from beginning to end and makes one process transform itself into another, that it is ubiquitous, and that struggle is therefore unconditional and absolute.

The combination of conditional, relative identity and unconditional, absolute struggle constitutes the movement of opposites in all things.

We Chinese often say, "Things that oppose each other also complement each other." That is, things opposed to each other have identity. This saying is dialectical and contrary to metaphysics. "Oppose each other" refers to the mutual exclusion or the struggle of two contradictory aspects. "Complement each other" means that in given conditions the two contradictory aspects unite and achieve identity. Yet struggle is inherent in identity and without struggle there can be no identity.

In identity there is struggle, in particularity there is universality, and in individuality there is generality. To quote Lenin, ". . . there *is* an absolute *in* the relative."

VI. PLACE OF ANTAGONISM IN CONTRADICTION

The question of the struggle of opposites includes the question of what is antagonism. Our answer is that antagonism is one form, but not the only form, of the struggle of opposites.

In human history, antagonism between classes exists as a particular manifestation of the struggle of opposites. Consider the contradiction between the exploiting and the exploited classes. Such contradictory classes coexist for a long time in the same society, be it slave society, feudal society or capitalist society, and they struggle with each other; but it is not until the contradiction between the two classes develops to a certain stage that it assumes the form of open antagonism and develops into revolution. The same holds for the transformation of peace into war in class society.

Before it explodes, a bomb is a single entity in which opposites coexist in given conditions. The explosion takes place only when a new condition, ignition, is present. An analogous situation arises in all those natural phenomena which finally assume the form of open conflict to resolve old contradictions and produce new things.

It is highly important to grasp this fact. It enables us to understand that revolutions and revolutionary wars are inevitable in class society and that without them, it is impossible to accomplish any leap in social development and to overthrow the reactionary ruling classes and therefore impossible for the people to win political power. Communists must expose the deceitful propaganda of the reactionaries, such as the assertion that social revolution is unnecessary and impossible. They must firmly uphold the Marxist-Leninist theory of social revolution and enable the people to understand that social revolution is not only entirely necessary but also entirely practicable, and that the whole history of mankind and the triumph of the Soviet Union have confirmed this scientific truth.

However, we must make a concrete study of the circumstances of each specific struggle of opposites and should not arbitrarily apply the formula discussed above to everything. Contradiction and struggle are universal and absolute, but the methods of resolving contradictions, that is, the forms of struggle, differ according to the differences in the nature of the contradictions. Some contradictions are characterized by open antagonism, others are not. In accordance with the concrete development of things, some contradictions which were originally non-antagonistic develop into antagonistic ones, while others which were originally antagonistic develop into non-antagonistic ones.

As already mentioned, so long as classes exist, contradictions between correct and incorrect ideas in the Communist Party are reflections within the Party of class contradictions. At first, with regard to certain issues, such contradictions may not manifest themselves as antagonistic. But with the development of the class struggle, they may grow and become antagonistic. The history of the Communist Party of the Soviet Union shows us that the contradictions between the correct thinking of Lenin and Stalin and the fallacious thinking of Trotsky, Bukharin and others did not at first manifest themselves in an antagonistic form, but that later they did develop into antagonism. There are similar cases in the history of the Chinese Communist Party. At first the contradictions between the correct thinking of many of our Party comrades and the fallacious thinking of Ch'en Tu-hsiu, Chang Kuo-t'ao and others also did not manifest themselves in an antagonistic form, but later they did develop into antagonism. At present the contradiction between correct and incorrect thinking in our Party does not manifest itself in an antagonistic form, and if comrades who have committed mistakes can correct them, it will not develop into antagonism. Therefore, the Party must on the one hand wage a serious struggle against erroneous thinking, and on the other give the comrades who have committed errors ample opportunity to wake up. This being the case, excessive struggle is obviously inappropriate. But if the people who have committed errors persist in them and aggravate them, there is the possibility that this contradiction will develop into antagonism.

Economically, the contradiction between town and country is an extremely antagonistic one both in capitalist society, where under the rule of the bourgeoisie the towns ruthlessly plunder the countryside, and in the Kuomintang areas in China, where under the rule of foreign imperialism and the Chinese big comprador bourgeoisie the towns most rapaciously plunder the countryside. But in a socialist country and in our revolutionary base areas, this antagonistic contradiction has changed into one that is non-antagonistic; and when communist society is reached it will be abolished.

Lenin said, "Antagonism and contradiction are not at all one and the same. Under socialism, the first will disappear, the second will remain." That is to say, antagonism is one form, but not the only form, of the struggle of opposites; the formula of antagonism cannot be arbitrarily applied everywhere.

VII. Conclusion

We may now say a few words to sum up. The law of contradiction in things, that is, the law of the unity of opposites, is the fundamental law of nature and of society and therefore also the fundamental law of thought. It stands opposed to the metaphysical world outlook. It represents a great revolution in the history of human knowledge. According to dialectical materialism, contradiction is present in all processes of objectively existing things and of subjective thought and permeates all these processes from beginning to end; this is the universality and absoluteness of contradiction. Each contradiction and each of its aspects have their respective characteristics; this is the particularity and relativity of contradiction. In given conditions, opposites possess identity, and consequently can coexist in a single entity and can transform themselves into each other; this again is the particularity and relativity of contradiction. But the struggle of opposites is ceaseless, it goes on both when the opposites are coexisting and when they are transforming themselves into each other, and becomes especially conspicuous when they are transforming themselves into one another; this again is the universality and absoluteness of contradiction. In studying the particularity and relativity of contradiction, we must give attention to the distinction between the principal contradiction and the non-principal contradictions and to the distinction between the principal aspect and the non-principal aspect of a contradiction; in studying the universality of contradiction and the struggle of opposites in contradiction, we must give attention to the distinction between the different forms of struggle. Otherwise we shall make mistakes. If, through study, we achieve a real understanding of the essentials explained above, we shall be able to demolish dogmatist ideas which are contrary to the basic principles of Marxism-Leninism and detrimental to our revolutionary cause, and our comrades with practical experience will be able to organize their experience into principles and avoid repeating empiricist errors. These are a few simple conclusions from our study of the law of contradiction.

Chapter Three

The Wartime Expansion

8. Mao Tse-tung: Problems of Strategy in Guerrilla War Against Japan (May, 1938)*

There are two basic elements in Mao's road to power: guerrilla warfare and agrarian revolution. The significance of the "anti-Japanese guerrilla war" is well illustrated in the official commentary:

> In the early days of the Anti-Japanese War, many people inside as well as outside the Party belittled the strategic role of guerrilla warfare, and pinned their hopes on regular warfare, particularly on the operations of the Kuomintang troops. Comrade Mao Tse-tung refuted their view and at the same time wrote the following article to point out the correct course for the development of the anti-Japanese guerrilla war. As a result, the Eighth Route Army and the New Fourth Army, totalling only a little more than 40,000 men in 1937, expanded to one million strong when Japan surrendered in 1945, established many revolutionary base areas, and played an important role in the Anti-Japanese War by making Chiang Kai-shek afraid to capitulate to Japan or launch a nation-wide civil war. When, in 1946, he did launch the nation-wide civil war, the People's Liberation Army formed out of the Eighth Route Army and the New Fourth Army had already built up enough strength to deal with his attacks.[1]

---

* From *Selected Works of Mao Tse-tung*, Peking: Foreign Language Press, 1965, II, 81–111. (The first chapter and footnotes omitted.)
[1] *The Selected Works of Mao Tse-tung*, Peking: Foreign Language Press, 1965, II, 119.

Indeed, by the end of the war, the Communists had succeeded, through the strategy of guerrilla warfare, in laying the foundation for later achievement of their primary objective throughout the early years—the conquest of power in China.

THE BASIC PRINCIPLE OF WAR IS TO PRESERVE ONESELF AND DESTROY THE ENEMY

Before discussing the question of strategy in guerrilla warfare in concrete terms, a few words are needed on the fundamental problem of war.

All the guiding principles of military operations grow out of the one basic principle: to strive to the utmost to preserve one's own strength and destroy that of the enemy. In a revolutionary war, this principle is directly linked with basic political principles. For instance, the basic political principle of China's War of Resistance Against Japan, *i.e.*, its political aim, is to drive out Japanese imperialism and build an independent, free and happy new China. In terms of military action this principle means the use of armed force to defend our motherland and to drive out the Japanese invaders. To attain this end, the operations of the armed units take the form of doing their utmost to preserve their own strength on the one hand and destroy the enemy's on the other. How then do we justify the encouragement of heroic sacrifice in war? Every war exacts a price, sometimes an extremely high one. Is this not in contradiction with "preserving oneself"? In fact, there is no contradiction at all; to put it more exactly, sacrifice and self-preservation are both opposite and complementary to each other. For such sacrifice is essential not only for destroying the enemy but also for preserving oneself—partial and temporary "non-preservation" (sacrifice, or paying the price) is necessary for the sake of general and permanent preservation. From this basic principle stems the series of principles guiding military operations, all of which—from the principles of shooting (taking cover to preserve oneself, and making full use of fire-power to destroy the enemy) to the principles of strategy—are permeated with the spirit of this basic principle. All technical, tactical and strategic principles represent applications of this basic principle. The principle of preserving oneself and destroying the enemy is the basis of all military principles.

SIX SPECIFIC PROBLEMS OF STRATEGY IN GUERRILLA WAR AGAINST JAPAN

Now let us see what policies or principles have to be adopted in guerrilla operations against Japan before we can attain the object of preserving ourselves and destroying the enemy. Since the guerrilla units in the War of Resistance (and in all other revolutionary wars) generally grow out of nothing and expand from a small to a large force, they must preserve themselves and, moreover, they must expand. Hence the question is, what policies or principles have to be adopted before we can attain the object of preserving and expanding ourselves and destroying the enemy?

Generally speaking, the main principles are as follows: (1) the use of initiative, flexibility and planning in conducting offensives within the defensive, battles of quick decision within protracted war, and exterior-line operations within interior-line operations; (2) co-ordination with regular warfare; (3) establishment of base areas; (4) the strategic defensive and the strategic offensive; (5) the development of guerrilla warfare into mobile warfare; and (6) correct relationship of command. These six items constitute the whole of the strategic programme for guerrilla war against Japan and are the means necessary for the preservation and expansion of our forces, for the destruction and expulsion of the enemy, for co-ordination with regular warfare and the winning of final victory.

INITIATIVE, FLEXIBILITY AND PLANNING IN CONDUCTING OFFENSIVES WITHIN THE DEFENSIVE, BATTLES OF QUICK DECISION WITHIN PROTRACTED WAR, AND EXTERIOR-LINE OPERATIONS WITHIN INTERIOR-LINE OPERATIONS

Here the subject may be dealt with under four headings: (1) the relationship between the defensive and the offensive, between protractedness and quick decision, and between the interior and exterior lines; (2) the initiative in all operations;

(3) flexible employment of forces; and (4) planning in all operations.

To start with the first.

If we take the War of Resistance as a whole, the fact that Japan is a strong country and is attacking while China is a weak country and is defending herself makes our war strategically a defensive and protracted war. As far as the operational lines are concerned, the Japanese are operating on exterior and we on interior lines. This is one aspect of the situation. But there is another aspect which is just the reverse. The enemy forces, though strong (in arms, in certain qualities of their men, and certain other factors), are numerically small, whereas our forces, though weak (likewise, in arms, in certain qualities of our men, and certain other factors), are numerically very large. Added to the fact that the enemy is an alien nation invading our country while we are resisting his invasion on our own soil, this determines the following strategy. It is possible and necessary to use tactical offensives within the strategic defensive, to fight campaigns and battles of quick decision within a strategically protracted war and to fight campaigns and battles on exterior lines within strategically interior lines. Such is the strategy to be adopted in the War of Resistance as a whole. It holds true both for regular and for guerrilla warfare. Guerrilla warfare is different only in degree and form. Offensives in guerrilla warfare generally take the form of surprise attacks. Although surprise attacks can and should be employed in regular warfare too, the degree of surprise is less. In guerrilla warfare, the need to bring operations to a quick decision is very great, and our exterior-line ring of encirclement of the enemy in campaigns and battles is very small. All these distinguish it from regular warfare.

Now let us discuss initiative, flexibility and planning in guerrilla warfare.

What is initiative in guerrilla warfare?

In any war, the opponents contend for the initiative, whether on a battlefield, in a battle area, in a war zone or in the whole war, for the initiative means freedom of action for an army. Any army which, losing the initiative, is forced into a passive position and ceases to have freedom of action, faces the danger of defeat or extermination. Naturally, gaining the initiative is harder in strategic defensive and interior-line operations and easier in offensive exterior-line operations.

However, Japanese imperialism has two basic weaknesses, namely, its shortage of troops and the fact that it is fighting on foreign soil. Moreover, its underestimation of China's strength and the internal contradictions among the Japanese militarists have given rise to many mistakes in command, such as piecemeal reinforcement, lack of strategic co-ordination, occasional absence of a main direction for attack, failure to grasp opportunities in some operations and failure to wipe out encircled forces, all of which may be considered the third weakness of Japanese imperialism. Thus, despite the advantage of being on the offensive and operating on exterior lines, the Japanese militarists are gradually losing the initiative, because of their shortage of troops (their small territory, small population, inadequate resources, feudalistic imperialism, etc.), because of the fact that they are fighting on foreign soil (their war is imperialist and barbarous) and because of their stupidities in command. Japan is neither willing nor able to conclude the war at present, nor has her strategic offensive yet come to an end, but, as the general trend shows, her offensive is confined within certain limits, which is the inevitable consequence of her three weaknesses; she cannot go on indefinitely till she swallows the whole of China. Already there are signs that Japan will one day find herself in an utterly passive position. China, on the other hand, was in a rather passive position at the beginning of the war, but, having gained experience, she is now turning to the new policy of mobile warfare, the policy of taking the offensive, seeking quick decisions and operating on exterior lines in campaigns and battles, which, together with the policy of developing widespread guerrilla warfare, is helping China to build up a position of initiative day by day.

Next, let us deal with flexibility.

Flexibility is a concrete expression of the initiative. The flexible employment of forces is more essential in guerrilla warfare than in regular warfare.

A guerrilla commander must understand that the flexible employment of his forces is the most important means of changing the situation as between the enemy and ourselves and of gaining the initiative. The nature of guerrilla warfare is such that guerrilla forces must be employed flexibly in accordance with the task in hand and with such circumstances as the state of the enemy, the terrain and the local population, and the chief ways of employing the forces are dispersal, concentration and shifting of position. In employing his forces, a guerrilla commander is like a fisherman casting his net, which he should be able to spread wide as well as draw in tight. When casting his net, the fisherman has to ascertain the depth of the water, the speed of the current and the presence or absence of obstructions; similarly, when dispersing his units, a guerrilla commander must take care not to incur losses through ignorance of the situation or through miscalculated action. Just as the fisherman must keep a grip on the cord in order to draw his net in tight, so the guerrilla commander must maintain liaison and communication with all his forces and keep enough of his main forces at hand. Just as a frequent change of position is necessary in fishing, so a frequent shift of position is necessary for a guerrilla unit. Dispersal, concentration and shifting of position are the three ways of flexibly employing forces in guerrilla warfare.

Generally speaking, the dispersal of guerrilla units, or "breaking up the whole into parts", is employed chiefly: (1) when we want to threaten the enemy with a wide frontal attack because he is on the defensive, and there is temporarily no chance to mass our forces for action; (2) when we want to harass and disrupt the enemy throughout an area where his forces are weak; (3) when we are unable to break through the enemy's encirclement and try to slip away by making ourselves less conspicuous; (4) when we are restricted by terrain or supplies; or (5) when we are carrying on mass work over a wide area. But whatever the circumstances, when dispersing for action we should pay attention to the following: (1) we should never make an absolutely even dispersal of forces, but should keep a fairly large part in an area convenient for manoeuvre, so that any possible exigency can be met and there is a centre of gravity for the task being carried out in dispersion; and (2) we should assign to the dispersed units clearly defined tasks, fields of operation, time limits for actions, places for reassembly and ways and means of liaison.

Concentration of forces, or "assembling the parts into a whole", is the method usually applied to destroy an enemy when he is on the offensive and sometimes to destroy some of his stationary forces when he is on the defensive. Concentration of forces does not mean absolute concentration, but the massing of the main forces for use in one important direction while retaining or dispatching part of the forces for use in other directions to contain, harass or disrupt the enemy, or to carry on mass work.

Although the flexible dispersal or concentration of forces according to circumstances is the principal method in guerrilla warfare, we must also know how to shift (or transfer) our forces flexibly. When the enemy feels seriously threatened by guerrillas, he will send troops to attack or suppress them. Hence the guerrilla units will have to take stock of the situation. If advisable, they should fight where they are; if not, they should lose no time in shifting elsewhere. Sometimes, in order to crush the enemy units one by one, guerrilla units which have destroyed an enemy force in one place may immediately shift to another so as to wipe out a second enemy force; sometimes, finding it inadvisable to fight in one place, they may have to disengage quickly and fight the enemy elsewhere. If the enemy's forces in a certain place present a particularly serious threat, the guerrilla units should not linger, but should move off with lightning speed. In general, shifts of position should be made with secrecy and speed. In order to mislead, decoy and confuse the enemy, they should constantly use stratagems, such as making a feint to the east but attacking in the west, appearing now in the south and now in the north, hit-and-run attacks, and night actions.

Flexibility in dispersal, concentration and shifts of position is a concrete expression of the initiative in guerrilla warfare, whereas rigidness and inertia inevitably lead to passivity and cause unnecessary losses. But a commander proves himself wise not just by recognition of the importance of employing his forces flexibly but by skill in dispersing, concentrating or shifting them in good time according to the specific circumstances. This wisdom in sensing changes and choosing the right moment to act is not easily acquired; it can be gained only by those who study with a receptive mind and investigate and ponder diligently. Prudent consideration of the circumstances is essential to prevent flexibility from turning into impulsive action.

Lastly, we come to planning.

Without planning, victories in guerrilla warfare are impossible. Any idea that guerrilla warfare can be conducted in haphazard fashion indicates either a flippant attitude or ignorance of guerrilla warfare. The operations in a guerrilla zone as a whole, or those of a guerrilla unit or formation, must be preceded by as thorough planning as possible, by preparation in advance for every action. Grasping the situation, setting the tasks, disposing the forces, giving military and political training, securing supplies, putting the equipment in good order, making proper use of the people's help, etc.—all these are part of the work of the guerrilla commanders, which they must carefully consider and conscientiously perform and check up on. There can be no initiative, no flexibility, and no offensive unless they do so. True, guerrilla conditions do not allow as high a degree of planning as do those of regular warfare, and it would be a mistake to attempt very thorough planning in guerrilla warfare. But it is necessary to plan as thoroughly as the objective conditions permit, for it should be understood that fighting the enemy is no joke.

Co-Ordination with Regular Warfare

The second problem of strategy in guerrilla warfare is its co-ordination with regular warfare. It is a matter of clarifying the relation between guerrilla and regular warfare on the operational level, in the light of the nature of actual guerrilla operations. An understanding of this relation is very important for effectiveness in defeating the enemy.

There are three kinds of co-ordination between guerrilla and regular warfare, co-ordination in strategy, in campaigns and in battles.

Taken as a whole, guerrilla warfare behind the enemy lines, which cripples the enemy, pins him down, disrupts his supply lines and inspires the regular forces and the people throughout the country, is co-ordinated with regular warfare in strategy.

The Establishment of Base Areas

The third problem of strategy in anti-Japanese guerrilla warfare is the establishment of base areas, which is important and essential because of the protracted nature and ruthlessness of the war. The recovery of our lost territories will have to await the nation-wide strategic counter-offensive; by then the enemy's front will have extended deep into central China and cut it in two from north to south, and a part or even a greater part of our territory will have fallen into the hands of the enemy and become his rear. We shall have to extend guerrilla warfare all over this vast enemy-occupied area, make a front out of the enemy's rear, and force him to fight ceaselessly throughout the territory he occupies. Until such time as our strategic counter-offensive is launched and so long as our lost territories are not recovered, it will be necessary to persist in guerrilla warfare in the enemy's rear, certainly for a fairly long time, though one cannot say definitely for how long. This is why the war will be a protracted one. And in order to safeguard his gains in the occupied areas, the enemy is bound to step up his anti-guerrilla measures and, especially after the halting of his strategic offensive, to embark on relentless suppression of the guerrillas. With ruthlessness thus added to protractedness, it will be impossible to sustain guerrilla warfare behind the enemy lines without base areas.

The fundamental conditions for establishing a base area are that there should be anti-Japanese armed forces, that these armed forces should be employed to inflict defeats on the enemy and that they should arouse the people to action. Thus the establishment of a base area is first and foremost a matter of building an armed force. Leaders in guerrilla war must devote their energy to building one or more guerrilla units, and must gradually develop them in the course of struggle into guerrilla formations or even into units and formations of regular troops. The building up of an armed force is the key to establishing a base area; if there is no armed force or if the armed force is weak, nothing can be done. This constitutes the first condition.

The second indispensable condition for establishing a base area is that the armed forces should be used in co-ordination with the people to defeat the enemy. All places under enemy control are enemy, and not guerrilla, base areas, and obviously cannot be transformed into guerrilla base areas unless the enemy is defeated. Unless we repulse the enemy's attacks and defeat him, even places held by the guerrillas will come under enemy control, and then it will be impossible to establish base areas.

The third indispensable condition for establishing a base area is the use of all our strength, including our armed forces, to arouse the masses for struggle against Japan. In the course of this struggle we must arm the people, *i.e.*, organize self-defence corps and guerrilla units. In the course of this struggle, we must form mass organizations, we must organize the workers, peasants, youth, women, children, merchants and professional people—according to the degree of their political consciousness and fighting enthusiasm—into the various mass organizations necessary for the struggle against Japanese aggression, and we must gradually expand them. Without organization, the people cannot give effect to their anti-Japanese strength. In the course of this struggle, we must weed out the open and the hidden traitors, a task which can be accomplished only by relying on the strength of the people. In this struggle, it is particularly important to arouse the people to establish, or to consolidate, their local organs of anti-Japanese political power. Where the original Chinese organs of political power have not been destroyed by the enemy, we must reorganize and strengthen them with the support of the broad masses, and where they have been destroyed by the enemy, we should rebuild them by the efforts of the masses. They are organs of political power for carrying out the policy of the Anti-Japanese National United Front and should unite all the forces of the people to fight against our sole enemy, Japanese imperialism, and its jackals, the traitors and reactionaries.

A base area for guerrilla war can be truly established only with the gradual fulfilment of the three basic conditions, *i.e.,* only after the anti-Japanese armed forces are built up, the enemy has suffered defeats and the people are aroused.

THE STRATEGIC DEFENSIVE
AND THE STRATEGIC OFFENSIVE
IN GUERRILLA WAR

The fourth problem of strategy in guerrilla war concerns the strategic defensive and the strategic offensive. This is the problem of how the policy of offensive warfare, which we mentioned in our discussion of the first problem, is to be carried out in practice, when we are on the defensive and when we are on the offensive in our guerrilla warfare against Japan.

Within the nation-wide strategic defensive or strategic offensive (to be more exact, the strategic counter-offensive), small-scale strategic defensives and offensives take place in and around each guerrilla base area. By strategic defensive we mean our strategic situation and policy when the enemy is on the offensive and we are on the defensive; by strategic offensive we mean our strategic situation and policy when the enemy is on the defensive and we are on the offensive.

DEVELOPMENT OF GUERRILLA WAR INTO MOBILE WAR

The fifth problem of strategy in guerrilla war against Japan is its development into mobile war, a development which is necessary and possible because the war is protracted and ruthless. If China could speedily defeat the Japanese invaders and recover her lost territories, and if the war were neither protracted nor ruthless, this would not be necessary. But as, on the contrary, the war is protracted and ruthless, guerrilla warfare cannot adapt itself to such a war except by developing into mobile warfare. Since the war is protracted and ruthless, it is possible for the guerrilla units to undergo the necessary steeling and gradually to transform themselves into regular forces, so that their mode of operations is gradually regularized and guerrilla warfare develops into mobile warfare. The necessity and possibility of this development must be clearly recognized by the guerrilla commanders if they are to persist in, and systematically carry out, the policy of turning guerrilla warfare into mobile warfare.

THE RELATIONSHIP OF COMMAND

The last problem of strategy in guerrilla war against Japan concerns the relationship of command. A correct solution of this problem is one of the prerequisites for the unhampered development of guerrilla warfare.

Since guerrilla units are a lower level of armed organization characterized by dispersed operations, the methods of command in guerrilla warfare do not allow as high a degree of centralization as in regular warfare. If any attempt is made to apply the methods of command in regular warfare to guerrilla warfare, its great flexibility will inevitably be restricted and its vitality sapped. A highly centralized command is in direct contradiction to the great flexibility of guerrilla warfare and must not and cannot be applied to it.

However, guerrilla warfare cannot be successfully developed without some centralized command. When extensive regular warfare and extensive guerrilla warfare are going on at the same time, their operations must be properly co-ordinated; hence the need for a command co-ordinating the two, *i.e.*, for a unified strategic command by the national general staff and the war-zone commanders. In a guerrilla zone or guerrilla base area with many guerrilla units, there are usually one or more guerrilla formations (sometimes together with regular formations) which constitute the main force, a number of other guerrilla units, big and small, which represent the supplementary force, and many armed units composed of people not withdrawn from production; the enemy forces there usually form a unified complex to concert their operations against the guerrillas. Consequently, the problem arises of setting up a unified or centralized command in such guerrilla zones or base areas.

Hence, as opposed both to absolute centralization and to absolute decentralization, the principle of command in guerrilla war should be centralized strategic command and decentralized command in campaigns and battles.

9.   *Mao Tse-tung: On Protracted War (May, 1938)**

This is a series of lectures delivered from May 26 to June 3, 1938, at the Association for the Study of the Anti-Japanese War in Yenan. "On Protracted War" was published "when Japan was launching her large-scale attack against Wuhan and when the absurd theories of national subjugation and of a quick victory were much in the air."[1] Applying the Marxist-Leninist theories of materialist dialectics, Mao refuted these "theories," laid down the strategic line for a protracted war, and predicted the course of this war through three stages of strategic defense, strategic stalemate and strategic counter-offensive, thus leading to final victory.

* From *Selected Works of Mao Tse-tung*, Peking: Foreign Language Press, 1965, II, 152–189. (Extract; footnotes omitted.)
[1] Ho Kan-chih, *A History of the Modern Chinese Revolution*, Peking: Foreign Language Press, 1959, p. 337.

Mao's "protracted war" is based on the principle of linking war with politics. " 'War is the continuation of politics.' In this sense war is politics and war itself is a political action," Mao wrote in this essay. This principle involves the mobilization of the masses. Mao's guerrilla operations in the early 1930's were indeed based on "a people's war, which is not merely to fight, but also to agitate among the masses, to organize them, to arm them, and to help them establish political power."[2] In the Anti-Japanese War, Mao's strategy and tactics were also based on a "people's war"; that is, the mobilization of the masses. "The mobilization of the common people throughout the country," Mao wrote in this essay, "will create a vast sea in which to drown the enemy."

WAR AND POLITICS

"War is the continuation of politics." In this sense war is politics and war itself is a political action; since ancient times there has never been a war that did not have a political character. The anti-Japanese war is a revolutionary war waged by the whole nation, and victory is inseparable from the political aim of the war—to drive out Japanese imperialism and build a new China of freedom and equality—inseparable from the general policy of persevering in the War of Resistance and in the united front, from the mobilization of the entire people, and from the political principles of the unity between officers and men, the unity between army and people and the disintegration of the enemy forces, and inseparable from the effective application of united front policy, from mobilization on the cultural front, and from the efforts to win international support and the support of the people inside Japan. In a word, war cannot for a single moment be separated from politics. Any tendency among the anti-Japanese armed forces to belittle politics by isolating war from it and advocating the idea of war as an absolute is wrong and should be corrected.

But war has its own particular characteristics and in this sense it cannot be equated with politics in general. "War is the continuation of politics by other . . . means." When politics develops to a certain stage beyond which it cannot

---

[2] A resolution of December, 1929, for the Ninth Conference of the Communist Party Organization of the Fourth Army of the Red Army.

proceed by the usual means, war breaks out to sweep the obstacles from the way. For instance, the semi-independent status
of China is an obstacle to the political growth of Japanese imperialism, hence Japan has unleashed a war of aggression to
sweep away that obstacle. What about China? Imperialist
oppression has long been an obstacle to China's bourgeois-
democratic revolution, hence many wars of liberation have
been waged in the effort to sweep it away. Japan is now using
war for the purpose of oppressing China and completely
blocking the advance of the Chinese revolution, and therefore
China is compelled to wage the War of Resistance in her
determination to sweep away this obstacle. When the obstacle is removed, our political aim will be attained and the
war concluded. But if the obstacle is not completely swept
away, the war will have to continue till the aim is fully
accomplished. Thus anyone who seeks a compromise before
the task of the anti-Japanese war is fulfilled is bound to fail,
because even if a compromise were to occur for one reason
or another, the war would break out again, since the broad
masses of the people would certainly not submit but would
continue the war until its political objective was achieved. It
can therefore be said that politics is war without bloodshed
while war is politics with bloodshed.

From the particular characteristics of war there arise a
particular set of organizations, a particular series of methods
and a particular kind of process. The organizations are the
armed forces and everything that goes with them. The methods are the strategy and tactics for directing war. The process
is the particular form of social activity in which the opposing
armed forces attack each other or defend themselves against
one another, employing strategy and tactics favourable to
themselves and unfavourable to the enemy. Hence war experience is a particular kind of experience. All who take part
in war must rid themselves of their customary ways and
accustom themselves to war before they can win victory.

POLITICAL MOBILIZATION FOR
THE WAR OF RESISTANCE

A national revolutionary war as great as ours cannot be
won without extensive and thoroughgoing political mobilization. Before the anti-Japanese war there was no political

mobilization for resistance to Japan, and this was a great drawback, as a result of which China has already lost a move to the enemy. After the war began, political mobilization was very far from extensive, let alone thoroughgoing. It was the enemy's gunfire and the bombs dropped by enemy aeroplanes that brought news of the war to the great majority of the people. That was also a kind of mobilization, but it was done for us by the enemy, we did not do it ourselves. Even now the people in the remoter regions beyond the noise of the guns are carrying on quietly as usual. This situation must change, or otherwise we cannot win in our life-and-death struggle. We must never lose another move to the enemy; on the contrary, we must make full use of this move, political mobilization, to get the better of him. This move is crucial; it is indeed of primary importance, while our inferiority in weapons and other things is only secondary. The mobilization of the common people throughout the country will create a vast sea in which to drown the enemy, create the conditions that will make up for our inferiority in arms and other things, and create the prerequisites for overcoming every difficulty in the war. To win victory, we must persevere in the War of Resistance, in the united front and in the protracted war. But all these are inseparable from the mobilization of the common people. To wish for victory and yet neglect political mobilization is like wishing to "go south by driving the chariot north", and the result would inevitably be to forfeit victory.

What does political mobilization mean? First, it means telling the army and the people about the political aim of the war. It is necessary for every soldier and civilian to see why the war must be fought and how it concerns him. The political aim of the war is "to drive out Japanese imperialism and build a new China of freedom and equality"; we must proclaim this aim to everybody, to all soldiers and civilians, before we can create an anti-Japanese upsurge and unite hundreds of millions as one man to contribute their all to the war. Secondly, it is not enough merely to explain the aim to them; the steps and policies for its attainment must also be given, that is, there must be a political programme. We already have the Ten-Point Programme for Resisting Japan and Saving the Nation and also the Programme of Armed Resistance and National Reconstruction; we should popularize both of them in the army and among the people and mobilize everyone to carry them out. Without a clear-cut, concrete political programme it is impossible to mobilize all the armed forces and the whole people to carry the war against Japan through to the end. Thirdly, how should we mobilize them? By word of mouth, by leaflets and bulletins, by newspapers, books and pamphlets, through plays and films, through schools, through the mass organizations and through our cadres. What has been done so far in the Kuomintang areas is only a drop in the ocean, and moreover it has been done in a manner ill-suited to the people's tastes and in a spirit uncongenial to them; this must be drastically changed. Fourthly, to mobilize once is not enough; political mobilization for the War of Resistance must be continuous. Our job is not to recite our political programme to the people, for nobody will listen to such recitations; we must link the political mobilization for the war with developments in the war and with the life of the soldiers and the people, and make it a continuous movement. This is a matter of immense importance on which our victory in the war primarily depends.

THE OBJECT OF WAR

Here we are not dealing with the political aim of war; the political aim of the War of Resistance Against Japan has been defined above as "to drive out Japanese imperialism and build a new China of freedom and equality". Here we are dealing with the elementary object of war, war as "politics with bloodshed", as mutual slaughter by opposing armies. The object of war is specifically "to preserve oneself and destroy the enemy" (to destroy the enemy means to disarm him or "deprive him of the power to resist", and does not mean to destroy every member of his forces physically). In ancient warfare, the spear and the shield were used, the spear to attack and destroy the enemy, and the shield to defend and preserve oneself. To the present day, all weapons are still an extension of the spear and the shield. The bomber, the machine-gun, the long-range gun and poison gas are developments of the spear, while the air-raid shelter, the steel helmet, the concrete fortification and the gas mask are developments of the shield. The tank is a new weapon combining the functions of both spear and shield. Attack is the chief means of destroying the enemy, but defence cannot be dispensed with. In attack the immediate object is to destroy the enemy, but at the same time it is self-preservation, because if the enemy is not destroyed, you will be destroyed. In defence the immediate object is to preserve yourself, but at the same time defence is a means of supplementing attack or preparing to go over to the attack. Retreat is in the category of defence and is a continuation of defence, while pursuit is a continuation of attack. It should be pointed out that destruction of the enemy is the primary object of war and self-preservation the secondary, because only by destroying the enemy in large numbers can one effectively preserve oneself. Therefore attack, the chief means of destroying the enemy, is primary, while defence, a supplementary means of destroying the enemy and a means of self-preservation, is secondary. In actual warfare the chief role is played by defence much of the time and by attack for the rest of the time, but if war is taken as a whole, attack remains primary.

How do we justify the encouragement of heroic sacrifice in war? Does it not contradict "self-preservation"? No, it does not; sacrifice and self-preservation are both opposite and complementary to each other. War is politics with bloodshed and exacts a price, sometimes an extremely high price. Partial and temporary sacrifice (non-preservation) is incurred for the sake of general and permanent preservation. This is precisely why we say that attack, which is basically a means of destroying the enemy, also has the function of self-preservation. It is also the reason why defence must be accompanied by attack and should not be defence pure and simple.

The object of war, namely, the preservation of oneself and the destruction of the enemy, is the essence of war and the basis of all war activities, an essence which pervades all war activities, from the technical to the strategic. The object of war is the underlying principle of war, and no technical, tactical, or strategic concepts or principles can in any way depart from it. What for instance is meant by the principle of "taking cover and making full use of fire-power" in shooting? The purpose of the former is self-preservation, of the latter the destruction of the enemy. The former gives rise to such techniques as making use of the terrain and its features, advancing in spurts, and spreading out in dispersed formation. The latter gives rise to other techniques, such as clearing the field of fire and organizing a fire-net. As for the assault force, the containing force and the reserve force in a tactical operation, the first is for annihilating the enemy, the second for

preserving oneself, and the third is for either purpose according to circumstances—either for annihilating the enemy (in
which case it reinforces the assault force or serves as a pursuit force), or for self-preservation (in which case it reinforces the containing force or serves as a covering force).
Thus, no technical, tactical, or strategical principles or operations can in any way depart from the object of war, and this
object pervades the whole of a war and runs through it from
beginning to end.

In directing the anti-Japanese war, leaders at the various
levels must lose sight neither of the contrast between the
fundamental factors on each side nor of the object of this
war. In the course of military operations these contrasting
fundamental factors unfold themselves in the struggle by each
side to preserve itself and destroy the other. In our war we
strive in every engagement to win a victory, big or small, and
to disarm a part of the enemy and destroy a part of his men
and *matériel*. We must accumulate the results of these partial
destructions of the enemy into major strategic victories and
so achieve the final political aim of expelling the enemy, protecting the motherland and building a new China.

THE ARMY AND THE PEOPLE ARE
THE FOUNDATION OF VICTORY

Japanese imperialism will never relax in its aggression
against and repression of revolutionary China; this is determined by its imperialist nature. If China did not resist, Japan
would easily seize all China without firing a single shot, as
she did the four northeastern provinces. Since China is resisting, it is an inexorable law that Japan will try to repress this
resistance until the force of her repression is exceeded by the
force of China's resistance. The Japanese landlord class and
bourgeoisie are very ambitious, and in order to drive south to
Southeast Asia and north to Siberia, they have adopted the
policy of breaking through in the centre by first attacking
China. Those who think that Japan will know where to stop
and be content with the occupation of northern China and of
Kiangsu and Chekiang Provinces completely fail to perceive
that imperialist Japan, which has developed to a new stage
and is approaching extinction, differs from the Japan of the
past. When we say that there is a definite limit both to the

number of men Japan can throw in and to the extent of her advance, we mean that with her available strength, Japan can only commit part of her forces against China and only penetrate China as far as their capacity allows, for she also wants to attack in other directions and has to defend herself against other enemies; at the same time China has given proof of progress and capacity for stubborn resistance, and it is inconceivable that there should be fierce attacks by Japan without inevitable resistance by China. Japan cannot occupy the whole of China, but she will spare no effort to suppress China's resistance in all the areas she can reach, and will not stop until internal and external developments push Japanese imperialism to the brink of the grave. There are only two possible outcomes to the political situation in Japan. Either the downfall of her entire ruling class occurs rapidly, political power passes to the people and war thus comes to an end, which is impossible at the moment; or her landlord class and bourgeoisie become more and more fascist and maintain the war until the day of their downfall, which is the very road Japan is now travelling. There can be no other outcome. Those who hope that the moderates among the Japanese bourgeoisie will come forward and stop the war are only harbouring illusions. The reality of Japanese politics for many years has been that the bourgeois moderates of Japan have fallen captive to the landlords and the financial magnates. Now that Japan has launched war against China, so long as she does not suffer a fatal blow from Chinese resistance and still retains sufficient strength, she is bound to attack Southeast Asia or Siberia, or even both. She will do so once war breaks out in Europe; in their wishful calculations, the rulers of Japan have it worked out on a grandiose scale. Of course, it is possible that Japan will have to drop her original plan of invading Siberia and adopt a mainly defensive attitude towards the Soviet Union on account of Soviet strength and of the serious extent to which Japan herself has been weakened by her war against China. But in that case, so far from relaxing her aggression against China she will intensify it, because then the only way left to her will be to gobble up the weak. China's task of persevering in the War of Resistance, the united front and the protracted war will then become all the more weighty, and it will be all the more necessary not to slacken our efforts in the slightest.

Under the circumstances the main prerequisites for China's

victory over Japan are nation-wide unity and all-round progress on a scale ten or even a hundred times greater than in the past. China is already in an era of progress and has achieved a splendid unity, but her progress and unity are still far from adequate. That Japan has occupied such an extensive area is due not only to her strength but also to China's weakness; this weakness is entirely the cumulative effect of the various historical errors of the last hundred years, and especially of the last ten years, which have confined progress to its present bounds. It is impossible to vanquish so strong an enemy without making an extensive and long-term effort. There are many things we have to exert ourselves to do; here I will deal only with two fundamental aspects, the progress of the army and the progress of the people.

The reform of our military system requires its modernization and improved technical equipment, without which we cannot drive the enemy back across the Yalu River. In our employment of troops we need progressive, flexible strategy and tactics, without which we likewise cannot win victory. Nevertheless, soldiers are the foundation of an army; unless they are imbued with a progressive political spirit, and unless such a spirit is fostered through progressive political work, it will be impossible to achieve genuine unity between officers and men, impossible to arouse their enthusiasm for the War of Resistance to the full, and impossible to provide a sound basis for the most effective use of all our technical equipment and tactics. When we say that Japan will finally be defeated despite her technical superiority, we mean that the blows we deliver through annihilation and attrition, apart from inflicting losses, will eventually shake the morale of the enemy army whose weapons are not in the hands of politically conscious soldiers. With us, on the contrary, officers and men are at one on the political aim of the War of Resistance. This gives us the foundation for political work among all the anti-Japanese forces. A proper measure of democracy should be put into effect in the army, chiefly by abolishing the feudal practice of bullying and beating and by having officers and men share weal and woe. Once this is done, unity will be achieved between officers and men, the combat effectiveness of the army will be greatly increased, and there will be no doubt of our ability to sustain the long, cruel war.

The richest source of power to wage war lies in the masses of the people. It is mainly because of the unorganized state of the Chinese masses that Japan dares to bully us. When this defect is remedied, then the Japanese aggressor, like a mad bull crashing into a ring of flames, will be surrounded by hundreds of millions of our people standing upright, the mere sound of their voices will strike terror into him, and he will be burned to death. China's armies must have an uninterrupted flow of reinforcements, and the abuses of press-ganging and of buying substitutes, which now exist at the lower levels, must immediately be banned and replaced by widespread and enthusiastic political mobilization, which will make it easy to enlist millions of men. We now have great difficulties in raising money for the war, but once the people are mobilized, finances too will cease to be a problem. Why should a country as large and populous as China suffer from lack of funds? The army must become one with the people so that they see it as their own army. Such an army will be invincible, and an imperialist power like Japan will be no match for it.

Many people think that it is wrong methods that make for strained relations between officers and men and between the army and the people, but I always tell them that it is a question of basic attitude (or basic principle), of having respect for the soldiers and the people. It is from this attitude that the various policies, methods and forms ensue. If we depart from this attitude, then the policies, methods and forms will certainly be wrong, and the relations between officers and men and between the army and the people are bound to be unsatisfactory. Our three major principles for the army's political work are, first, unity between officers and men; second, unity between the army and the people; and third, the disintegration of the enemy forces. To apply these principles effectively, we must start with this basic attitude of respect for the soldiers and the people, and of respect for the human dignity of prisoners of war once they have laid down their arms. Those who take all this as a technical matter and not one of basic attitude are indeed wrong, and they should correct their view.

At this moment when the defence of Wuhan and other places has become urgent, it is a task of the utmost importance to arouse the initiative and enthusiasm of the whole army and the whole people to the full in support of the war. There is no doubt that the task of defending Wuhan and other places must be seriously posed and seriously performed. But whether we can be certain of holding them depends not on our subjective desires but on concrete conditions. Among the most important of these conditions is the political mobilization of the whole army and people for the struggle. If a strenuous effort is not made to secure all the necessary conditions, indeed even if one of these conditions is missing, disasters like the loss of Nanking and other places are bound to be repeated. China will have her Madrids in places where the conditions are present. So far China has not had a Madrid, and from now on we should work hard to create several, but it all depends on the conditions. The most fundamental of these is extensive political mobilization of the whole army and people.

In all our work we must persevere in the Anti-Japanese National United Front as the general policy. For only with this policy can we persevere in the War of Resistance and in protracted warfare, bring about a widespread and profound improvement in the relations between officers and men and between the army and the people, arouse to the full the initiative and enthusiasm of the entire army and the entire people in the fight for the defence of all the territory still in our hands and for the recovery of what we have lost, and so win final victory.

This question of the political mobilization of the army and the people is indeed of the greatest importance. We have dwelt on it at the risk of repetition precisely because victory is impossible without it. There are, of course, many other conditions indispensable to victory, but political mobilization is the most fundamental. The Anti-Japanese National United Front is a united front of the whole army and the whole people, it is certainly not a united front merely of the headquarters and members of a few political parties; our basic objective in initiating the Anti-Japanese National United Front is to mobilize the whole army and the whole people to participate in it.

CONCLUSIONS

What are our conclusions? They are:

"Under what conditions do you think China can defeat and destroy the forces of Japan?" "Three conditions are required: first, the establishment of an anti-Japanese united front in China; second, the formation of an international anti-Japanese united front; third, the rise of the revolutionary movement of the people in Japan and the Japanese colonies. From the standpoint of the Chinese people, the unity of the people of China is the most important of the three conditions."

"How long do you think such a war would last?" "That depends on the strength of China's anti-Japanese united front and many other conditioning factors involving China and Japan."

"If these conditions are not realized quickly, the war will be prolonged. But in the end, just the same, Japan will certainly be defeated and China will certainly be victorious. Only the sacrifices will be great and there will be a very painful period."

"Our strategy should be to employ our main forces to operate over an extended and fluid front. To achieve success, the Chinese troops must conduct their warfare with a high degree of mobility on extensive battlefields."

"Besides employing trained armies to carry on mobile warfare, we must organize great numbers of guerrilla units among the peasants."

"In the course of the war, China will be able to . . . reinforce the equipment of her troops gradually. Therefore China will be able to conduct positional warfare in the latter period of the war and make positional attacks on the Japanese-occupied areas. Thus Japan's economy will crack under the strain of China's long resistance and the morale of the Japanese forces will break under the trial of innumerable battles. On the Chinese side, however, the growing latent power of resistance will be constantly brought into play and large numbers of revolutionary people will be pouring into the front lines to fight for their freedom. The combination of all these and other factors will enable us to make the final and decisive attacks on the fortifications and bases in the Japanese-occupied areas and drive the Japanese forces of aggression out of China." (From an interview with Edgar Snow in July 1936.)

"Thus a new stage has opened in China's political situation. . . . In the present stage the central task is to mobilize all the nation's forces for victory in the War of Resistance."

"The key to victory in the war now lies in developing the resistance that has already begun into a war of total resistance by the whole nation. Only through such a war of total resistance can final victory be won."

"The existence of serious weaknesses in the War of Resistance may lead to setbacks, retreats, internal splits, betrayals, temporary and partial compromises and other such reverses. Therefore it should be realized that the war will be arduous and protracted. But we are confident that, through the efforts of our Party and the whole people, the resistance already started will sweep aside all obstacles and continue to advance and develop." ("Resolution on the Present Situation and the Tasks of the Party", adopted by the Central Committee of the Communist Party of China, August 1937.)

These are our conclusions. In the eyes of the subjugationists the enemy are supermen and we Chinese are worthless, while in the eyes of the theorists of quick victory we Chinese are supermen and the enemy are worthless. Both are wrong. We take a different view; the War of Resistance Against Japan is a protracted war, and the final victory will be China's. These are our conclusions.

My lectures end here. The great War of Resistance Against Japan is unfolding, and many people are hoping for a summary of experience to facilitate the winning of complete victory. What I have discussed is simply the general experience of the past ten months, and it may perhaps serve as a kind of summary. The problem of protracted war deserves wide attention and discussion; what I have given is only an outline, which I hope you will examine and discuss, amend and amplify.

10. *Mao Tse-tung: Problems of War and Strategy (November, 1938)**

This is part of Mao's concluding speech delivered at the Central Committee's plenary session. The work was published for the purpose of overcoming the "right opportunists" who "opposed the Party's line on war and strategy." In Mao's own mind, there were two goals: the conquest of power in China and the expulsion of the Japanese from Chinese soil. To this end, Mao considered the link between guerrilla tactics and their political context to be indispensable. This is consistent with the basic principle of his classic on guerrilla warfare. In the preceding two works, Mao spoke on the subject through his analysis of the Party's role against the Japanese. In view of the importance of "the problems of war and strategy in the Chinese revolution," Mao here again "explained the problem, approaching it from the angle of the history of China's political struggles."

In this work, Mao complimented Chiang Kai-shek for having "held firmly to the vital point that whoever has an army has power and that war decides everything." However, he contrasted the military history of the Kuomintang with that of the Chinese Communist Party and thereby

---

* From *Selected Works of Mao Tse-tung*, Peking: Foreign Language Press, 1965, II, 219–232. (Footnotes omitted.)

stressed that there were political objectives besides victory in war. Then he reiterated his conviction that "the organizational [military] task must be subordinated to the political task." In his mind, these two goals—military victory and achievement of political objectives—fall into place in a coherent system of strategy and tactics.

I. China's Characteristics and Revolutionary War

The seizure of power by armed force, the settlement of the issue by war, is the central task and the highest form of revolution. This Marxist-Leninist principle of revolution holds good universally, for China and for all other countries.

But while the principle remains the same, its application by the party of the proletariat finds expression in varying ways according to the varying conditions. Internally, capitalist countries practise bourgeois democracy (not feudalism) when they are not fascist or not at war; in their external relations, they are not oppressed by, but themselves oppress, other nations. Because of these characteristics, it is the task of the party of the proletariat in the capitalist countries to educate the workers and build up strength through a long period of legal struggle, and thus prepare for the final overthrow of capitalism. In these countries, the question is one of a long legal struggle, of utilizing parliament as a platform, of economic and political strikes, of organizing trade unions and educating the workers. There the form of organization is legal and the form of struggle bloodless (non-military). On the issue of war, the Communist Parties in the capitalist countries oppose the imperialist wars waged by their own countries; if such wars occur, the policy of these Parties is to bring about the defeat of the reactionary governments of their own countries. The one war they want to fight is the civil war for which they are preparing. But this insurrection and war should not be launched until the bourgeoisie becomes really helpless, until the majority of the proletariat are determined to rise in arms and fight, and until the rural masses are giving willing help to the proletariat. And when the time comes to launch such an insurrection and war, the first step will be to seize the cities, and then advance into the countryside, and not the other way about. All this has been done by Communist Parties in capitalist countries, and it has been proved correct by the October Revolution in Russia.

China is different however. The characteristics of China are that she is not independent and democratic but semi-colonial and semi-feudal, that internally she has no democracy but is under feudal oppression and that in her external relations she has no national independence but is oppressed by imperialism. It follows that we have no parliament to make use of and no legal right to organize the workers to strike. Basically, the task of the Communist Party here is not to go through a long period of legal struggle before launching insurrection and war, and not to seize the big cities first and then occupy the countryside, but the reverse.

When imperialism is not making armed attacks on our country, the Chinese Communist Party either wages civil war jointly with the bourgeoisie against the warlords (lackeys of imperialism), as in 1924–27 in the wars in Kwangtung Province and the Northern Expedition, or unites with the peasants and the urban petty bourgeoisie to wage civil war against the landlord class and the comprador bourgeoisie (also lackeys of imperialism), as in the War of Agrarian Revolution of 1927–36. When imperialism launches armed attacks on China, the Party unites all classes and strata in the country opposing the foreign aggressors to wage a national war against the foreign enemy, as it is doing in the present War of Resistance Against Japan.

All this shows the difference between China and the capitalist countries. In China war is the main form of struggle and the army is the main form of organization. Other forms such as mass organization and mass struggle are also extremely important and indeed indispensable and in no circumstances to be overlooked, but their purpose is to serve the war. Before the outbreak of a war all organization and struggle are in preparation for the war, as in the period from the May 4th Movement of 1919 to the May 30th Movement of 1925. After war breaks out, all organization and struggle are co-ordinated with the war either directly or indirectly, as, for instance, in the period of the Northern Expedition when all organization and struggle in the rear areas of the revolutionary army were co-ordinated with the war directly, and those in the Northern warlord areas were co-ordinated with the war indirectly. Again in the period of the War of Agrarian

Revolution all organization and struggle inside the Red areas were co-ordinated with the war directly, and outside the Red areas indirectly. Yet again in the present period, the War of Resistance, all organization and struggle in the rear areas of the anti-Japanese forces and in the areas occupied by the enemy are directly or indirectly co-ordinated with the war.

"In China the armed revolution is fighting the armed counter-revolution. That is one of the specific features and one of the advantages of the Chinese revolution." This thesis of Comrade Stalin's is perfectly correct and is equally valid for the Northern Expedition, the War of Agrarian Revolution, and the present War of Resistance Against Japan. They are all revolutionary wars, all directed against counter-revolutionaries and all waged mainly by the revolutionary people, differing only in the sense that a civil war differs from a national war, and that a war conducted by the Communist Party differs from a war it conducts jointly with the Kuomintang. Of course, these differences are important. They indicate the breadth of the main forces in the war (an alliance of the workers and peasants, or of the workers, peasants and bourgeoisie) and whether our antagonist in the war is internal or external (whether the war is against domestic or foreign foes, and, if domestic, whether against the Northern warlords or against the Kuomintang); they also indicate that the content of China's revolutionary war differs at different stages of its history. But all these wars are instances of armed revolution fighting armed counter-revolution, they are all revolutionary wars, and all exhibit the specific features and advantages of the Chinese revolution. The thesis that revolutionary war "is one of the specific features and one of the advantages of the Chinese revolution" fits China's conditions perfectly. The main task of the party of the Chinese proletariat, a task confronting it almost from its very inception, has been to unite with as many allies as possible and, according to the circumstances, to organize armed struggles for national and social liberation against armed counter-revolution, whether internal or external. Without armed struggle the proletariat and the Communist Party would have no standing at all in China, and it would be impossible to accomplish any revolutionary task.

Our Party did not grasp this point fully during the first five or six years after it was founded, that is, from 1921 to its participation in the Northern Expedition in 1926. It did not then understand the supreme importance of armed struggle in China, or seriously prepare for war and organize armed forces, or apply itself to the study of military strategy and tactics. During the Northern Expedition it neglected to win over the army but laid one-sided stress on the mass movement, with the result that the whole mass movement collapsed the moment the Kuomintang turned reactionary. For a long time after 1927 many comrades continued to make it the Party's central task to prepare for insurrections in the cities and to work in the White areas. It was only after our victory in repelling the enemy's third "encirclement and suppression" campaign in 1931 that some comrades fundamentally changed their attitude on this question. But this was not true of the whole Party, and there were other comrades who did not think along the lines presented here.

Experience tells us that China's problems cannot be settled without armed force. An understanding of this point will help us in successfully waging the War of Resistance Against Japan from now on. The fact that the whole nation is rising in armed resistance in the war against Japan should inculcate a better understanding of the importance of this question in the whole Party, and every Party member should be prepared to take up arms and go to the front at any moment. Moreover, our present session has clearly defined the direction for our efforts by deciding that the Party's main fields of work are in the battle zones and in the enemy's rear. This is also an excellent antidote against the tendency of some Party members to be willing only to work in Party organizations and in the mass movement but to be unwilling to study or participate in warfare, and against the failure of some schools to encourage students to go to the front, and other such phenomena. In most of China, Party organizational work and mass work are directly linked with armed struggle; there is not, and cannot be, any Party work or mass work that is isolated and stands by itself. Even in rear areas remote from the battle zones (like Yunnan, Kweichow and Szechuan) and in enemy-occupied areas (like Peiping, Tientsin, Nanking and Shanghai), Party organizational work and mass work are co-ordinated with the war, and should and must exclusively serve the needs of the front. In a word, the whole Party must pay great attention to war, study military matters and prepare itself for fighting.

II. THE WAR HISTORY OF THE KUOMINTANG

It will be useful for us to look at the history of the Kuomintang and see what attention it pays to war.

From the start, when he organized a small revolutionary group, Sun Yat-sen staged armed insurrections against the Ching Dynasty. The period of *Tung Meng Hui* (the Chinese Revolutionary League) was replete with armed insurrections, right up to the armed overthrow of the Ching Dynasty by the Revolution of 1911. Then, during the period of the Chinese Revolutionary Party, he carried out a military campaign against Yuan Shih-k'ai. Subsequent events such as the southern movement of the naval units, the northern expedition from Kweilin and the founding of the Whampoa Military Academy were also among Sun Yat-sen's military undertakings.

After Sun Yat-sen came Chiang Kai-shek, who brought the Kuomintang's military power to its zenith. He values the army as his very life and has had the experience of three wars, namely, the Northern Expedition, the Civil War and the War of Resistance Against Japan. For the last ten years Chiang Kai-shek has been a counter-revolutionary. He has created a huge "Central Army" for counter-revolutionary purposes. He has held firmly to the vital point that whoever has an army has power and that war decides everything. In this respect we ought to learn from him. In this respect both Sun Yat-sen and Chiang Kai-shek are our teachers.

Since the Revolution of 1911, all the warlords have clung to their armies for dear life, setting great store by the principle, "Whoever has an army has power."

Tan Yen-kai, a clever bureaucrat who had a chequered career in Hunan, was never a civil governor pure and simple but always insisted on being both the military governor and the civil governor. Even when he became President of the National Government first in Canton and then in Wuhan, he was concurrently the commander of the Second Army. There are many such warlords who understand this peculiarity of China's.

There have also been parties in China, notably the Progressive Party, which did not want to have an army; yet even this party recognized that it could not get government positions without some warlord backing. Among its successive patrons have been Yuan Shih-k'ai, Tuan Ch'i-jui and Chiang Kai-shek (to whom the Political Science Group, formed out of a section of the Progressive Party, has attached itself).

A few small political parties with a short history, *e.g.*, the Youth Party, have no army, and so have not been able to get anywhere.

In other countries there is no need for each of the bourgeois parties to have an armed force under its direct command. But things are different in China, where, because of the feudal division of the country, those landlord or bourgeois groupings or parties which have guns have power, and those which have more guns have more power. Placed in such an environment, the party of the proletariat should see clearly to the heart of the matter.

Communists do not fight for personal military power (they must in no circumstances do that, and let no one ever again follow the example of Chang Kuo-t'ao), but they must fight for military power for the Party, for military power for the people. As a national war of resistance is going on, we must also fight for military power for the nation. Where there is naivety on the question of military power, nothing whatsoever can be achieved. It is very difficult for the labouring people, who have been deceived and intimidated by the reactionary ruling classes for thousands of years, to awaken to the importance of having guns in their own hands. Now that Japanese imperialist oppression and the nation-wide resistance to it have pushed our labouring people into the arena of war, Communists should prove themselves the most politically conscious leaders in this war. Every Communist must grasp the truth, "Political power grows out of the barrel of a gun." Our principle is that the Party commands the gun, and the gun must never be allowed to command the Party. Yet, having guns, we can create Party organizations, as witness the powerful Party organizations which the Eighth Route Army has created in northern China. We can also create cadres, create schools, create culture, create mass movements. Everything in Yenan has been created by having guns. All things grow out of the barrel of a gun. According to the Marxist theory of the state, the army is the chief component of state power. Whoever wants to seize and retain state power must have a strong army. Some people ridicule us as advocates of the "omnipotence of war". Yes, we are advocates of the omnipotence of revolutionary war; that is good, not bad, it is Marxist. The guns of the Russian Communist Party created socialism. We shall create a democratic republic. Experience in the class struggle in the era of imperialism teaches us that it is only by the power of the gun that the working class and the labouring masses can defeat the armed bourgeoisie and landlords; in this sense we may say that only with guns can the whole world be transformed. We are advocates of the abolition of war, we do not want war; but war can only be abolished through war, and in order to get rid of the gun it is necessary to take up the gun.

III. The War History of the Chinese Communist Party

Our Party failed to grasp the importance of engaging itself directly in preparations for war and in the organization of armed forces for a period of three or four years, that is, from 1921 (when the Chinese Communist Party was founded) to 1924 (when the First National Congress of the Kuomintang was held), and it still lacked adequate understanding of this issue in the 1924–27 period and even later; nevertheless, after 1924, when it began to participate in the Whampoa Military Academy, it entered a new stage and began to see the importance of military affairs. Through helping the Kuomintang in the wars in Kwangtung Province and participating in the Northern Expedition, the Party gained leadership over some armed forces. Then, having learned a bitter lesson from the failure of the revolution, the Party organized the Nanchang Uprising, the Autumn Harvest Uprising and the Canton Uprising, and entered on a new period, the founding of the Red Army. That was the crucial period in which our Party arrived at a thorough understanding of the importance of the army. Had there been no Red Army and no war fought by the Red Army in this period, that is, had the Communist Party adopted Chen Tu-hsiu's liquidationism, the present War of Resistance would have been inconceivable or could not have been sustained for long.

At its emergency meeting held on August 7, 1927, the Central Committee of the Party combated Right opportunism in the political sphere, thus enabling the Party to take a big stride forward. At its fourth plenary session in January 1931, the Sixth Central Committee nominally combated "Left" opportunism in the political sphere, but in fact itself committed the error of "Left" opportunism anew. The two meetings differed in their content and historical role, but neither of them dealt seriously with the problems of war and strategy, a fact which showed that war had not yet been made the centre of gravity in the Party's work. After the central leadership of the Party moved into the Red areas in 1933, this situation underwent a radical change, but mistakes in principle were again committed on the problem of war (and all other major problems), bringing serious losses to the revolutionary war. The Tsunyi Meeting of 1935, on the other hand, was mainly a fight against opportunism in the military sphere and gave top priority to the question of war, and this was a reflection of the war conditions of the time. Today we can say with confidence that in the struggles of the past seventeen years the Chinese Communist Party has forged not only a firm Marxist political line but also a firm Marxist military line. We have been able to apply Marxism in solving not only political but also military problems; we have trained not only a large core of cadres capable of running the Party and the state, but also a large core of cadres capable of running the army. These achievements are the flower of the revolution, watered by the blood of countless martyrs, a glory that belongs not only to the Chinese Communist Party and the Chinese people, but also to the Communist Parties and the peoples of the whole world. There are only three armies in the whole world which belong to the proletariat and the labouring people, the armies led by the Communist Parties of the Soviet Union, of China and of Spain, and as yet Communist Parties in other countries have had no military experience; hence our army and our military experience are all the more precious.

In order to carry the present War of Resistance Against Japan to victory, it is extremely important to expand and consolidate the Eighth Route Army, the New Fourth Army and all the guerrilla forces led by our Party. Acting on this principle, the Party should dispatch a sufficient number of its best members and cadres to the front. Everything must serve victory at the front, and the organizational task must be subordinated to the political task.

IV. Changes in the Party's Military Strategy in the Civil War and the National War

The changes in our Party's military strategy are worth studying. Let us deal separately with the two processes, the civil war and the national war.

The civil war can be roughly divided into two strategic periods. Guerrilla warfare was primary in the first period and regular warfare in the second. But this regular warfare was of the Chinese type, regular only in its concentration of forces for mobile warfare and in a certain degree of centralization and planning in command and organization; in other respects it retained a guerrilla character and, as regular warfare, was on a low level and not comparable with the regular warfare of foreign armies or, in some ways, even with that of the Kuomintang army. Thus, in a sense, this type of regular warfare was only guerrilla warfare raised to a higher level.

The War of Resistance Against Japan can also be roughly divided into two strategic periods, so far as our Party's military tasks are concerned. In the first period (comprising the stages of the strategic defensive and strategic stalemate) it is guerrilla warfare which is primary, while in the second (the stage of the strategic counter-offensive) it is regular warfare which will be primary. However, the guerrilla warfare of the first period of the War of Resistance differs considerably in content from that of the first period of the civil war, because the dispersed guerrilla tasks are being carried out by the regular (*i.e.*, regular to a certain degree) Eighth Route Army. Likewise, the regular warfare of the second period of the War of Resistance will be different from that of the second period of the civil war because we can assume that, given up-to-date equipment, a great change will take place both in the army and in its operations. Our army will then attain a high degree of centralization and organization, and its operations will lose much of their guerrilla character and attain a high degree of regularity; what is now on a low level will then be raised to a higher level, and the Chinese type of regular warfare will change into the general type. That will be our task in the stage of the strategic counter-offensive.

Thus we see that the two processes, the civil war and the War of Resistance Against Japan, and their four strategic periods, contain three changes in strategy. The first was the change from guerrilla warfare to regular warfare in the civil war. The second was the change from regular warfare in the civil war to guerrilla warfare in the War of Resistance. And the third will be the change from guerrilla warfare to regular warfare in the War of Resistance.

The first of the three changes encountered great difficulties. It involved a twofold task. On the one hand, we had to combat the Right tendency of localism and guerrilla-ism, which consisted in clinging to guerrilla habits and refusing to make the turn to regularization, a tendency which arose because our cadres underestimated the changes in the enemy's situation and our own tasks. In the Central Red Area it was only after much painstaking education that this tendency was gradually corrected. On the other hand, we also had to combat the "Left" tendency of over-centralization and adventurism which put undue stress on regularization, a tendency which arose because some of the leading cadres overestimated the enemy, set the tasks too high and mechanically applied foreign experience regardless of the actual conditions. For three long years (before the Tsunyi Meeting) this tendency imposed enormous sacrifices on the Central Red Area, and it was corrected only after we had learned lessons for which we paid in blood. Its correction was the achievement of the Tsunyi Meeting.

The second change in strategy took place in the autumn of 1937 (after the Lukouchiao Incident), at the juncture of the two different wars. We faced a new enemy, Japanese imperialism, and had as our ally our former enemy, the Kuomintang (which was still hostile to us), and the theatre of war was the vast expanse of northern China (which was temporarily our army's front but would soon be the enemy's rear and would remain so for a long time). In this special situation, our change in strategy was an extremely serious one. In this special situation we had to transform the regular army of the past into a guerrilla army (in respect to its dispersed operations, and not to its sense of organization or to its discipline), and transform the mobile warfare of the past into guerrilla warfare, so that we could adapt ourselves to the kind of enemy facing us and to the tasks before us. But this change was, to all appearances, a step backward and therefore necessarily very difficult. Both underestimation and morbid fear of Japan, tendencies likely to occur at such a time, did actually occur among the Kuomintang. When the

Kuomintang changed over from civil war to national war, it suffered many needless losses mainly because of its underestimation of the enemy, but also because of its morbid fear of Japan (as exemplified by Han Fu-chu and Liu Chih). On the other hand, we have effected the change fairly smoothly and, instead of suffering losses, have won big victories. The reason is that the great majority of our cadres accepted the correct guidance of the Central Committee in good time and skilfully sized up the actual situation, even though there were serious arguments between the Central Committee and some of the army cadres. The extreme importance of this change for persevering in, developing and winning the War of Resistance as a whole, as well as for the future of the Communist Party of China, can be seen immediately if we think of the historic significance of anti-Japanese guerrilla warfare in determining the fate of the national liberation struggle in China. In its extraordinary breadth and protractedness, China's anti-Japanese guerrilla war is without precedent, not only in the East but perhaps in the whole history of mankind.

The third change, from guerrilla to regular warfare against Japan, belongs to the future development of the war, which will presumably give rise to new circumstances and new difficulties. We need not discuss it now.

V. THE STRATEGIC ROLE OF GUERRILLA WARFARE AGAINST JAPAN

In the anti-Japanese war as a whole, regular warfare is primary and guerrilla warfare supplementary, for only regular warfare can decide the final outcome of the war. Of the three strategic stages (the defensive, the stalemate and the counter-offensive) in the entire process of the war in the country as a whole, the first and last are stages in which regular warfare is primary and guerrilla warfare supplementary. In the intermediate stage guerrilla warfare will become primary and regular warfare supplementary, because the enemy will be holding on to the areas he has occupied and we will be preparing for the counter-offensive but will not yet be ready to launch it. Though this stage will possibly be the longest, it is still only one of the three stages in the entire war. If we take the war as a whole, therefore, regular warfare is primary and guerrilla warfare supplementary. Unless we understand this, unless we recognize that regular warfare will decide the final outcome of the war, and unless we pay attention to building a regular army and to studying and directing regular warfare, we shall be unable to defeat Japan. This is one aspect of the matter.

All the same, guerrilla warfare has its important strategic place throughout the war. Without guerrilla warfare and without due attention to building guerrilla units and guerrilla armies and to studying and directing guerrilla warfare, we shall likewise be unable to defeat Japan. The reason is that, since the greater part of China will be converted into the enemy's rear, in the absence of the most extensive and persistent guerrilla warfare the enemy will entrench himself securely without any fear of attacks from behind, will inflict heavy losses on our main forces fighting at the front and will launch increasingly fierce offensives; thus it will be difficult for us to bring about a stalemate, and the very continuation of the War of Resistance may be jeopardized. But even if things do not turn out that way, other unfavourable circumstances will ensue, such as the inadequate building up of strength for our counter-offensive, the absence of supporting actions during the counter-offensive, and the possibility that the enemy will be able to replace his losses. If these circumstances arise and are not overcome by the timely development of extensive and persistent guerrilla warfare, it will likewise be impossible to defeat Japan. Hence, though guerrilla warfare occupies a supplementary place in the war as a whole, it does have an extremely important place in strategy. In waging the War of Resistance Against Japan it is undoubtedly a grave error to neglect guerrilla warfare. This is the other aspect of the matter.

Given a big country, guerrilla warfare is possible; hence there was guerrilla warfare in the past too. But guerrilla warfare can be persevered in only when led by the Communist Party. That is why guerrilla warfare generally failed in the past and why it can be victorious only in modern times and only in big countries in which Communist Parties have emerged, as in the Soviet Union during its civil war and in China at present. Considering the present circumstances and the general situation with respect to the war, the division of labour between the Kuomintang and the Communist Party in the anti-Japanese war, in which the former carries on frontal regular warfare and the latter carries on guerrilla warfare behind the enemy lines, is both necessary and proper, and is a matter of mutual need, mutual co-ordination and mutual assistance.

It can thus be understood how important and necessary it was for our Party to change its military strategy from the regular warfare of the latter period of the civil war to the guerrilla warfare of the first period of the War of Resistance. The favourable effects of this change can be summed up in the following eighteen points:

(1) reduction of the areas occupied by the enemy forces;

(2) expansion of the base areas of our own forces;

(3) in the stage of the defensive, co-ordination with operations at the regular front, so as to pin down the enemy;

(4) in the stage of stalemate, maintenance of a firm hold on the base areas behind the enemy lines, so as to facilitate the training and reorganization of troops at the regular front;

(5) in the stage of the counter-offensive, co-ordination with the regular front in recovering lost territory;

(6) the quickest and most effective expansion of our forces;

(7) the widest expansion of the Communist Party, so that a Party branch may be organized in every village;

(8) the broadest development of the mass movements, so that all the people behind the enemy lines, except for those in his strongholds, may be organized;

(9) the most extensive establishment of organs of anti-Japanese democratic political power;

(10) the widest development of anti-Japanese cultural and educational work;

(11) the most extensive improvement of the people's livelihood;

(12) the most effective disintegration of the enemy troops;

(13) the most extensive and enduring impact on popular feeling and stimulation of morale throughout the country;

(14) the most extensive impetus to progress in the friendly armies and parties;

(15) adaptation to the situation in which the enemy is strong and we are weak, so that we suffer fewer losses and win more victories;

(16) adaptation to the fact that China is large and Japan small, so as to make the enemy suffer more losses and win fewer victories;

(17) the quickest and most effective training of large numbers of cadres for leadership; and

(18) the most effective solution of the problem of provisions.

It is also beyond doubt that in the long course of struggle the guerrilla units and guerrilla warfare will not remain as they are but will develop to a higher stage and evolve gradually into regular units and regular warfare. Through guerrilla warfare, we shall build up our strength and turn ourselves into a decisive element in the crushing of Japanese imperialism.

VI. PAY GREAT ATTENTION TO THE STUDY OF MILITARY MATTERS

All the issues between two hostile armies depend on war for their solution, and China's survival or extinction depends on her victory or defeat in the present war. Hence our study of military theory, of strategy and tactics and of army political work brooks not a moment's delay. Though our study of tactics is still inadequate, our comrades who are engaged in military work have achieved a great deal in the last ten years and, on the basis of Chinese conditions, have brought forth much that is new; the shortcoming here is that there has been no general summing-up. But so far only a few people have taken up the study of the problems of strategy and the theory of war. First-rate results have been achieved in the study of our political work, which, in wealth of experience and in the number and quality of its innovations, ranks second only to that of the Soviet Union; here too the shortcoming is insufficient synthesis and systematization. The popularization of military knowledge is an urgent task for the Party and the whole country. We must now pay great attention to all these things, but most of all to the theory of war and strategy. I deem it imperative that we arouse interest in the study of military theory and direct the attention of the whole membership to the study of military matters.

11. *Liu Shao-chi: How to Be a Good Communist (July, 1939)**

LIU SHAO-CHI, a veteran Communist who was trained in the Soviet Union and joined the Party in 1921, is well

* From translation of article so titled, made from the Chinese text published in the double issue of *Honggi* (Red Flag), Nos. 15–16, in which the author has made a number of stylistic changes and additions. 4th rev. ed., Peking: Foreign Language Press, 1964, pp. 45–95. (The first five sections and most footnotes omitted.)

known to be especially well versed in Marxist doctrine. Since 1922, he had led the revolutionary trade union movement in China. After the 1927 debacle he went to Kiangsi and took charge of the workers' movement in the Red Areas. Since 1932 he has been a member of the Political Bureau of the Central Committee, and from 1943 onward he has been a member of the Secretariat of the Central Committee. When the People's Republic was established in 1949, he became Vice-Chairman of the Central People's Government. In 1959 he succeeded Mao as Chairman of the People's Republic. He was for many years Mao's right-hand man, but in a 1966 list of the top leaders announced by the Central Committee he was dropped to seventh position in the Standing Committee of the Politburo.[1]

"How to Be a Good Communist"[2] was for more than twenty years a basic statement on the model of ideal Communist behavior, delivered first as a series of lectures at the Institute of Marxism-Leninism in Yenan, July, 1939. The article reflects the aim of the 1942–1943 *cheng-feng* campaign for the "correction of unorthodox tendencies" by reasserting the basic Leninist conception of Party discipline.

If it is true that this work contains little that is original, this does not imply that there is nothing significant in it. Its chief contribution lies in the fact that, while the Party determines to maintain its discipline and unity along orthodox Leninist lines, it encourages Party members to discipline themselves according to the Chinese tradition of self-cultivation, as expressed in the passages from Confucian classics.

A PARTY MEMBER'S PERSONAL INTERESTS MUST BE UNCONDITIONALLY SUBORDINATED TO THE INTERESTS OF THE PARTY

Personal interests must be subordinated to the Party's interests, the interests of the local Party organization to those of the entire Party, the interests of the part to those of the whole, and temporary to long-term interests. This is a Marxist-Leninist principle which must be followed by every Communist.

---

[1] For details, see Selection 29.

[2] Its original title is literally "The Cultivation of Communist Party Members."

A Communist must be clear about the correct relationship between personal and Party interests.

The Communist Party is the political party of the proletariat and has no interests of its own other than those of the emancipation of the proletariat. The final emancipation of the proletariat will also inevitably be the final emancipation of all mankind. Unless the proletariat emancipates all working people and all nations—unless it emancipates mankind as a whole—it cannot fully emancipate itself. The cause of the emancipation of the proletariat is identical with and inseparable from the cause of the emancipation of all working people, all oppressed nations and all mankind. Therefore, the interests of the Communist Party are the emancipation of the proletariat and of all mankind, are communism and social progress. When a Party member's personal interests are subordinated to those of the Party, they are subordinated to the interests of the emancipation of the class and the nation, and those of communism and social progress.

Comrade Mao Tse-tung has said:

> At no time and in no circumstances should a Communist place his personal interests first; he should subordinate them to the interests of the nation and of the masses of the people. Hence, selfishness, slacking, corruption, striving for the limelight, etc. are most contemptible, while selflessness, working with all one's energy, whole-hearted devotion to public duty, and quiet hard work are the qualities that command respect.

The test of a Party member's loyalty to the Party, the revolution and the cause of communism is whether or not he can subordinate his personal interests absolutely and unconditionally to the interests of the Party, whatever the circumstances.

At all times and on all questions, a Party member should give first consideration to the interests of the Party as a whole, and put them in the forefront and place personal matters and interests second. The supremacy of the Party's interests is the highest principle that must govern the thinking and actions of the members of our Party. In accordance with this principle, every Party member must completely identify his personal interests with those of the Party both in his thinking and in his actions. He must be able to yield to the interests of the Party without any hesitation or reluctance and sacrifice his personal interests whenever the two are at variance. Unhesitating readiness to sacrifice personal interests, and even one's life, for the Party and the proletariat and for the emancipation of the nation and of all mankind—this is one expression of what we usually describe as "Party spirit", "Party sense" or "sense of organization". It is the highest expression of communist morality, of the principled nature of the party of the proletariat, and of the purest proletarian class consciousness.

Members of our Party should not have personal aims which are independent of the Party's interests. Their personal aims must harmonize with the Party's interests. If the aim they set themselves is to study Marxist-Leninist theory, to develop their ability in work, to establish revolutionary organizations and to lead the masses in successful revolutionary struggles—if their aim is to do more for the Party—then this personal aim harmonizes with the interests of the Party. The Party needs many such members and cadres. Apart from this aim, Party members should have no independent personal motives such as attaining position or fame, or playing the individual hero, otherwise they will depart from the interests of the Party and may even become careerists within the Party.

If a Party member thinks only of the communist interests and aims of the Party, is really selfless and has no personal aims and considerations divorced from those of the Party, and if he ceaselessly raises the level of his political consciousness through revolutionary practice and through the study of Marxism-Leninism, then the following ensues.

First, he has a high communist morality. Taking a clear-cut, firm proletarian stand, he is able to show loyalty to and love for all comrades, all revolutionaries and working people, help them unreservedly and act towards them as his equals, and he will never allow himself to hurt a single one of them for his own interests. He is able to feel for others, place himself in their position, and be considerate of them. On the other hand, he is able to wage resolute struggle against the pernicious enemies of mankind and persevere in the fight for the interests of the Party, the proletariat, and the emancipation of the nation and all mankind. He is "the first to worry and the last to enjoy himself". Whether in the Party or among the people, he is the first to suffer hardship and the last to enjoy comfort; he compares himself with others not with respect to material enjoyment but to the amount of work done for the revolution and the spirit of hard endurance in struggle. In times of adversity he steps forward boldly, and in times of difficulty he does his duty to the full. He has such revolutionary firmness and integrity that "neither riches nor honours can corrupt him, neither poverty nor lowly condition can make him swerve from principle, neither threats nor force can bend him".

Second, he has the greatest revolutionary courage. Having no selfish motives, he has nothing to fear. Having done nothing to give himself a guilty conscience, he can lay bare and courageously correct his mistakes and shortcomings, which are like "an eclipse of the sun or the moon". Because he has the courage of righteous conviction, he never fears the truth, courageously upholds it, spreads it and fights for it. Even if it is temporarily to his disadvantage and if, in upholding the truth, he suffers blows of all kinds, is opposed or censured by most other people and so finds himself in temporary (and honourable) isolation, even to the point where he may have to give up his life, he will still breast the waves to uphold the truth and will never drift with the tide.

Third, he learns how best to grasp the theory and method of Marxism-Leninism. He is able to apply them in keenly observing problems and in knowing and changing reality. Because he takes a clear-cut, firm proletarian stand and is tempered in Marxism-Leninism, he is free from personal apprehensions and self-interest, so that there is no impediment to his observation of things or distortion of his understanding of the truth. He seeks the truth from the facts, and he tests all theories and distinguishes what is true from what is false in revolutionary practice. He does not take a dogmatist or empiricist approach to Marxism-Leninism but integrates the universal truth of Marxism-Leninism with concrete revolutionary practice.

Fourth, he is the most sincere, most candid and happiest of men. Because he has no private axe to grind, nothing to conceal from the Party and nothing he cannot tell others, he has no problems of personal gain or loss and no personal anxieties other than for the interests of the Party and the revolution. Even when he is working on his own without supervision and is therefore in a position to do something bad, he is just as "watchful over himself when he is alone" and does not do anything harmful. His work bears examination and he is not afraid of having it checked. He does not fear criticism and at the same time is able to criticize others with courage and sincerity.

Fifth, he has the greatest self-respect and self-esteem. For the sake of the Party and the revolution he can be most forbearing and tolerant towards comrades and can suffer wrong in the general interest, even enduring misunderstanding and humiliation without bitterness if the occasion so demands. No personal aims lead him to flatter anyone or to desire flattery from others. When it comes to personal matters, he knows how to conduct himself and has no need to humble himself in order to get help from others. He knows how to take good care of himself in the interests of the Party and the revolution and how to strengthen both his grasp of theory and his practical effectiveness. But when it is necessary to swallow humiliation and bear a heavy load for some important purpose in the cause of the Party and the revolution, he can take on the most difficult and vital tasks without the slightest reluctance, never passing the difficulties to others.

A member of the Communist Party should possess the finest and highest human virtues and take a clear-cut and firm Party and proletarian stand (that is, possess Party spirit and class spirit). Ours is a fine morality precisely because it is proletarian and communist. It is founded not on the protection of the interests of individuals or of the exploiting few, but on those of the proletariat and the great mass of working people, of the cause of the final emancipation of all mankind, the liberation of the whole world from the calamities of capitalism, and the building of a happy and beautiful communist world—it is a morality founded on the Marxist-Leninist theory of scientific communism. As we Communists see it, nothing can be more worthless or indefensible than to sacrifice oneself in the interests of an individual or a small minority. But it is the worthiest and justest thing in the world to sacrifice oneself for the Party, for the proletariat, for the emancipation of the nation and of all mankind, for social progress and for the highest interests of the overwhelming majority of the people. Indeed, countless members of the Communist Party have looked death calmly in the face and made the ultimate sacrifice without the slightest hesitation. Most Communists consider it a matter of course to die for the sake of the cause, to lay down their life for justice, when that is necessary. This does not stem from any revolutionary fanaticism or hunger for fame but from their scientific understanding of social development and their deep political consciousness. There is no morality in class society to compare with this high communist morality. The universal morality which supposedly transcends class is sheer deceptive nonsense and is in fact a morality designed to protect the interests of the exploiting few. Such a concept of morality is always idealist. It is only we Communists who build our morality on the scientific basis of historical materialism, and publicly proclaim its purpose to be the protection of the interests of the proletariat in the struggle for the emancipation of itself and of all mankind.

The Communist Party represents the general and long-range interests of the proletariat and all mankind in their struggle for emancipation; the Party's interests are the concentrated expression of this cause. One must never regard the Communist Party as a narrow clique, like a guild pursuing the interests of its members. Anyone who does so is no Communist.

A Party member has interests of his own, which may be inconsistent with or even run counter to the interests of the Party in certain circumstances. Should this happen, it is incumbent on him to sacrifice his personal interests and unconditionally subordinate them to the interests of the Party; under no pretence or excuse may he sacrifice the Party's interests by clinging to his own. At all times and in all circumstances, he should fight heart and soul for the Party's interests and for the Party's development, regarding every success and victory won by the Party and the proletariat as his very own. Every Party member should strive to increase his effectiveness and ability in the service of the people. But this must be done in the fight for the advancement, success and victory of the Party's cause, and there must be no striving for individual development divorced from the fight to advance the Party's cause. The facts prove that only by complete devotion in the fight for the advancement, success and victory of the Party's cause can a Party member heighten his effectiveness and ability, and that he cannot possibly make progress or heighten his ability in any other way. Hence a Party member can and must completely merge his personal interests with those of the Party.

Members of our Party are no ordinary people but the awakened vanguard fighters of the proletariat. They must consciously represent the class interests and class ideology of the proletariat. Therefore, their personal interests must never project beyond those of the Party and the proletariat. It is all the more necessary for each cadre and leader of the Party to be a living embodiment of the general interests of the Party and the proletariat, and to merge his personal interests completely in their general interests and aims. In present-day China, it is the proletariat that best represents the interests of national liberation, and therefore our Party members must be worthy champions of the interests of the nation as a whole.

Members of our Party must subordinate personal to Party interests and are required to sacrifice them to Party interests if necessary. But this by no means implies that our Party does not recognize, or brushes aside, the personal interests of its members or that it wants to wipe out their individuality. Party members do have their personal problems to attend to, and, moreover, they should develop themselves according to their individual inclinations and aptitudes. Therefore, so long as the interests of the Party are not violated, a Party member can have his private and family life, and develop his individual inclinations and aptitudes. At the same time, the Party will use every possibility to help members develop their individual inclinations and aptitudes in conformity with its interests, furnish them with suitable work and working conditions and commend and reward them. As far as possible, the Party will attend to and safeguard its members' essential interests; for example, it will give them the opportunity to study and to acquire an education, it will help them cope with health and family problems and, when necessary, it will even give up some of its work in order to preserve comrades working under the rule of reaction. But all this has no other purpose than the over-all interests of the Party. For the fulfilment of its tasks the Party must ensure that members have the conditions necessary for life, work and education so that they can perform their tasks with enthusiasm and without worry. Comrades in responsible Party positions must bear all this in mind when they deal with Party members' problems.

To sum up, on his side, every Party member should completely submit himself to the interests of the Party and self-sacrificingly devote himself to the public duty. He should forgo all personal aims and private considerations which conflict with the Party's interests. He should not think of himself all the time, make endless personal demands on the Party or blame the Party for not promoting or rewarding him.

Whatever the circumstances, he should study hard, try to make progress, be courageous in struggle and make ceaseless efforts to raise the level of his political consciousness and his understanding of Marxism-Leninism, so as to be able to contribute more to the Party and the revolution. On their side, all Party organizations and comrades in responsible positions, in dealing with the problems of Party members, should see how they work, live and study, and enable them to work better for the Party, ceaselessly develop themselves and raise their level in the course of the revolutionary struggle of the proletariat. In particular, attention should be paid to comrades who are really selfless and who serve the people well. Only so, through combined attention and effort by both sides can the interests of the Party be well served.

EXAMPLES OF WRONG IDEOLOGY
IN THE PARTY

In the light of what has been said, we can see that if an understanding of communism and a correct correlation between personal and Party interests are taken as the standard for evaluating Party members and cadres, many measure up to it and can serve as models, but some do not yet measure up to this standard and still have various wrong ideas to some degree or other. It may not be amiss if I outline these wrong ideas for our comrades' attention.

What are the fundamentally wrong ideas to be found among comrades in our Party?

First. The people joining our Party not only differ in class origin and personal class status but also carry with them aims and motives of every description. Many, of course, join the Party in order to bring about communism and attain the great goal of the emancipation of the proletariat and all mankind, but some do so for other reasons and with other aims. For example, some comrades of peasant background used to think that communism meant "expropriation of local tyrants and distribution of the land". When they first joined, they had no understanding of the real meaning of communism. Today, quite a number of people join the Party chiefly because it is resolute in resisting Japan and advocates the National United Front Against Japan. Others join our ranks because they admire the Communist Party for its good reputation or because they realize in a vague way that it can save China. Still others are seeking a future for themselves, chiefly because they have no other way out—they have no fixed occupation, are out of work, lack the means to study, or want to escape from family bondage or forced marriage, etc. A few even join because they count on the Party to get their taxes reduced, or because they hope to "make their mark" some day, or because their relatives or friends have brought them in, etc. Naturally, such comrades do not have a clear-cut and stable communist world outlook, do not understand the greatness of the communist cause and the difficulties besetting it, and lack a firm proletarian standpoint. Naturally, too, some of them will waver or change somewhat in certain circumstances at certain critical turning points. Since they bring all sorts of ideas with them into the Party, it is most important that they should be educated and should train and temper themselves. Otherwise, they cannot become revolutionary fighters of the proletariat.

Nevertheless, there is no terrible problem here. After all, it is not a bad thing that people turn to the Communist Party, enter it seeking a way out of their predicament and approve of its policy. They are not mistaken in coming to us. We welcome them—everyone except for enemy agents, traitors, careerists and ambitious climbers. Provided they accept and are ready to abide by the Party's Programme and Constitution, work in one of the Party organizations and pay membership dues, they may be admitted into the Communist Party. As for deepening their study and understanding of communism and the Party's Programme and Constitution, they can do so after joining the Party, and can temper and train themselves in revolutionary struggle on the basis of what they learn; in this way they have every possibility of becoming very good Communists. Indeed, for most people it is impossible to have a profound understanding of communism and the Party's Programme and Constitution before joining the Party. That is why we only prescribe acceptance, and not a thorough understanding, of the Party's Programme and Constitution as a condition for admission. Although many people do not have a thorough understanding of communism before joining, it is possible for them to become active fighters in the communist and revolutionary movements of the time. They can become politically conscious Communists provided they study hard after joining the Party. Furthermore, our Party Constitution stipulates that members are free to withdraw from the Party (there is no freedom of admission). Any member is free to notify the Party that he is withdrawing if he lacks a profound belief in communism, or cannot live a strict Party life, or for any other reason, and the Party gives him the freedom to withdraw. It will do nothing against him, unless he gives away Party secrets or engages in wrecking activities against the Party after he leaves. As for careerists and spies who have wormed their way into the Party, of course they have to be expelled. Only thus can we preserve the purity of our Party.

Second. Fairly strong individualism and selfishness are still to be found in some members of our Party.

The individualism expresses itself as follows. Some people habitually place their personal interests above those of the Party when it comes to practical matters; they are preoccupied with personal gain and loss and always calculate in terms of personal interests; they abuse the public trust, turning their Party work to private advantage of one kind or another; or they attack comrades they dislike and wreak private vengeance, on high-sounding pretexts of principle or Party interests. When it comes to status, material benefits and other questions affecting everyday life, they invariably try to get more than others, compare themselves with those at the top, diligently strive after greater personal benefits and crow when they get them. But when it comes to work, they like to compare themselves with those who are less capable. When there are hardships to bear, they make themselves scarce. In times of danger they want to run away. When it comes to orderlies, they always want more. Their living quarters must be of the best, and they want to show off and to bask in the Party's glory. They want to grab all the good things of life, but when it comes to the "unpleasant things", they think these are for others. The heads of such people are stuffed with the ideology of the exploiting classes. They believe that "Every man is for himself, or Heaven and Earth will destroy him", "Man is a selfish animal", and "No one in the world is genuinely unselfish, unless he is a simpleton or an idiot". They even use such exploiting class rubbish to justify their own selfishness and individualism. There are such people in our Party.

This type of self-seeking individualism often manifests itself inside the Party in unprincipled quarrelling, factional struggle, sectarianism and departmentalism; it manifests itself in disrespect for and wilful violation of Party discipline. Most unprincipled struggles originate in personal interests. Those who go in for factional struggle and are given to sectarianism usually place their own individual interests, or the interests of a small minority, above those of the Party. Often, in their unprincipled factional struggles they deliberately undermine Party organization and discipline, making unprincipled and sometimes calculated attacks on certain people, while contracting unprincipled friendships to avoid giving offence, to cover up for one another, to sing each other's praises, etc.

Departmentalism within the Party arises chiefly because some comrades only see the interests of the part, *i.e.*, the work of their own department or locality, and fail to see the interests of the whole, *i.e.*, the interests of the entire Party and the work of other departments and localities. Politically and ideologically, this resembles the guild outlook. Not all comrades who make the mistake of departmentalism are necessarily prompted by individualism, but people with an individualist ideology usually make the mistake of departmentalism.

Third. Conceit, the idea of individualistic heroism, ostentatiousness, etc. are still to be found, to a greater or lesser extent, in the minds of quite a few Party comrades.

The first consideration of people with such notions is their position in the Party. They like to show off and to have people sing their praises and flatter them. They are ambitious, they like to cut a dash, to claim credit for themselves and to get into the limelight, and they like to keep everything in their own hands and lack a democratic style of work. They are extremely vain, and are unwilling to immerse themselves in hard work or do routine or technical jobs. They are arrogant, and whenever they accomplish something they throw their weight about, become overbearing and try to domineer, and they do not treat others as equals in a modest and friendly way. They are complacent, talk down to and lecture people and order others about, and they are always trying to tread on people's necks; they do not learn modestly from others, particularly from the masses, and do not accept even well-grounded opinions and criticisms. They can bear promotion but not demotion, they can bear fair weather but not foul, and they cannot bear being misunderstood or wronged. As their baneful yearning for fame has not yet been uprooted, they try to dress themselves up as "great men" and "heroes" in the communist movement, and stop at nothing to gratify their desire. When they fail to achieve this object, or when they are misunderstood or wronged, there is a danger that they will vacillate. Quite a number of people have vacillated and left our Party for such reasons in the course of its history. Exploiting class ideas still linger in the minds of such people, who fail to understand the greatness of the cause of communism and who lack the communist breadth of vision.

Communists must not be in the least complacent or arrogant. Granted that some comrades are very capable, have done some good work and have to their credit considerable achievements, which may be reckoned "great" and on which they might well preen themselves (for example, our army commanders who have led thousands and tens of thousands of men in battle and won victories, or the leaders of our Party and mass work in various places who have brought about fairly significant changes in the situation). Yet after all, how great are these achievements compared with the communist cause as a whole? And for people with a communist world outlook, what is there worth preening oneself about in these achievements?

For a Communist to do his work properly and well is no more than his duty. He should guard against complacency and arrogance and do his best to make no mistakes, or as few as possible.

What is there in personal position for a Communist to bother about? No one's position is higher than an emperor's, and yet what is an emperor compared with a fighter in the cause of communism? Is he not just a "drop in the ocean" as Comrade Stalin put it? So what is there in personal position worth bothering or bragging about?

Yes, we need countless communist heroes and many mass leaders of great prestige in our Party and in the communist movement. At present, we really have too few of them and have yet to train and temper large numbers of good communist revolutionary leaders and heroes in all fields. This is indeed very important for our cause and must not be neglected. Whoever takes it lightly is ignorant of how to advance the cause of communism. Its advancement requires that we should greatly enhance the revolutionary spirit of enterprise among our Party members and bring their vitality into full play. We have to admit that so far we have not done enough in this respect. This is shown, for instance, by the fact that some Party members do not study hard and have little interest in politics and theory. Therefore, while we are opposed to individualistic heroism and to ostentatiousness, we are certainly not opposed to a spirit of enterprise in the Party members. The desire to make progress in the interests of the people is a most precious quality in a Communist. But the communist, proletarian, spirit of enterprise is entirely different from the individualist "spirit of enterprise". The former means seeking the truth, upholding it and fighting for it with the greatest effectiveness. It is progressive and opens up unlimited prospects of development, while the latter offers no prospects even for the individual. For people with an individualist ideology are usually driven by their personal interests into deliberately brushing aside, covering up or distorting the truth.

Our comrades must understand that genuine leaders and heroes in the communist movement are never individualistic, nor are they ever self-styled or self-appointed. Anyone who styles himself a leader or reaches after leadership can never become a leader in our Party. The rank and file of our Party will not make leaders of people who are prone to conceit, individualistic heroism, ostentatiousness, personal ambition and vanity. No member of our Party has any right to demand that the rank and file should support or keep him as a leader. Only those who are entirely selfless and devoted to the Party, only those with an excellent communist morality and fine communist qualities, who have grasped the theory and method of Marxism-Leninism, who have considerable practical ability, who can direct Party work correctly and who study hard and make constant progress, can win the trust of the Party and the confidence and support of the rank and file, and so become leaders and heroes in the communist movement.

Our comrades must also understand that a member, or a leader and hero, whoever he may be, can only do part of the work, can only carry part of the responsibility, in the communist movement. The communist cause is an undertaking which requires the collective efforts of tens of millions of people over a long period of time, and which cannot be encompassed by any one individual alone. Even such great men as Marx, Engels, Lenin and Stalin could only perform part of the work needed by the communist cause. The cause for which they worked requires the joint efforts and sustained labour of tens of millions of us. We ordinary Communists are also doing part of the work of the communist cause and carrying part of the responsibility. Of course, our part is much smaller than that of Marx, Engels, Lenin or Stalin. Nevertheless, we all have a *part*. Big or small, it is all part of the great cause. Therefore, if only we do our part of the work well, we can consider that we have done our duty. Naturally, we should try our best to do more, but if we cannot and can only do a little, that is also useful and just as honourable. In any case, we should at least not hamper the progress of the communist cause, but should do our part, whether big or small, and perform our work well, be it heavy or light; that is the correct attitude for every member of our Party. Comrades who are unwilling to undertake technical work think that it stifles their talents, that it prevents them from becoming famous (actually it does not, as witness the technical worker Stakhanov) and from giving full play to their abilities and that it kills some of the enterprising spirit which all Communists should have. This view is wrong. Technical work occupies a very important place in our Party work, and comrades engaged in it are doing their share in the communist cause no less than comrades engaged in other jobs. The proper attitude for a Communist is to do whatever work the Party requires of him and do it happily and well, whether it suits his inclinations or not.

Naturally, in assigning work to members, the Party organization and the responsible Party comrades should, as far as possible, take their individual inclinations and aptitudes into consideration, develop their strong points and stimulate their zeal to go forward. However, no Communist must refuse a Party assignment on the grounds of personal preference.

Fourth. A small number of comrades are deeply imbued with the ideology of the exploiting classes. They are usually unscrupulous in dealing with comrades and in handling problems inside the Party, and are utterly devoid of the great and sincere proletarian communist spirit of mutual help and solidarity.

People with this ideology always want to climb over the heads of others in the Party and, to this end, resort to attacking others and doing them harm. They are jealous of those more capable than themselves. They always try to pull down those who are moving ahead of them. They cannot bear playing second fiddle and think only of themselves and never of others. When other comrades are suffering difficulties or setbacks, they gloat or secretly rejoice and have no comradely sympathy at all. They even scheme to injure comrades, "drop stones on one who has fallen into a well", and take advantage of comrades' weaknesses and difficulties to attack and harm them. They "crawl through any crack" and exploit and exacerbate any weakness in Party organization and work for their personal advantage. They love to stir up trouble in the Party, speak ill of others behind their backs and engage in intrigues in order to sow dissension between comrades. They love to join in any unprincipled dispute that may occur in the Party and take great interest in unprincipled quarrels. They are especially active in stirring up and aggravating such quarrels when the Party is in difficulties. In short, they are thoroughly crooked and lack all integrity. Would it not be absurd to describe such people as being able to grasp the Marxist-Leninist theory and method and to give expression to proletarian ideology? It is only too clear that all they express is the ideology of the declining exploiting classes.

All exploiters must do harm to other people in order to expand. To increase their wealth, or to avoid bankruptcy in an economic crisis, bigger capitalists must squeeze many smaller capitalists out of existence and drive countless workers to starvation. To enrich themselves, landlords must exploit peasants and deprive many of them of their land. In order to expand, fascist Germany, Italy and Japan must devastate other countries; they have subjugated Austria, Czechoslovakia, and Abyssinia and are committing aggression against China. Exploiters always harm and ruin other people as a necessary precondition for their own expansion; their happiness is founded on the suffering of others. Among the exploiters, therefore, genuine firm unity, genuine mutual help, and genuine human sympathy are impossible; they inevitably engage in intrigues and underhand activities in order to ruin others. Yet they have to lie and pose as saints and pillars of justice before the people. Such are the distinguishing characteristics of all declining exploiting classes. These may be models of "fine" ethical conduct for the exploiters, but they are most criminal from the point of view of the proletariat and the masses.

The proletariat is absolutely different from any exploiting class. It does not exploit others but is itself exploited. There is no conflict of basic interests within its ranks or between it and the other oppressed and exploited working people. So far from needing to harm other working people or impede their development for the sake of its own development and emancipation, the proletariat must forge the closest unity with them in common struggle. If the proletariat is to emancipate itself, it must at the same time emancipate all other working people and emancipate all mankind. There can be no such thing as the separate emancipation of a single worker or section of workers. The proletariat must carry the cause of the emancipation of humanity through to the end, fighting step by step for the liberation of all mankind, and there can be no giving up or compromising half-way.

As a result of this objective position occupied by the proletariat, the ideology of the politically conscious workers is the diametrical opposite of that of the exploiters. Communists are vanguard fighters of the proletariat, who arm themselves with Marxism-Leninism and are ruthless towards the people's enemies but never towards the toilers, their class brothers and comrades. They differentiate clearly and sharply between the attitudes and methods to be adopted against the enemy and those to be adopted towards their comrades and friends. They cherish great and sincere friendship, warmth and sympathy for other members of their own class and for all oppressed and exploited working people, towards whom they show a fine spirit of mutual help, firm unity and genuine equality. They are absolutely opposed to privileges of any kind for anyone, consider it impermissible to think in terms of privileges for themselves, and would deem it unthinkable, and indeed a disgrace, to occupy a privileged position among the people. If they themselves are to develop and improve their own status, they must develop others and improve the status of all the working people at the same time. They are anxious not to fall behind, whether ideologically or politically or in their work, and they have a sturdy spirit of enterprise, but at the same time they esteem, cherish and support those who are ahead of them in these respects and, without any jealousy, do their best to learn from them. They are deeply concerned with the sufferings and privations of their own class and of all working people, they are concerned with all the struggles of the working people for emancipation anywhere in the world, regarding every victory or defeat for the working people anywhere as their own victory or defeat, and therefore displaying the greatest solidarity. They consider it wrong to be indifferent to the struggle of the working and oppressed people for liberation, and criminal to gloat over their setbacks. They cherish their own comrades and brothers, whose weaknesses and mistakes they criticize frankly and sincerely (and this shows genuine affection); in matters of principle they never gloss over and accommodate, let alone encourage, mistakes (to accommodate or even to encourage others' mistakes does not betoken genuine affection for one's comrades). They do everything possible to help comrades overcome weaknesses and correct mistakes and never exploit or aggravate these weaknesses and mistakes to get comrades into trouble, let alone cause the mistakes to develop beyond correction. Not harbouring any desire to settle old scores, they can return good for evil to their own comrades and brothers and help them straighten themselves out. They can be strict with themselves and lenient with others. The stand they take is firm, strict and principled, their attitude is frank, upright and responsible, they do not give way on matters of principle, they do not tolerate anyone who harms the Party, they do not permit anyone to insult them and are particularly contemptuous of adulation and flattery as contrary to all principle. They oppose all unprincipled struggles; they do not let themselves become involved in such struggles, and are not so swayed or affected by irresponsible or casual criticism made behind their backs as to depart from principle, become incapable of thinking calmly or lose their composure. Such are the proletarian qualities of mind every Party member must learn to acquire and foster. The great founders of Marxism-Leninism epitomize these proletarian qualities in the most concentrated, exemplary and concrete form. These qualities represent everything of integrity in present-day society. Indeed it is the Communist Party that represents human integrity. We must foster and enhance such proletarian integrity and overcome all that is crooked and evil.

Fifth. Pettiness, fussing over trifles and ignoring the general interest are faults still prevalent among some Party members. These comrades lack the stature and breadth of vision of Communists and are blind to the bigger things; they relish only the immediate and the petty. They do not take much interest in the great problems and events in the Party and the revolution, but are always fussing over the merest trifles about which they enter into ponderous and endless arguments and become highly disturbed. Such people are also easily led by the nose when they receive some small favour or kindness.

They have the petty-mindedness characteristic of small rural producers.

There are other people who do not seem to have a clear-cut and definite attitude in their Party life, people who shift and hedge. They are actually of two kinds; for one kind the question is one of understanding, and for the other, of moral character. The latter are always opportunistic in their personal behaviour, curry favour with all sides and try to please everybody. They tailor their words to the person and the circumstances, tack with the wind and show no principle whatsoever. Such are their characteristics. Sometimes, they wait and see what will suit the occasion, like the bat in *Aesop's Fables*,[1] and then move over to the winning side. Such double-faced creatures, who are neither fish nor fowl, are not altogether unknown in our ranks. They have the traits of the old-fashioned merchant. In addition, there are some individuals who, unable to resist the lure of the old society's exploiting classes, with their glittering world, their money and their women, begin to waver, go wrong and eventually betray the Party and the revolution.

Finally, the ideology of some of our Party comrades often reflects the impetuosity and vacillation of the petty bourgeoisie and the destructiveness of the *lumpen*-proletariat and certain bankrupt peasants, but I shall not go into this question here.

To sum up, our Party represents the great and powerful proletarian communist ideology, but it must be noted that all kinds of non-proletarian ideology—including even the ideology of the declining exploiting classes—are still reflected to a greater or lesser degree in the minds of certain comrades. At times such ideology is dormant in the Party, revealing itself only in insignificant matters of everyday life; but at other times it becomes active, systematically revealing itself in a whole variety of questions of Party principle, in major political questions and in problems of inner-Party struggle. Certain sections or links in the Party organization may come to be dominated and corroded by such erroneous ideology, and in

---

[1] See "The Bat and the Weasels", *Aesop's Fables*. A bat once fell down and was caught by a weasel. He begged the weasel to spare his life. The weasel said, "I hate birds. I will not let you go." The bat said, "I am not a bird but a mouse," and was set free. Some time later, the bat again fell to the ground and was caught by another weasel. He begged the weasel not to kill him. The weasel said he hated mice. The bat argued he was not a mouse but a bat, and so he was set free a second time. The bat thus save his life twice by changing his name.

extreme cases it may even temporarily dominate key links in the Party leadership, as in the periods when people like Chen Tu-hsiu and Chang Kuo-tao were in control. In normal periods, however, it is held in check by the correct proletarian ideology. These are all manifestations within the Party of the struggle between proletarian and non-proletarian ideology. Similarly with some individual Party members. At times what is wrong in their ideology lies dormant and under control, but at other times it may grow and even dominate their actions. This is a manifestation among individual Party members of the contradiction and struggle between proletarian and non-proletarian ideology. For our Party members, ideological self-cultivation means that they must consciously use the proletarian ideology and the Communist world outlook to overcome and eliminate all the various kinds of incorrect, non-proletarian ideology.

12. Mao Tse-tung: On New Democracy (January, 1940)*

"On New Democracy," published in January, 1940, was a persuasive propaganda document, justifying the united front as a temporary measure and reaffirming the Party's long-term mission. The Chinese Revolution, Mao reaffirmed, would be divided into two stages—the democratic and the socialist. The two stages, though different in nature, could be blended into a continuous process, as conducted by a coalition of all revolutionary classes.

There was nothing essentially new in this concept. But Mao's technique was aimed at seizing political power by collaborating with all who were willing to work along with the Communists. To this end, he worked out a concrete program for political, economic and cultural development under a New Democratic regime, as a cloak for his conquest of power in China. In political form, the New Democracy envisages a system of government known as "democratic centralism"—a system of government in which all

* From *Selected Works of Mao Tse-tung*, Peking: Foreign Language Press, 1965, II, 339–382. (Extract; footnotes omitted.)

power is centralized, but it is "democratic," Mao claimed, because it is jointly ruled by the various "revolutionary classes." In economic terms, Mao conceived of the New Democracy as involving a moderate program of land reform and nationalization of key industry. And the cultural program defined the New Democratic culture as a national, scientific and mass culture, to oppose imperialist oppression and uphold the dignity and independence of the Chinese nation. All this was designed to make Communist leadership acceptable and to prepare the way for isolating the Kuomintang.

The major significance of this work lies in two points: (1) not merely providing the united front strategy with a theoretical framework, but also preparing the Party for the possible disintegration of the alliance in the future; (2) not only pointing out the "bourgeois-democratic" nature of the Chinese Revolution at its present stage, but also to reemphasizing the fact that the Party had its own ultimate aims and its own separate destiny.

WHITHER CHINA?

A lively atmosphere has prevailed throughout the country ever since the War of Resistance began, there is a general feeling that a way out of the impasse has been found, and people no longer knit their brows in despair. Of late, however, the dust and din of compromise and anti-communism have once again filled the air, and once again the people are thrown into bewilderment. Most susceptible, and the first to be affected, are the intellectuals and the young students. The question once again arises: What is to be done? Whither China? On the occasion of the publication of *Chinese Culture,* it may therefore be profitable to clarify the political and cultural trends in the country. I am a layman in matters of culture; I would like to study them, but have only just begun to do so. Fortunately, there are many comrades in Yenan who have written at length in this field, so that my rough and ready words may serve the same purpose as the beating of the gongs before a theatrical performance. Our observations may contain a grain of truth for the nation's advanced cultural workers and may serve as a modest spur to induce them to come forward with valuable contributions of their own, and we hope that they will join in the discussion to reach correct conclusions which will meet our national needs. To "seek truth from facts" is the scientific approach, and presumptuously to claim infallibility and lecture people will never settle anything. The troubles that have befallen our nation are extremely serious, and only a scientific approach and a spirit of responsibility can lead it on to the road of liberation. There is but one truth, and the question of whether or not one has arrived at it depends not on subjective boasting but on objective practice. The only yardstick of truth is the revolutionary practice of millions of people. This, I think, can be regarded as the attitude of *Chinese Culture*.

WE WANT TO BUILD A NEW CHINA

For many years we Communists have struggled for a cultural revolution as well as for a political and economic revolution, and our aim is to build a new society and a new state for the Chinese nation. That new society and new state will have not only a new politics and a new economy but a new culture. In other words, not only do we want to change a China that is politically oppressed and economically exploited into a China that is politically free and economically prosperous, we also want to change the China which is being kept ignorant and backward under the sway of the old culture into an enlightened and progressive China under the sway of a new culture. In short, we want to build a new China. Our aim in the cultural sphere is to build a new Chinese national culture.

CHINA'S HISTORICAL CHARACTERISTICS

What are China's old politics and economics? And what is her old culture?

From the Chou and Chin Dynasties onwards, Chinese society was feudal, as were its politics and its economy. And the dominant culture, reflecting the politics and economy, was feudal culture.

Since the invasion of foreign capitalism and the gradual growth of capitalist elements in Chinese society, the country has changed by degrees into a colonial, semi-colonial and semi-feudal society. China today is colonial in the Japanese-occupied areas and basically semi-colonial in the Kuomintang areas, and it is predominantly feudal or semi-feudal in both. Such, then, is the character of present-day Chinese society and the state of affairs in our country. The politics and the economy of this society are predominantly colonial, semi-colonial and semi-feudal, and the predominant culture, reflecting the politics and economy, is also colonial, semi-colonial and semi-feudal.

It is precisely against these predominant political, economic and cultural forms that our revolution is directed. What we want to get rid of is the old colonial, semi-colonial and semi-feudal politics and economy and the old culture in their service. And what we want to build up is their direct opposite, *i.e.*, the new politics, the new economy and the new culture of the Chinese nation.

What, then, are the new politics and the new economy of the Chinese nation, and what is its new culture?

In the course of its history the Chinese revolution must go through two stages, first, the democratic revolution, and second, the socialist revolution, and by their very nature they are two different revolutionary processes. Here democracy does not belong to the old category—it is not the old democracy, but belongs to the new category—it is New Democracy.

It can thus be affirmed that China's new politics are the politics of New Democracy, that China's new economy is the economy of New Democracy and that China's new culture is the culture of New Democracy.

Such are the historical characteristics of the Chinese revolution at the present time. Any political party, group or person taking part in the Chinese revolution that fails to understand this will not be able to direct the revolution and lead it to victory, but will be cast aside by the people and left to grieve out in the cold.

THE CHINESE REVOLUTION IS PART OF THE WORLD REVOLUTION

The historical characteristic of the Chinese revolution lies in its division into the two stages, democracy and socialism, the first being no longer democracy in general, but democracy of the Chinese type, a new and special type, namely, New Democracy. How, then, has this historical characteristic come into being? Has it been in existence for the past hundred years, or is it of recent origin?

A brief study of the historical development of China and of the world shows that this characteristic did not emerge immediately after the Opium War, but took shape later, after the first imperialist world war and the October Revolution in Russia. Let us now examine the process of its formation.

Clearly, it follows from the colonial, semi-colonial and semi-feudal character of present-day Chinese society that the Chinese revolution must be divided into two stages. The first step is to change the colonial, semi-colonial and semi-feudal form of society into an independent, democratic society. The second is to carry the revolution forward and build a socialist society. At present the Chinese revolution is taking the first step.

The preparatory period for the first step began with the Opium War in 1840, *i.e.*, when China's feudal society started changing into a semi-colonial and semi-feudal one. Then came the Movement of the Taiping Heavenly Kingdom, the Sino-French War, the Sino-Japanese War, the Reform Movement of 1898, the Revolution of 1911, the May 4th Movement, the Northern Expedition, the War of the Agrarian Revolution and the present War of Resistance Against Japan. Together these have taken up a whole century and in a sense they represent that first step, being struggles waged by the Chinese people, on different occasions and in varying degrees, against imperialism and the feudal forces in order to build up an independent, democratic society and complete the first revolution. The Revolution of 1911 was in a fuller sense the beginning of that revolution. In its social character, this revolution is a bourgeois-democratic and not a proletarian-socialist revolution. It is still unfinished and still demands great efforts, because to this day its enemies are still very strong. When Dr. Sun Yat-sen said, "The revolution is not yet completed, all my comrades must struggle on", he was referring to the bourgeois-democratic revolution.

A change, however, occurred in China's bourgeois-democratic revolution after the outbreak of the first imperialist world war in 1914 and the founding of a socialist state on one-sixth of the globe as a result of the Russian October Revolution of 1917.

Before these events, the Chinese bourgeois-democratic revolution came within the old category of the bourgeois-democratic world revolution, of which it was a part.

Since these events, the Chinese bourgeois-democratic revolution has changed, it has come within the new category of bourgeois-democratic revolutions and, as far as the alignment of revolutionary forces is concerned, forms part of the proletarian-socialist world revolution.

Why? Because the first imperialist world war and the first victorious socialist revolution, the October Revolution, have changed the whole course of world history and ushered in a new era.

It is an era in which the world capitalist front has collapsed in one part of the globe (one-sixth of the world) and has fully revealed its decadence everywhere else, in which the remaining capitalist parts cannot survive without relying more than ever on the colonies and semi-colonies, in which a socialist state has been established and has proclaimed its readiness to give active support to the liberation movement of all colonies and semi-colonies, and in which the proletariat of the capitalist countries is steadily freeing itself from the social-imperialist influence of the social-democratic parties and has proclaimed its support for the liberation movement in the colonies and semi-colonies. In this era, any revolution in a colony or semi-colony that is directed against imperialism, *i.e.*, against the international bourgeoisie or international capitalism, no longer comes within the old category of the bourgeois-democratic world revolution, but within the new category. It is no longer part of the old bourgeois, or capitalist, world revolution, but is part of the new world revolution, the proletarian-socialist world revolution. Such revolutionary colonies and semi-colonies can no longer be regarded as allies of the counter-revolutionary front of world capitalism; they have become allies of the revolutionary front of world socialism.

Although such a revolution in a colonial and semi-colonial country is still fundamentally bourgeois-democratic in its social character during its first stage or first step, and although its objective mission is to clear the path for the development of capitalism, it is no longer a revolution of the old type led by the bourgeoisie with the aim of establishing a capitalist society and a state under bourgeois dictatorship. It belongs to the new type of revolution led by the proletariat with the aim, in the first stage, of establishing a new-democratic society and a state under the joint dictatorship of all the revolutionary classes. Thus this revolution actually serves the purpose of clearing a still wider path for the development of socialism. In the course of its progress, there may be a number of further sub-stages, because of changes on the enemy's side and within the ranks of our allies, but the fundamental character of the revolution remains unchanged.

Such a revolution attacks imperialism at its very roots, and is therefore not tolerated but opposed by imperialism. However, it is favoured by socialism and supported by the land of socialism and the socialist international proletariat.

Therefore, such a revolution inevitably becomes part of the proletarian-socialist world revolution.

The correct thesis that "the Chinese revolution is part of the world revolution" was put forward as early as 1924–27 during the period of China's First Great Revolution. It was put forward by the Chinese Communists and endorsed by all those taking part in the anti-imperialist and anti-feudal struggle of the time. However, the significance of this thesis was not fully expounded in those days, and consequently it was only vaguely understood.

The "world revolution" no longer refers to the old world revolution, for the old bourgeois world revolution has long been a thing of the past; it refers to the new world revolution, the socialist world revolution. Similarly, to form "part of" means to form part not of the old bourgeois but of the new socialist revolution. This is a tremendous change unparalleled in the history of China and of the world.

This correct thesis advanced by the Chinese Communists is based on Stalin's theory.

As early as 1918, in an article commemorating the first anniversary of the October Revolution, Stalin wrote:

> The great world-wide significance of the October Revolution chiefly consists in the fact that:
>   1) It has widened the scope of the national question and converted it from the particular question of combating national oppression in Europe into the general question of emancipating the oppressed peoples, colonies and semi-colonies from imperialism;
>   2) It has opened up wide possibilities for their emancipation and the right paths towards it, has thereby greatly facilitated the cause of the emancipation of the oppressed peoples of the West and the

East, and has drawn them into the common current of the victorious struggle against imperialism;

3) *It has thereby erected a bridge between the socialist West and the enslaved East*, having created a new front of revolutions *against* world imperialism, extending from the proletarians of the West, through the Russian Revolution, to the oppressed peoples of the East.

Since writing this article, Stalin has again and again expounded the theory that revolutions in the colonies and semi-colonies have broken away from the old category and become part of the proletarian-socialist revolution.

From this it can be seen that there are two kinds of world revolution, the first belonging to the bourgeois or capitalist category. The era of this kind of world revolution is long past, having come to an end as far back as 1914 when the first imperialist world war broke out, and more particularly in 1917 when the October Revolution took place. The second kind, namely, the proletarian-socialist world revolution, thereupon began. This revolution has the proletariat of the capitalist countries as its main force and the oppressed peoples of the colonies and semi-colonies as its allies. No matter what classes, parties or individuals in an oppressed nation join the revolution, and no matter whether they themselves are conscious of the point or understand it, as long as they oppose imperialism, their revolution becomes part of the proletarian-socialist world revolution and they become its allies.

Today, the Chinese revolution has taken on still greater significance. This is a time when the economic and political crises of capitalism are dragging the world more and more deeply into the Second World War, when the Soviet Union has reached the period of transition from socialism to communism and is capable of leading and helping the proletariat and oppressed nations of the whole world in their fight against imperialist war and capitalist reaction, when the proletariat of the capitalist countries is preparing to overthrow capitalism and establish socialism, and when the proletariat, the peasantry, the intelligentsia and other sections of the petty bourgeoisie in China have become a mighty independent political force under the leadership of the Chinese Communist Party. Situated as we are in this day and age, should we not make the appraisal that the Chinese revolution has taken on still greater world significance? I think we should. The Chinese revolution has become a very important part of the world revolution.

THE POLITICS OF NEW DEMOCRACY

In China, it is perfectly clear that whoever can lead the people in overthrowing imperialism and the forces of feudalism can win the people's confidence, because these two, and especially imperialism, are the mortal enemies of the people. Today, whoever can lead the people in driving out Japanese imperialism and introducing democratic government will be the saviours of the people. History has proved that the Chinese bourgeoisie cannot fulfil this responsibility, which inevitably falls upon the shoulders of the proletariat.

Therefore, the proletariat, the peasantry, the intelligentsia and the other sections of the petty bourgeoisie undoubtedly constitute the basic forces determining China's fate. These classes, some already awakened and others in the process of awakening, will necessarily become the basic components of the state and governmental structure in the democratic republic of China, with the proletariat as the leading force. The Chinese democratic republic which we desire to establish now must be a democratic republic under the joint dictatorship of all anti-imperialist and anti-feudal people led by the proletariat, that is, a new-democratic republic, a republic of the genuinely revolutionary new Three People's Principles with their Three Great Policies.

This new-democratic republic will be different from the old European-American form of capitalist republic under bourgeois dictatorship, which is the old democratic form and already out of date. On the other hand, it will also be different from the socialist republic of the Soviet type under the dictatorship of the proletariat which is already flourishing in the U.S.S.R., and which, moreover, will be established in all the capitalist countries and will undoubtedly become the dominant form of state and governmental structure in all the industrially advanced countries. However, for a certain historical period, this form is not suitable for the revolutions in the colonial and semi-colonial countries. During this period, therefore, a third form of state must be adopted in the revolutions of all colonial and semi-colonial countries, namely, the new-democratic republic. This form suits a certain historical period and is therefore transitional; nevertheless, it is a form which is necessary and cannot be dispensed with.

Thus the numerous types of state system in the world can be reduced to three basic kinds according to the class character of their political power: (1) republics under bourgeois dictatorship; (2) republics under the dictatorship of the proletariat; and (3) republics under the joint dictatorship of several revolutionary classes.

The first kind comprises the old democratic states. Today, after the outbreak of the second imperialist war, there is hardly a trace of democracy in many of the capitalist countries, which have come or are coming under the bloody militarist dictatorship of the bourgeoisie. Certain countries under the joint dictatorship of the landlords and the bourgeoisie can be grouped with this kind.

The second kind exists in the Soviet Union, and the conditions for its birth are ripening in capitalist countries. In the future, it will be the dominant form throughout the world for a certain period.

The third kind is the transitional form of state to be adopted in the revolutions of the colonial and semi-colonial countries. Each of these revolutions will necessarily have specific characteristics of its own, but these will be minor variations on a general theme. So long as they are revolutions in colonial or semi-colonial countries, their state and governmental structure will of necessity be basically the same, *i.e.,* a new-democratic state under the joint dictatorship of several anti-imperialist classes. In present-day China, the anti-Japanese united front represents the new-democratic form of state. It is anti-Japanese and anti-imperialist; it is also a united front, an alliance of several revolutionary classes. But unfortunately, despite the fact that the war has been going on for so long, the work of introducing democracy has hardly started in most of the country outside the democratic anti-Japanese base areas under the leadership of the Communist Party, and the Japanese imperialists have exploited this fundamental weakness to stride into our country. If nothing is done about it, our national future will be gravely imperilled.

As for the question of "the system of government", this is a matter of how political power is organized, the form in which one social class or another chooses to arrange its apparatus of political power to oppose its enemies and protect itself. There is no state which does not have an appropriate apparatus of political power to represent it. China may now adopt a system of people's congresses, from the national people's congress down to the provincial, county, district and township people's congresses, with all levels electing their respective governmental bodies. But if there is to be a proper representation for each revolutionary class according to its status in the state, a proper expession of the people's will, a proper direction for revolutionary struggles and a proper manifestation of the spirit of New Democracy, then a system of really universal and equal suffrage, irrespective of sex, creed, property or education, must be introduced. Such is the system of democratic centralism. Only a government based on democratic centralism can fully express the will of all the revolutionary people and fight the enemies of the revolution most effectively. There must be a spirit of refusal to be "privately owned by the few" in the government and the army; without a genuinely democratic system this cannot be attained and the system of government and the state system will be out of harmony.

The state system, a joint dictatorship of all the revolutionary classes and the system of government, democratic centralism—these constitute the politics of New Democracy, the republic of New Democracy, the republic of the anti-Japanese united front, the republic of the new Three People's Principles with their Three Great Policies, the Republic of China in reality as well as in name. Today we have a Republic of China in name but not in reality, and our present task is to create the reality that will fit the name.

Such are the internal political relations which a revolutionary China, a China fighting Japanese aggression, should and must establish without fail; such is the orientation, the only correct orientation, for our present work of national reconstruction.

THE ECONOMY OF NEW DEMOCRACY

If such a republic is to be established in China, it must be new-democratic not only in its politics but also in its economy.

It will own the big banks and the big industrial and commercial enterprises.

> Enterprises, such as banks, railways and airlines, whether Chinese-owned or foreign-owned, which are either monopolistic in character or too big for private management, shall be operated and administered by the state, so that private capital cannot dominate the livelihood of the people: this is the main principle of the regulation of capital.

This is another solemn declaration in the Manifesto of the Kuomintang's First National Congress held during the period of Kuomintang-Communist co-operation, and it is the correct policy for the economic structure of the new-democratic republic. In the new-democratic republic under the leadership of the proletariat, the state enterprises will be of a socialist character and will constitute the leading force in the whole national economy, but the republic will neither confiscate capitalist private property in general nor forbid the development of such capitalist production as does not "dominate the livelihood of the people", for China's economy is still very backward.

The republic will take certain necessary steps to confiscate the land of the landlords and distribute it to those peasants having little or no land, carry out Dr. Sun Yat-sen's slogan of "land to the tiller," abolish feudal relations in the rural areas, and turn the land over to the private ownership of the peasants. A rich peasant economy will be allowed in the rural areas. Such is the policy of "equalization of landownership". "Land to the tiller" is the correct slogan for this policy. In general, socialist agriculture will not be established at this stage, though various types of co-operative enterprises developed on the basis of "land to the tiller" will contain elements of socialism.

China's economy must develop along the path of the "regulation of capital" and the "equalization of landownership", and must never be "privately owned by the few"; we must never permit the few capitalists and landlords to "dominate the livelihood of the people"; we must never establish a capitalist society of the European-American type or allow the old semi-feudal society to survive. Whoever dares to go counter to this line of advance will certainly not succeed but will run into a brick wall.

Such are the internal economic relations which a revolutionary China, a China fighting Japanese aggression, must and necessarily will establish.

Such is the economy of New Democracy.

And the politics of New Democracy are the concentrated expression of the economy of New Democracy.

THE CULTURE OF NEW DEMOCRACY

In the foregoing we have explained the historical characteristics of Chinese politics in the new period and the question of the new-democratic republic. We can now proceed to the question of culture.

A given culture is the ideological reflection of the politics and economics of a given society. There is in China an imperialist culture which is a reflection of imperialist rule, or partial rule, in the political and economic fields. This culture is fostered not only by the cultural organizations run directly by the imperialists in China but by a number of Chinese who have lost all sense of shame. Into this category falls all culture embodying a slave ideology. China also has a semifeudal culture which reflects her semi-feudal politics and economy, and whose exponents include all those who advocate the worship of Confucius, the study of the Confucian canon, the old ethical code and the old ideas in opposition to the new culture and new ideas. Imperialist culture and semi-feudal culture are devoted brothers and have formed a reactionary cultural alliance against China's new culture. This kind of reactionary culture serves the imperialists and the feudal class and must be swept away. Unless it is swept away, no new culture of any kind can be built up. There is no construction without destruction, no flowing without damning and no motion without rest; the two are locked in a life-and-death struggle.

THE HISTORICAL CHARACTERISTICS OF CHINA'S CULTURAL REVOLUTION

On the cultural or ideological front, the two periods preceding and following the May 4th Movement form two distinct historical periods.

Before the May 4th Movement, the struggle on China's cultural front was one between the new culture of the bourgeoisie and the old culture of the feudal class. The struggles between the modern school system and the imperial examination system, between the new learning and the old learning, and between Western learning and Chinese learning, were all of this nature. The so-called modern schools or new learning or Western learning of that time concentrated mainly (we say mainly, because in part pernicious vestiges of Chinese feudalism still remained) on the natural sciences and bourgeois social and political theories, which were needed by the representatives of the bourgeoisie. At the time, the ideology of the new learning played a revolutionary role in fighting the Chinese feudal ideology, and it served the bourgeois-democratic revolution of the old period. However, because the Chinese bourgeoisie lacked strength and the world had already entered the era of imperialism, this bourgeois ideology was only able to last out a few rounds and was beaten back by the reactionary alliance of the enslaving ideology of foreign imperialism and the "back to the ancients" ideology of Chinese feudalism; as soon as this reactionary ideological alliance started a minor counter-offensive, the so-called new learning lowered its banners, muffled its drums and beat a retreat, retaining its outer form but losing its soul. The old bourgeois-democratic culture became enervated and decayed in the era of imperialism, and its failure was inevitable.

But since the May 4th Movement things have been different. A brand-new cultural force came into being in China, that is, the communist culture and ideology guided by the Chinese Communists, or the communist world outlook and theory of social revolution. The May 4th Movement occurred in 1919, and in 1921 came the founding of the Chinese Communist Party and the real beginning of China's labour movement—all in the wake of the First World War and the October Revolution, *i.e.,* at a time when the national problem and the colonial revolutionary movements of the world underwent a change, and the connection between the Chinese revolution and the world revolution became quite obvious. The new political force of the proletariat and the Communist Party entered the Chinese political arena, and as a result, the new cultural force, in new uniform and with new weapons, mustering all possible allies and deploying its ranks in battle array, launched heroic attacks on imperialist culture and feudal culture. This new force has made great strides in the domain of the social sciences and of the arts and letters, whether of philosophy, economics, political science, military science, history, literature or art (including the theatre, the cinema, music, sculpture and painting). For the last twenty years, wherever this new cultural force has directed its attack, a great revolution has taken place both in ideological content and in form (for example, in the written language). Its influence has been so great and its impact so powerful that it is invincible wherever it goes. The numbers it has rallied behind it have no parallel in Chinese history. Lu Hsun was the greatest and the most courageous standard-bearer of this new cultural force. The chief commander of China's cultural revolution, he was not only a great man of letters but a great thinker and revolutionary. Lu Hsun was a man of unyielding integrity, free from all sycophancy or obsequiousness; this quality is invaluable among colonial and semi-colonial peoples. Representing the great majority of the nation, Lu Hsun breached and stormed the enemy citadel; on the cultural front he was the bravest and most correct, the firmest, the most loyal and the most ardent national hero, a hero without parallel in our history. The road he took was the very road of China's new national culture.

Prior to the May 4th Movement, China's new culture was a culture of the old-democratic kind and part of the capitalist cultural revolution of the world bourgeoisie. Since the May 4th Movement, it has become new-democratic and part of the socialist cultural revolution of the world proletariat.

Prior to the May 4th Movement, China's new cultural movement, her cultural revolution, was led by the bourgeoisie, which still had a leading role to play. After the May 4th Movement, its culture and ideology became even more backward than its politics and were incapable of playing any leading role; at most, they could serve to a certain extent as an ally during revolutionary periods, while inevitably the responsibility for leading the alliance rested on proletarian culture and ideology. This is an undeniable fact.

The new-democratic culture is the anti-imperialist and anti-feudal culture of the broad masses; today it is the culture of the anti-Japanese united front. This culture can be led only by the culture and ideology of the proletariat, by the ideology of communism, and not by the culture and ideology of any other class. In a word, new-democratic culture is the proletarian-led, anti-imperialist and anti-feudal culture of the broad masses.

SOME WRONG IDEAS ABOUT
THE NATURE OF CULTURE

Everything new comes from the forge of hard and bitter struggle. This is also true of the new culture which has followed a zigzag course in the past twenty years, during which both the good and the bad were tested and proved in struggle.

The bourgeois die-hards are as hopelessly wrong on the question of culture as on that of political power. They neither understand the historical characteristics of this new period in China, nor recognize the new-democratic culture of the masses. Their starting point is bourgeois despotism, which in culture becomes the cultural despotism of the bourgeoisie. It seems that a section (and I refer only to a section) of educated people from the so-called European-American school who in fact supported the Kuomintang government's "Communist suppression" campaign on the cultural front in the past are now supporting its policy of "restricting" and "corroding" the Communist Party. They do not want the workers and the peasants to hold up their heads politically or culturally. This bourgeois die-hard road of cultural despotism leads nowhere; as in the case of political despotism, the domestic and international pre-conditions are lacking. Therefore this cultural despotism, too, had better be "folded up".

So far as the orientation of our national culture is concerned, communist ideology plays the guiding role, and we should work hard both to disseminate socialism and communism throughout the working class and to educate the peasantry and other sections of the people in socialism properly and step by step. However, our national culture as a whole is not yet socialist.

Because of the leadership of the proletariat, the politics, the economy and the culture of New Democracy all contain an element of socialism, and by no means a mere casual element but one with a decisive role. However, taken as a whole, the political, economic and cultural situation so far is new-democratic and not socialist. For the Chinese revolution in its present stage is not yet a socialist revolution for the overthrow of capitalism but a bourgeois-democratic revolution, its central task being mainly that of combating foreign imperialism and domestic feudalism. In the sphere of national culture, it is wrong to assume that the existing national culture is, or should be, socialist in its entirety. That would amount to confusing the dissemination of communist ideology with the carrying out of an immediate programme of action, and to confusing the application of the communist standpoint and method in investigating problems, undertaking research, handling work and training cadres with the general policy for national education and national culture in the democratic stage of the Chinese revolution. A national culture with a socialist content will necessarily be the reflection of a socialist politics and a socialist economy. There are socialist elements in our politics and our economy, and hence these socialist elements are reflected in our national culture; but taking our society as a whole, we do not have a socialist politics and a socialist economy yet, so that there cannot be a wholly socialist national culture. Since the present Chinese revolution is part of the world proletarian-socialist revolution, the new culture of China today is part of the world proletarian-socialist new culture and is its great ally. While this part contains vital elements of socialist culture, the national culture as a whole joins the stream of the world proletarian-socialist new culture not entirely as a socialist culture, but as the anti-imperialist and anti-feudal new-democratic culture of the broad masses. And since the Chinese revolution today cannot do without proletarian leadership, China's new culture cannot do without the leadership of proletarian culture and ideology, of communist ideology. At the present stage, however, this kind of leadership means leading the masses of the people in an anti-imperialist and anti-feudal political and cultural revolution, and therefore, taken as a whole, the content of China's new national culture is still not socialist but new-democratic.

A NATIONAL, SCIENTIFIC AND MASS CULTURE

New-democratic culture is national. It opposes imperialist oppression and upholds the dignity and independence of the Chinese nation. It belongs to our own nation and bears our own national characteristics. It links up with the socialist and new-democratic cultures of all other nations and they are related in such a way that they can absorb something from each other and help each other to develop, together forming a new world culture; but as a revolutionary national culture it can never link up with any reactionary imperialist culture of whatever nation. To nourish her own culture China needs to assimilate a good deal of foreign progressive culture, not enough of which was done in the past. We should assimilate whatever is useful to us today not only from the present-day socialist and new-democratic cultures but also from the earlier cultures of other nations, for example, from the culture of the various capitalist countries in the Age of Enlightenment. However, we should not gulp any of this foreign material down uncritically, but must treat it as we do our food—first chewing it, then submitting it to the working of the stomach and intestines with their juices and secretions, and separating it into nutriment to be absorbed and waste matter to be discarded—before it can nourish us. To advocate "wholesale westernization" is wrong. China has suffered a great deal from the mechanical absorption of foreign material. Similarly, in applying Marxism to China, Chinese communists must fully and properly integrate the universal truth of Marxism with the concrete practice of the Chinese revolution, or in other words, the universal truth of Marxism must be combined with specific national characteristics and acquire a definite national form if it is to be useful, and in no circumstances can it be applied subjectively as a mere formula. Marxists who make a fetish of formulas are simply playing the fool with Marxism and the Chinese revolution, and there is no room for them in the ranks of the Chinese revolution. Chinese culture should have its own form, its own national form. National in form and new-democratic in content—such is our new culture today.

New-democratic culture is scientific. Opposed as it is to all feudal and superstitious ideas, it stands for seeking truth from facts, for objective truth and for the unity of theory and practice. On this point, the possibility exists of a united front against imperialism, feudalism and superstition between the scientific thought of the Chinese proletariat and those Chinese bourgeois materialists and natural scientists who are progressive, but in no case is there a possibility of a united front with any reactionary idealism. In the field of political action Communists may form an anti-imperialist and anti-feudal united front with some idealists and even religious people, but we can never approve of their idealism or religious doctrines. A splendid old culture was created during the long period of Chinese feudal society. To study the development of this old culture, to reject its feudal dross and assimilate its democratic essence is a necessary condition for developing our new national culture and increasing our national self-confidence, but we should never swallow anything and everything uncritically. It is imperative to separate the fine old culture of the people which had a more or less democratic and revolutionary character from all the decadence of the old feudal ruling class. China's present new politics and new economy have developed out of her old politics and old economy, and her present new culture, too, has developed out of her old culture; therefore, we must respect our own history and must not lop it off. However, respect for history means giving it its proper place as a science, respecting its dialectical development, and not eulogizing the past at the expense of the present or praising every drop of feudal poison. As far as the masses and the young students are concerned, the essential thing is to guide them to look forward and not backward.

New-democratic culture belongs to the broad masses and is therefore democratic. It should serve the toiling masses of workers and peasants who make up more than 90 per cent of the nation's population and should gradually become their very own. There is a difference of degree, as well as a close link, between the knowledge imparted to the revolutionary cadres and the knowledge imparted to the revolutionary masses, between the raising of cultural standards and popularization. Revolutionary culture is a powerful revolutionary weapon for the broad masses of the people. It prepares the ground ideologically before the revolution comes and is an important, indeed essential, fighting front in the general revolutionary front during the revolution. People engaged in revolutionary cultural work are the commanders at various levels on this cultural front. "Without revolutionary theory there can be no revolutionary movement"; one can thus see how important the cultural movement is for the practical revolutionary movement. Both the cultural and practical movements must be of the masses. Therefore all progressive cultural workers in the anti-Japanese war must have their own cultural battalions, that is, the broad masses. A revolutionary cultural worker who is not close to the people is a commander without an army, whose fire-power cannot bring the enemy down. To attain this objective, written Chinese must be reformed, given the requisite conditions, and our spoken language brought closer to that of the people, for the people, it must be stressed, are the inexhaustible source of our revolutionary culture.

A national, scientific and mass culture—such is the anti-imperialist and anti-feudal culture of the people, the culture of New Democracy, the new culture of the Chinese nation.

Combine the politics, the economy and the culture of New Democracy, and you have the new-democratic republic, the Republic of China both in name and in reality, the new China we want to create.

Behold, New China is within sight. Let us all hail her!

Her masts have already risen above the horizon. Let us all cheer in welcome!

Raise both your hands. New China is ours!

13. *Liu Shao-chi: On the Intra-Party Struggle (July, 1941)**

This essay, delivered as a series of lectures to a Party school in July, 1941, is a companion piece to "How to Be a Good Communist" in the series of documents issued by the Party in the early 1940's under the name of *Cheng-Feng Documents*. The *cheng-feng* movement concerned itself with learning, the Party, and art and literature. It was launched with the purpose of tightening Party discipline and strengthening Party organization, in order to prevent or correct deviations from proper ideological practice. Where earlier work stressed the individual Party member and his self-discipline, emphasis here is placed on the proper relationships among Party members and their proper attitudes and views within the Party. The whole essay is designed to distinguish the intra-Party struggle, which is necessary to maintain the Party's purity and independence, from the open or outward Party struggle, which aims at the attainment of factional supremacy over others. This intra-Party struggle, according to Liu, is "a method of strengthening Party uni-

---

* From Boyd Compton, *Mao's China: Party Reform Documents, 1942–1944*, Seattle and London: University of Washington Press (Washington Paperbacks), 1966, pp. 188–238. (Extract.)

formity," not "of encouraging independent views." This is to reassert the Leninist nature of the Party.

However, Liu insisted that intra-Party struggle is primarily ideological and should be conducted in a spirit of solidarity and organizational discipline, but the emphasis should be placed on self-confession (self-criticism) and comradeship rather than on accusation and individual grievances.

The dynamism of Chinese Communism, especially in this early period, owes much to its concept of struggle both inside and outside the Party. Two important functions of ceaseless internal struggle may be singled out. First, it has strengthened Party spirit by keeping Party members on the alert, sensitive to Party interests and needs. And secondly, it has built up a disciplined Party organization by thwarting undesirable tendencies in the Party. Cadres selected during this period staffed the Party and the military apparatus throughout the final stages of the war with Japan and then during the post–1945 campaigns against the Kuomintang. And it was these cadres who took the major posts when in 1949 the Communists took control of China.

Ironically, twenty-five years after Liu Shao-chi wrote this major work for the Party, he became a victim of his own ideology in the Chinese Cultural Revolution of 1967.

I. INTRODUCTION

Comrades! Recently we have raised the problem of strengthening the Party spirit among Party members. I have heard that before long we shall be able to obtain the resolution passed by the Central Committee on "Strengthening the Party Spirit." In order to strengthen the Party spirit among Party members, we must develop a series of concrete struggles in thought so that all types of improper tendencies transgressing that spirit will be opposed. But what is to be considered the correct method for developing the struggles in thought within the Party and what is to be considered the incorrect method? This is the question I would now like to discuss.

Everyone knows that our Party is a Party of the proletariat, that it leads the broad masses to battle. In order to carry out the historical task which it has taken upon itself, the Party must struggle against all who are revolutionary enemies in a given period and unite with the various revolutionary groups and classes. Since its origin, the Party has not experienced a minute free from serious conflict. The Party and the proletariat have been constantly encircled by the power of the nonproletarian classes: the big and petty bourgeoisie, the farmers, and even the remnants of feudal forces. These classes are either struggling against the proletariat or in alliance with it. Unstable elements, having passed into the Party and proletariat and penetrated to their heart, have constantly influenced them in ideology, living habits, theory, and action. This, then, is the source of all undesirable mistaken tendencies within the Party. It is the social origin of all opportunism within the Party and also the source of the intra-Party struggle.

The intra-Party struggle is a reflection of the struggle outside the Party.

Since the day of its origin the Party has not only fought enemies outside the Party, but has also fought the nonproletarian influences of enemies within the Party. The two struggles are to be distinguished, but both are necessary and, in class substance, they are one and the same. If the Party does not engage in the second struggle, if it does not constantly struggle to oppose all undesirable tendencies within the Party, does not constantly reject all nonproletarian ideologies and overcome "left" and right opportunism, then nonproletarian ideologies and "left" and right opportunism will be able to develop in the Party and influence and guide the Party. They will make it impossible for the Party to develop stability and maintain its independent existence. They will endanger the Party and make it fall into decay. Nonproletarian ideologies and "left" and right opportunism can cause our Party or certain parts of the Party to rot away, can cause a transformation in their very nature and give them a nonproletarian organization. For example, it was in this manner that the European Social Democratic parties were rotted away by bourgeois ideology, were transformed into parties of the bourgeoisie and important pillars for them in society. Thus the intra-Party struggle is entirely necessary and unavoidable. It is therefore completely incorrect to attempt to avoid the intra-Party struggle or to refuse to criticize others' mistakes in order to escape their criticism.

The most important aspect of the intra-Party struggle is the struggle in thought, which consists of divergencies and mutual opposition in ideological principles. Even though divergencies and mutual opposition can lead to political divergencies and even, under certain conditions, unavoidably lead to divergencies on Party organization, the thought struggle remains its basic substance and content. Therefore, if a struggle within the Party does not reveal diverging ideological principles, if there is not divergence in principle or mutual contention among comrades, the struggle is then without principle and without content. Within the Party, this type of struggle—without principle and without content—is entirely unnecessary. It harms the Party and should be completely avoided by Party members.

The object of the intra-Party struggle is to maintain the Party's purity and independence, to guarantee that Party activities represent the highest interests of the proletariat, and to maintain the Party's indispensable proletarian substance. With this aim, the intra-Party struggle must proceed in two directions and advance on two fronts. This is because enemy thought influences the Party from two directions, because it attacks the Party from the right and from the "left," and because it is manifested in the Party as right and "left" opportunism. In the intra-Party struggle, we must therefore oppose right opportunism and at the same time oppose "left" opportunism. We must struggle against both, and then only will we be able to maintain the proletarian substance of our Party. If we do not do this, if we merely struggle on one front, and if we are careless and fail to remain vigilant and ready to fight at any one point, the enemy will be able to attack and will certainly attack us at that point which we have neglected; in that case we would not be able to maintain the Party's purity and independence, nor would we be able to stabilize the Party. Thus the Party stabilizes and develops in a continuous inner struggle on two fronts.

II. Special Conditions of the Chinese Communist Party and Tendencies in the Intra-Party Struggle

But if we speak of the concrete conditions under which the Chinese Communist Party was established, we must realize that they were completely different from those encountered by Lenin before the October Revolution.

First. The Chinese Party was established after the October Revolution and after the Russian Bolshevik Party had already achieved victory and a living form. Therefore, from the beginning, it was under the guidance of the Communist International and was established according to the principles of Lenin.

Second. From the beginning, in thought and organization, the Chinese Communist Party has not been influenced by the Second International of the European Social Democratic parties.

Third. China has not gone through the period of the "peaceful" development of capitalism, such as was experienced in Europe, which allowed the working classes to engage in a peaceful parliamentary struggle, nor does China have Europe's distinction between worker and aristocrat.

Fourth. A comparatively large segment of the membership of the Chinese Communist Party comes from the petty bourgeoisie, and there are in addition certain elements from the "roaming population." This is the social foundation for "left" opportunism in the Party.

Under the four above conditions, our Party's development has automatically been, from the beginning, according to the path and principles of Lenin. A great many Party members can recite the organizational principles of the Bolshevik Party from memory. The traditions and usages of the Social Democratic parties are not to be found in ours. As a consequence, we have traveled a straight path. From the time of its organization, our Party has exhibited self-criticism and a struggle in thought, has had a system of democratic-centralism, strict organization and discipline, has not allowed the existence of factions, and has rigorously opposed liberalism, syndicalism, and the tendencies of the Economists, etc. Because of this, a systematic theory of right opportunism in organization has not yet been advocated openly in the Party. It is generally recognized that opposition either to self-criticism, the intra-Party struggle, strict organization and discipline, a workers' political party or trade union independence has not been able to develop openly within the Party. If the thought struggle in the Party is in certain respects deficient, it is because the low theoretical level hides divergencies in principle, or because individuals in the Party utilize unusual means to suppress the results of self-criticism; it is not because of any systematic theory in the Party in opposition to the thought struggle.

However, the special conditions and circumstances of the period in which the Chinese Communist Party was established gave rise to two influences; one was a good influence and enabled us, at the very beginning, to establish a Chinese Communist Party of Leninist form which, subjectively, complied strictly with the principles of Lenin, for from the outset the Party had a combination of rigorous self-criticism and internal struggle which enabled it to progress rapidly and which acted as a force motivating the Party's advance. But there was another influence which caused our comrades to go frequently to another extreme and commit another error, an influence which frequently caused the Party struggle to become violent and excessive, to go beyond limits and move toward "left" deviation. . . .

A great many comrades mechanically and erroneously conceive of the principles of Lenin as absolutes. They believe that a high degree of centralism in Party organization precludes democracy within the Party, that the necessity for an intra-Party struggle precludes peace within the Party, that the Party's position as the highest form of proletarian organization, leading all other proletarian mass organizations in political affairs, precludes the independent nature of trade unions and other organizations of the workers and laboring masses and furthermore believe that consolidated, iron discipline destroys the individuality of Party members and their initiative and creativity. . . .

Many comrades do not realize that the intra-Party struggle is a struggle in principle, a struggle to uphold one principle or another, to establish one battle objective or another, to select one method or another for attaining the battle objective. They do not understand that in questions of everyday political affairs, in questions of a purely practical nature, compromise can and should be made with those in the Party holding different views. They do not understand that in questions of principle, in questions of battle objectives, and in questions of the selection of methods for the attainment of these battle objectives, they should struggle uncompromisingly with those in the Party holding different views but should make all kinds of compromises. This, then, is the fundamental spirit of the Party of Lenin and Stalin, but it has not been mastered by a great many of our comrades. In questions on which full compromise should be made, they carry out an uncompromising struggle; there is, therefore, no question on which they do not offer opposition, there is no time at which they do not offer opposition, there is no person whom they do not oppose. On all points where there is disagreement, they offer opposition and compel absolute agreement—they are completely and absolutely uncompromising. They take all contradictions as opposition; opposition is all. This, then, is their absolutism.

A great many comrades have no comprehension of the nature of principles or questions of principle, or the nature of questions of the Party's strategical plan and tactical line. They carry on a struggle by seizing on divergencies in questions of principle and questions of strategical plan and tactical line. Their theoretical level and political experience is still extremely low, for they wrangle on these relatively important questions, but do not understand them. They have memorized the fact, however, that the intra-Party struggle is necessary and that it is wrong not to struggle. Although they do not succeed in grasping important questions and cannot raise a question from principle, they still struggle. Accordingly, able only to grasp individual facts and individual questions, they proceed to carry on a struggle or debate that is without principle or content with those in the Party holding different views, and thus create disunity, mutual opposition, and organizational divergencies among our comrades. This abominable phenomenon exists in the struggle within our Party.

What has been described above is a deviation in the struggle within the Chinese Communist Party; in our Party it is a deviation of special seriousness (although it also exists in foreign parties). It is a case of the struggle within the Party going too far, going beyond limits, traveling to another extreme—"left" opportunism in the intra-Party struggle and in Party organization (precluding democracy in the Party, precluding a uniform peace on principle in the Party, precluding the mutual independence of trade unions and other mass organization, cancelling out the Party member's individuality, his initiative, and creativity). It has been produced under the special environment and special conditions of the Chinese Communist Party.

It should also be noted that a great many comrades have not given their attention to Lenin's struggle in principle against "left" opportunism after the October Revolution. At that time a faction of "left"-wing Communists arose in the

Russian Communist Party, who opposed the peace of Brest-Litovsk, and afterward carried on discussions on the trade union question. Although there was a faction of "recallists," of leftist appearance in the Bolshevik Party before the October Revolution, they were soon subdued and their "left"-wing communism was not as serious as that of the Brest-Litovsk period. It was not long before the "left" faction of the Russian Communist Party was overcome by Lenin, but "left"-wing communism also appeared in the countries of western Europe. Its adherents raised the slogan, "Make No Compromise," opposed participation in national assemblies, opposed struggling within the limits of the law, and opposed the conclusion of the necessary alliance with the left wings of the Social Democratic parties. Under these conditions, Lenin wrote *Left-wing Communism, an Infantile Disease,* to correct this deviation. The living fact of the victory of the October Revolution dealt a mortal blow to the right opportunism of those who did not believe that the proletariat could seize political power, and under those conditions was produced the "left" opportunism which believed that the revolution could attain victory in a day without traveling a winding path.

This is exactly the feeling which has been produced in the Chinese Communist Party, and in certain periods it has been a dominating tendency. Those who commit this error completely disregard the importance of Lenin's treatise on the infantile disease of the left faction. They oppose "winding" and waiting and advocate that a small vanguard carry out an adventurous attack and disregard the fact that the masses have not yet given their support; yet they have the gall to scold others as "right opportunists." All right or "left" opportunism in organizational matters springs from right or "left" political deviations. Since the errors of right or "left" deviation in political matters have been committed at certain times within the Chinese party, the same errors have also been committed in organizational matters. The adventurous "leftist" error was committed especially at the time of the Civil War, and the "excessive intra-Party struggle" appeared as a consequence on the organizational level.

Thus, the following three deviations exist in the intra-Party struggle in the Chinese Communist Party: (1) Liberalism and centrism, (2) a mechanical and excessive intra-Party struggle, expressed as "left" opportunism in Party organization and in the struggle itself, and (3) unprincipled dispute and conflict within the Party.

In essence, the above three deviations are not to be differentiated, because unprincipled disputes, unprincipled conflict, struggling to excess, and liberalism are not Marxist-Leninist, but the manifested forms of anti-Marxism-Leninism. These, then, are the tendencies in the intra-Party struggle which developed under the special conditions of the Chinese Communist Party.

III. MANIFESTATIONS OF THE MECHANICAL AND EXCESSIVE STRUGGLE WITHIN THE PARTY

What are the manifestations of a mechanical and excessive struggle in the Party? The following facts should be noted:

First, in local subdivisions of the Party and in Party branches, "struggle meetings" are frequently held. They are even held in such non-Party bodies as government organs and mass organizations. These meetings are arranged beforehand so that the principal object is not to discuss work accomplished, but to attack certain men, not to struggle primarily against "things," but against individuals, not to struggle against certain incorrect thoughts and principles, but against certain persons. The object of the so-called "struggle against Mr. X or Mr. Y" is to attack certain comrades who are in error. The "struggle meetings" are essentially courts of justice set up by Party members, the principal object of which is not the resolution of questions on the basis of thought but on the basis of organizational process, with the object of suppressing those comrades who dare to hold views of their own (without any certainty that these views are incorrect), or those comrades who get in the way. In a great majority of the cases where attacks are launched against individuals in "struggle meetings," organizational conclusions result. It is quite clearly incorrect to utilize this method.

Second, the mechanical and excessive form of intra-Party struggle is manifested in the following conditions: some comrades think that the more savage the intra-Party struggle, the better, the more serious the questions raised, the better, the more mistakes discovered, the more terms used, the more blame laid on others, the sharper the criticism, the more severe and rude the method and attitude of criticism, the better . . . and if the words are louder, the expressions more violent, and the fangs longer . . . they consider this better and the "most revolutionary thing possible." In the intra-Party struggle and self-criticism, they do not endeavor to do what is proper, do not weigh their opinions, or stop when they have gone far enough; they struggle on with no limit. It is clear that this attitude is also completely incorrect.

Third, some comrades do not understand that the intra-Party struggle is basically a struggle in thought, and that only if unanimity is obtained in thought can it then be maintained and strengthened in political affairs, organization, and Party activities. Only after questions are resolved on the basis of thought and principle can they then be resolved in organization and Party activities. However, it is not an easy matter to obtain unanimity and resolve questions in thought and principle, to overcome the false principles held by others, to correct their false principles, to transform their thoughts, and correct their long-cherished principles, views, and prejudices. Nor can this end be reached by simple means, whether they be a few words, the struggle meeting method, or simply oppression and force. This end can be achieved only by experience in the difficult work of persuasion and education, experience in the complexities of the struggle, and by rather long-term experience in education and actual revolutionary work.

The fourth case is a failure to make a distinction between the methods to be employed in the struggles within and outside the Party. Some comrades take the methods of the intra-Party struggle and use them mechanically in mass organizations and organs outside the Party and use the methods of the intra-Party struggle in the struggle of non-Party cadres and masses; in addition, some comrades use the methods of the struggle outside the Party, the methods of the struggle against the enemy and oppositional elements in struggling with their own comrades, use the methods used against the enemy and opposition, and apply them against comrades in the Party. Incitements to dissension and cunning schemes of all types are being used. Administrative devices—investigation, arrest, imprisonment, and trial—are also put to use in the intra-Party struggle.

If some comrades engaged in the liquidation of traitors commit "leftist" errors, these are the result of failure to discriminate strictly between the struggles within and outside the Party, a confusion of the intra-Party thought struggle, and the work of liquidation. There are frequently enemies cunningly hidden within the Party; to expose and expel this hidden enemy from the Party, it is necessary to carry on a struggle based on actual conditions. But this struggle and the educational struggle which must be carried on against Communist Party members who commit errors are to be clearly distinguished. The struggles within and outside the Party are closely connected, but the methods and forms are different.

There are also some comrades (although they cannot still actually be called comrades) who openly avail themselves of and rely on resources outside the Party to engage in the intra-Party struggle and terrorize the Party. For example, some rely on certain of their achievements, on the troops they command or their weapons, on their mass support or certain of their connections in the United Front, to carry on a struggle against the Party and higher organs and force them to accept their demands and views, propagandize and agitate for independence from the Party. Or who take advantage of non-Party, and even bourgeois and enemy newspapers and magazines and various conferences, to criticize the Party and carry on a struggle against higher Party and certain comrades and cadres. It is clear that this error is as grave as that committed by those who rely on the power of the Party to coerce, dominate, and oppress the non-Party masses, and engage in extortion and blackmail against men outside the Party. Such men struggle against the Party from a position outside the Party; although they still bear the name of Communist Party members, they have already divorced themselves completely from the views of the Party, and have become Party enemies.

Fifth, within our Party, a great many questions are being or have been settled in meetings; this is an excellent thing. But since, in every organization, many meetings are held for which the work of preparation, investigation, and research has not been done beforehand, many different views and arguments often spring up.

In all meetings, the task of forming conclusions must fall on the most responsible participants, and the conclusions of these meetings amount to resolutions; here, also, a great many defects often arise. In the debates held at some meetings, I have seen that the instructors, branch clerks, and other responsible comrades eventually form the conclusions. Yet these responsible comrades themselves have no grasp of the situation, and the question has not been at all clarified; however, they are compelled to form the conclusions; if they don't, they cannot be responsible comrades. Since these responsible comrades have to form the conclusions, there are some who are extremely distressed, break out in a sweat, and make very rough conclusions; these conclusions then amount to resolutions and determine events.

This procedure naturally gives rise to a great many errors. Some comrades who do not yet have a firm grasp of questions are still unwilling to make this fact clear when they make decisions, unwilling to request a period for consideration and research, or time to ask higher echelons for instruction. In order to save face and maintain their position, they claim with determination that they do have a firm grasp on the situation; then they make decisions carelessly, and the results are often incorrect. Such a situation should be corrected.

What have been the results in the Party of this type of incorrect and inappropriate intra-Party struggle? The following unfavorable results have been produced:

First, it has assisted the development of paternalism in the Party. Under this form of intra-Party struggle, individual leaders and guiding organs have oppressed many Party members so that they have not dared speak or criticize. It has created a dictatorship of individuals or minorities within the Party.

Second, another aspect is that it has assisted the development of extreme democratic tendencies and liberalism within the Party. A formal kind of peace and unity have been manifested in the Party, for many comrades ordinarily do not dare speak or criticize. But once the continued concealment of contradictions becomes impossible, once the situation becomes serious and mistakes are exposed, they criticize and fight recklessly; opposition, schism, and organizational confusion develop in the Party, and it is difficult to reëstablish order. This, then, is the reverse side of the system of Party paternalism.

Third, its influence has been to make the correct establishment of intra-Party democratic-centralism impossible, and Party democracy exceptionally abnormal or extremely deficient.

Fourth, it has obstructed the development of positivism,

initiative, and creativity on the part of Party members, and has weakened their spirit of responsibility toward the Party and their work. Comrades under its influence do not dare take active responsibility, do not dare work or create freely, and do not examine and study problems and conditions carefully. It cultivates their tendency to depend on protocol and follow along with the crowd.

Fifth, it has assisted the development of Party sectarianism, the development of an unprincipled sectarian struggle among Party members, and the creation of a state of mind which fears criticism and conflict. For certain Party members, it has cultivated the tendency to "pay attention solely to personal affairs," and the attitude that "one more is worse than one less."

Sixth, it gives Trotskyite spies and counterrevolutionary spies all the more opportunity to destroy the Party, and gives the counterrevolution all the more slogans with which to attack the Party. Trotskyite spies take special advantage of contradictions in the Party and shortcomings in the intra-Party struggle to further their activities for the destruction of the Party and seize those elements which have been attacked and are dissatisfied with the Party. The counterrevolution takes advantage of the struggle against opportunism in the Party to spread propaganda and stir up trouble, to influence sympathizers outside the Party and unstable elements within the Party, and to destroy the Party's solidarity and unity.

The evils in the Party described above arose in the past, yet, in part, they still exist and have not been eliminated.

For a rather long period, these excessive and mechanical forms in the intra-Party struggle have been creating abnormalities in Party life and causing the Party great injury. Despite the fact that the highest leading organs of the Party have already corrected their errors and these forms do not now dominate the struggle being conducted throughout the Party, these forms still have not been corrected in certain middle- and lower-level or certain individual organizations; they still exist more or less universally. Thus, as before, these aspects of organizational life are still abnormal. We must as a consequence call strict attention to these deviations and thoroughly eradicate them from our organizations, so that our comrades will not repeat these mistakes, so that there will be a correct and genuine development of the Party thought struggle, and the Party program will be pushed ahead.

IV. ON THE UNPRINCIPLED INTER-PARTY STRUGGLE

Comrades! I am now going to speak on another deviation in the intra-Party struggle—the struggle without principle. The prevalence of this phenomenon is especially universal and grave within the Chinese Party. Although the so-called "gossip movement" exists in foreign Communist parties, in my opinion it is not so serious abroad as in the Chinese Communist Party. Therefore we must see that our comrades recognize this phenomenon clearly and adopt the measures necessary to deal with it; otherwise, the obstructions to Party solidarity and work will be exceedingly great.

What can be called unprincipled dispute and conflict in the Party?

I consider the following instances of dispute and conflict within the Party to be without principle and to run counter to those principles and common standpoints which promote the interests of our Party and the proletarian revolution.

First, some comrades do not raise questions and struggle with other comrades from a Party standpoint or for the sake of the interests of the entire Party, but do so from the standpoint of individual and group interests. This is to say that the standpoint from which they engage in the intra-Party struggle is incorrect. As a consequence, their views on problems and their orientations and methods in dealing with them are also incorrect. Only if their individual or minority interests are benefited do they give approval or support in dealing with a matter. If their individual or minority interests are not benefited, they stand in opposition and refuse to give their approval. They are unconcerned with the interests of the Party or the revolution, and assign these to a place of secondary importance. Thus, the decision of such a person to advocate or oppose is always without principle and apart from the interests of the Party and the revolution. If all considered their own interests as principles, their interests and principles would then necessarily be in contradiction and mutual conflict.

Second, some comrades provoke conflicts and disputes in the Party, not to improve the situation, but with the opposite purpose in mind. For example, some comrades foment disputes in the Party and struggle with their comrades in order to show off, improve their position, save face, or even to vent their hatred and seek revenge. They upset their comrades' work and plans and wreck the order and solidarity of the Party, but fail to give their attention to prevailing circumstances and conditions. Such are the characteristics of this form of unprincipled struggle.

Third, some comrades do not start from a basis of principle in raising questions for acceptance or rejection by the Party. It is only on the basis of their own feelings, likes, and dislikes that they raise questions and struggle, only for the fun of the moment or the soothing of their ruffled tempers that they revile others and give vent to their anger. This is also a form of struggle without principle. On the other hand, because their experience is limited or their theoretical level low, some comrades cannot raise questions for debate on the basis of principle. It is only on particular or miscellaneous questions, questions of a purely practical nature, or everyday political questions, which do not involve principle, that they start to debate with an absolute refusal to compromise. But since this does not involve general questions of principle, it is also an unprincipled form of struggle which should be eliminated.

For example, some comrades might develop oppositional views regarding a particular battle, action, form of struggle, or organization formula, views which do not involve general principles of strategy, tactical plans, general lines of action, general forms of struggle or organization. And each side might go on debating indefinitely, maintaining its own viewpoint. Since the problems have been formulated incorrectly, they frequently arrive at conclusions which are either incorrect or ambiguous. Thus, the debate becomes a discussion with no conclusion.

The fourth is to engage in the intra-Party struggle without observing rules or correct organizational procedures, to implicate or attack comrades in an unprincipled way, provoking dissension, betraying or plotting against comrades, or not speaking to a man's face, but speaking wildly behind his back, irresponsibly criticizing the Party, broadcasting unfounded opinions against it, spreading rumors, telling lies, and calumniating others.

The cases cited above are all examples of the struggle without principle. Next, there are also some comrades who infuse certain elements of the unprincipled struggle into the struggle in principle, or who, under the protective banner of the struggle in principle, engage in a struggle which is without principle. In addition, there are some comrades who pay special attention to the quarrels between certain persons, or to the discordant relations between certain persons, instead of the substance of their debate.

All of these instances of unprincipled struggle are harmful to the Party.

What are the origins of the unprincipled and the mechanical and excessive struggle within the Party? They spring from the following sources:

First is the generally low theoretical level of comrades in the Party, and, in many respects, the insufficiency of their experience. For a long time, a leadership and nucleus for the entire Party did not actually materialize, and in the various regions, a Party leadership and nucleus have, to the present, materialized to only a very slight degree.

Second, since petty bourgeois elements within the Party are strong, the acute maladies and madness of the petty bourgeoisie, and the farmers' petty bourgeois spirit of vengeance, have constantly influenced the intra-Party struggle.

Third, since democratic life within the Party has been abnormal, a tendency toward objective, mutual discussion of problems has not developed among our comrades, and the tendency to decide and dispose of problems in a crudely subjective manner is prevalent to a serious degree.

Fourth, speculating elements have crept into the Party, and a certain speculative psychology is held by a group of comrades within the Party. In order to prove their own "bolshevization," they will often intentionally go a little to the "left," since they consider the "left" slightly preferable to the right, or will attack others in order to better their own position.

Fifth, spying Trotskyite counterrevolutionary elements have crept into the Party, making use of the intra-Party struggle to destroy the Party. Under the protection of the Party banner, traitorous Trotskyite elements often attack certain comrades, and after the attack, still other traitorous Trotskyite elements absorb the comrades who thus have been attacked into the Trotskyite group as traitors.

These sources have produced the deviations in the intra-Party struggle described above.

V. How to Carry Out the Intra-Party Struggle

Comrades! The question before us now is already quite clear! What is the correct and proper way to carry out the intra-Party struggle?

In this problem, the Communist Party of the Soviet Union and the various national parties have had a great deal of experience, as has the Chinese Party. Lenin and Stalin have given many instructions, and so has the Central Committee of the Chinese Party. Comrades should study these carefully, but since they will also be discussed in connection with the development of the Party, I shall not speak on them today. I shall raise only the few opinions listed below which have been taken from the experience of the struggle within the Chinese Communist Party for our comrades' reference.

First, our comrades must realize at the outset that the intra-Party struggle is a most serious and important matter. It must be carried out with a grave and responsible attitude, certainly not in a slipshod manner. In carrying out the struggle we must ourselves first of all take a completely correct Party standpoint, a public-spirited, unselfish standpoint which is completely in the interest of the Party, for the sake of progress in Party work, and of assistance to other comrades in correcting their errors and solving problems. We ourselves must first see things clearly, see the problems clearly, carry out systematic investigation and research, and at the same time carry out the struggle in a well-organized, well-directed, and well-planned manner.

Our comrades should know that you can correct others' mistakes only if you yourself first adopt a correct standpoint, that you can rectify heterodoxy in others only if you yourself are first completely orthodox. "You must first rectify yourself, then you can rectify others."

Second, comrades should understand that the intra-Party struggle is a struggle between differing thoughts and principles, and the mutual opposition between differing thoughts and principles within the Party. It is entirely necessary that clear boundaries be drawn in thought and principle. But in organization, in the methods of the struggle, in attitudes of speech and criticism, there should be the least possible opposition, the greatest possible use of moderate forms of discussion and debate. If at all possible, neither organizational means nor organizational decisions should be adopted. If possible, the intra-Party struggle should be carried on with a sincere, fair, educational attitude, so that unity can be achieved in thought and principle. Only when it is completely and one hundred per cent necessary should we adopt the method of opposition in the struggle or adopt organizational devices.

Opposition in thought and principle, and the least possible opposition in questions of organization and form: this is the correct method which we should adopt in the intra-Party struggle. A great many comrades' errors consist of the following tendencies: on one hand, they do not develop clear-cut opposition and divergence in thought and principle, and on the other hand, they oppose and struggle confusingly on organization operations and on the methods of the struggle; they struggle until they are red in the face, revile until the opposition is battered, fight until the two sides are irreconcilable and the seeds of hate are planted deep; yet among them, you cannot find a clear-cut divergence in thought or principle.

Third, criticism of Party organization, Party members, and Party work should be appropriate and measured. Bolshevik self-criticism has its own Bolshevik standards. Excessive criticism, the exaggeration of others' mistakes, and excessive praise are all incorrect. It is not true that the fiercer the intra-Party struggle, the better; it should have appropriate limits and seek a suitable level. Both "excessive" and "insufficient" struggle are undesirable.

Fourth is the general cessation of struggle meetings both within and outside the Party. On the basis of summation and investigation we should indicate defects and errors. First "against things," and afterward, "against men." We should first make sure of the facts, clarify the questions, clarify the essential nature of defects and errors, their degree of seriousness, and the reasons for their origin, and only afterward point out the men who are responsible for these defects and errors, and who is primarily and secondarily responsible; we should not start off by going after the men responsible for the mistakes. If the comrade did not commit the error intentionally, and, moreover, if he really understands the mistake and corrects it, we should welcome him and not take up the matter again or go into minute detail. In the intra-Party struggle, our policy is not one of aggression toward cadres and comrades, or of attacks and aggression toward others. This is, in substance, the "whip" policy of the exploiting classes against the workers, the policy of oppression. Our policy is mutual assistance and mutual examination among comrades.

Fifth, a comrade who is being criticized or punished must be given every possible opportunity to state his case. When testimony is given against a comrade and when organizational decisions are being made, the comrade himself should ordinarily be informed and the decisions should be made in his presence. When the comrade does not accept the decision, the case should be referred to higher authorities. (In all cases where nonacceptance is voiced after the punishment is announced, the Party organization should appeal, even for those who do not wish to appeal.) The Party organization cannot forbid a comrade who has received punishment to appeal to higher echelons. A Party member's right of appeal is inalienable. No Party organization can suppress appeals, and in questions of thought and principle a Party member can bypass regular channels and appeal directly to the Central Committee or a higher-level Party committee. However, comrades who appeal should fully clarify their own position, arguments, and diverging views at the lower levels. After that is done, they can appeal. They cannot be silent at the lower levels, then speak wildly to their superiors and purposely confuse them to make the situation easier for themselves. In all cases, after appeal, the power of decision rests at the higher level. A higher-ranking Party committee can cancel, lighten, or increase the punishment meted out to a comrade by a lower Party committee.

Sixth, a clear line should be drawn between the intra-Party and the extra-Party struggles, yet at the same time, an appropriate relationship should be established. The methods of the intra-Party struggle should not be carried over to the struggle outside the Party, and the methods of the extra-Party struggle should not be carried over to the intra-Party struggle; even less should forces and conditions outside the Party be utilized for struggling and intimidation within the Party. All Party members must be strictly attentive and cautious lest hidden Trotskyite spies and counterrevolutionary elements take advantage of contradictions and the struggle within the Party to carry on activities ruinous to the Party. In the intra-Party struggle, no Party member should be victimized by these elements. This can be avoided only if all strictly observe Party discipline and engage correctly in the intra-Party struggle.

Within the Party, only a legal struggle is permitted; only a struggle in thought is permitted. Any type of struggle contrary to the Party programs and Party discipline is not to be tolerated.

Seventh is the prohibition of disputes without principle within the Party.

1. If any Party member has an opinion about the leading organs of the Party or any Party organization, he can offer criticism only to the proper Party organization. He is not permitted to speak irresponsibly among the masses.

2. If any Party member has an opinion about another Party member or about a responsible man in the Party, he can express criticism only to their faces or in certain organizations. He is not permitted to chatter recklessly.

3. If any Party member or low-ranking committee has an opinion about a high-ranking Party committee, it can be expressed only to high-ranking Party committees; a request can be made to call a meeting for examination, or a charge can be made to the higher-ranking committees. They are not permitted to speak wildly or carry reports to the lower ranks.

4. If any Party member discovers that another member is acting incorrectly or in such a way as to endanger Party interests, he must report to the proper Party organization; there may be no covering up or mutual screening.

5. All Party members should support correct influences and orthodoxy, and oppose incorrect influences and all heterodox speeches and actions. They should seriously reprimand those Party members who like to gossip, broadcast, discover people's secrets, or spread rumors. Leading organs of the Party should issue orders as the occasion demands forbidding Party members to discuss certain questions.

6. As the occasion demands, leading organs at every level should take to task those comrades who like to gossip or stir up unprincipled disputes, and correct them, issue warnings, or otherwise adjust their conduct.

7. Party committees at all levels should respect the opinions raised by all comrades. They should call meetings regularly, discuss questions, investigate work, and give Party members sufficient opportunity to express their views.

Unprincipled disputes should be generally forbidden with no judgment as to whether they are right or wrong. Because they are without principle, there is no right or wrong involved which can be judged.

When we wish to settle an unprincipled dispute among our comrades, we should certainly not be content to make a decision on the dispute itself, but should examine and summarize the relevant work, and indicate future tasks, work directives, the general line, plans, etc., directly and on the basis of principle. Within the framework of these summaries, tasks, directives, lines, and plans, we should criticize the comrades' incorrect views, and afterward solicit their views to find whether or not they still differ. If they still differ, it has become a dispute in principle, and an unprincipled dispute among comrades has been raised to the level of principle. If the comrades have no difference of opinion on principle, they should be requested to unite under these summaries, tasks, and directives, and strive unanimously for their complete fulfillment.

In brief, the intra-Party struggle consists basically of divergences and conflict in thought and principle. All in the Party should speak reasonably, work out their lines of reasoning, and have some line of reasoning to speak about. Otherwise nothing can be accomplished. If lines of reasoning are worked out, there is nothing which cannot be done well and easily. In the Party, we should cultivate the tendency to be reasonable. The standards to use in judging the correctness or incorrectness of a line of reasoning are the interest of the struggle being carried on by the Party and the proletariat, the subordination of the interest of the part to the interest of the whole, and the subordination of the short-range interest to the long-range interest.

All reasoning and all proposals which are in the interest of the struggle of the Party and proletariat—in the long-range interest of the struggle of the entire Party and proletariat—are correct. Those which are counter to these interests are all incorrect. Where there is no line of reasoning, or where there is none which can be worked out, the struggle is without principle. Failure to speak reasonably, or to work out lines of reasoning, is incorrect and can lead to no final conclusion nor to any fundamental solution of the problem.

A Bolshevik is reasonable, a supporter of the truth, a person who understands reason and who is able to be reasonable with others; he is not an aggressive, unreasonable, irrational fighter.

Comrades! These are the methods I have proposed for carrying on the intra-Party struggle.

I believe that our comrades should rely on these methods in carrying on the intra-Party struggle, in opposing the various incorrect deviations within the Party, and in examining the Party spirit of individual Party members and especially of cadres. The progressive strengthening of our Party in thought and organization: this is our goal.

14. Mao Tse-tung: Talks at the Yenan Forum on Art and Literature (May, 1942)*

The so-called *cheng-feng* movement was designed particularly to rectify unorthodox tendencies in the cultural sphere. To this end, Mao called in May, 1942, a conference of literary and art workers at Yenan to expound the objectives of Communist literature and art and outline methods for their implementation. His inaugural and concluding speeches at the meetings, published in pamphlet form as "Talks at the Yenan Forum on Art and Literature," became the new oracle for all literary and art workers in Communist areas.

In the talks, Mao initiated sharp criticism against various "petty-bourgeois ideas and tendencies" existing in art and literature. By reasserting the orthodox Communist view that art and literature must subserve the political ends of the revolution, Mao exhorted artists and writers to measure themselves against five yardsticks: standpoint, attitude, audience, work and study. The five yardsticks constitute control over ideological content in order to ensure the appearance of "a correct literature."

In the talks, Mao further discussed the problem of whether the literary cadres should aim at the achievement of a higher literary quality or a broader literary dissemination. He admitted the primacy of popularization, but stressed that "no hard and fast line can be drawn between popularization and the raising of standards." In effect, he was unaware that the elevation of literary quality relies on the freedom of expression—that Mao never allows! Likewise, he acknowledged the distinction between artistic standards and political standards, but he stressed that the former should be subordinate to the latter. After all, correct ideology is all that counts;

---

* From *Selected Works of Mao Tse-tung*, Peking: Foreign Language Press, 1965, III, 75–97. (Extract; introduction and footnotes omitted.)

as a result, art and literature have been subverted into a mechanical form of propaganda.

What then is the crux of the matter? In my opinion, it consists fundamentally of the problems of working for the masses and how to work for the masses. Unless these two problems are solved, or solved properly, our writers and artists will be ill-adapted to their environment and their tasks and will come up against a series of difficulties from without and within. My concluding remarks will centre on these two problems and also touch upon some related ones.

I

The first problem is: literature and art for whom?

This problem was solved long ago by Marxists, especially by Lenin. As far back as 1905 Lenin pointed out emphatically that our literature and art should "serve . . . the millions and tens of millions of working people". For comrades engaged in literary and artistic work in the anti-Japanese base areas it might seem that this problem is already solved and needs no further discussion. Actually, that is not the case. Many comrades have not found a clear solution. Consequently their sentiments, their works, their actions and their views on the guiding principles for literature and art have inevitably been more or less at variance with the needs of the masses and of the practical struggle. Of course, among the numerous men of culture, writers, artists and other literary and artistic workers engaged in the great struggle for liberation together with the Communist Party and the Eighth Route and New Fourth Armies, a few may be careerists who are with us only temporarily, but the overwhelming majority are working energetically for the common cause. By relying on these comrades, we have achieved a great deal in our literature, drama, music and fine arts. Many of these writers and artists have begun their work since the outbreak of the War of Resistance; many others did much revolutionary work before the war, endured many hardships and influenced broad masses of the people by their activities and works. Why do we say, then, that even among these comrades there are some who have not reached a clear solution of the problem of whom literature and art are for? Is it conceivable that there are still some who maintain that revolutionary literature and art are not for the masses of the people but for the exploiters and oppressors?

Indeed literature and art exist which are for the exploiters and oppressors. Literature and art for the landlord class are feudal literature and art. Such were the literature and art of the ruling class in China's feudal era. To this day such literature and art still have considerable influence in China. Literature and art for the bourgeoisie are bourgeois literature and art. People like Liang Shih-chiu, whom Lu Hsun criticized, talk about literature and art as transcending classes, but in fact they uphold bourgeois literature and art and oppose proletarian literature and art. Then literature and art exist which serve the imperialists—for example, the works of Chou Tso-jen, Chang Tzu-ping and their like—which we call traitor literature and art. With us, literature and art are for the people, not for any of the above groups. We have said that China's new culture at the present stage is an anti-imperialist, anti-feudal culture of the masses of the people under the leadership of the proletariat. Today, anything that is truly of the masses must necessarily be led by the proletariat. Whatever is under the leadership of the bourgeoisie cannot possibly be of the masses. Naturally, the same applies to the new literature and art which are part of the new culture. We should take over the rich legacy and the good traditions in literature and art that have been handed down from past ages in China and foreign countries, but the aim must still be to serve the masses of the people. Nor do we refuse to utilize the literary and artistic forms of the past, but in our hands these old forms, remoulded and infused with new content, also become something revolutionary in the service of the people.

Who, then, are the masses of the people? The broadest sections of the people, constituting more than 90 per cent of our total population, are the workers, peasants, soldiers and urban petty bourgeoisie. Therefore, our literature and art are first for the workers, the class that leads the revolution. Secondly, they are for the peasants, the most numerous and most steadfast of our allies in the revolution. Thirdly, they are for the armed workers and peasants, namely, the Eighth Route and New Fourth Armies and the other armed units of the people, which are the main forces of the revolutionary war. Fourthly, they are for the labouring masses of the urban petty bourgeoisie and for the petty-bourgeois intellectuals, both of whom are also our allies in the revolution and capable of long-term co-operation with us. These four kinds of people constitute the overwhelming majority of the Chinese nation, the broadest masses of the people.

II

Having settled the problem of whom to serve, we come to the next problem, how to serve. To put it in the words of some of our comrades: should we devote ourselves to raising standards, or should we devote ourselves to popularization?

Although man's social life is the only source of literature and art and is incomparably livelier and richer in content, the people are not satisfied with life alone and demand literature and art as well. Why? Because, while both are beautiful, life as reflected in works of literature and art can and ought to be on a higher plane, more intense, more concentrated, more typical, nearer the ideal, and therefore more universal than actual everyday life. Revolutionary literature and art should create a variety of characters out of real life and help the masses to propel history forward. For example, there is suffering from hunger, cold and oppression on the one hand, and exploitation and oppression of man by man on the other. These facts exist everywhere and people look upon them as commonplace. Writers and artists concentrate such everyday phenomena, typify the contradictions and struggles within them and produce works which awaken the masses, fire them with enthusiasm and impel them to unite and struggle to transform their environment. Without such literature and art, this task could not be fulfilled, or at least not so effectively and speedily.

What is meant by popularizing and by raising standards in works of literature and art? What is the relationship between these two tasks? Popular works are simpler and plainer, and therefore more readily accepted by the broad masses of the people today. Works of a higher quality, being more polished, are more difficult to produce and in general do not circulate so easily and quickly among the masses at present. The problem facing the workers, peasants and soldiers is this: they are now engaged in a bitter and bloody struggle with the enemy but are illiterate and uneducated as a result of long years of rule by the feudal and bourgeois classes, and therefore they are eagerly demanding enlightenment, education and works of literature and art which meet their urgent needs and which are easy to absorb, in order to heighten their enthusiasm in struggle and confidence in victory, strengthen their unity and fight the enemy with one heart and one mind. For them the prime need is not "more flowers on the brocade" but "fuel in snowy weather". In present conditions, therefore, popularization is the more pressing task. It is wrong to belittle or neglect popularization.

Nevertheless, no hard and fast line can be drawn between popularization and the raising of standards. Not only is it possible to popularize some works of higher quality even now, but the cultural level of the broad masses is steadily rising. If popularization remains at the same level for ever, with the same stuff being supplied month after month and year after year, always the same "Little Cowherd" and the same "man, hand, mouth, knife, cow, goat", will not the educators and those being educated be six of one and half a dozen of the other? What would be the sense of such popularization? The people demand popularization and, following that, higher standards; they demand higher standards month by month and year by year. Here popularization means popularizing for the people and raising of standards means raising the level for the people. And such raising is not from mid-air, or behind closed doors, but is actually based on popularization. It is determined by and at the same time guides popularization. In China as a whole the development of the revolution and of revolutionary culture is uneven and their spread is gradual. While in one place there is popularization and then raising of standards on the basis of popularization, in other places popularization has not even begun. Hence good experience in popularization leading to higher standards in one locality can be applied in other localities and serve to guide popularization and the raising of standards there, saving many twists and turns along the road. Internationally, the good experience of foreign countries, and especially Soviet experience, can also serve to guide us. With us, therefore, the raising of standards is based on popularization, while popularization is guided by the raising of standards. Precisely for this reason, so far from being an obstacle to the raising of standards, the work of popularization we are speaking of supplies the basis for the work of raising standards which we are now doing on a limited scale, and prepares the necessary conditions for us to raise standards in the future on a much broader scale.

Besides such raising of standards as meets the needs of the

masses directly, there is the kind which meets their needs indirectly, that is, the kind which is needed by the cadres. The cadres are the advanced elements of the masses and generally have received more education; literature and art of a higher level are entirely necessary for them. To ignore this would be a mistake. Whatever is done for the cadres is also entirely for the masses, because it is only through the cadres that we can educate and guide the masses. If we go against this aim, if what we give the cadres cannot help them educate and guide the masses, our work of raising standards will be like shooting at random and will depart from the fundamental principle of serving the masses of the people.

To sum up: through the creative labour of revolutionary writers and artists, the raw materials found in the life of the people are shaped into the ideological form of literature and art serving the masses of the people. Included here are the more advanced literature and art as developed on the basis of elementary literature and art and as required by those sections of the masses whose level has been raised, or, more immediately, by the cadres among the masses. Also included here are elementary literature and art which, conversely, are guided by more advanced literature and art and are needed primarily by the overwhelming majority of the masses at present. Whether more advanced or elementary, all our literature and art are for the masses of the people, and in the first place for the workers, peasants and soldiers; they are created for the workers, peasants and soldiers and are for their use.

III

Since our literature and art are for the masses of the people, we can proceed to discuss a problem of inner-Party relations, *i.e.*, the relation between the Party's work in literature and art and the Party's work as a whole, and in addition a problem of the Party's external relations, *i.e.*, the relation between the Party's work in literature and art and the work of non-Party people in this field, a problem of the united front in literary and art circles.

Let us consider the first problem. In the world today all culture, all literature and art belong to definite classes and are geared to definite political lines. There is in fact no such thing as art for art's sake, art that stands above classes or art that is detached from or independent of politics. Proletarian literature and art are part of the whole proletarian revolutionary cause; they are, as Lenin said, cogs and wheels in the whole revolutionary machine. Therefore, Party work in literature and art occupies a definite and assigned position in Party revolutionary work as a whole and is subordinated to the revolutionary tasks set by the Party in a given revolutionary period. Opposition to this arrangement is certain to lead to dualism or pluralism, and in essence amounts to "politics—Marxist, art—bourgeois", as with Trotsky. We do not favour overstressing the importance of literature and art, but neither do we favour underestimating their importance. Literature and art are subordinate to politics, but in their turn exert a great influence on politics. Revolutionary literature and art are part of the whole revolutionary cause, they are cogs and wheels in it, and though in comparison with certain other and more important parts they may be less significant and less urgent and may occupy a secondary position, nevertheless, they are indispensable cogs and wheels in the whole machine, an indispensable part of the entire revolutionary cause. If we had no literature and art even in the broadest and most ordinary sense, we could not carry on the revolutionary movement and win victory. Failure to recognize this is wrong. Furthermore, when we say that literature and art are subordinate to politics, we mean class politics, the politics of the masses, not the politics of a few so-called statesmen. Politics, whether revolutionary or counter-revolutionary, is the struggle of class against class, not the activity of a few individuals. The revolutionary struggle on the ideological and artistic fronts must be subordinate to the political struggle because only through politics can the needs of the class and the masses find expression in concentrated form. Revolutionary statesmen, the political specialists who know the science or art of revolutionary politics, are simply the leaders of millions upon millions of statesmen—the masses. Their task is to collect the opinions of these mass statesmen, sift and refine them, and return them to the masses, who then take them and put them into practice. They are therefore not the kind of aristocratic "statesmen" who work behind closed doors and fancy they have a monopoly of wisdom. Herein lies the difference in principle between proletarian statesmen and decadent bourgeois statesmen. This is precisely why there can be complete unity between the political character of our literary and artistic works and their truthfulness. It would be wrong to fail to realize this and to debase the politics and the statesmen of the proletariat.

Let us consider next the question of the united front in the world of literature and art. Since literature and art are subordinate to politics and since the fundamental problem in China's politics today is resistance to Japan, our Party writers and artists must in the first place unite on this issue of resistance to Japan with all non-Party writers and artists (ranging from Party sympathizers and petty-bourgeois writers and artists to all those writers and artists of the bourgeois and landlord classes who are in favour of resistance to Japan). Secondly, we should unite with them on the issue of democracy. On this issue there is a section of anti-Japanese writers and artists who do not agree with us, so the range of unity will unavoidably be somewhat more limited. Thirdly, we should unite with them on issues peculiar to the literary and artistic world, questions of method and style in literature and art; here again, as we are for socialist realism and some people do not agree, the range of unity will be narrower still. While on one issue there is unity, on another there is struggle, there is criticism. The issues are at once separate and interrelated, so that even on the very ones which give rise to unity, such as resistance to Japan, there are at the same time struggle and criticism. In a united front, "all unity and no struggle" and "all struggle and no unity" are both wrong policies—as with the Right capitulationism and tailism, or the "Left" exclusivism and sectarianism, practised by some comrades in the past. This is as true in literature and art as in politics.

The petty-bourgeois writers and artists constitute an important force among the forces of the united front in literary and art circles in China. There are many shortcomings in both their thinking and their works, but, comparatively speaking, they are inclined towards the revolution and are close to the working people. Therefore, it is an especially important task to help them overcome their shortcomings and to win them over to the front which serves the working people.

IV

Literary and art criticism is one of the principal methods of struggle in the world of literature and art. It should be developed and, as comrades have rightly pointed out, our past work in this respect has been quite inadequate. Literary and art criticism is a complex question which requires a great deal of special study. Here I shall concentrate only on the basic problem of criteria in criticism. I shall also comment briefly on a few specific problems raised by some comrades and on certain incorrect views.

In literary and art criticism there are two criteria, the political and the artistic. According to the political criterion, everything is good that is helpful to unity and resistance to Japan, that encourages the masses to be of one heart and one mind, that opposes retrogression and promotes progress; on the other hand, everything is bad that is detrimental to unity and resistance to Japan, foments dissension and discord among the masses and opposes progress and drags people back. How can we tell the good from the bad—by the motive (the subjective intention) or by the effect (social practice)? Idealists stress motive and ignore effect, while mechanical materialists stress effect and ignore motive. In contradistinction to both, we dialectical materialists insist on the unity of motive and effect. The motive of serving the masses is inseparably linked with the effect of winning their approval; the two must be united. The motive of serving the individual or a small clique is not good, nor is it good to have the motive of serving the masses without the effect of winning their approval and benefiting them. In examining the subjective intention of a writer or artist, that is, whether his motive is correct and good, we do not judge by his declarations but by the effect of his actions (mainly his works) on the masses in society. The criterion for judging subjective intention or motive is social practice and its effect. We want no sectarianism in our literary and art criticism and, subject to the general principle of unity for resistance to Japan, we should tolerate literary and art works with a variety of political attitudes. But at the same time, in our criticism we must adhere firmly to principle and severely criticize and repudiate all works of literature and art expressing views in opposition to the nation, to science, to the masses and to the Communist Party, because these so-called works of literature and art proceed from the motive and produce the effect of undermining unity for resistance to Japan. According to the artistic criterion, all works of a higher artistic quality are good or comparatively good, while those of a lower artistic quality are bad or comparatively bad. Here, too, of course, social effect must be taken into account. There is hardly a writer or artist who does not consider his own work beautiful, and our criticism ought to permit the free competition of all varieties of works of art; but it is also entirely necessary to subject these works to correct criticism according to the criteria of the science of aesthetics, so that art of a lower level can be gradually raised to a higher and art which does not meet the demands of the struggle of the broad masses can be transformed into art that does.

There is the political criterion and there is the artistic criterion; what is the relationship between the two? Politics cannot be equated with art, nor can a general world outlook be equated with a method of artistic creation and criticism. We deny not only that there is an abstract and absolutely unchangeable political criterion, but also that there is an abstract and absolutely unchangeable artistic criterion; each class in every class society has its own political and artistic criteria. But all classes in all class societies invariably put the political criterion first and the artistic criterion second. The bourgeoisie always shuts out proletarian literature and art, however great their artistic merit. The proletariat must similarly distinguish among the literary and art works of past ages and determine its attitude towards them only after examining their attitude to the people and whether or not they had any progressive significance historically. Some works which politically are downright reactionary may have a certain artistic quality. The more reactionary their content and the higher their artistic quality, the more poisonous they are to the people, and the more necessary it is to reject them. A common characteristic of the literature and art of all exploiting classes in their period of decline is the contradiction between their reactionary political content and their artistic form. What we demand is the unity of politics and art, the unity of content and form, the unity of revolutionary political content and the highest possible perfection of artistic form. Works of art which lack artistic quality have no force, however progressive they are politically. Therefore, we oppose both the tendency to produce works of art with a wrong political viewpoint and the tendency towards the "poster and slogan style" which is correct in political viewpoint but lacking in artistic power. On questions of literature and art we must carry on a struggle on two fronts.

Both these tendencies can be found in the thinking of many comrades. A good number of comrades tend to neglect artistic technique; it is therefore necessary to give attention to the raising of artistic standards. But as I see it, the political side is more of a problem at present. Some comrades lack elementary political knowledge and consequently have all sorts of muddled ideas.

V

The problems discussed here exist in our literary and art circles in Yenan. What does that show? It shows that wrong styles of work still exist to a serious extent in our literary and art circles and that there are still many defects among our comrades, such as idealism, dogmatism, empty illusions, empty talk, contempt for practice and aloofness from the masses, all of which call for an effective and serious campaign of rectification.

Since integration into the new epoch of the masses is essential, it is necessary thoroughly to solve the problem of the relationship between the individual and the masses. This couplet from a poem by Lu Hsun should be our motto:

> *Fierce-browed, I coolly defy a thousand pointing fingers,*
> *Head-bowed, like a willing ox I serve the children.*

The "thousand pointing fingers" are our enemies, and we will never yield to them, no matter how ferocious. The "children" here symbolize the proletariat and the masses. All Communists, all revolutionaries, all revolutionary literary and art workers should learn from the example of Lu Hsun and be "oxen" for the proletariat and the masses, bending their backs to the task until their dying day. Intellectuals who want to integrate themselves with the masses, who want to serve the masses, must go through a process in which they and the masses come to know each other well. This process may, and certainly will, involve much pain and friction, but if you have the determination, you will be able to fulfil these requirements.

Today I have discussed only some of the problems of fundamental orientation for our literature and art movement; many specific problems remain which will require further study. I am confident that comrades here are determined to move in the direction indicated. I believe that in the course of the rectification movement and in the long period of study and work to come, you will surely be able to bring about a transformation in yourselves and in your works, to create many fine works which will be warmly welcomed by the masses of the people, and to advance the literature and art movement in the revolutionary base areas and throughout China to a glorious new stage.

15. Mao Tse-tung: Some Questions Concerning Methods of Leadership (June, 1943)*

This is a resolution on methods of leadership drafted on behalf of the Central Committee in June, 1943.

During the early years of the Anti-Japanese War, the Party built its military and political forces and summarized and codified the lessons of the previous period in training cadres and members in mass-line operation.

The mass line is the basic working method "to integrate the leadership with the masses," and "to develop energetic mass movements under the guidance of the leadership."[1] This method includes two techniques of "combining the general with the particular" and "combining the leadership with the masses," as given by Mao in this article. Highly organized and concrete, this mass-line method of operation served the Party well in its quest for military victory prior to 1949. The whole work, in effect, reflects Mao's strategy and tactics for the mobilization of the masses, as illustrated in his early works.

There are two methods which we Communists must employ in whatever work we do. One is to combine the general with the particular; the other is to combine the leadership with the masses.

In any task, if no general and widespread call is issued, the broad masses cannot be mobilized for action. But if persons in leading positions confine themselves to a general call—if they do not personally, in some of the organizations, go deeply and

---

* From *Selected Works of Mao Tse-tung,* Peking: Foreign Language Press, 1965, III, 117–122. (Footnotes omitted.)
[1] See Teng Hsiao-p'ing, *The Great Unity of the Chinese People and the Great Unity of the Peoples of the World! Ten Glorious Years,* Peking: Foreign Language Press, 1960.

concretely into the work called for, make a break-through at some single point, gain experience and use this experience for guiding other units—then they will have no way of testing the correctness or of enriching the content of their general call, and there is the danger that nothing may come of it. In the rectification movement of 1942, for example, there were achievements wherever the method of combining the general call with particular and specific guidance was used, but there were no achievements wherever this method was not used. In the rectification movement of 1943, each bureau and sub-bureau of the Central Committee and each area and prefectural Party committee, in addition to making a general call (a rectification plan for the whole year), must do the following things, gaining experience in the process. Select two or three units (but not too many) from the organization itself and from other organizations, schools or army units in the vicinity. Make a thorough study of those units, acquire a detailed knowledge of the development of the rectification movement in them and a detailed knowledge of the political history, the ideological characteristics, the zeal in study and the strong and weak points in the work of some (again not too many) representative members of their personnel. Furthermore, give personal guidance to those in charge to find concrete solutions for the practical problems facing those units. The leaders in every organization, school or army unit must do likewise, as each of these has a number of subordinate units. Moreover, this is the method by which the leaders combine leading and learning. No one in a leading position is competent to give general guidance to all the units unless he derives concrete experience from particular individuals and events in particular subordinate units. This method must be promoted everywhere so that leading cadres at all levels learn to apply it.

Experience in the 1942 rectification movement also proves it is essential for the success of the rectification that a leading group should be formed in each unit in the course of the movement, made up of a small number of activists and with the heads of the given unit as its nucleus, and that this leading group should link itself closely with the masses taking part in the movement. However active the leading group may be, its activity will amount to fruitless effort by a handful of people unless combined with the activity of the masses. On the other hand, if the masses alone are active without a strong leading group to organize their activity properly, such activity cannot be sustained for long, or carried forward in the right direction, or raised to a high level. The masses in any given place are generally composed of three parts, the relatively active, the intermediate and the relatively backward. The leaders must therefore be skilled in uniting the small number of active elements around the leadership and must rely on them to raise the level of the intermediate elements and to win over the backward elements. A leading group that is genuinely united and linked with the masses can be formed only gradually in the process of mass struggle, and not in isolation from it. In the process of a great struggle, the composition of the leading group in most cases should not and cannot remain entirely unchanged throughout the initial, middle and final stages; the activists who come forward in the course of the struggle must constantly be promoted to replace those original members of the leading group who are inferior by comparison or who have degenerated. One fundamental reason why the work in many places and many organizations cannot be pushed ahead is the lack of a leading group which is united, linked with the masses and kept constantly healthy. A school of a hundred people certainly cannot be run well if it does not have a leading group of several people, or a dozen or more, which is formed in accordance with the actual circumstances (and not thrown together artificially) and is composed of the most active, upright and alert of the teachers, the other staff and the students. In every organization, school, army unit, factory or village, whether large or small, we should give effect to the ninth of Stalin's twelve conditions for the bolshevization of the Party, namely, that on the establishment of a nucleus of leadership. The criteria for such a leading group should be the four which Dimitrov enumerated in his discussion of cadres policy —absolute devotion to the cause, contact with the masses, ability independently to find one's bearings and observance of discipline. Whether in carrying out the central tasks—war, production, education (including rectification)—or in checking-up on work, examining the cadres' histories, or in other activities, it is necessary to adopt the method of linking the leading group with the masses, in addition to that of linking the general call with particular guidance.

In all the practical work of our Party, all correct leadership is necessarily "from the masses, to the masses". This means: take the ideas of the masses (scattered and unsystematic ideas) and concentrate them (through study turn them into concentrated and systematic ideas), then go to the masses and propagate and explain these ideas until the masses embrace them as their own, hold fast to them and translate them into action, and test the correctness of these ideas in such action. Then once again concentrate ideas from the masses and once again go to the masses so that the ideas are persevered in and carried through. And so on, over and over again in an endless spiral, with the ideas becoming more correct, more vital and richer each time. Such is the Marxist theory of knowledge.

The concept of a correct relationship between the leading group and the masses in an organization or in a struggle, the concept that correct ideas on the part of the leadership can only be "from the masses, to the masses", and the concept that the general call must be combined with particular guidance when the leadership's ideas are being put into practice—these concepts must be propagated everywhere during the present rectification movement in order to correct the mistaken viewpoints among our cadres on these questions. Many comrades do not see the importance of, or are not good at, drawing together the activists to form a nucleus of leadership, and they do not see the importance of, or are not good at, linking this nucleus of leadership closely with the masses, and so their leadership becomes bureaucratic and divorced from the masses. Many comrades do not see the importance of, or are not good at, summing up the experience of mass struggles, but fancying themselves clever, are fond of voicing their subjectivist ideas, and so their ideas become empty and impractical. Many comrades rest content with making a general call with regard to a task and do not see the importance of, or are not good at, following it up immediately with particular and concrete guidance, and so their call remains on their lips, or on paper or in the conference room, and their leadership becomes bureaucratic. In the present rectification movement we must correct these defects and learn to use the methods of combining the leadership with the masses and the general with the particular in our study, in the check-up on work and in the examination of cadres' histories; and we must also apply these methods in all our future work.

Take the ideas of the masses and concentrate them, then go to the masses, persevere in the ideas and carry them through, so as to form correct ideas of leadership—such is the basic method of leadership. In the process of concentrating ideas and persevering in them, it is necessary to use the method of combining the general call with particular guidance, and this is a component part of the basic method. Formulate general ideas (general calls) out of the particular guidance given in a number of cases, and put them to the test in many different units (not only doing so yourself, but by telling others to do the same); then concentrate the new experience (sum it up) and draw up new directives for the guidance of the masses generally. Comrades should do this in the present rectification movement, and also in every other kind of work. Better leadership comes with greater skill in doing this.

In relaying to subordinate units any task (whether it concerns the revolutionary war, production or education; the rectification movement, check-up on work or the examination of cadres' histories; propaganda work, organizational work or anti-espionage, or other work), a higher organization and its departments should in all cases go through the leader of the lower organization concerned so that he may assume responsibility; in this way both division of labour and unified centralized leadership are achieved. A department at a higher level should not go solely to its counterpart at the lower level (for instance, a higher department concerned with organization, propaganda or anti-espionage should not go solely to the corresponding department at the lower level), leaving the person in over-all charge of the lower organization (such as the secretary, the chairman, the director or the school principal) in ignorance or without responsibility. Both the person in over-all charge and the person with specific responsibility should be informed and given responsibility. This centralized method, combining division of labour with unified leadership, makes it possible, through the person with over-all responsibility, to mobilize a large number of cadres—on occasion even an organization's entire personnel—to carry out a particular task, and thus to overcome shortages of cadres in individual departments and turn a good number of people into active cadres for the work in hand. This, too, is a way of combining the leadership with the masses. Take, for instance, the examining of cadres' histories. If the job is done in isolation, if it is done only by the few people in the organization department in charge of such work, it certainly cannot be done well. But if it is done through the administrative head of a particular orgánization or school, who mobilizes many or even all of his staff, or many or even all of his students, to take part in the work, while at the same time the leading members of the organization department at the higher level give correct guidance, applying the principle of linking the leadership with the masses, then undoubtedly the task of examining the cadres' histories will be satisfactorily accomplished.

In any given place, there cannot be a number of central tasks at the same time. At any one time there can be only one central task, supplemented by other tasks of a second or third order of importance. Consequently, the person with over-all responsibility in the locality must take into account the history and circumstances of the struggle there and put the different tasks in their proper order; he should not act upon each instruction as it comes from the higher organization without any planning of his own, and thereby create a multitude of "central tasks" and a state of confusion and disorder. Nor should a higher organization simultaneously assign many tasks to a lower organization without indicating their relative importance and urgency or without specifying which is central, for that will lead to confusion in the steps to be taken by the lower organizations in their work and thus no definite results will be achieved. It is part of the art of leadership to take the whole situation into account and plan accordingly in the light of the historical conditions and existing circumstances of each locality, decide correctly on the centre of gravity and the sequence of the work for each period, steadfastly carry through the decision, and make sure that definite results are achieved. This is also a problem of method of leadership, and care must be taken to solve it when applying the principles of combining the leadership with the masses and the general with the particular.

Details concerning methods of leadership are not dealt with here; it is hoped that comrades in all localities will themselves do some hard thinking and give full play to their own creativeness on the basis of the principles here set forth. The harder the struggle, the greater the need for Communists to link their leadership closely with the demands of the vast masses, and to combine general calls closely with particular guidance, so as to smash the subjectivist and bureaucratic methods of leadership completely. All the leading comrades of our Party must at all times counterpose scientific, Marxist methods of leadership to subjectivist, bureaucratic methods of leadership and use the former to overcome the latter. Subjectivists and bureaucrats do not understand the principles of combining the leadership with the masses and the general with the particular; they greatly impede the development of the work of the Party. To combat subjectivist and bureaucratic methods of leadership, we must promote scientific, Marxist methods of leadership both extensively and intensively.

Chapter Four

The Communist Triumph on the Mainland

THE FOURTH period (1945–1949), bringing victory to the Communists, marked a critical transformation in the Communist leaders' thoughts as reflected in their writings. For instance, in his 1945 report on "Coalition Government" (Selection 16), Mao stressed the need for free competition in politics; four years later, with complete power within his grasp, Mao said no more about free competition and stressed instead the need for the so-called "people's Democratic dictatorship" (Selection 18). This shows how Mao compromised and shifted to account for the change in the Party's role. These writings illuminate key ideological problems that have confronted the Party for the past two decades in its attempt to exercise power for economic and social development.

16. Mao Tse-tung: On Coalition Government (April, 1945)*

This is a political report made at the Seventh National Congress of the Communist Party held at Yenan on April

* From *Selected Works of Mao Tse-tung,* Peking: Foreign Language Press, 1965, III, 277–288. (Extract; footnotes omitted.)

23, 1945.[1] In his report, Mao demanded that the Kuomintang dictatorship should be ended and a coalition government created in its place. The demand for a coalition government was in fact an extension of his classic strategy of the united front: it would give the Communists a chance to compete for support from outside the government while infiltrating the government from within. It is therefore understandable that Mao had kept the idea so firmly and so steadily in mind, insisting on the need for free competition in politics. Mao's political platform consisted of two parts: a general outline and specific stipulations. The general outline in the period of the bourgeois-democratic revolution was to establish a "state system which we call New Democracy, namely, a united-front democratic alliance," following victory in the war of aggression. Mao stressed that his view on "politics of New Democracy" was "completely in accord with the revolutionary views of Dr. Sun Yat-sen."

His specific stipulations dealt with vital wartime and postwar problems. But to carry out these measures, "the most important thing is the immediate abolition of the Kuomintang one-party dictatorship and the establishment of a democratic provisional central government, a coalition government." Thus the central theme of Mao's report was the coalition government. Mao reasoned that since China is still in the "stage of the bourgeois-democratic revolution," it needs a coalition government "including representatives of all the anti-Japanese parties and people without party affiliation."[2]

The Policy of the Chinese Communist Party

In China's present grave situation, the people, the democrats and democratic parties at home and the people in other countries who are concerned about the Chinese situation all hope that unity will replace disunity and that democratic reforms will be introduced, and they all want to know what the policy of the Chinese Communist Party is for solving the

[1] The Congress of the Communist Party had not held any meetings since the Sixth Congress in July, 1928.

[2] As noted in the Introduction, from the end of 1941 to 1947 American policy toward China aimed (1) to encourage the unification of China by political means; and (2) to urge Chiang to enter into a political arrangement with Mao in order to form a coalition government.

many vital problems of today. The members of our Party, of course, have a still deeper interest in these matters.

Our policies of the Anti-Japanese National United Front in the war have always been clear and definite, and they have been tested in the eight years of war. Our congress should draw conclusions from them as a guide for our future struggles.

Here I shall explain a number of the definite conclusions arrived at by our Party concerning the major policies for solving China's problems.

Our General Programme. An agreed common programme is urgently needed by the Chinese people, the Chinese Communist Party and all the anti-Japanese democratic parties for the purpose of mobilizing and uniting all the anti-Japanese forces of the Chinese people, completely wiping out the Japanese aggressors and building a new China that is independent, free, democratic, united, prosperous and powerful.

Such a common programme may be divided into two parts, the general and the specific. Let us consider first the general and then the specific programme.

On the major premise that the Japanese aggressors must be completely destroyed and a new China must be built, we Communists and the overwhelming majority of the population are agreed on the following fundamental propositions at the present stage of China's development. First, China should not have a feudal, fascist and anti-popular state system under the dictatorship of the big landlords and big bourgeoisie, because eighteen years of government by the chief ruling clique of the Kuomintang have already proved its complete bankruptcy. Second, China cannot possibly establish the old type of democratic dictatorship—a purely national-bourgeois state—and therefore should not attempt to do so, because on the one hand the Chinese national bourgeoisie has proved itself very flabby economically and politically, and on the other, for a long time now a new factor has been present, namely, the awakened Chinese proletariat with its leader, the Chinese Communist Party, which has demonstrated great capacity in the political arena and assumed leadership of the peasant masses, the urban petty bourgeoisie, the intelligentsia and other democratic forces. Third, it is likewise impossible for the Chinese people to institute a socialist state system at the present stage when it is still their task to fight foreign and feudal oppression and the necessary social and economic conditions for a socialist state are still lacking.

What then do we propose? We propose the establishment, after the thorough defeat of the Japanese aggressors, of a state system which we call New Democracy, namely, a united-front democratic alliance based on the overwhelming majority of the people, under the leadership of the working class.

It is this kind of state system that truly meets the demands of the overwhelming majority of the Chinese population, because it can win and indeed has been winning the approval, first, of millions of industrial workers and tens of millions of handicraftsmen and farm labourers, second, of the peasantry, which constitutes 80 per cent of China's population, *i.e.*, 360 million out of a population of 450 million, and third, of the large numbers of the urban petty bourgeoisie as well as the national bourgeoisie, the enlightened gentry and other patriots.

Of course, there are still contradictions among these classes, notably the contradiction between labour and capital, and consequently each has its own particular demands. It would be hypocritical and wrong to deny the existence of these contradictions and differing demands. But throughout the stage of New Democracy, these contradictions, these differing demands, will not grow and transcend the demands which all have in common and should not be allowed to do so; they can be adjusted. Given such adjustment, these classes can together accomplish the political, economic and cultural tasks of the new-democratic state.

The politics of New Democracy which we advocate consists in the overthrow of external oppression and of internal feudal and fascist oppression, and then the setting up not of the old type of democracy but of a political system which is a united front of all the democratic classes. These views of ours are completely in accord with the revolutionary views of Dr. Sun Yat-sen. In the Manifesto of the First National Congress of the Kuomintang, Dr. Sun wrote:

> The so-called democratic system in modern states is usually monopolized by the bourgeoisie and has become simply an instrument for oppressing the common people. On the other hand, the Kuomintang's Principle of Democracy means a democratic system shared by all the common people and not privately owned by the few.

This is a great political injunction of Dr. Sun's. The Chinese people, the Chinese Communist Party and all other democrats must respect it, firmly put it into practice and wage a determined fight against all individuals and groups that violate or oppose it, and so defend and develop this perfectly correct political principle of New Democracy.

The organizational principle of the new-democratic state should be democratic centralism, with the people's congresses determining the major policies and electing the governments at the various levels. It is at once democratic and centralized, that is, centralized on the basis of democracy and democratic under centralized guidance. This is the only system that can give full expression to democracy with full powers vested in the people's congresses at all levels and, at the same time, guarantee centralized administration with the governments at each level exercising centralized management of all the affairs entrusted to them by the people's congresses at the corresponding level and safeguarding whatever is essential to the democratic life of the people.

The army and the other armed forces constitute an important part of the apparatus of the new-democratic state power, without which the state cannot be defended. As with all other organs of power, the armed forces of the new-democratic state belong to the people and protect the people; they have nothing in common with the army, police, etc. of the old type which belong to the few and oppress the people.

The economy of New Democracy which we advocate is likewise in accord with Dr. Sun's principles. On the land question, Dr. Sun championed "land to the tiller". On the question of industry and commerce, Dr. Sun stated in the Manifesto quoted above:

> Enterprises, such as banks, railways and airlines, whether Chinese-owned or foreign-owned, which are either monopolistic in character or too big for private management, shall be operated and administered by the state, so that private capital cannot dominate the livelihood of the people: this is the main principle of the regulation of capital.

In the present stage, we fully agree with these views of Dr. Sun's on economic questions.

Some people suspect that the Chinese Communists are opposed to the development of individual initiative, the growth of private capital and the protection of private property, but they are mistaken. It is foreign oppression and feudal oppression that cruelly fetter the development of the individual initiative of the Chinese people, hamper the growth of private capital and destroy the property of the people. It is the very task of the New Democracy we advocate to remove these fetters and stop this destruction, to guarantee that the people can freely develop their individuality within the framework of society and freely develop such private capitalist economy as will benefit and not "dominate the livelihood of the people", and to protect all appropriate forms of private property.

In accordance with Dr. Sun's principles and the experience of the Chinese revolution, China's national economy at the present stage should be composed of the state sector, the private sector and the co-operative sector. But the state here must certainly not be one "privately owned by the few", but a new-democratic state "shared by all the common people" under the leadership of the proletariat.

The culture of New Democracy should likewise be "shared by all the common people", that is, it should be a national, scientific and mass culture, and must under no circumstances be a culture "privately owned by the few".

Such is the general or fundamental programme which we Communists advocate for the present stage, the entire stage of the bourgeois-democratic revolution. This is our minimum programme as against our future or maximum programme of socialism and communism. Its realization will carry the Chinese state and Chinese society a step forward, from a colonial, semi-colonial and semi-feudal to a new-democratic state and society.

Our Specific Programme. Our Party must also have a specific programme for each period based on this general programme. Our general programme of New Democracy will remain unchanged throughout the stage of the bourgeois-democratic revolution, that is, for several decades. But from phase to phase during this stage, conditions have changed or are changing and it is only natural that we have to change our specific programme accordingly. For example, our general programme of New Democracy has remained the same throughout the periods of the Northern Expedition, the Agrarian Revolutionary War and the War of Resistance Against Japan, but there have been changes in our specific programme, because our friends and enemies have not remained the same in the three periods.

The Chinese people now find themselves in the following situation:

> (1) the Japanese aggressors have not yet been defeated;
> (2) the Chinese people urgently need to work together for a democratic change in order to achieve national unity, rapidly mobilize and unite all anti-Japanese forces, and defeat the Japanese aggressors in co-operation with the allies; and
> (3) the Kuomintang government is disrupting national unity and obstructing such a democratic change.

What is our specific programme in the circumstances or, in other words, what are the immediate demands of the people?

We consider the following to be appropriate and minimum demands:

> Mobilize all available forces for the thorough defeat of the Japanese aggressors and the establishment of international peace in co-operation with the allies;
>
> Abolish the Kuomintang one-party dictatorship and establish a democratic coalition government and a joint supreme command;
>
> Punish the pro-Japanese elements, fascists and defeatists who are opposing the people and disrupting national unity, and so help to build national unity;
>
> Punish the reactionaries who are creating the danger of civil war, and so help to ensure internal peace;
>
> Punish the traitors, take punitive action against officers who surrender to the enemy, and punish the agents of the Japanese;
>
> Liquidate the reactionary secret service and all its repressive activities and abolish the concentration camps;
>
> Revoke all reactionary laws and decrees aimed at suppressing the people's freedom of speech, press, assembly, association, political conviction and religious belief and freedom of the person, and guarantee full civil rights to the people;
>
> Recognize the legal status of all democratic parties and groups;
>
> Release all patriotic political prisoners;
>
> Withdraw all troops encircling and attacking China's Liberated Areas and dispatch them to the anti-Japanese front;
>
> Recognize the anti-Japanese armed forces and popularly elected governments of China's Liberated Areas;
>
> Consolidate and expand the Liberated Areas and their armed forces, and recover all lost territory;
>
> Help the people in the Japanese-occupied areas to organize underground armed forces for armed uprisings;
>
> Allow the Chinese people to arm themselves and defend their homes and their country;
>
> Bring about the political and military transformation of those armies directly under the Kuomintang supreme command, which con-

stantly lose battles, oppress the people and discriminate against armies not directly under it, and punish the commanders who are responsible for disastrous defeats;

Improve the recruiting system and the living conditions of the officers and men;

Give preferential treatment to the families of the soldiers fighting in the anti-Japanese war, so that the officers and men at the front are free from domestic worries;

Provide preferential treatment for disabled soldiers and for the families of the soldiers who give their lives for the country, and help demobilized soldiers to settle down and earn a living;

Develop war industries to facilitate the prosecution of the war;

Distribute the military and financial aid received from the allies impartially to all the armies fighting in the War of Resistance;

Punish corrupt officials and institute clean government;

Improve the pay of the middle and lower grade government employees;

Give the Chinese people democratic rights;

Abolish the oppressive *pao-chia* system;

Provide the war refugees and the victims of natural disasters with relief;

Appropriate substantial funds after the recovery of China's lost territory for the extensive relief of people who have suffered under enemy occupation;

Abolish exorbitant taxes and miscellaneous levies and establish a consolidated progressive tax;

Introduce rural reforms, reduce rent and interest, provide suitable safeguards for the rights of tenants, grant low-interest loans to impoverished peasants and help the peasants to organize, in order to facilitate the expansion of agricultural production;

Outlaw bureaucrat-capital;

Abolish the present policy of economic controls;

Check the unbridled inflation and rocketing prices;

Assist private industry and provide it with facilities for obtaining loans, purchasing raw materials and marketing its products;

Improve the livelihood of the workers, provide relief for the unemployed and help the workers to organize, in order to facilitate the expansion of industrial production;

Abolish Kuomintang indoctrination in education and promote a national, scientific and mass culture and education;

Guarantee the livelihood of the teachers and other staff members of educational institutions and guarantee academic freedom;

Protect the interests of the youth, women and children—provide assistance to young student refugees, help the youth and women to organize in order to participate on an equal footing in all work useful to the war effort and to social progress, ensure freedom of marriage and equality as between men and women, and give young people and children a useful education;

Give the minority nationalities in China better treatment and grant them autonomous rights;

Protect the interests of the overseas Chinese and assist those who have returned to the motherland;

Protect foreign nationals who have fled to China from the Japanese oppression and support their struggle against the Japanese aggressors;

Improve Sino-Soviet relations.

To achieve these demands, the most important thing is the immediate abolition of the Kuomintang one-party dictatorship and the establishment of a democratic provisional central government, a coalition government enjoying nation-wide support and including representatives of all the anti-Japanese parties and people without party affiliation. Without this prerequisite it is impossible to make any genuine change in the Kuomintang areas, and therefore in the country as a whole.

These demands voice the desires of the Chinese masses and also of broad sections of democratic public opinion in the allied countries.

A minimum specific programme which is agreed upon by all the anti-Japanese democratic parties is absolutely indispensable, and we are prepared to consult with them on the basis of the programme outlined above. Different parties may have different demands, but all should reach agreement on a common programme.

As far as the Kuomintang areas are concerned, such a programme is still at the stage of being a demand of the people; as far as the Japanese-occupied areas are concerned, it is a programme whose fulfilment must await their recovery, except for the item on the organization of underground forces for armed uprisings; as far as the Liberated Areas are concerned, it is a programme which has already been, is being and should continue to be, put into practice.

17. Liu Shao-chi: On the Party
(May, 1945)*

At the Seventh National Congress of the Chinese Communist Party, Liu Shao-chi, as a member of the Secretariat of the Central Committee of the Party, made a report on the revision of the Party Constitution. This report, entitled "On the Party," reflects a number of trends as provided in

* From book so titled, Peking: Foreign Language Press, 1954, pp. 88–107.

the Constitution of 1945. Liu laid special stress on the theory of "democratic centralism" as the basic principle of governing Party organization, and on the mass line as the basic political and organizational line of the Party. The Chinese Communist Party, after all, is a membership organization which selectively recruits potential cadres who must abide by rigid standards of initiative and indoctrination, which guarantee that the Party will always rid itself of the wrong attitude and views of doctrinairism and empiricism. The General Program of the Party Constitution states that the Chinese Communist Party "guides its entire work by the teachings which unite the theories of Marxism-Leninism with the actual practice of the Chinese revolution— Mao Tse-tung's theory of the Chinese revolution—and fights against any dogmatist or empiricist deviations." However, during the 1966–1967 Cultural Revolution, the Chinese Communist Party under Chairman Mao Tse-tung had to rely upon the Red Guards to get rid of the "wrong attitudes."

DEMOCRATIC CENTRALISM WITHIN THE PARTY

Our Party is not simply the aggregate of its membership. It is a unified organic body established according to a definite principle. It is a combination of leaders and rank and file. It is an integration of the Party headquarters (the Central Committee), the Party organizations at all levels, and the broad membership constituted according to a definite principle of inner-Party democratic centralism.

Three Party members in a factory or village do not necessarily constitute a Party organization. They must be organized according to the principle of democratic centralism. Under ordinary conditions, one of the three should be the group leader and the other two the members of the group, so that in all activities there will be a leader and two followers. Only then can this group become a Party organization. This type of organization generates new strength. The strength of the proletariat lies in organization.

As laid down in the Party Constitution, democratic centralism means centralism on the basis of democracy and democracy under centralized leadership. It is both democratic and centralized. It reflects the relationship between the leadership and the followers, between higher and lower Party organizations, between individual Party members and the Party as a whole, and between the Party's Central Committee and Party organizations at all levels on the one hand and the rank-and-file Party members on the other.

What does it mean when we say that Party centralism is centralism based on democracy? It means that the leading bodies of the Party are elected by the membership on a democratic basis and enjoy their confidence. It means that the rank and file, or its representatives, decide on the resolutions and policies of the Party, which are centralized from the rank and file on a democratic basis, and are then persistently maintained and carried out by the leadership in conjunction with the rank and file. The authority of a leading body of the Party is given by the Party membership. Therefore, the leading body is empowered, on behalf of the membership, to give centralized leadership in the management of all Party affairs and to command obedience from the lower organizations and the Party membership. Order within the Party is built on the principle of the subordination of the individual to the organization, the subordination of the minority to the majority, the subordination of lower organizations to higher organizations, and the subordination of all the constituent Party organizations to the Central Committee. This means that the Party's centralism is based on, instead of separated from, democracy. It is not individual autocracy.

Why do we say that the Party's democracy is democracy under centralized leadership? It means that every Party meeting must be convened by a leading body and carried through under proper leadership. The adoption of every resolution or ruling is preceded by thorough preparation and careful deliberation. Every election has a carefully prepared list of nominees. The Party as a whole has a unified Party Constitution and unified discipline which all Party members must observe, and a unified leading body which must be obeyed by the entire membership. This means that inner-Party democracy is neither democracy without leadership, ultrademocracy, nor anarchy within the Party.

Democratic centralism within the Party is a system which unites the leadership of the Party with the broad rank and file of the Party membership. In other words, it is a process of synthesis of the opinions of the rank and file by the leading body and the carrying out of such synthesized opinions among the rank and file. It is the expression of the mass line within the Party.

Some comrades do not understand that the centralism of the Party is based on democracy. Consequently, they separate their leadership from inner-Party democracy, and from the rank and file of the Party membership, and call this "centralism." They think that their authority as leaders needs no mandate from the Party membership but can be arrogated by them. They think their leading positions require neither election nor the confidence of the Party membership and the lower Party organizations but can be assumed by themselves. They think that their policies and resolutions need not be centralized from the rank and file on a democratic basis and then decided by them but can be issued arbitrarily. They stand above the rank and file of the Party membership, instead of joining with the rank and file. They command and control the Party, lording it over the Party organizations, instead of acting within the organization of the Party and obeying and submitting to the control of the Party. They want to act independently of the upper Party organizations in the name of inner-Party democracy, but they suppress the democratic rights of the Party membership and lower Party organizations in the name of inner-Party centralism. In fact, they observe neither democracy towards their subordinates nor centralism towards their superiors.

While others must obey and observe majority decisions and Party discipline, they, as leaders, feel entitled to do otherwise. They observe none of such basic organizational principles as the subordination by the individual to the organization, the subordination of the minority to the majority, and the subordination of lower Party organizations to higher Party organizations. Party rules and resolutions, in their opinion, are written for ordinary Party members but not for those who are leaders. This is an anti-democratic, autocratic tendency in the Party and a reflection of the ideology of the privileged classes in society. It has nothing in common with our Party's centralism. It is a deviation which does however exist within our Party and should therefore be completely wiped out.

There are other comrades who do not understand that democracy inside the Party is democracy under centralized leadership. They therefore divorce their actions from the

Party's centralized leadership and from the Party as a whole. They pay no attention to the overall situation or to the long-range interests of the Party as a whole. They act freely and without restraint within the Party, guided solely by their own interests and views. They neither abide by Party discipline nor carry out the decisions of the Party's leading bodies. They indulge in all kinds of non-organizational, non-political, and unprincipled utterances and actions. They either deliberately resort to exaggeration in order to spread dissension within the Party or engage in endless gossip or wrangling, never taking the trouble to see whether or not there is a critical situation or an emergency. They even take advantage of some temporary lack of understanding among the Party membership, due to insufficient consideration of their proposals, to take the vote on their own proposals and fulfil their own designs in the name of "the majority."

This represents the idea of ultra-democracy which has nothing in common with our Party's democracy. The danger of such an idea, as Comrade Mao Tse-tung has pointed out, "lies in the tendency to damage and even completely destroy the Party organization, to weaken and even completely destroy the Party's fighting capacity."

The root of this idea "lies in the nature of the petty bourgeoisie which is easy-going and averse to discipline. Such a characteristic, having found its way into the Party, manifests itself politically and organizationally as the idea of ultra-democracy. This idea is basically incompatible with the fighting tasks of the proletariat." (Mao Tse-tung: *On the Rectification of Incorrect Ideas in the Party*.)

The tendency to anti-democratic absolutism and the presence of ultra-democracy inside the Party are two extremes of inner-Party life; yet the latter often appears as a kind of retaliation against the former. Thus wherever there is a serious tendency to absolutism, there ultra-democracy may arise. Both are wrong tendencies detrimental to and destructive of genuine Party unity and solidarity. The sharp vigilance of the whole Party is required to guard against their occurrence.

Now we must fully develop the democratic way of life in our Party and bring about a high degree of inner-Party democracy. At the same time a high degree of centralism in Party leadership must also be achieved on the basis of this highly developed democracy.

In his report to the Sixth Plenum of the Central Committee elected by the Sixth Party Congress, Comrade Mao Tsetung said:

> "The patriarchal system born of small-scale production is predominant in our country, and there is so far scarcely any democratic life on a nation-wide scale. This state of affairs, when reflected in our Party, accounts for an inadequacy of democratic life. It impedes the full development of the activity of the whole Party. Meanwhile it contributes to insufficient democracy in the mass movement and the united front."

The situation has changed since the Sixth Plenum. Considerable progress has been made both in the democratic movement in China's liberated areas and in inner-Party democracy, especially through the Rectification of Three Styles and the review of Party work. A free and penetrating examination of Party history and the Party line by the cadres prior to the Seventh Party Congress contributed to a substantial development of inner-Party democracy and ensured adequate preparations for the Congress. However, whether we view the Party as a whole or take the local Party organizations separately, it must be said that democratic life within the Party is still insufficient and needs to be developed further. This is why many provisions for the extension of inner-Party democracy are included in the Party Constitution.

Our Party is still waging a war and it must be stressed that this war is of a protracted nature. Until there are changes in our technical conditions and in the situation of our enemy, this war remains basically a kind of guerilla warfare. Therefore, meetings and elections must be held in so far as conditions of guerilla warfare permit. There should be no unwarranted curtailment of inner-Party democracy on the pretext of the war situation.

In the liberated areas, whenever large meetings and elections can be held, Party congresses at all levels and membership meetings must be called according to the provisions of the Constitution in order to elect the Party's leading bodies at all levels.

It is provided in the Party Constitution that in electing a leading body of the Party, not only does the presidium of the Congress have the right to submit a list of candidates, but every delegation and every delegate must be assured of the right to nominate candidates and every elector must have the right to criticize any candidate or candidates or propose alternative ones. The candidate list must be fully discussed. Voting must be carried out on the basis of the list either by secret ballot or by open vote.

It is provided in the Party Constitution that congresses of lower Party organizations shall be convened once in every two years. This means that there must be a new election of the leading bodies of the lower Party organizations once in every two years. Between congresses, the convocation of conferences to deliberate and decide on immediate tasks is necessary and possible. In the past we have held various kinds of cadres' meetings to review and decide on our work, but in future this work should be carried out by conferences and congresses. Elections should be held only once in every two years, as too many elections are unnecessary and will handicap our work. Therefore, in addition to Party congresses, Party conferences are needed to review and plan our work. Such conferences may be held once or twice a year according to local needs, with representatives selected by lower Party committees. Such conferences have the power to remove members of a Party committee and to replace them by by-election, but the removal or replacement of Party committee members must be approved by the Party committee in question. This is because such a conference, although its power is greater than that of the cadres' meetings of the past, remains a lower organ than the Party committee.

Provincial or border area, region, county or sub-district Party congresses and conferences may be held in rotation. For instance, this year the province, border region and county may hold congresses while the region and the sub-district hold conferences. Next year the region and the sub-district may hold congresses while the province, border region and county hold conferences.

The Party committees at various levels should be broadened so as to include people in charge of various lines of work and cadres who maintain good connections with the masses of the people. According to the Constitution, a standing committee should be organized within each Party committee to take charge of the day to day work. The standing committee should also include cadres in charge of various lines of work so that it may become a regular leading nucleus of the various lines of work in its territory. A leading Party committee may, when necessary, avail itself of one or two assistant secretaries to help the secretary, so that all

Party work may be taken care of without hitch. No committee at any level should confine its activities to inner-Party organizational work; each should strive to become a body directing all the activities in its territory. Inner-Party organizational work is only part of the work of a Party committee and it should be specially assigned to the committee's organizational department. Therefore, every Party committee's decisions and plans of work, if they are of a general character, should be discussed and decided upon by meetings of the entire committee. After decisions have been reached collectively, assignment of individuals should be made to put these decisions into effect.

A crucial factor in broadening inner-Party democracy lies in the fostering of criticism and self-criticism among Party members and cadres. Comrade Mao Tse-tung stresses self-criticism in his report, pointing out that serious self-criticism is an outstanding feature which distinguishes us from other political parties. We must develop a positive sense of responsibility among our Party members and cadres in regard to Party policy and Party work, thus enabling them to use their reasoning power, raise problems boldly and properly and express their views. Those in charge of the leading bodies of the Party at all levels must be the first to practise thoroughgoing self-criticism on the defects and errors in the work carried out under their leadership. They must set an example to the Party membership and the cadres and be fully prepared in their minds to accept criticism from others, without becoming resentful or insolent when so confronted, or resorting to repression or punishment of their critics. Only in this way can the development of inner-Party democracy be encouraged. Otherwise, Party congresses and conferences, even if held regularly, may just be lifeless, undemocratic gatherings filled with dull and repetitious speeches, while listening to reports and voting may be nothing but pure routine.

Many of our comrades, including some in responsible positions, still do not know how to conduct a meeting or make it successful. Thus many meetings have ended in failure or produced poor results. Sometimes meetings become a serious burden on the Party membership and the masses. It is obvious that the holding of too many meetings does not in itself constitute democracy. Meetings must be well conducted, and be permeated with a spirit of democracy, criticism, and self-criticism. In this connection we must observe Comrade

Mao Tse-tung's directives on "How to Make Party Members Interested in Attending Meetings," embodied in the *Resolution of the Kutien Conference.*

Experience proves that wherever a comrade in a responsible position seriously practises sincere and necessary self-criticism before the Party membership and the masses, the people and the Party membership there will develop their criticism and self-criticism and their activity will be heightened, their internal solidarity will develop, their work will improve and their defects will be overcome; while the prestige of the responsible comrade will increase instead of being undermined. There is a great deal of evidence both in the Party and among the masses, to prove this. On the other hand, wherever a responsible comrade lacks the spirit of self-criticism, refuses or fears to criticize or reveal his own defects or mistakes, or tries to cover them up; when he expresses no gratitude for criticism and, instead of being pleased to be told of his faults blushes to the ears and makes acrimonious retorts or looks for a chance to revenge himself on his critics, the result is just the opposite. Democracy and self-criticism among the Party members and the people will not develop, their activity will not be heightened, their internal solidarity will not be achieved, the defects will not be overcome and the work will not improve; furthermore, the prestige of that comrade will vanish. Therefore, the responsible personnel of all local Party organizations have a tremendous responsibility for the promotion and broadening of democracy within the Party.

The Party Constitution provides that the leading bodies and responsible personnel of the Party organizations at all levels should submit reports on their work at stated intervals to the Party members and lower Party organizations which have elected them. In any such report, not only the current situation and the accomplishments but also the defects, weaknesses, and mistakes in the work should be discussed, with a request that the electors and lower Party organizations should give their opinions and comments. Experience shows that the responsibility for errors and shortcomings in the work of many lower Party organizations or cadres does not always rest with them but with the higher leading bodies. Many such errors and shortcomings are due to the failure of the higher leading bodies to assign the tasks and clarify the policy at the right moment, or, if they have defined the tasks and clarified the policy, to a failure to tackle the pertinent problems systematically and thoroughly. Sometimes mistakes are due to errors in the tasks and policies defined by the higher leading bodies. When this happens, it is not right to "pass the buck" and lay too much of the blame on the lower Party organizations, on the membership or on the cadres, for this will undoubtedly undermine their confidence and activity. Of course, the lower Party committees, the Party members and the cadres must show a similar spirit of self-criticism towards their own defects and mistakes.

The essential aim of inner-Party democracy is to allow full rein to the initiative and activity of the Party members, raise their sense of responsibility towards the cause of the Party and encourage them or their representatives to express their opinions fully, within the scope of the Party Constitution. In this way they can take an active part in the Party's work of leading the people and the unity and discipline of the Party will be strengthened. Only through a genuine extension of inner-Party democracy can voluntary Party discipline be strengthened, inner-Party centralism established and consolidated and correct leadership given by the leading bodies. Therefore the Party Constitution provides that the leading bodies of the Party at all levels shall carry on their work in accordance with the principle of inner-Party democracy.

To allow the practice of a high degree of democracy within the Party is not intended to weaken inner-Party centralism in any way. On the contrary, a high degree of democracy goes hand in hand with a high degree of centralism. A high degree of democracy and a high degree of centralism should be combined and should not be counterposed. Only through the practice of a high degree of democracy can a high degree of centralism of leadership be attained, and only under a high degree of centralism of leadership based on democracy can a high degree of democracy prevail. It is wrong to assert that centralized leadership will be weakened by practising a high degree of democracy. Thus, the Constitution provides that when a leading body at any level carries on its work in accordance with the principle of inner-Party democracy, it should not hamper inner-Party centralism or distort inner-Party democracy, which is proper and beneficial to centralized action, into anarchistic tendencies—acts of autonomism and ultra-democracy.

Inner-Party democracy must be encouraged to proceed along lines beneficial to the cause of the Party, that is, the cause of the people, and it should neither weaken the fighting will and fighting solidarity of the Party nor become a tool for saboteurs, anti-Party elements, splitters, opportunists and adventurists. Thus the Constitution provides that a thorough review of and debate on the policy and line of the whole Party or of a lower Party organization may be undertaken only under proper leadership, and when conditions permit. In other words, it must not be carried out in a state of emergency but must be properly decided by the central organs of the Party or by lower bodies as the case may be, or must be demanded by a majority of the lower organizations or a higher organization.

Inner-Party democracy must be broadened, but Party decisions must be carried out unconditionally. The subordination of the Party membership to the Party organization, of lower Party organizations to higher Party organizations, of the minority to the majority and the constituent organizations of the Party to the Central Committee—these principles as laid down in the Constitution must be observed unconditionally.

Some comrades make the carrying out of these principles contingent on such matters as their own acceptance of the correctness of the resolutions or instructions; or the ability, position, length of Party membership and cultural level of their superior, whether he has treated them well or badly, or whether he belongs to the same group. It must be clearly stated that no conditions such as these apply. A Communist best expresses his spirit of discipline precisely when he is in danger or when there are serious differences between him and the Party over matters of principle or personal matters. It is only when he unconditionally carries out organizational principles even when he is in a minority that he can be considered a highly disciplined and principled Party member who is mindful of the whole situation and understands the subordination of partial interests to those of the whole, the subordination of a small truth to a big truth and the need to submit differences over secondary principles and personal matters to the supreme principle of Party unity and Party discipline.

In no circumstance should we Communists encourage blind obedience. Since we are now in the midst of guerilla warfare, conducted over dispersed rural districts, whose internal and external conditions differ widely from each other, in carrying on our work we should pursue a policy of "decentralized operations under centralized leadership." Over-centralized operations and equalitarianism are both erroneous. But, decentralized operations do not mean autonomism. They mean independent actions and the ability to do independent work. They must not be separated from centralized leadership, indeed, they must have centralized leadership.

Conditions being what they are, it often happens that the decisions and instructions of a leading body do not cover every situation in every place, but are only of a general character. Consequently, while they are applicable to ordinary areas, they do not suit certain special areas. It also often happens that they contain mistakes and are impracticable. In such conditions, we should not advocate blind performance or obedience. Instead, we should encourage intelligent and sincere action. This means that a serious study of both the circumstances and the decisions and instructions is necessary. When the latter are found to contain mistakes or to be at variance with the local situation, one should have the courage to bring them to the attention of a higher body with a request for their withdrawal or amendment, instead of trying to enforce them blindly and obstinately, which leads to waste of the people's time and money and isolates us from the masses. In so doing the lower Party organizations are by no means being insubordinate. Nor are they committing autonomism, but they are sincerely carrying out the decisions and instructions. The outstanding Party members are those who are capable not merely of independent deliberation but also of helping to correct the errors and defects of a higher body. They should be especially encouraged.

In carrying out the decisions and instructions of the higher bodies, there may be three kinds of approach. The first is to carry out only those decisions and instructions which suit one's taste and disregard others which do not. This is autonomism pure and simple and is impermissible, whatever may be the pretext. The second is blind, mechanical fulfilment of decisions, without taking the trouble to examine whether or not the particular decisions and instructions are applicable, or to study the existing circumstances. This is a blind rather than a serious carrying out of decisions and instructions of a higher body and is consequently also impermissible. The third is to study the decisions and instructions on the one hand and the circumstances on the other, to resolutely carry out what is practicable, and to report what is impracticable to the higher body, giving detailed reasons and requesting amendments. This is an intelligent and sincere manner of carrying out decisions and instructions and it is the only correct approach. We not only do not oppose, but should by all means encourage, this kind of creative power and activity on the part of a Communist. The Party opposes disregard for discipline and the practice of autonomism, but advocates and encourages initiative on the part of every Party member in tackling problems and in doing his work independently under the general direction of the Party.

A leading body should allow its lower organizations and membership to set forth their suggestions and questions and to propose revisions to its decisions and instructions, which, when found really to contain mistakes or defects, should be corrected accordingly. If the lower ranks are wrong, satisfactory explanation should be given to straighten out their ideas, while the wrong practice of taking harsh measures against them should be definitely avoided. If the higher body insists on the execution of a decision or instruction, despite appeal for revision, then it should be carried out, and the lower ranks should cease persisting in their own stand or resisting the decision.

The discipline of the Communist Party is based on voluntary subordination. It should not be mechanical nor should it restrict the activity and initiative of the membership. There should be a combination of the membership's discipline and initiative.

The Party Constitution provides that a Party organization at any level shall ensure that publications under its guidance popularize the decisions and policy of its higher organizations and of the central bodies. This is necessitated by the Party's unity and its national character. The decisions and policy of the Central Committee and other higher Party organizations should be disseminated everywhere, and no ideas contrary to these should be publicized. The ideology of Marxism should be disseminated while ideologies contrary to it should not. This is not being satisfactorily carried out by some of our lower Party organizations. Some papers do not give sufficient publicity to the decisions and policy of the Central Committee, and it even happens that they carry articles at variance with the decisions and policy of the Central Committee.

Therefore, Party organizations at all levels must check up on this and correct such practices.

With regard to issues which are of a national character the Party Constitution provides that prior to a statement or decision by the Central Committee no lower Party organizations or their responsible personnel shall take the liberty of making their views public or issuing decisions on such issues, although they may hold discussions among themselves and raise their proposals to the Central Committee. This, too, is essential to the Party's unity and its national character. The Party as a whole can have only one orientation or line, not several. It can adopt only one attitude or take one viewpoint on a national issue, not several. Lower Party organizations should not exceed their powers by publicly issuing their views in place of or prior to the Central Committee on issues which should and must be decided upon and made public by the Central Committee. No responsible Party leader, including members of the Central Committee, should publicize their views on national issues without the Central Committee's approval. They may discuss their views at the meetings of lower Party committees and make suggestions to the Central Committee. But it is impermissible for them to make public, either inside or outside the Party, views not yet made known by the Central Committee or to circulate and disseminate these views among other lower Party committees. The reason is that should such views or decisions conflict with those of the Central Committee it would leave a very bad impression in the Party and among the people, or before our enemy. We did not stress this point when we had only very limited wireless facilities. But now when such facilities are ample this point must be emphasized. The Central Committee has called attention to this point a number of times during the War of Resistance to Japanese Aggression.

As to local questions, the Constitution authorizes lower Party organizations to make independent decisions, provided these decisions do not conflict with the decisions of the Central Committee and other higher organizations. In this connection, undue interference or making of decisions for the lower Party organizations on the part of a higher body should also be avoided. While it is necessary for a higher body to make suggestions to a lower organization in order to help it reach correct decisions, the power of decision must rest with the latter.

At present our Party is still underground in many areas. A Party organization in such circumstances must adopt special forms to carry out its work. Hence the Constitution provides that open organizational forms and methods of work of the Party which are unsuitable for a Party organization operating in secret may be modified. This provision is necessary. Organizational principles provided in the Constitution must be carried out by the whole Party, but the organizational forms and methods of work of the Party should be modified according to the changing circumstances and conditions. This is a point which has already been dealt with.

18. *Mao Tse-tung: On People's Democratic Dictatorship (July, 1949)**

This essay was written to commemorate the twenty-eighth anniversary of the Communist Party on July 1, 1949, on the eve of the complete conquest of power on the mainland. In the main it reinstates ideas Mao had set forth in his famous text "On New Democracy" (Selection 12), affirming that the new government would be a dictatorship of the "people," which Mao defined as being made up of the four classes: the proletariat, the peasantry, the petty bourgeoisie and the national bourgeoisie. During this period state power would be vested in a coalition of the four classes under the leadership of the working class, by which was meant, of course, the Communist Party, with the purpose of wiping out feudal vestiges and imperialism.

Amplifying his earlier formula, Mao now defined "the people's democratic dictatorship" as "democracy for the people and dictatorship over the reactionaries." He made a sharp distinction between the "people" (those who accept Communist leadership) and the "national," including among the latter all "reactionaries" (those who do not). Mao stressed that only the "people" were to have the rights to vote and to voice their opinions while "reactionaries" were to be suppressed.

---

* From *Selected Works of Mao Tse-tung*, Peking: Foreign Language Press, 1965, IV, 411–423. (Footnotes omitted.)

Thus we see that the New Democracy was designed primarily to support the Communist demand for a "coalition government," made during the war years (1937–1945). Now, however, with all final powers within the grasp of the Party, Mao considered a single, uniform policy to be indispensable, and thereby used the concept of the "people's dictatorship" to justify the dictatorial character of the People's Government, established on October 1, 1949.

These views of Mao, which represent the crystallization of Communist political philosophy, were incorporated into the Common Program of the Chinese People's Political Consultative Conference, convened by the Communist Party on September 21, 1949, in Peking immediately after their conquest of the country.

The first of July 1949 marks the fact that the Communist Party of China has already lived through twenty-eight years. Like a man, a political party has its childhood, youth, manhood and old age. The Communist Party of China is no longer a child or a lad in his teens but has become an adult. When a man reaches old age, he will die; the same is true of a party. When classes disappear, all instruments of class struggle —parties and the state machinery—will lose their function, cease to be necessary, therefore gradually wither away and end their historical mission; and human society will move to a higher stage. We are the opposite of the political parties of the bourgeoisie. They are afraid to speak of the extinction of classes, state power and parties. We, on the contrary, declare openly that we are striving hard to create the very conditions which will bring about their extinction. The leadership of the Communist Party and the state power of the people's dictatorship are such conditions. Anyone who does not recognize this truth is no communist. Young comrades who have not studied Marxism-Leninism and have only recently joined the Party may not yet understand this truth. They must understand it— only then can they have a correct world outlook. They must understand that the road to the abolition of classes, to the abolition of state power and to the abolition of parties is the road all mankind must take; it is only a question of time and conditions. Communists the world over are wiser than the bourgeoisie, they understand the laws governing the existence and development of things, they understand dialectics and they can see farther. The bourgeoisie does not welcome this truth because it does not want to be overthrown. To be overthrown is painful and is unbearable to contemplate for those overthrown, for example, for the Kuomintang reactionaries whom we are now overthrowing and for Japanese imperialism which we together with other peoples overthrew some time ago. But for the working class, the labouring people and the Communist Party the question is not one of being overthrown, but of working hard to create the conditions in which classes, state power and political parties will die out very naturally and mankind will enter the realm of Great Harmony. We have mentioned in passing the long-range perspective of human progress in order to explain clearly the problems we are about to discuss.

As everyone knows, our Party passed through these twenty-eight years not in peace but amid hardships, for we had to fight enemies, both foreign and domestic, both inside and outside the Party. We thank Marx, Engels, Lenin and Stalin for giving us a weapon. This weapon is not a machine-gun, but Marxism-Leninism.

In his book *"Left-Wing" Communism, an Infantile Disorder* written in 1920, Lenin described the quest of the Russians for revolutionary theory. Only after several decades of hardship and suffering did the Russians find Marxism. Many things in China were the same as, or similar to, those in Russia before the October Revolution. There was the same feudal oppression. There was similar economic and cultural backwardness. Both countries were backward, China even more so. In both countries alike, for the sake of national regeneration progressives braved hard and bitter struggles in their quest for revolutionary truth.

From the time of China's defeat in the Opium War of 1840, Chinese progressives went through untold hardships in their quest for truth from the Western countries. Hung Hsiu-chuan, Kang Yu-wei, Yen Fu and Sun Yat-sen were representative of those who had looked to the West for truth before the Communist Party of China was born. Chinese who then sought progress would read any book containing the new knowledge from the West. The number of students sent to Japan, Britain, the United States, France and Germany was amazing. At home, the imperial examinations were abolished and modern schools sprang up like bamboo shoots after a spring rain; every effort was made to learn from the West. In my youth, I too engaged in such studies. They represented the culture of Western bourgeois democracy, including the social theories and natural sciences of that period, and they were called "the new learning" in contrast to Chinese feudal culture, which was called "the old learning". For quite a long time, those who had acquired the new learning felt confident that it would save China, and very few of them had any doubts on this score, as the adherents of the old learning had. Only modernization could save China, only learning from foreign countries could modernize China. Among the foreign countries, only the Western capitalist countries were then progressive, as they had successfully built modern bourgeois states. The Japanese had been successful in learning from the West, and the Chinese also wished to learn from the Japanese. The Chinese in those days regarded Russia as backward, and few wanted to learn from her. That was how the Chinese tried to learn from foreign countries in the period from the 1840s to the beginning of the 20th century.

Imperialist aggression shattered the fond dreams of the Chinese about learning from the West. It was very odd—why were the teachers always committing aggression against their pupil? The Chinese learned a good deal from the West, but they could not make it work and were never able to realize their ideals. Their repeated struggles, including such a country-wide movement as the Revolution of 1911, all ended in failure. Day by day, conditions in the country got worse, and life was made impossible. Doubts arose, increased and deepened. World War I shook the whole globe. The Russians made the October Revolution and created the world's first socialist state. Under the leadership of Lenin and Stalin, the revolutionary energy of the great proletariat and labouring people of Russia, hitherto latent and unseen by foreigners, suddenly erupted like a volcano, and the Chinese and all mankind began to see the Russians in a new light. Then, and only then, did the Chinese enter an entirely new era in their thinking and their life. They found Marxism-Leninism, the universally applicable truth, and the face of China began to change.

It was through the Russians that the Chinese found Marxism. Before the October Revolution, the Chinese were not only ignorant of Lenin and Stalin, they did not even know of Marx and Engels. The salvoes of the October Revolution brought us Marxism-Leninism. The October Revolution helped progressives in China, as throughout the world, to adopt the proletarian world outlook as the instrument for studying a nation's destiny and considering anew their own problems. Follow the path of the Russians—that was their conclusion. In 1919, the May 4th Movement took place in China. In 1921, the Communist Party of China was founded. Sun Yat-sen, in the depths of despair, came across the October Revolution and the Communist Party of China. He welcomed the October Revolution, welcomed Russian help to the Chinese and welcomed co-operation with the Communist Party of China. Then Sun Yat-sen died and Chiang Kai-shek rose to power. Over a long period of twenty-two years, Chiang Kai-shek dragged China into ever more hopeless straits. In this period, during the anti-fascist Second World War in which the Soviet Union was the main force, three big imperialist powers were knocked out, while two others were weakened. In the whole world only one big imperialist power, the United States of America, remained uninjured. But the United States faced a grave domestic crisis. It wanted to enslave the whole world; it supplied arms to help Chiang Kai-shek slaughter several million Chinese. Under the leadership of the Communist Party of China, the Chinese people, after driving out Japanese imperialism, waged the People's War of Liberation for three years and have basically won victory.

Thus Western bourgeois civilization, bourgeois democracy and the plan for a bourgeois republic have all gone bankrupt in the eyes of the Chinese people. Bourgeois democracy has given way to people's democracy under the leadership of the working class and the bourgeois republic to the people's republic. This has made it possible to achieve socialism and communism through the people's republic, to abolish classes and enter a world of Great Harmony. Kang Yu-wei wrote *Ta Tung Shu*, or the *Book of Great Harmony*, but he did not and could not find the way to achieve Great Harmony. There are bourgeois republics in foreign lands, but China cannot have a bourgeois republic because she is a country suffering under imperialist oppression. The only way is through a people's republic led by the working class.

All other ways have been tried and failed. Of the people who hankered after those ways, some have fallen, some have awakened and some are changing their ideas. Events are developing so swiftly that many feel the abruptness of the change and the need to learn anew. This state of mind is understandable and we welcome this worthy desire to learn anew.

The vanguard of the Chinese proletariat learned Marxism-Leninism after the October Revolution and founded the Communist Party of China. It entered at once into political struggles and only now, after a tortuous course of twenty-eight years, has it won basic victory. From our twenty-eight years' experience we have drawn a conclusion similar to the one Sun Yat-sen drew in his testament from his "experience of forty years"; that is, we are deeply convinced that to win victory, "we must arouse the masses of the people and unite in a common struggle with those nations of the world which treat us as equals". Sun Yat-sen had a world outlook different from ours and started from a different class standpoint in studying and tackling problems; yet, in the 1920s he reached a conclusion basically the same as ours on the question of how to struggle against imperialism.

Twenty-four years have passed since Sun Yat-sen's death, and the Chinese revolution, led by the Communist Party of China, has made tremendous advances both in theory and practice and has radically changed the face of China. Up to now the principal and fundamental experience the Chinese people have gained is twofold:

(1) Internally, arouse the masses of the people. That is, unite the working class, the peasantry, the urban petty bourgeoisie and the national bourgeoisie, form a domestic united front under the leadership of the working class, and advance from this to the establishment of a state which is a people's democratic dictatorship under the leadership of the working class and based on the alliance of workers and peasants.

(2) Externally, unite in a common struggle with those nations of the world which treat us as equals and unite with the peoples of all countries. That is, ally ourselves with the Soviet Union, with the People's Democracies and with the proletariat and the broad masses of the people in all other countries, and form an international united front.

"You are leaning to one side." Exactly. The forty years' experience of Sun Yat-sen and the twenty-eight years' experience of the Communist Party have taught us to lean to one side, and we are firmly convinced that in order to win victory and consolidate it we must lean to one side. In the light of the experiences accumulated in these forty years and these twenty-eight years, all Chinese without exception must lean either to the side of imperialism or to the side of socialism. Sitting on the fence will not do, nor is there a third road. We oppose the Chiang Kai-shek reactionaries who lean to the side of imperialism, and we also oppose the illusions about a third road.

"You are too irritating." We are talking about how to deal with domestic and foreign reactionaries, the imperialists and their running dogs, not about how to deal with anyone else. With regard to such reactionaries, the question of irritating them or not does not arise. Irritated or not irritated, they will remain the same because they are reactionaries. Only if we draw a clear line between reactionaries and revolutionaries, expose the intrigues and plots of the reactionaries, arouse the vigilance and attention of the revolutionary ranks, heighten our will to fight and crush the enemy's arrogance can we isolate the reactionaries, vanquish them or supersede them. We must not show the slightest timidity before a wild beast. We must learn from Wu Sung on the Chingyang Ridge. As Wu Sung saw it, the tiger on Chingyang Ridge was a man-eater, whether irritated or not. Either kill the tiger or be eaten by him—one or the other.

"We want to do business." Quite right, business will be done. We are against no one except the domestic and foreign reactionaries who hinder us from doing business. Everybody should know that it is none other than the imperialists and their running dogs, the Chiang Kai-shek reactionaries, who hinder us from doing business and also from establishing diplomatic relations with foreign countries. When we have beaten the internal and external reactionaries by uniting all domestic and international forces, we shall be able to do business and establish diplomatic relations with all foreign countries on the basis of equality, mutual benefit and mutual respect for territorial integrity and sovereignty.

"Victory is possible even without international help." This is a mistaken idea. In the epoch in which imperialism exists, it is impossible for a genuine people's revolution to win victory in any country without various forms of help from the international revolutionary forces, and even if victory were won, it could not be consolidated. This was the case with the victory and consolidation of the great October Revolution, as Lenin and Stalin told us long ago. This was also the case with the overthrow of the three imperialist powers in World War II and the establishment of the People's Democracies. And this is also the case with the present and the future of People's China. Just imagine! If the Soviet Union had not existed, if there had been no victory in the anti-fascist Second World War, if Japanese imperialism had not been defeated, if the People's Democracies had not come into being, if the oppressed nations of the East were not rising in struggle and if there were no struggle of the masses of the people against their reactionary rulers in the United States, Britain, France, Germany, Italy, Japan and other capitalist countries—if not for all these in combination, the international reactionary forces bearing down upon us would certainly be many times greater than now. In such circumstances, could we have won victory? Obviously not. And even with victory, there could be no consolidation. The Chinese people have had more than enough experience of this kind. This experience was reflected long ago in Sun Yat-sen's death-bed statement on the necessity of uniting with the international revolutionary forces.

"We need help from the British and U.S. governments." This, too, is a naive idea in these times. Would the present rulers of Britain and the United States, who are imperialists, help a people's state? Why do these countries do business with us and, supposing they might be willing to lend us money on terms of mutual benefit in the future, why would they do so? Because their capitalists want to make money and their bankers want to earn interest to extricate themselves from their own crisis—it is not a matter of helping the Chinese people. The Communist Parties and progressive groups in these countries are urging their governments to establish trade and even diplomatic relations with us. This is goodwill, this is help, this cannot be mentioned in the same breath with the conduct of the bourgeoisie in the same countries. Throughout his life, Sun Yat-sen appealed countless times to the capitalist countries for help and got nothing but heartless rebuffs. Only once in his whole life did Sun Yat-sen receive foreign help, and that was Soviet help. Let readers refer to Dr. Sun Yat-sen's testament; his earnest advice was not to look for help from the imperialist countries but to "unite with those nations of the world which treat us as equals". Dr. Sun had experience; he had suffered, he had been deceived. We should remember his words and not allow ourselves to be deceived again. Internationally, we belong to the side of the anti-imperialist front headed by the Soviet Union, and so we can turn only to this side for genuine and friendly help, not to the side of the imperialist front.

"You are dictatorial." My dear sirs, you are right, that is just what we are. All the experience the Chinese people have accumulated through several decades teaches us to enforce the people's democratic dictatorship, that is, to deprive the reactionaries of the right to speak and let the people alone have that right.

Who are the people? At the present stage in China, they are the working class, the peasantry, the urban petty bourgeoisie and the national bourgeoisie. These classes, led by the working class and the Communist Party, unite to form their own state and elect their own government; they enforce their dictatorship over the running dogs of imperialism—the landlord class and bureaucrat-bourgeoisie, as well as the representatives of those classes, the Kuomintang reactionaries and their accomplices—suppress them, allow them only to behave themselves and not to be unruly in word or deed. If they speak or act in an unruly way, they will be promptly stopped and punished. Democracy is practised within the ranks of the people, who enjoy the rights of freedom of speech, assembly, association and so on. The right to vote belongs only to the people, not to the reactionaries. The combination of these two aspects, democracy for the people and dictatorship over the reactionaries, is the people's democratic dictatorship.

Why must things be done this way? The reason is quite clear to everybody. If things were not done this way, the revolution would fail, the people would suffer, the country would be conquered.

"Don't you want to abolish state power?" Yes, we do, but not right now; we cannot do it yet. Why? Because imperialism still exists, because domestic reaction still exists, because classes still exist in our country. Our present task is to strengthen the people's state apparatus—mainly the people's army, the people's police and the people's courts—in order to consolidate national defence and protect the people's interests. Given this condition, China can develop steadily, under the leadership of the working class and the Communist Party, from an agricultural into an industrial country and from a new-democratic into a socialist and communist society, can abolish classes and realize the Great Harmony. The state apparatus, including the army, the police and the courts, is the instrument by which one class oppresses another. It is an instrument for the oppression of antagonistic classes; it is violence and not "benevolence". "You are not benevolent!" Quite so. We definitely do not apply a policy of benevolence to the reactionaries and towards the reactionary activities of the reactionary classes. Our policy of benevolence is applied only within the ranks of the people, not beyond them to the reactionaries or to the reactionary activities of reactionary classes.

The people's state protects the people. Only when the people have such a state can they educate and remould themselves on a country-wide scale by democratic methods and, with everyone taking part, shake off the influence of domestic and foreign reactionaries (which is still very strong, will survive for a long time and cannot be quickly destroyed), rid themselves of the bad habits and ideas acquired in the old society, not allow themselves to be led astray by the reactionaries, and continue to advance—to advance towards a socialist and communist society.

Here, the method we employ is democratic, the method of persuasion, not of compulsion. When anyone among the people breaks the law, he too should be punished, imprisoned or even sentenced to death; but this is a matter of a few individual cases, and it differs in principle from the dictatorship exercised over the reactionaries as a class.

As for the members of the reactionary classes and individual reactionaries, so long as they do not rebel, sabotage or create trouble after their political power has been overthrown, land and work will be given to them as well in order to allow them to live and remould themselves through labour into new people. If they are not willing to work, the people's state will compel them to work. Propaganda and educational work will be done among them too and will be done, moreover, with as much care and thoroughness as among the captured army officers in the past. This, too, may be called a "policy of benevolence" if you like, but it is imposed by us on the members of the enemy classes and cannot be mentioned in the same breath with the work of self-education which we carry on within the ranks of the revolutionary people.

Such remoulding of members of the reactionary classes can be accomplished only by a state of the people's democratic dictatorship under the leadership of the Communist Party. When it is well done, China's major exploiting classes, the landlord class and the bureaucrat-bourgeoisie (the monopoly capitalist class), will be eliminated for good. There remain the national bourgeoisie; at the present stage, we can already do a good deal of suitable educational work with many of them. When the time comes to realize socialism, that is, to nationalize private enterprise, we shall carry the work of educating and remoulding them a step further. The people have a powerful state apparatus in their hands—there is no need to fear rebellion by the national bourgeoisie.

The serious problem is the education of the peasantry. The

peasant economy is scattered, and the socialization of agriculture, judging by the Soviet Union's experience, will require a long time and painstaking work. Without socialization of agriculture, there can be no complete, consolidated socialism. The steps to socialize agriculture must be co-ordinated with the development of a powerful industry having state enterprise as its backbone. The state of the people's democratic dictatorship must systematically solve the problems of industrialization. Since it is not proposed to discuss economic problems in detail in this article, I shall not go into them further.

In 1924 a famous manifesto was adopted at the Kuomintang's First National Congress, which Sun Yat-sen himself led and in which Communists participated. The manifesto stated:

> The so-called democratic system in modern states is usually monopolized by the bourgeoisie and has become simply an instrument for oppressing the common people. On the other hand, the Kuomintang's Principle of Democracy means a democratic system shared by all the common people and not privately owned by the few.

Apart from the question of who leads whom, the Principle of Democracy stated above corresponds as a general political programme to what we call People's Democracy or New Democracy. A state system which is shared only by the common people and which the bourgeoisie is not allowed to own privately—add to this the leadership of the working class, and we have the state system of the people's democratic dictatorship.

Chiang Kai-shek betrayed Sun Yat-sen and used the dictatorship of the bureaucrat-bourgeoisie and the landlord class as an instrument for oppressing the common people of China. This counter-revolutionary dictatorship was enforced for twenty-two years and has only now been overthrown by the common people of China under our leadership.

The foreign reactionaries who accuse us of practising "dictatorship" or "totalitarianism" are the very persons who practise it. They practise the dictatorship or totalitarianism of one class, the bourgeoisie, over the proletariat and the rest of the people. They are the very persons Sun Yat-sen spoke of as the bourgeoisie of modern states who oppress the common people. And it is from these reactionary scoundrels that Chiang Kai-shek learned his counter-revolutionary dictatorship.

Chu Hsi, a philosopher of the Sung Dynasty, wrote many

books and made many remarks which are now forgotten, but one remark is still remembered, "Deal with a man as he deals with you." This is just what we do; we deal with the imperialists and their running dogs, the Chiang Kai-shek reactionaries, as they deal with us. That is all there is to it!

Revolutionary dictatorship and counter-revolutionary dictatorship are by nature opposites, but the former was learned from the latter. Such learning is very important. If the revolutionary people do not master this method of ruling over the counter-revolutionary classes, they will not be able to maintain their state power, domestic and foreign reaction will overthrow that power and restore its own rule over China, and disaster will befall the revolutionary people.

The people's democratic dictatorship is based on the alliance of the working class, the peasantry and the urban petty bourgeoisie, and mainly on the alliance of the workers and the peasants, because these two classes comprise 80 to 90 per cent of China's population. These two classes are the main force in overthrowing imperialism and the Kuomintang reactionaries. The transition from New Democracy to socialism also depends mainly upon their alliance.

The people's democratic dictatorship needs the leadership of the working class. For it is only the working class that is most farsighted, most selfless and most thoroughly revolutionary. The entire history of revolution proves that without the leadership of the working class revolution fails and that with the leadership of the working class revolution triumphs. In the epoch of imperialism, in no country can any other class lead any genuine revolution to victory. This is clearly proved by the fact that the many revolutions led by China's petty bourgeoisie and national bourgeoisie all failed.

The national bourgeoisie at the present stage is of great importance. Imperialism, a most ferocious enemy, is still standing alongside us. China's modern industry still forms a very small proportion of the national economy. No reliable statistics are available, but it is estimated, on the basis of certain data, that before the War of Resistance Against Japan the value of output of modern industry constituted only about 10 per cent of the total value of output of the national economy. To counter imperialist oppression and to raise her backward economy to a higher level, China must utilize all the factors of urban and rural capitalism that are beneficial and not harmful to the national economy and the people's livelihood; and we must unite with the national bourgeoisie in common struggle. Our present policy is to regulate capitalism, not to detroy it. But the national bourgeoisie cannot be the leader of the revolution, nor should it have the chief role in state power. The reason it cannot be the leader of the revolution and should not have the chief role in state power is that the social and economic position of the national bourgeoisie determines its weakness; it lacks foresight and sufficient courage and many of its members are afraid of the masses.

Sun Yat-sen advocated "arousing the masses of the people" or "giving assistance to the peasants and workers". But who is to "arouse" them or "give assistance" to them? Sun Yat-sen had the petty bourgeoisie and the national bourgeoisie in mind. As a matter of fact, they cannot do so. Why did forty years of revolution under Sun Yat-sen end in failure? Because in the epoch of imperialism the petty bourgeoisie and the national bourgeoisie cannot lead any genuine revolution to victory.

Our twenty-eight years have been quite different. We have had much valuable experience. A well-disciplined Party armed with the theory of Marxism-Leninism, using the method of self-criticism and linked with the masses of the people; an army under the leadership of such a Party; a united front of all revolutionary classes and all revolutionary groups under the leadership of such a Party—these are the three main weapons with which we have defeated the enemy. They distinguish us from our predecessors. Relying on them, we have won basic victory. We have travelled a tortuous road. We have struggled against opportunist deviations in our Party, both Right and "Left". Whenever we made serious mistakes on these three matters, the revolution suffered setbacks. Taught by mistakes and setbacks, we have become wiser and handle our affairs better. It is hard for any political party or person to avoid mistakes, but we should make as few as possible. Once a mistake is made, we should correct it, and the more quickly and thoroughly the better.

To sum up our experience and concentrate it into one point, it is: the people's democratic dictatorship under the leadership of the working class (through the Communist Party) and based upon the alliance of workers and peasants. This dictatorship must unite as one with the international revolutionary forces. This is our formula, our principal experience, our main programme.

Twenty-eight years of our Party are a long period, in which

we have accomplished only one thing—we have won basic victory in the revolutionary war. This calls for celebration, because it is the people's victory, because it is a victory in a country as large as China. But we still have much work to do; to use the analogy of a journey, our past work is only the first step in a long march of ten thousand *li*. Remnants of the enemy have yet to be wiped out. The serious task of economic construction lies before us. We shall soon put aside some of the things we know well and be compelled to do things we don't know well. This means difficulties. The imperialists reckon that we will not be able to manage our economy; they are standing by and looking on, awaiting our failure.

We must overcome difficulties, we must learn what we do not know. We must learn to do economic work from all who know how, no matter who they are. We must esteem them as teachers, learning from them respectfully and conscientiously. We must not pretend to know when we do not know. We must not put on bureaucratic airs. If we dig into a subject for several months, for a year or two, for three or five years, we shall eventually master it. At first some of the Soviet Communists also were not very good at handling economic matters and the imperialists awaited their failure too. But the Communist Party of the Soviet Union emerged victorious and, under the leadership of Lenin and Stalin, it learned not only how to make the revolution but also how to carry on construction. It has built a great and splendid socialist state. The Communist Party of the Soviet Union is our best teacher and we must learn from it. The situation both at home and abroad is in our favour, we can rely fully on the weapon of the people's democratic dictatorship, unite the people throughout the country, the reactionaries excepted, and advance steadily to our goal.

Chapter Five

Construction and Controversy

THE TWO important stages that currently divide the years after the establishment of the Chinese People's Republic in 1949 may be analyzed in terms of the attempt to make China a Communist nation. During the first stage (1949–1957), one of construction and controversy, efforts were made to lift the Chinese people from the old order to the threshold of a new order—an order of "socialist transformation" and "socialist construction." Of all the accomplishments, the first and foremost was the creation of a strong central government, under the supervision of the Communist Party, with authority directly reaching the people. It took the new regime five years to accomplish this task (see Selection 19). Meanwhile, the Chinese Communists reorganized the powerful organs of Party machinery to strengthen Party leadership and make it the real driving force behind the new regime (see Selections 20 and 21). However, progress followed a fluctuating curve, showing that "socialist construction" had been accompanied by "controversy," which, according to the Communist ideology, is inherent in human institutions (Selection 22).

As a result of the "controversy," there was the 1957–1958 rectification campaign—which reached its climax in the "hundred flowers" adventure when extended to intellectuals and "democratic personalities"—and thence the political line that was to set the tone for the second stage of the new regime, "the quest for new ideology."

19. *The Constitution of the People's Republic of China (September, 1954)**

When the Chinese Communists established their new regime at Peking in September, 1949, they called a People's Political Consultative Conference, from September 21 to October 30, to adopt three important documents—the Organic Law of the People's Political Consultative Conference, the Organic Law of the Central People's Government, and the Common Program of the People's Political Consultative Conference—which represented a detailed statement of the theory and structure of the Chinese Communist government. The People's Political Consultative Conference continued to function until 1954, when it was turned into a National People's Congress. This congress, which met in Peking from September 15 to September 28, consisted of 1,226 deputies from the provincial congresses, the large cities, the national minorities, the armed forces and overseas Chinese. It duly adopted the draft Constitution, on September 20, which had been drawn up by the Central Committee of the Communist Party and issued by the draft committee headed by Mao Tse-tung.

The 1954 Constitution, which consists of a preamble and 106 articles in four chapters, is, in fact, the continuation of the Organic Law and the Common Program of 1949.[1] It contains much of the content of Western constitutions. For example, it defines functions and powers, and provides for popular election of government officials. (The People's Congresses are elected by the people—by direct vote at the village level, and by indirect vote from the county level up through the provincial level to the highest legislative organ, the National People's Congress. But the candidates are

---

* From book so titled, Peking: Foreign Language Press, 1961, pp. 1–45.
[1] For the institutional and technical changes, see H. Arthur Steiner, "Constitutionalism in Communist China," Part V, *American Political Science Review*, March, 1955.

nominated under the supervision of the Party. This kind of representation is merely stage-managed exercise in mass participation rather than popular control of government.) In addition, there is a chapter on "Fundamental Rights and Duties of Citizens" (Articles 85–103).

All these would represent essential features of democratic system, so that the new regime would have entered the "constitutional stage." In effect, the 1954 Constitution is a form of the Communist mandate by which to organize the public power of the Chinese state. So long as the Party is "the core of the leadership of our country," the Constitution is not the "supreme law of the land," rather it is an instrument of the Party in the transition period. As Liu Shao-chi asserted, "China's advance along the road to socialism is fixed and unalterable," and the purpose of the Constitution is "to set down in legal form the central task of our country in the transition period." This statement reveals the extent to which the Constitution is conceived as "a weapon," and not an end in itself. In other words, as soon as the socialist objective is attained, the present Constitution will be superseded.

In fact, much of the 1954 Constitution was copied directly from the Soviet Constitution of 1936, using a different terminology. For instance, the People's Republic of China is described as "a people's democratic state led by the working class and based on the alliance of workers and peasants" (Article 1), whereas, according to the Soviet Constitution, the "Union of Soviet Republics is a socialist state of workers and peasants" (Article 1). And again, the so-called "people's democratic dictatorship" in the preamble of the Chinese Communist Constitution is just another version of the Soviet Russian "proletarian dictatorship."

However, there are differences in the government structures. First, the Supreme Soviet of the USSR is bicameral, providing for constituent republics, whereas the Chinese National People's Congress is unicameral; secondly, in the USSR the Council of Ministers, including its Chairman or Premier, is appointed by the Presidium of the Supreme Soviet, whereas in Communist China the Premier, the head of the State Council, is nominated and appointed by the Chairman of the People's Republic with the consent of the National People's Congress; and thirdly, the National People's Congress, like the Supreme Soviet of the USSR, is the supreme organ of the state power, but it differs from the latter in that the Chairman of its Standing Committee is not the titular head of the government, but is subordinate to the Chairman of the People's Republic. Moreover, the Chairman of the People's Republic presides over the Supreme State Conference and the National Defense Council—two policy-planning organs of full constitutional status through which he can exert a dominant influence in political and military affairs of the state. We see, therefore, that the 1954 Constitution creates an office for which no parallel is found in the Soviet Constitution.

Now let us further examine the state structure as provided in the 1954 Constitution. While the National People's Congress is "the highest organ of state power" (Article 21), the State Council is "the executive organ of the highest organ of state power" (Article 47). Similarly, on lower levels, the local people's congresses are "local organs of state power" (Article 55), and the local people's councils are "local organs of state administration" (Article 62). This parallel system of people's congresses and people's councils, which extends through the entire Communist governmental hierarchy, is built upon the distinction between "state power" as represented by the people's congresses and "state administration" as represented by the people's councils.

Having made clear the distinction between "state power" and "state administration," there remains the question of how this parallel system actually works in the Chinese Communist government. The underlying spirit of the Communist government is the principle of democratic centralism; that is, "centralized on the basis of democracy and democratic under centralized guidance."[2] This system of "democratic centralism," as adopted in the 1954 Constitution (Article 2), is mainly a system of concentration of power by the central authority. For example, the local people's councils, designed to be "the executive organs of local people's congresses at the corresponding levels," represent in reality the downward movement of authority from the central government, because they take orders from the State Council at the apex of hierarchy.

The real driving force behind the government, however, is the Party leadership—the Standing Committee of the Party Politburo and the men who hold major positions in the government. At the summit, Party and state machine

[2] "On Coalition Government," *Selected Works of Mao Tse-tung*, Peking: Foreign Language Press, 1965, IV, 272. (Selection 16.)

merge in a common nucleus of leadership, thus giving a hollow note to the constitutional rhetoric about the "supremacy" of the National People's Congress. In effect, policies are made in the inner councils of these men rather than in the National People's Congress. The same is true of the State Council, which, designed as the "highest organ" of administrative authority, is in reality under the control of the inner circle of the Party Politburo. Whatever the Party leaders decide upon, the state machine is expected to endorse it and carry it out, under the cloak of proper constitutional and legal forms and procedures.

PREAMBLE

In the year 1949, after more than a century of heroic struggle, the Chinese people, led by the Communist Party of China, finally won their great victory in the people's revolution against imperialism, feudalism and bureaucrat-capitalism, and thereby brought to an end the history of the oppression and enslavement they had undergone for so long and founded the People's Republic of China—a people's democratic dictatorship. The system of people's democracy—the system of new democracy—of the People's Republic of China guarantees that our country can in a peaceful way eliminate exploitation and poverty and build a prosperous and happy socialist society.

From the founding of the People's Republic of China to the attainment of a socialist society is a period of transition. The general tasks of the state during the transition period are, step by step, to bring about the socialist industrialization of the country and, step by step, to accomplish the socialist transformation of agriculture, handicrafts and capitalist industry and commerce. In the last few years our people have successfully carried out the reform of the agrarian system, resistance to United States aggression and aid to Korea, the suppression of counter-revolutionaries, the rehabilitation of the national economy, and other large-scale struggles, thereby preparing the necessary conditions for planned economic construction and the gradual transition to a socialist society.

The First National People's Congress of the People's Republic of China, at its First Session held in Peking, the capital, solemnly adopted the Constitution of the People's Republic of China on September 20, 1954. This Constitution is based on the Common Programme of the Chinese People's Political Consultative Conference of 1949 and is a development of it. This Constitution consolidates the gains of the Chinese people's revolution and the new victories won in the political and economic fields since the founding of the People's Republic of China; and, moreover, it reflects the basic needs of the state in the period of transition, as well as the common desire of the broad masses of the people to build a socialist society.

In the course of the great struggle to establish the People's Republic of China, the people of our country forged a broad people's democratic united front led by the Communist Party of China and composed of all democratic classes, democratic parties and groups, and people's organizations. This people's democratic united front will continue to play its part in mobilizing and rallying the whole people in the struggle to fulfil the general tasks of the state during the transition period and to oppose enemies within and without.

All the nationalities in our country have been united in one great family of free and equal nationalities. The unity of our country's nationalities will continue to gain in strength on the basis of the further development of the fraternal bonds and mutual aid among them, and on the basis of opposition to imperialism, opposition to public enemies within their own ranks, and opposition to both big-nation chauvinism and local nationalism. In the course of economic construction and cultural development, the state will concern itself with the needs of the different nationalities, and, in the matter of socialist transformation, pay full attention to the special characteristics in the development of each nationality.

Our country has already built an indestructible friendship with the great Union of Soviet Socialist Republics and the People's Democracies; and the friendship between our people and other peace-loving peoples all over the world is growing day by day. These friendships will continue to be developed and consolidated. Our country's policy of establishing and extending diplomatic relations with all countries on the principles of equality, mutual benefit and respect for each other's sovereignty and territorial integrity has already yielded success and will continue to be carried out. In international affairs the firm and consistent policy of our country is to strive for the noble aims of world peace and the progress of mankind.

CHAPTER 1: GENERAL PRINCIPLES

Article 1

The People's Republic of China is a people's democratic state led by the working class and based on the alliance of workers and peasants.

Article 2

All power in the People's Republic of China belongs to the people. The organs through which the people exercise power are the National People's Congress and the local people's congresses at various levels.

The National People's Congress, the local people's congresses and other organs of state practise democratic centralism.

Article 3

The People's Republic of China is a unitary multi-national state.

All the nationalities are equal. Discrimination against or oppression of any nationality, and acts which undermine the unity of the nationalities, are prohibited.

All the nationalities have the freedom to use and develop their own spoken and written languages, and to preserve or reform their own customs and ways.

Regional autonomy applies in areas where a minority nationality live in a compact community. All the national autonomous areas are inseparable parts of the People's Republic of China.

Article 4

The People's Republic of China, by relying on the organs of state and the social forces, and through socialist industrialization and socialist transformation, ensures the gradual abolition of systems of exploitation and the building of a socialist society.

Article 5

At present, the main categories of ownership of means of production in the People's Republic of China are the following: state ownership, that is, ownership by the whole people; co-operative ownership, that is, collective ownership by the masses of working people; ownership by individual working people; and capitalist ownership.

Article 6

The state sector of the economy is the socialist sector owned by the whole people. It is the leading force in the national economy and the material basis on which the state carries out socialist transformation. The state ensures priority for the development of the state sector of the economy.

All mineral resources and waters, as well as forests, undeveloped land and other resources which the state owns by law, are the property of the whole people.

Article 7

The co-operative sector of the economy is either socialist, when collectively owned by the masses of working people, or semi-socialist, when in part collectively owned by the masses of working people. Partial collective ownership by the masses of working people is a transitional form by means of which individual peasants, individual handicraftsmen and other individual working people organize themselves in their advance towards collective ownership by the masses of working people.

The state protects the property of the co-operatives, and encourages, guides and helps the development of the co-operative sector of the economy. It regards the development of co-operation in production as the chief means of the transformation of individual farming and individual handicrafts.

Article 8

The state protects according to law the right of peasants to own land and other means of production.

The state guides and helps individual peasants to increase production and encourages them, on the voluntary principle, to organize co-operation in the fields of production, supply and marketing, and credit.

The policy of the state towards the rich-peasant economy is to restrict and gradually eliminate it.

Article 9

The state protects according to law the right of handicrafts-men and other individual working people in non-agricultural pursuits to own means of production.

The state guides and helps individual handicraftsmen and other individual working people in non-agricultural pursuits to improve their operations, and encourages them, on the voluntary principle, to organize co-operation in production, and supply and marketing.

Article 10

The state protects according to law the right of capitalists to own means of production and other capital.

The policy of the state towards capitalist industry and commerce is to use, restrict and transform them. Through control exercised by organs of state administration, leadership by the state sector of the economy, and supervision by the masses of the workers, the state makes use of the positive aspects of capitalist industry and commerce which are beneficial to national welfare and the people's livelihood, restricts their negative aspects which are detrimental to national welfare and the people's livelihood, and encourages and guides their transformation into various forms of state-capitalist economy, gradually replacing capitalist ownership with ownership by the whole people.

The state prohibits capitalist from engaging in any unlawful activities which injure the public interest, disturb the social-economic order, or undermine the economic plan of the state.

Article 11

The state protects the right of citizens to own lawfully-earned income, savings, houses and other means of subsistence.

Article 12

The state protects according to law the right of citizens to inherit private property.

Article 13

The state may, in the public interest, requisition by purchase, take over for use or nationalize both urban and rural land as well as other means of production on the conditions provided by law.

Article 14

The state prohibits the use of private property by any person to the detriment of the public interest.

Article 15

By economic planning, the state directs the growth and transformation of the national economy in order to bring about the constant increase of productive forces, thereby improving the material and cultural life of the people and consolidating the independence and security of the state.

Article 16

Work is a matter of honour for every citizen of the People's Republic of China who is capable of working. The state encourages the working enthusiasm and creativeness of citizens.

Article 17

All organs of state must rely on the masses of the people, constantly maintain close contact with them, heed their opinions and accept their supervision.

Article 18

All personnel of organs of state must be loyal to the system of people's democracy, observe the Constitution and the law and strive to serve the people.

Article 19

The People's Republic of China safeguards the system of people's democracy, suppresses all treasonable and counterrevolutionary activities and punishes all traitors and counterrevolutionaries.

The state deprives feudal landlords and bureaucrat-capitalists of political rights for a specific period of time according to law; at the same time it gives them a way to earn a living, in order to enable them to reform through labour and become citizens who earn their livelihood by their own labour.

Article 20

The armed forces of the People's Republic of China belong to the people; their duty is to safeguard the gains of the people's revolution and the achievements of national construction, and to defend the sovereignty, territorial integrity and security of the state.

CHAPTER 2: THE STATE STRUCTURE

Section 1. The National People's Congress.

Article 21

The National People's Congress of the People's Republic of China is the highest organ of state power.

Article 22

The National People's Congress is the sole organ exercising the legislative power of the state.

Article 23

The National People's Congress is composed of deputies elected by provinces, autonomous regions, cities directly under the central authority, the armed forces and Chinese who live abroad.

The number of deputies to the National People's Congress, including those representing minority nationalities, and the manner of their election, are prescribed by the electoral law.

Article 24

The National People's Congress is elected for a term of four years.

Two months before the term of office of the National People's Congress expires, its Standing Committee must complete the election of deputies to the succeeding National People's Congress. Should exceptional circumstances arise that prevent such an election, the term of office of the National People's Congress may be prolonged until the first session of the succeeding National People's Congress.

Article 25

The National People's Congress holds the session once a year, convened by its Standing Committee. It may also be convened whenever its Standing Committee deems this necessary or one-fifth of the deputies so propose.

Article 26

When the National People's Congress meets, it elects a presidium to conduct the session.

Article 27

The National People's Congress exercises the following functions and powers:
(1) to amend the Constitution;
(2) to make laws;
(3) to supervise the enforcement of the Constitution;
(4) to elect the Chairman and the Vice-Chairman of the People's Republic of China;
(5) to decide on the choice of the Premier of the State Council upon recommendation by the Chairman of the People's Republic of China, and of the component members of the State Council upon recommendation by the Premier;
(6) to decide on the choice of the Vice-Chairmen and members of the Council of National Defence upon recommendation by the Chairman of the People's Republic of China;
(7) to elect the President of the Supreme People's Court;
(8) to elect the Chief Procurator of the Supreme People's Procuratorate;
(9) to decide on the national economic plan;
(10) To examine and approve the state budget and the final state accounts;
(11) to ratify the following administrative divisions: provinces, autonomous regions, and cities directly under the central authority;
(12) to decide on amnesties;
(13) to decide on questions of war and peace;
(14) to exercise such other functions and powers as the National People's Congress considers it should exercise.

Article 28

The National People's Congress has the power to remove from office:

(1) the Chairman and the Vice-Chairman of the People's Republic of China;

(2) the Premier and Vice-Premiers, Ministers, Chairmen of Commissions and the Secretary-General of the State Council;

(3) the Vice-Chairmen and members of the Council of National Defence;

(4) the President of the Supreme People's Court;

(5) the Chief Procurator of the Supreme People's Procuratorate.

Article 29

Amendments to the Constitution require a two-thirds majority vote of all the deputies to the National People's Congress.

Decisions on laws and other proposals require a simple majority vote of all the deputies to the National People's Congress.

Article 30

The Standing Committee of the National People's Congress is the permanent working organ of the National People's Congress.

The Standing Committee of the National People's Congress is composed of the following persons, elected by the National People's Congress:

the Chairman;
the Vice-Chairmen;
the Secretary-General;
the members.

Article 31

The Standing Committee of the National People's Congress exercises the following functions and powers:

(1) to conduct the election of deputies to the National People's Congress;

(2) to convene the sessions of the National People's Congress;

(3) to interpret laws;

(4) to make decrees;

(5) to supervise the work of the State Council, the Supreme People's Court and the Supreme People's Procuratorate;

(6) to annul decisions and orders of the State Council which contravene the Constitution, laws or decrees;

(7) to alter or annul inappropriate decisions of the organs of state power of provinces, autonomous regions, and cities directly under the central authority;

(8) to decide on the individual appointment and removal of Vice-Premiers, Ministers, Chairmen of Commissions or the Secretary-General of the State Council when the National People's Congress is not in session;

(9) to appoint and remove Vice-Presidents and judges of the Supreme People's Court, and members of its Judicial Committee;

(10) to appoint and remove Deputy Chief Procurators and procurators of the Supreme People's Procuratorate, and members of its Procuratorial Committee;

(11) to decide on the appointment and removal of plenipotentiary representatives abroad;

(12) to decide on the ratification and denunciation of treaties concluded with foreign states;

(13) to institute military, diplomatic and other special titles and ranks;

(14) to institute state orders and titles of honour and decide on their conferment;

(15) to decide on the granting of pardons;

(16) to decide, when the National People's Congress is not in session, on the proclamation of a state of war in the event of armed attack on the country or in case of necessity to execute an international treaty for joint defence against aggression;

(17) to decide on general or partial mobilization;

(18) to decide on the enforcement of martial law throughout the country or in certain areas;

(19) to exercise such other functions and powers as are vested in it by the National People's Congress.

Article 32

The Standing Committee of the National People's Congress exercises its functions and powers until a new Standing Committee is elected by the succeeding National People's Congress.

Article 33

The Standing Committee of the National People's Congress is responsible and accountable to the National People's Congress.

The National People's Congress has the power to recall component members of its standing Committee.

Article 34

The National People's Congress establishes a Nationalities Committee, a Bills Committee, a Budget Committee, a Credentials Committee and such other committees as may be necessary.

The Nationalities Committee and the Bills Committee are under the direction of the Standing Committee of the National People's 'Congress when the National People's Congress is not in session.

Article 35

The National People's Congress, or its Standing Committee when the National People's Congress is not in session, may, if it deems necessary, appoint commissions of investigation on specific questions.

All organs of state, people's organizations and citizens concerned are obliged to supply the necessary material to these commissions when they conduct investigations.

Article 36

Deputies to the National People's Congress have the right to address questions to the State Council, or to the Ministries and Commissions of the State Council, which are under obligation to answer.

Article 37

No deputy to the National People's Congress may be arrested or placed on trial without the consent of the National People's Congress or, when the National People's Congress is not in session, of its Standing Committee.

Article 38

Deputies to the National People's Congress are subject to the supervision of the units which elect them. These electoral units have the power to replace the deputies they elect at any time according to the procedure prescribed by law.

Section II. The Chairman of the People's Republic of China.

Article 39

The Chairman of the People's Republic of China is elected by the National People's Congress. Any citizen of the People's Republic of China who has the right to vote and stand for election and has reached the age of thirty-five is eligible for election as Chairman of the People's Republic of China.

The term of office of the Chairman of the People's Republic of China is four years.

Article 40

The Chairman of the People's Republic of China, in pursuance of decisions of the National People's Congress or its Standing Committee, promulgates laws and decrees; appoints and removes the Premier, Vice-Premiers, Ministers, Chairmen of Commissions or the Secretary-General of the State Council; appoints and removes the Vice-Chairmen and members of the Council of National Defence; confers state orders and titles of honour; proclaims amnesties and grants pardons; proclaims martial law; proclaims a state of war; and orders mobilization.

Article 41

The Chairman of the People's Republic of China represents the People's Republic of China in its foreign relations, receives foreign diplomatic representatives and, in pursuance of decisions of the Standing Committee of the National People's Congress, dispatches and recalls plenipotentiary representatives abroad and ratifies treaties concluded with foreign states.

Article 42

The Chairman of the People's Republic of China commands the armed forces of the state, and is Chairman of the Council of National Defence.

Article 43

The Chairman of the People's Republic of China, whenever necessary, convenes a Supreme State Conference and acts as its chairman.

The Vice-Chairman of the People's Republic of China, the Chairman of the Standing Committee of the National People's Congress, the Premier of the State Council and other persons concerned take part in the Supreme State Conference.

The Chairman of the People's Republic of China submits the views of the Supreme State Conference on important affairs of state to the National People's Congress, its Standing Committee, the State Council, or other bodies concerned for their consideration and decision.

Article 44

The Vice-Chairman of the People's Republic of China assists the Chairman in his work. The Vice-Chairman may exercise such part of the functions and powers of the Chairman as the Chairman may entrust to him.

The provisions of Article 39 of the Constitution governing the election and term of office of the Chairman of the People's Republic of China apply also to the election and term of office of the Vice-Chairman of the People's Republic of China.

Article 45

The Chairman and the Vice-Chairman of the People's Republic of China exercise their functions and powers until the new Chairman and Vice-Chairman elected by the succeeding National People's Congress take office.

Article 46

Should the Chairman of the People's Republic of China be incapacitated for a prolonged period by reason of health, the functions and powers of Chairman shall be exercised by the Vice-Chairman.

Should the office of Chairman of the People's Republic of

China fall vacant, the Vice-Chairman succeeds to the office of Chairman.

Section III. The State Council.

Article 47

The State Council of the People's Republic of China, that is, the Central People's Government, is the executive organ of the highest organ of state power; it is the highest organ of state administration.

Article 48

The State Council is composed of the following persons:
the Premier;
the Vice-Premiers;
the Ministers;
the Chairmen of Commissions;
the Secretary-General.
The organization of the State Council is determined by law.

Article 49

The State Council exercises the following functions and powers:

(1) to formulate administrative measures, issue decisions and orders and verify their execution in accordance with the Constitution, laws and decrees;

(2) to submit proposals on laws and other matters to the National People's Congress or its Standing Committee;

(3) to co-ordinate and lead the work of Ministries and Commissions;

(4) to co-ordinate and lead the work of local organs of state administration at various levels throughout the country;

(5) to alter or annul inappropriate orders and directives issued by Ministers or by Chairmen of Commissions;

(6) to alter or annul inappropriate decisions and orders issued by local organs of state administration at various levels;

(7) to put into effect the national economic plan and the state budget;

(8) to administer foreign and domestic trade;

(9) to administer cultural, educational and public health work;

(10) to administer affairs concerning the nationalities;

(11) to administer affairs concerning Chinese who live abroad;

(12) to protect the interests of the state, to maintain public order and to safeguard the rights of citizens;

(13) to administer the conduct of external affairs;

(14) to direct the building up of the armed forces;

(15) to ratify the following administrative divisions; autonomous *chou*, counties, autonomous counties, and cities;

(16) to appoint and remove administrative personnel according to provisions of law;

(17) to exercise such other functions and powers as are vested in it by the National People's Congress or its Standing Committee.

Article 50

The Premier directs the work of the State Council and presides over its meetings.

The Vice-Premiers assist the Premier in his work.

Article 51

The Ministers and Chairmen of Commissions direct the work of their respective departments. They may issue orders and directives within the jurisdiction of their respective departments and in accordance with laws and decrees and with the decisions and orders of the State Council.

Article 52

The State Council is responsible and accountable to the National People's Congress or, when the National People's Congress is not in session, to its Standing Committee.

Section IV. The Local People's Congresses and the Local People's Councils.

Article 53

The administrative division of the People's Republic of China is as follows:

(1) The country is divided into provinces, autonomous regions, and cities directly under the central authority;

(2) Provinces and autonomous regions are divided into autonomous *chou*, counties, autonomous counties, and cities;

(3 Counties and autonomous counties are divided into *hsiang*, nationality *hsiang*, and towns.

Cities directly under the central authority and other large cities are divided into districts. Autonomous *chou* are divided into counties, autonomous counties, and cities.

Autonomous regions, autonomous *chou* and autonomous counties are all national autonomous areas.

Article 54

People's congresses and people's councils are established in provinces, cities directly under the central authority, counties, cities, city districts, *hsiang*, nationality *hsiang*, and towns.

Organs of self-government are established in autonomous regions, autonomous *chou* and autonomous counties. The organization and work of organs of self-government are specified in Chapter Two, Section V of the Constitution.

Article 55

Local people's congresses at various levels are local organs of state power.

Article 56

Deputies to the people's congresses of provinces, cities directly under the central authority, counties, and cities divided into districts are elected by people's congresses at the next lower level; deputies to the people's congresses of cities not divided into districts, and of city districts, *hsiang*, nationality *hsiang*, and towns are directly elected by the voters.

The number of deputies to local people's congresses at various levels and the manner of their election are prescribed by the electoral law.

Article 57

The term of office of the provincial people's congresses is four years. The term of office of the people's congresses of cities directly under the central authority, counties, cities, city districts, *hsiang*, nationality *hsiang*, and towns is two years.

Article 58

Local people's congresses in their respective administrative areas ensure the observance and execution of laws and decrees; make plans for local economic construction and cultural development and for public utilities; examine and approve local budgets and final accounts; protect public property; maintain public order; and safeguard the rights of citizens and the equal rights of minority nationalities.

Article 59

Local people's congresses elect, and have the power to remove, component members of people's councils at the corresponding levels.

People's congresses at county level and above elect, and have the power to remove, the presidents of people's courts at the corresponding levels.

Article 60

Local people's congresses adopt and issue decisions within the limits of their authority as prescribed by law.

The people's congresses of nationality *hsiang* may, within the limits of their authority as prescribed by law, take specific measures suited to the characteristics of the nationalities concerned.

Local people's congresses have the power to alter or annul inappropriate decisions and orders of people's councils at the corresponding levels.

People's congresses at county level and above have the power to alter or annul inappropriate decisions of people's congresses at the next lower level as well as inappropriate decisions and orders of people's councils at the next lower level.

Article 61

Deputies to the people's congresses of provinces, cities directly under the central authority, counties, and cities divided into districts are subject to supervision by the units which elect them; deputies to the people's congresses of cities not divided into districts, and of city districts, *hsiang*, nationality *hsiang*, and towns are subject to supervision by their electors. The electoral units and electorates which elect the deputies to the local people's congresses have the power to replace their deputies at any time according to the procedure prescribed by law.

Article 62

Local people's councils, that is, local people's governments, are the executive organs of local people's congresses at the corresponding levels, and are local organs of state administration.

Article 63

A local people's council is composed, according to its level, of the provincial governor and deputy provincial governors, or the mayor and deputy mayors of cities, or the county head and deputy county heads, or the district head and deputy district heads, or the *hsiang* head and deputy *hsiang* heads, or the mayor or deputy mayors of towns, as the case may be; together with council members.

The term of office of a local people's council is the same as that of the people's congress at the corresponding level.

The organization of local people's councils is determined by law.

Article 64

Local people's councils direct the administrative work of their respective areas within the limits of their authority as prescribed by law.

Local people's councils carry out decisions of people's congresses at the corresponding levels as well as decisions and orders of organs of state administration at the higher levels.

Local people's councils issue decisions and orders within the limits of their authority as prescribed by law.

Article 65

People's councils at county level and above direct the work of all their subordinate departments and of people's councils at the lower levels, as well as appoint and remove the personnel of organs of state according to provisions of law.

People's councils at county level and above have the power to suspend the carrying out of inappropriate decisions of people's congresses at the next lower level; and to alter or annul inappropriate orders and directives of their subordinate departments as well as inappropriate decisions and orders of people's councils at the lower levels.

Article 66

Local people's councils are responsible and accountable to people's congresses at the corresponding levels and to organs of state administration at the next higher level.

Local people's councils throughout the country are local organs of state administration under the co-ordinating leadership of the State Council and are subordinate to it.

Section V. The Organs of Self-Government of National Autonomous Areas.

Article 67

The organization of the organs of self-government of autonomous regions, autonomous *chou* and autonomous counties should conform to the basic principles governing the organization of local organs of state as specified in Chapter 2, Section IV of the Constitution. The form of each organ of self-government may be determined in accordance with the wishes of the majority of the people of the nationality or nationalities enjoying regional autonomy in a given area.

Article 68

In autonomous regions, autonomous *chou* and autonomous counties where a number of nationalities live together, each nationality is entitled to appropriate representation in the organs of self-government.

Article 69

The organs of self-government of autonomous regions, autonomous *chou* and autonomous counties exercise the functions and powers of local organs of state as specified in Chapter 2, Section IV of the Constitution.

Article 70

The organs of self-government of autonomous regions, autonomous *chou* and autonomous counties exercise autonomy within the limits of their authority as prescribed by the Constitution and by law.

The organs of self-government of autonomous regions, autonomous *chou* and autonomous counties administer the finances of their areas within the limits of their authority as prescribed by law.

The organs of self-government of autonomous regions, autonomous *chou* and autonomous counties organize the public security forces of their areas in accordance with the military system of the state.

The organs of self-government of autonomous regions, autonomous *chou* and autonomous counties may, in the light of the political, economic and cultural characteristics of the nationality or nationalities in a given area, make regulations on the exercise of autonomy as well as specific regulations and submit them to the Standing Committee of the National People's Congress for approval.

Article 71

In performing their functions, organs of self-government of autonomous regions, autonomous *chou* and autonomous counties employ the spoken and written language or languages commonly used by the nationality or nationalities in the locality.

Article 72

The higher organs of state should fully safeguard the exercise of autonomy by organs of self-government of autonomous regions, autonomous *chou* and autonomous counties, and should assist all the minority nationalities in their political, economic and cultural development.

Section VI. The People's Courts and the People's Procuratorates.

Article 73

The Supreme People's Court of the People's Republic of China, local people's courts at various levels and special people's courts exercise judicial authority.

Article 74

The term of office of the President of the Supreme People's Court and presidents of local people's courts is four years.

The organization of people's courts is determined by law.

Article 75

The people's courts, in administering justice, apply the system of people's assessors in accordance with law.

Article 76

All cases in the people's courts are heard in public except those involving special circumstances as prescribed by law. The accused has the right to defence.

Article 77

Citizens of all nationalities have the right to use their own spoken and written languages in judicial proceedings. The people's courts are required to provide interpretation for any party unacquainted with the spoken or written language commonly used in the locality.

In an area where people of a minority nationality live in a compact community or where a number of nationalities live together, hearings in people's courts should be conducted in the language commonly used in the locality, and judgements, notices and other documents of people's courts should be made public in that language.

Article 78

The people's courts administer justice independently and are subject only to the law.

Article 79

The Supreme People's Court is the highest judicial organ.

The Supreme People's Court supervises the administration of justice by local people's courts at various levels and special people's courts; people's courts at the higher levels supervise the administration of justice by people's courts at the lower levels.

Article 80

The Supreme People's Court is responsible and accountable to the National People's Congress or, when the National People's Congress is not in session, to its Standing Committee. Local people's courts are responsible and accountable to local people's congresses at the corresponding levels.

Article 81

The Supreme People's Procuratorate of the People's Republic of China exercises procuratorial authority to ensure observance of the law by all the departments under the State Council, local organs of state at various levels, persons working in organs of state and citizens. Local people's procuratorates and special people's procuratorates exercise procuratorial authority within the limits prescribed by law.

Local people's procuratorates and special people's procuratorates work under the leadership of people's procuratorates at the higher levels, and all of them work under the coordinating leadership of the Supreme People's Procuratorate.

Article 82

The term of office of the Chief Procurator of the Supreme People's Procuratorate is four years.

The organization of people's procuratorates is determined by law.

Article 83

Local people's procuratorates at various levels exercise their functions and powers independently and are not subject to interference by local organs of state.

Article 84

The Supreme People's Procuratorate is responsible and accountable to the National People's Congress or, when the National People's Congress is not in session, to its Standing Committee.

CHAPTER 3: FUNDAMENTAL RIGHTS AND DUTIES OF CITIZENS

Article 85

All citizens of the People's Republic of China are equal before the law.

Article 86

All citizens of the People's Republic of China, who have reached the age of eighteen, have the right to vote and stand for election, irrespective of their nationality, race, sex, occupation, social origin, religious belief, education, property status, or length of residence, except insane persons and persons deprived by law of the right to vote and stand for election.

Women have equal rights with men to vote and stand for election.

Article 87

Citizens of the People's Republic of China enjoy freedom of speech, freedom of the press, freedom of assembly, freedom of association, freedom of procession and freedom of demonstration. To ensure that citizens can enjoy these freedoms, the state provides the necessary material facilities.

Article 88

Citizens of the People's Republic of China enjoy freedom of religious belief.

Article 89

The freedom of person of citizens of the People's Republic of China is inviolable. No citizen may be arrested except by decision of a people's court or with the sanction of a people's procuratorate.

Article 90

The homes of citizens of the People's Republic of China are inviolable, and privacy of correspondence is protected by law.

Citizens of the People's Republic of China enjoy freedom of residence and freedom to change their residence.

Article 91

Citizens of the People's Republic of China have the right to work. To ensure that citizens can enjoy this right, the state, by planned development of the national economy, gradually provides more employment, improves working conditions and increases wages, amenities and benefits.

Article 92

Working people in the People's Republic of China have the right to rest and leisure. To ensure that working people can enjoy this right, the state prescribes working hours and systems of vacations for workers and office personnel, and gradually expands material facilities for the working people to rest and build up their health.

Article 93

Working people in the People's Republic of China have the right to material assistance in old age, and in case of illness or disability. To ensure that working people can enjoy this right, the state provides social insurance, social assistance and public health services and gradually expands these facilities.

Article 94

Citizens of the People's Republic of China have the right to education. To ensure that citizens can enjoy this right, the state establishes and gradually expands schools of various types and other cultural and educational institutions.

The state pays special attention to the physical and mental development of young people.

Article 95

The People's Republic of China safeguards the freedom of citizens to engage in scientific research, literary and artistic creation and other cultural activities. The state encourages and assists the creative endeavours of citizens in science, education, literature, art and other cultural pursuits.

Article 96

Women in the People's Republic of China enjoy equal rights with men in all spheres of political, economic, cultural, social and family life.

The state protects marriage, the family, and the mother and child.

Article 97

Citizens of the People's Republic of China have the right to make written or oral complaints to organs of state at any level against any person working in an organ of state for transgression of law or neglect of duty. People suffering loss by reason of infringement of their rights as citizens by persons working in organs of state have the right to compensation.

Article 98

The People's Republic of China protects the just rights and interests of Chinese who live abroad.

Article 99

The People's Republic of China grants asylum to any foreign national persecuted for supporting a just cause, for taking part in the peace movement or for scientific activities.

Article 100

Citizens of the People's Republic of China must abide by the Constitution and the law, observe labour discipline, observe public order and respect public morality.

Article 101

The public property of the People's Republic of China is sacred and inviolable. It is the duty of every citizen to take care of and protect public property.

Article 102

Citizens of the People's Republic of China have the duty to pay taxes according to law.

Article 103

It is the sacred responsibility of every citizen of the People's Republic of China to defend the motherland.

It is the honourable duty of citizens of the People's Republic of China to perform military service according to law.

CHAPTER 4: NATIONAL FLAG, NATIONAL EMBLEM, CAPITAL

Article 104

The national flag of the People's Republic of China is a red flag with five stars.

Article 105

The national emblem of the People's Republic of China is: in the centre, Tien An Men under the light of five stars, and encircled by ears of grain and a cogwheel.

Article 106

The capital of the People's Republic of China is Peking.

20. *The Constitution of the Communist Party of China (September, 1956)**

This revised Constitution was adopted by the Eighth National Congress on September 26, 1956. It was based on the Party Constitution of 1945. It consists of a General Program and sixty articles arranged in nine chapters. In the General Program the Chinese Communist Party is defined as "the vanguard of the Chinese working class," guided by the principles of Marxism-Leninism.

The revised Constitution deals mainly with the Party structure and system. It stipulates the organization of central, provincial and local Party congresses and the election of congresses and committees at all levels, while abolishing the old Party conferences under the Constitution of 1945. In addition, it provides for election of the Central Control Commission by the Central Committee plenum and the election of regional control commissions by regional committees. The main function of these commissions is to tighten Party discipline and to strengthen Party leadership.

The Central Committee is in fact the supreme organ of the Chinese Communist Party. It elects the Political Bureau and its Standing Committee and the Secretariat. The Eighth Congress enlarged the membership in the Central Committee to 170, with 97 full members and 73 alternates. During the 1966–1967 Cultural Revolution, the Committee was divided into pro-Mao and anti-Mao groups. According to a recent study,[1] the pro-Mao group consists of only 52 members, about one-third of the total membership. As a result, Mao Tse-tung has by-passed the Central Committee and es-

---

* From book so titled, Peking: Foreign Language Press, 1965, pp. 10–44. (Chapter on General Program omitted.)
[1] Fang Chun-kuei, "Current Situation of the Eighth Central Committee of the Chinese Communist Party," *Studies on Chinese Communism* (No. 5) May 31, 1967, I, 1–18.

tablished new "Revolutionary Committees," mostly military men, to replace the Party structure and system.

CHAPTER 1: MEMBERSHIP

Article 1

Membership in the Party is open to any Chinese citizen who works and does not exploit the labour of others, accepts the programme and Constitution of the Party, joins and works in one of the Party organizations, carries out Party decisions, and pays membership dues as required.

Article 2

Party members have the following duties:

(1) To study Marxism-Leninism diligently and strive unceasingly to raise the level of their understanding;

(2) To safeguard the Party's solidarity and consolidate its unity;

(3) To faithfully carry out Party policy and decisions and energetically fulfil the tasks assigned them by the Party;

(4) To strictly observe the Party Constitution and the laws of the state and behave in accordance with communist ethics, no exception being made for any Party member, whatever his services and position;

(5) To place the interests of the Party and the state, that is, the interests of the masses of the people, above their own, and in the event of any conflict between the two, to submit unswervingly to the interests of the Party and the state, that is, the interests of the people;

(6) To serve the masses of the people heart and soul, strengthen their ties with them, learn from them, listen with an open mind to their wishes and opinions and report these without delay to the Party, and explain Party policy and decisions to the people;

(7) To set a good example in their work and constantly raise their productive skill and professional ability;

(8) To practise criticism and self-criticism, expose shortcomings and mistakes in work and strive to overcome and correct them; to report such shortcomings and mistakes to the leading Party bodies, up to and including the Central Committee; and to fight both inside and outside the Party against

everything which is detrimental to the interests of the Party and the people;

(9) To be truthful and honest with the Party and not to conceal or distort the truth;

(10) To be constantly on the alert against the intrigues of the enemy, and to guard the secrets of the Party and the state.

Party members who fail to fulfil any of the above-mentioned duties shall be criticized and educated. Any serious infraction of these duties, involving the splitting of Party unity, breaking state laws, violating Party decisions, damaging Party interests, or deceiving the Party, constitutes a violation of Party discipline, and disciplinary action shall be taken against it.

Article 3

Party members enjoy the following rights:

(1) To participate in free and practical discussion at Party meetings or in the Party press on theoretical and practical questions relating to Party policy;

(2) To make proposals regarding Party work and give full play to their creative ability in their work;

(3) To elect and be elected within the Party;

(4) To criticize any Party organization or any functionary at Party meetings;

(5) To ask to attend in person when a Party organization decides to take disciplinary action against them or to make an appraisal of their character and work;

(6) To reserve their opinions or submit them to a leading body of the Party, in case they disagree with any Party decision, which, in the meanwhile, they must carry out unconditionally;

(7) To address any statement, appeal or complaint to any Party organization, up to and including the Central Committee.

Party members and responsible members of Party organizations who fail to respect these rights of a member shall be criticized and educated. Infringement of these rights constitutes a violation of Party discipline, and disciplinary action shall be taken against it.

Article 4

Only persons over 18 years of age are eligible for Party membership.

Applicants for Party membership must each undergo the procedure of admission individually.

New members are admitted to the Party through a Party branch. An applicant must be recommended by two full Party members, and is admitted as a probationary member after being accepted by the general membership meeting of a Party branch and approved by the next higher Party committee; he may become a full Party member only after the completion of a probationary period of one year.

Under special conditions, Party committees at county or municipal level and above have the power to recruit new Party members directly.

Article 5

Party members who recommend an applicant for admission to the Party must be highly conscientious in furnishing the Party with truthful information about the applicant's ideology, character and personal history and must explain the Party programme and Constitution to the applicant.

Article 6

Before approving the admission of an applicant for Party membership, the Party committee concerned must assign a Party functionary to have a detailed conversation with the applicant and carefully examine his application form, the opinions of his sponsors and the decision made by the Party branch on his admission.

Article 7

During the probationary period, the Party organization concerned shall give the probationary member an elementary Party education and observe his political qualities.

Probationary members have the same duties as full members. They enjoy the same rights as full members except that they have no right to elect or be elected or to vote on any motion.

Article 8

When the probationary period has expired, the Party branch to which a probationary member belongs must discuss without delay whether he is qualified to be transferred to full membership. Such a transfer must be accepted by a general membership meeting of the said Party branch and approved by the next higher Party committee.

When the probationary period has expired, the Party organization concerned may prolong it for a period not exceeding a year if it finds it necessary to continue to observe a probationary member. If such a member is found to be unfit for transfer to full membership, his status as a probationary member shall be annulled.

Any decision by a Party branch to prolong the probationary period or to deprive a probationary member of his status must be approved by the next higher Party committee.

Article 9

The probationary period begins from the day when the general membership meeting of a Party branch accepts a probationary member. The Party standing of a member dates from the day when the general membership meeting of a Party branch accepts his transfer to full membership.

Article 10

Party members transferring from one Party organization to another become members of the latter organization.

Article 11

Party members are free to withdraw from the Party. When a Party member asks to withdraw, the Party branch to which he belongs shall, by a decision of its general membership meeting, strike his name off the Party rolls and report the matter to the next higher Party committee for registration.

Article 12

A Party member who, over a period of six months and without proper reasons, fails to take part in Party life or to pay membership dues is regarded as having quitted the Party himself. The Party branch to which this member belongs shall, by a decision of its general membership meeting, strike his name off the Party rolls and report the matter to the next higher Party committee for registration.

Article 13

Party organizations at all levels may, according to each individual case, take disciplinary measures against any Party member who violates Party discipline, by issuing a warning, a serious warning, removing him from posts in the Party, placing him on probation within the Party, or expelling him from the Party.

The period in which a Party member is placed on probation shall not exceed two years. During this period, the rights and duties of the Party member concerned are the same as those of a probationary member. If after a Party member has been placed on probation the facts show that he has corrected his mistakes, his rights as full Party member shall be restored and the period in which he is placed on probation will be reckoned in his Party standing. If he is found to be unfit for Party membership, he shall be expelled from the Party.

Article 14

Any disciplinary measure taken against a Party member must be decided on by a general membership meeting of the Party branch to which he belongs and must be approved by a higher Party control commission or higher Party committee.

Under special conditions, a Party branch committee or a higher Party committee has the power to take disciplinary measures against a Party member, but it must be subject to approval by a higher Party control commission or higher Party committee.

Article 15

Any decision to remove a member or alternate member from any Party committee—such as that of a county, an autonomous county, a municipality, a province, an autonomous region or a municipality directly under the central authority, or an autonomous *chou* [national minority area] —to place him on probation or to expel him from the Party must be taken by the Party congress that elected the said member. In conditions of urgency, such a decision may be taken by a two-thirds majority vote at a plenary session of the Party committee to which the member belongs, but it must be subject to approval by the next higher Party committee. A primary Party organization has no power to decide upon the removal of a member or alternate member of a higher Party committee, to place him on probation or to expel him from the Party.

Article 16

Any decision to remove a member or alternate member from the Central Committee of the Party, to place him on probation or to expel him from the Party must be taken by the National Party Congress. In conditions of urgency, such a decision may be taken by a two-thirds majority vote of the Central Committee at its plenary session, but it must be subject to subsequent confirmation by the next session of the National Party Congress.

Article 17

Expulsion from the Party is the most severe of all inner-Party disciplinary measures. In taking or approving such a decision, all Party organizations must exercise the utmost caution, thoroughly investigate and study the facts and material evidence of the case, and listen carefully to the statement made in his own defence by the Party member concerned.

Article 18

When a Party organization discusses or decides on a disciplinary measure against a Party member, it must, barring special circumstances, notify the member concerned to attend the meeting to defend himself. When disciplinary action is decided on, the person against whom such action is taken must be told the reasons for it. If he disagrees, he may ask for a reconsideration of his case and address an appeal to higher Party committees, to Party control commissions, up to and including the Central Committee. Party organizations at all levels must deal with such appeals seriously or forward them promptly; no suppression is permitted.

CHAPTER 2: ORGANIZATIONAL STRUCTURE AND ORGANIZATIONAL PRINCIPLES OF THE PARTY

Article 19

The Party is formed on the principle of democratic centralism.

Democratic centralism means centralism on the basis of democracy and democracy under centralized guidance. Its basic conditions are as follows:

(1) The leading bodies of the Party at all levels are elected.

(2) The highest leading body of the Party is the National Party Congress, and the highest leading body in each local Party organization is the local Party congress. The National Party Congress elects the Central Committee and the local Party congresses elect their respective local Party committees. The Central Committee and local Party committees are responsible to their respective Party congresses to which they should report on their work.

(3) All leading bodies of the Party must pay constant heed to the views of their lower organizations and the rank-and-file Party members, study their experience and promptly help to solve their problems.

(4) Lower Party organizations must present periodical reports on their work to the Party organizations above them and ask in good time for instructions on questions which need a decision by higher Party organizations.

(5) All Party organizations operate on the principle of collective leadership combined with individual responsibility. All important issues are decided on collectively, and at the same time, each individual is enabled to play his part to the fullest possible extent.

(6) Party decisions must be carried out unconditionally. Individual Party members shall obey the Party organization, the minority shall obey the majority, the lower Party organizations shall obey higher ones, and all constituent Party organizations throughout the country shall obey the National Party Congress and the Central Committee.

Article 20

Party organizations are formed on a geographical or industrial basis.

The Party organization in charge of Party work in a defined area is regarded as the highest of all the constituent Party organizations there.

The Party organization in charge of Party work in a particular production or work unit is regarded as the highest of all the constituent Party organizations in it.

Article 21

The highest leading bodies in Party organizations at various levels are as follows:

(1) For the whole country, it is the National Party Congress. When the National Party Congress is not in session, it is the Central Committee elected by the National Party Congress;

(2) For a province, autonomous region, or municipality directly under the central authority, it is the provincial, autonomous regional or municipal Party congress. When the congress is not in session, it is the provincial, autonomous regional or municipal Party committee elected by the congress.

For an autonomous *chou*, it is the autonomous *chou* Party congress. When the congress is not in session, it is the autonomous *chou* committee elected by the congress;

(3) For a county, autonomous county or municipality, it is the county, autonomous county or municipal Party congress. When the congress is not in session, it is the county, autonomous county or municipal committee elected by the congress;

(4) For primary units (factories, mines and other enterprises, *hsiang* [small rural administrative unit], nationality *hsiang*, towns and agricultural producers' co-operatives, offices, schools, streets, companies of the People's Liberation Army and other primary units), it is the delegate meeting or the general membership meeting of the particular primary unit. When the delegate meeting or general membership meeting of the primary unit is not in session, it is the primary Party committee, the committee of a general Party branch, or the committee of a Party branch elected by the delegate meeting or the general membership meeting.

Article 22

Party elections must fully reflect the will of the electors. The lists of candidates for election put forward by the Party organization or by electors must be discussed by the electors.

Election is by secret ballot. Electors shall be ensured of the right to criticize or reject any candidate, or nominate a person who is not on the list.

In an election in a primary Party organization, voting may be by a show of hands if a ballot vote is impossible. In such cases, each candidate shall be voted for separately, and voting for a whole list of candidates is forbidden.

Article 23

Party electing units have the power to replace any member they have elected to a Party congress or Party committee during his term of office.

When a local Party congress is not in session, a higher Party committee, if it deems it necessary, may transfer or appoint responsible members of a lower Party organization.

Article 24

In places where, because of special circumstances, it is impossible for the time being to call Party congresses or general membership meetings to elect Party committees, such Party committees may be elected at Party conferences or appointed by higher Party organizations.

Article 25

The functions and powers of the central Party organizations and those of the local Party organizations shall be appropriately divided. All questions of a national character or questions that require a uniform decision for the whole country shall be handled by the central Party organizations so as to contribute to the centralism and unity of the Party. All questions of a local character or questions that need to be decided locally shall be handled by the local Party organizations so as to find solutions appropriate to the local conditions. The functions and powers of higher local Party organizations and those of lower local Party organizations shall be appropriately divided according to the same principle.

Decisions taken by lower Party organizations must not run counter to those made by higher ones.

Article 26

Before decisions on Party policy are made by leading bodies of the Party, lower Party organizations and members of the Party committees may hold free and practical discussions inside Party organizations and at Party meetings and submit their proposals to the leading bodies of the Party. However, once a decision is taken by the leading bodies of the Party, it must be accepted. Should a lower Party organization find that a decision made by a higher one does not suit the actual conditions in its locality or in its particular department, it should request the higher Party organization concerned to modify the decision. If the higher Party organization still upholds its decision, then the lower one must carry it out unconditionally.

On policy of a national character, before the central leading bodies of the Party have made any statement or decision, departmental and local Party organizations and their responsible members are not permitted to make any public statement or make a decision at will, although they may discuss it among themselves and make suggestions to the central leading bodies.

Article 27

The newspapers issued by Party organizations at all levels must publicize the decisions and policy of the central Party organizations and those made by other higher Party organizations as well as their own.

Article 28

The formation of a new Party organization or the dissolution of an existing one must be decided on by the next higher Party organization.

Article 29

To facilitate the direction of the work in various localities, the Central Committee may, if it deems it necessary, establish a bureau of the Central Committee as its representative body for an area embracing several provinces, autonomous regions and municipalities directly under the central authority. A provincial or autonomous regional committee may, if it deems it necessary, establish a regional committee or an organization of equal status as its representative body for an area embracing a number of counties, autonomous counties and municipalities. The Party committee of a municipality directly under the central authority, or of a municipality, county or autonomous county may, if it deems it necessary, establish a number of district committees as its representative bodies within its area.

Article 30

Party committees at all levels may, as the situation requires, set up a number of departments, commissions or other bodies to carry on work under their own direction.

CHAPTER 3: CENTRAL ORGANIZATIONS OF THE PARTY

Article 31

The National Party Congress is elected for a term of five years.

The number of delegates to the National Party Congress and the procedure governing their election, replacement and the filling of vacancies shall be determined by the Central Committee.

A session of the National Party Congress shall be convened once a year by the Central Committee. Under extraordinary conditions, it may be postponed or convened before its due date as the Central Committee may decide. The Central Committee must convene a session of the National Party Congress if one-third of the delegates to the Congress or one-third of the Party organizations at provincial level so request.

Article 32

The functions and powers of the National Party Congress are as follows:

(1) To hear and examine the reports of the Central Committee and other central organs;

(2) To determine the Party's line and policy;

(3) To revise the Constitution of the Party;

(4) To elect the Central Committee.

Article 33

The Central Committee of the Party is elected for a term of five years. The number of members and alternate members of the Central Committee shall be determined by the National Party Congress. Vacancies on the Central Committee shall be filled by alternate members in order of established precedence.

Article 34

When the National Party Congress is not in session the Central Committee directs the entire work of the Party, carries out the decisions of the National Party Congress, represents the Party in its relations with other parties and organizations, sets up various Party organs and directs their activities, takes charge of and allocates Party cadres.

The Central Committee guides the work of the central state organs and people's organizations of a national character through leading Party members' groups within them.

Article 35

The Party organizations in the Chinese People's Liberation Army carry on their work in accordance with the instructions of the Central Committee. The General Political Department in the People's Liberation Army, under the direction of the Central Committee, takes charge of the ideological and organizational work of the Party in the army.

Article 36

The plenary sessions of the Central Committee are to be convened by the Political Bureau of the Central Committee at least twice a year.

Article 37

The Central Committee elects at its plenary session the Political Bureau, the Standing Committee of the Political Bureau and the Secretariat, as well as the chairman, vice-chairmen and general secretary of the Central Committee.

When the Central Committee is not in plenary session, the Political Bureau and its Standing Committee exercise the powers and functions of the Central Committee.

The Secretariat attends to the daily work of the Central Committee under the direction of the Political Bureau and its Standing Committee.

The chairman and vice-chairmen of the Central Committee are concurrently chairman and vice-chairmen of the Political Bureau.

The Central Committee may, when it deems it necessary, have an honorary chairman.

CHAPTER 4: PARTY ORGANIZATIONS IN PROVINCES,
AUTONOMOUS REGIONS, MUNICIPALITIES DIRECTLY
UNDER THE CENTRAL AUTHORITY,
AND AUTONOMOUS "CHOU"

Article 38

The Party congress for a province, autonomous region, or municipality directly under the central authority is elected for a term of three years.

The number of delegates to such a Party congress and the procedure governing their election, replacement and the filling of vacancies shall be determined by the Party committee in the given area.

The Party congress for a province, autonomous region, or municipality directly under the central authority shall be convened once a year by the Party committee in the area.

Article 39

The Party congress for a province, autonomous region, or municipality directly under the central authority hears and examines the reports of the Party committee and other organs in the area, discusses and decides on questions relating to the policy and work of a local character in its area, elects the Party committee for the area, and elects delegates to the National Party Congress.

Article 40

The Party committee of a province, autonomous region, or municipality directly under the central authority is elected for a term of three years. The number of members and alternate members of the committee shall be determined by the Central Committee. Vacancies on the committee shall be filled by alternate members of the committee in order of established precedence.

The Party committee of a province, autonomous region, or municipality directly under the central authority shall, when the Party congress for the given area is not in session, carry out the decisions and directives of the Party in its area, direct all work of a local character, set up various Party organs and direct their activities, take charge of and allocate Party cadres in accordance with the regulations laid down by the Central Committee, direct the work of leading Party members' groups in local state organs and people's organizations and systematically report on its work to the Central Committee.

Article 41

The Party committee of a province, autonomous region, or municipality directly under the central authority shall meet in full session at least three times a year.

The Party committee of a province, autonomous region, or municipality directly under the central authority elects at its plenary session its standing committee and secretariat. The standing committee exercises the powers and functions of the Party committee when the latter is not in plenary session. The secretariat attends to the daily work under the direction of the standing committee.

The members of the secretariat and those of the standing committee of the Party committee of a province, autonomous region or municipality directly under the central authority, must be approved by the Central Committee. Members of the secretariat must be Party members of at least five years' standing.

Article 42

Party organizations in an autonomous *chou* carry on their work under the direction of a provincial or autonomous regional Party committee.

The Party congress and Party committee for an autonomous *chou* are constituted in the same manner as those for a province, autonomous region or municipality directly under the central authority.

The Party congress and Party committee for an autonomous *chou* are elected for a term of two years.

An autonomous *chou* Party congress elects delegates to the provincial or autonomous regional Party congress.

The members of the secretariat and those of the standing committee of an autonomous *chou* Party committee must be approved by the Central Committee. The secretaries must be Party members of at least three years' standing.

CHAPTER 5: COUNTY, AUTONOMOUS COUNTY AND MUNICIPAL PARTY ORGANIZATIONS

Article 43

The Party congress for a county, autonomous county or municipality is elected for a term of two years.

The number of delegates to the congress and the procedure governing their election, replacement and the filling of vacancies shall be determined by the Party committee in the area.

The Party congress for a county, autonomous county or municipality shall be convened once a year by the Party committee in the area.

Article 44

The Party congress for a county, autonomous county or municipality hears and examines the reports of the Party committee and other organs in the area, discusses and decides on questions relating to the policy and work of a local character in its area, elects the Party committee for the area and elects delegates to the provincial or autonomous regional Party congress.

The Party congress for a county, autonomous county or municipality under the jurisdiction of an autonomous *chou* elects delegates only to the Party congress of the autonomous *chou.*

Article 45

The Party committee of a county, autonomous county or municipality is elected for a term of two years. The number of members and alternate members of the committee shall be determined by the provincial or autonomous regional Party committee. Vacancies on the committee shall be filled by alternate members of the committee in order of established precedence.

When the Party congress for a county, autonomous county or municipality is not in session, the Party committee in the area carries out Party decisions and directives in its area, directs all work of a local character, sets up various Party organs and directs their activities, takes charge of and allocates

Party cadres in accordance with the regulations laid down by the Central Committee, directs the work of leading Party members' groups in local government organs and people's organizations and systematically reports on its work to higher Party committees.

Article 46

The Party committee of a county, autonomous county or municipality shall meet in plenary session at least four times a year.

The county, autonomous county or municipal Party committee elects at its plenary session its standing committee and secretary, and, if necessary, a secretariat. The standing committee exercises the powers and functions of the Party committee when the latter is not in plenary session. The secretary or the secretariat attends to the daily work under the direction of the standing committee.

The members of the secretariat and those of the standing committee must be approved by the provincial or autonomous regional Party committee. In the case of a city with a population of 500,000 or more or in the case of a key industrial city, such members must be approved by the Central Committee. The secretaries of the Party committee of a county, autonomous county or municipality must be Party members of at least two years' standing. In the case of a city with a population of 500,000 or more or in the case of a key industrial city, the secretaries of the Party committee must be Party members of at least five years' standing.

CHAPTER 6: PRIMARY ORGANIZATIONS OF THE PARTY

Article 47

Primary Party organizations are formed in factories, mines and other enterprises, in *hsiang* and nationality *hsiang*, in towns, in agricultural producers' co-operatives, in offices, schools and streets, in companies of the People's Liberation Army and in other primary units where there are three or more full Party members. When a primary unit contains less than three full Party members, no primary Party organization should be established, but these members together with the probationary members in their unit may either form a group or join the primary Party organization of a nearby unit.

Article 48

Primary Party organizations take the following organizational forms:

(1) A primary Party organization with one hundred or more Party members may, by decision of the next higher Party committee, hold a delegate meeting or a general membership meeting to elect a primary Party committee. Under the primary Party committee a number of general branches or branches may be formed in accordance with divisions based on production, work or residence. Under a general Party branch a number of Party branches may be formed. The committee of a general Party branch is elected by a general membership meeting or a delegate meeting of the general branch. The committee of a Party branch is elected by the general membership meeting of the branch. The committee of the primary Party organization or of the general Party branch has the power to approve decisions made by a branch on the admission of new members and on disciplinary measures against Party members.

Under special conditions, individual primary Party organizations with less than one hundred members may, by decision of the next higher Party committee, establish a committee of the primary Party organization.

(2) A primary Party organization with fifty or more Party members may, by decision of the next higher Party committee, set up a general branch committee to be elected by a general membership meeting or a delegate meeting. Under a general branch committee a number of branches may be formed in accordance with divisions based on production, work or residence. The general branch committee has the power to approve decisions made by a branch on the admission of new members and on disciplinary measures against Party members.

Under special conditions, a general branch committee may, by decision of the next higher Party committee, be set up in a primary Party organization whose membership is less than fifty but whose work requires a general branch committee, or in a primary Party organization whose membership numbers one hundred or more but whose work does not require a primary Party committee.

(3) A primary Party organization with less than fifty members may, by decision of the next higher Party committee, set up a branch committee to be elected by a general membership meeting. Such a primary Party organization has the power to make decisions on the admission of new members and on disciplinary measures against Party members.

(4) Groups may be formed under a general Party branch or a Party branch.

Article 49

A primary Party organization which has set up its own primary committee shall convene a delegate meeting at least once a year. A general Party branch shall hold a general membership meeting or a delegate meeting at least twice a year. A Party branch shall hold a general membership meeting at least once in three months.

The delegate meeting or general membership meeting of a primary Party organization hears and examines the reports of the primary Party committee, the general branch committee or the branch committee; it discusses and decides on questions relating to work in its own unit, elects the primary Party committee, the general Party branch committee, or the branch committee, and elects delegates to the higher Party congress.

The primary Party committee, the general Party branch committee and the branch committee are elected for a term of one year. The number of members of these committees shall be determined by their next higher Party committees.

A primary Party committee shall elect a secretary and from one to four deputy secretaries. If necessary, it may elect a standing committee. The general branch committee and the branch committee shall each elect a secretary, and, if necessary, one to three deputy secretaries.

A Party branch with less than ten members only elects a secretary or in addition a deputy secretary, but no branch committee needs to be formed.

A Party group shall elect a leader and, if necessary, a deputy leader.

Article 50

Primary Party organizations must cement the ties of the workers, peasants, intellectuals and other patriotic people with the Party and its leading bodies. The general tasks of primary Party organizations are as follows:

(1) To carry on propaganda and organizational work among the masses and put into practice what the Party advocates, and the decisions of higher Party organizations;

(2) To pay constant heed to the sentiments and demands of the masses and report them to higher Party organizations, to pay constant attention to the material and cultural life of the masses and strive to improve it;

(3) To recruit new Party members, to collect membership dues, to examine and appraise Party members and to maintain Party discipline among the membership;

(4) To organize Party members to study Marxism-Leninism and the Party's policy and experience and raise the levels of their ideology and political understanding;

(5) To lead the masses of the people to take an active part in the political life of the country;

(6) To lead the masses so that they can give full play to their initiative and creative ability, to strengthen labour discipline and ensure the fulfilment of production and work plans;

(7) To promote criticism and self-criticism, to expose and eliminate shortcomings and mistakes in work, and wage struggles against the violation of laws and discipline, against corruption, waste and bureaucracy;

(8) To educate Party members and the masses to sharpen their revolutionary vigilance and be constantly on the alert to combat the disruptive activities of the class enemy.

Article 51

Primary Party organizations in the enterprises, villages, schools and army units should guide and supervise the administrative bodies and mass organizations in their respective units so that they may energetically fulfil the decisions of higher Party organizations and higher state organs and ceaselessly improve their work.

Since special conditions obtain in public institutions and organizations, the primary Party organizations therein are in no position to guide and supervise their work, but they should supervise ideologically and politically all Party members in the said institutions and organizations, including those who hold leading administrative posts. The primary Party organizations should also take a constant interest in improving the work in their respective units, strengthen labour discipline, combat bureaucracy, and report without delay any shortcomings in the work to the administrative chiefs of the given units and to higher Party organizations.

CHAPTER 7: CONTROL ORGANS OF THE PARTY

Article 52

The Party's Central Committee, the Party committees of the provinces, autonomous regions, municipalities directly under the central authority, and autonomous *chou*, and the Party committees of the counties, autonomous counties and municipalities shall set up control commissions. The Central Control Commission shall be elected by the Central Committee at its plenary session. A local control commission shall be elected by a plenary session of the Party committee for that locality, subject to approval by the next higher Party committee.

Article 53

The tasks of the central and local control commissions are as follows: regularly to examine and deal with cases of violation by Party members of the Party Constitution, Party discipline, communist ethics and state laws and decrees; to decide on or cancel disciplinary measures against Party members; and to deal with appeals and complaints from Party members.

Article 54

The control commissions at all levels function under the direction of the Party committees at corresponding levels.

Higher control commissions have the power to check up on the work of lower ones, and to approve or modify their decisions on any case. Lower control commissions must report on their work to higher ones, and present accurate reports on the violation of discipline by Party members.

CHAPTER 8: RELATION BETWEEN THE PARTY AND THE COMMUNIST YOUTH LEAGUE

Article 55

The Communist Youth League of China carries on its activities under the guidance of the Communist Party of China. The Central Committee of the League accepts the leadership of the Party's Central Committee. The League's local organizations are simultaneously under the leadership of the Party organizations at corresponding levels and of higher League organizations.

Article 56

The Communist Youth League is the Party's assistant. In all spheres of socialist construction the League organizations should play an active role in publicizing and carrying out Party policy and decisions. In the struggle to promote production, improve work, and expose and eliminate shortcomings and mistakes in work, the League organizations should render effective help to the Party and have the duty to make suggestions to the Party organizations concerned.

Article 57

Party organizations at all levels must take a deep interest in the Communist Youth League's ideological and organizational work, give guidance to the League in imbuing all its members with communist spirit and educating them in Marxist-Leninist theory, see to it that close contact is maintained between the League and the broad masses of young people and pay constant attention to the selection of members for the leading core of the League.

Article 58

Members of the Communist Youth League shall withdraw from the League when they have been admitted to the Party and have become full Party members, provided they do not hold leading posts or engage in specific work in the League organizations.

CHAPTER 9: LEADING PARTY MEMBERS' GROUPS IN NON-PARTY ORGANIZATIONS

Article 59

In the leading body of a state organ or people's organization, where there are three or more Party members holding responsible posts, a leading Party members' group shall be formed. The tasks of such a group in the organ or organization are: to assume the responsibility of carrying out Party policy and decisions, to fortify unity with non-Party cadres, to cement ties with the masses, to strengthen Party and state discipline and to combat bureaucracy.

Article 60

The composition of a leading Party members' group shall be decided by a competent Party committee. The group shall have a secretary, and may, in case of need, also have a deputy secretary.

A leading Party members' group must in all matters accept the leadership of the competent Party committee.

21. *Teng Hsiao-p'ing: Report on the Revision of the Constitution of the Communist Party of China (September, 1956)**

At the time when this report was presented to the Party, Teng Hsiao-p'ing, also known as Teng Wen-pin, was one of the most influential members of the Politburo Standing Committee and the General Secretary of the Party.

Teng studied in France in 1920 and helped Chou En-lai to found the Chinese Communist group in Paris in 1920–1922. After his return to China in 1926, he served in the Red Army as a political commissar. When the People's Government was established in Peking, Teng became a

---

* From book so titled, Peking: Foreign Language Press, 1956, pp. 57–104. (Extract.)

Vice-Premier of the State Council as well as a Vice-Chairman of the National Defense Council. However, during the 1966–1967 Cultural Revolution he sided with President Liu Shao-chi and thereby aroused the displeasure of Chairman Mao Tse-tung.

This report by Teng was delivered at the Eighth National Congress on September 16, 1956. In it, Teng particularly stresses (1) the mass line as a Communist method of work, (2) democratic centralism as the Party's Leninist organizational principle, and (3) membership solidarity as the key concept in formulation of the Party's structure.

THE MASS LINE

What is the mass line in Party work? Briefly stated, it has two aspects. In one respect, it maintains that the people must liberate themselves, that the Party's entire task is to serve the people heart and soul, and that the Party's role in leading the masses lies in pointing out to them the correct path of struggle and helping them to struggle for and build a happy life by their own effort. Consequently, the Party must keep in close contact with the masses and rely on them, and must in no circumstances lose touch with them or place itself above them. For the same reason every Party member must cultivate a style of work of serving the people, holding himself responsible to the masses, never failing to consult them, and being ever ready to share their joys and sorrows.

In another respect, the mass line maintains that the Party's ability to go on exercising correct leadership hinges upon its ability to adopt the method of "coming from the masses and going back to the masses." This means—to quote from the Central Committee's "Resolution on Methods of Leadership," drafted by Comrade Mao Tse-tung—"summing up (i.e. coordinating and systematizing after careful study) the views of the masses (i.e. views scattered and unsystematic), then taking the resulting ideas back to the masses, explaining and popularizing them until the masses embrace the ideas as their own, stand up for them and act on them and then testing the correctness of these ideas in mass activity. Then it is necessary once more to sum up the views of the masses, and once again take the resulting ideas back to the masses so that the masses give them their whole-hearted support. . . . And so on, over and over again, so that each time these ideas emerge with greater correctness and become more vital and meaningful."

The mass line in Party work is of profound theoretical and practical significance. Marxism has always maintained that history, in the last analysis, is made by the people. Only by relying on its own mass strength and that of all labouring people will the working class be able to fulfil its historical mission—the mission of liberating itself and, with it, all labouring people. The greater the awakening, activity and creative ability of the masses, the more flourishing the cause of the working class. Consequently, a political party of the working class, unlike the political parties of the bourgeoisie, never regards the masses as its tools, but consciously regards itself as their tool for carrying out their given historical mission in a given historical period. The Communist Party is the collective body of the advanced elements among the working class and the labouring people, and there can be no doubt as to its great role in leading the masses. But the Party can play its part as vanguard and lead the masses forward precisely and solely because it whole-heartedly serves the masses, represents their will and interests, and strives to help them organize themselves to fight for their own interests and for the fulfilment of their will. To fully affirm this concept of the Party is to affirm that the Party has no right whatever to place itself above the masses, that is, no right to act towards the masses as if it were dispensing "favours," to take everything into its own hands and impose its will "by decree," or rather no right to lord it over the people.

Unless we understand from a correct ideological approach that our Party policy must of necessity be "coming from the masses and going back to the masses," we can obtain no real solution to the problem of the Party's relations with the masses. Practice has shown that there are many people who do not lack the desire to serve the masses and yet bungle their work in a way that does great harm to the masses. This is because they regard themselves as advanced elements, or as leaders knowing a great deal more than the masses. Therefore, they neither learn from the masses nor consult them, with the result that their ideas more often than not prove impracticable. Far from learning from their mistakes and failures, they blame them on the backwardness of the masses or other accidental factors, abuse the Party's prestige, and wilfully and arbitrarily persist in their actions, thereby aggravating their mistakes and failures. The history of our Party furnishes us with instances of such subjectivists causing incalculable losses to our Party, to the Chinese revolution and the Chinese people. The subjectivists do not understand that only those who really know how to be students of the masses can ever become their teachers, and only by continuing to be students can they continue to be teachers. Only by carefully summing up the experience of the masses and bringing their wisdom together, can a party and its members point to the correct path and lead the masses forward. We do not tail behind the masses, and we know quite well that the opinions which come from the masses cannot be all correct and mature. What we mean by summing up the experience and bringing together the wisdom of the masses is by no means a simple process of accumulation; there must be classification, analysis, critical judgment and synthesis. But without investigation and study of the experience and opinions of the masses, no leader, however talented, can lead correctly. Mistakes may still be made even after classification, analysis, critical judgment and synthesis have been made. But by constantly consulting the masses and studying their practice, the Party will be able to make fewer mistakes and to discover and correct them in time so as to prevent them from becoming serious.

The mass line in Party work, therefore, demands that the Party leadership should conduct themselves with modesty and prudence. Arrogance, arbitrariness, rashness, and habits of pretending to be clever, of not consulting the masses, of forcing one's opinions on others, of persisting in errors to keep up one's prestige—all these are utterly incompatible with the Party's mass line.

This task is set forth both in the General Programme and in all the relevant articles of the draft Party Constitution. Of course, these provisions by themselves cannot solve the problem. We must in addition adopt a series of practical measures. What measures must we take?

First, we must vigorously expound the mass line throughout the Party's educational network, in the educational literature for Party members, and in all Party newspapers and periodicals.

Secondly, we must systematically improve the working methods of the leading bodies at all levels so that the leading personnel will have ample time to go deep into the midst of the masses, and study their conditions, their experience and their opinions by investigating typical situations. This should replace the present practice of spending most of the time in offices, handling papers and documents and holding meetings inside the leading bodies. The staff of the leading bodies should be cut down and the number of organizational levels be reduced. The leading bodies should send as many of their superfluous working personnel as possible to lower bodies and let the remaining ones handle practical work themselves, so as to guard against the danger of the leading bodies turning bureaucratic.

Thirdly, we must see to it that the democratic life of the Party and the state is fully developed so that the lower organizations of the Party and government will have adequate facilities and the assurance to make timely and fearless criticism of all mistakes and shortcomings in the work of the higher bodies, and that all kinds of Party or state meetings, especially Party congresses and people's congresses at all levels, will serve as the forum where the opinions of the masses can be fully voiced and criticism and debate freely used.

Fourthly, we must strengthen supervision by the Party and the state, discover and correct in time all kinds of bureaucratic practices, and mete out due and prompt punishment to those who have contravened law and discipline or seriously damaged the interests of the masses.

Fifthly, the Party organizations in various localities and departments must check up at regular intervals on the working style of all Party members through criticism by the masses and through self-criticism, drawing on the experience gained in Party rectification campaigns of the past. In particular, they must carefully check up on how the mass line is being carried out.

In the struggle to carry out the mass line and combat bureaucracy, it is of vital importance to strengthen still further our co-operation with non-Party people, and to draw as many of them as possible into the struggle. At present, however, there are a good many comrades in our Party, including some in fairly responsible positions, who still have the defect of being either reluctant or unaccustomed to co-operate with non-Party people. This, in fact, is a very harmful sectarian tendency, and only when such a tendency is overcome can the Party's united front policy be carried out thoroughly.

DEMOCRATIC CENTRALISM

Democratic centralism is our Party's Leninist organizational principle. It is the fundamental organizational principle of the Party, the mass line in Party work applied to the life of the Party itself. In the General Programme and in Chapter Two of the draft Constitution, more detailed provisions are made concerning democratic centralism in the Party. These provisions are the result of many years' experience gained in the organizational life of our Party.

The Party depends on all its members and organizations to maintain contact with the broad masses of the people. The collection of opinions and experiences from among the masses, the publicizing of the Party's policy so as to turn it into the views of the masses, and the organization of the masses to put the Party's policy into effect—all this must be done, generally speaking, through the efforts of the Party members and lower Party organizations. Therefore, with regard to the question of democratic centralism in the Party, what is of special significance is to correctly regulate the relations between the Party organization and its members, between higher and lower Party organizations, and between central and local Party organizations.

In the light of the various kinds of experience mentioned above, the draft Constitution makes the following additional provisions in regard to the relationship between higher and lower organizations under democratic centralism:

Firstly, with regard to the basic conditions of democratic centralism, the following provisions are added: "All leading bodies of the Party must pay constant heed to the views of their lower organizations and the rank-and-file Party members, study their experiences and give prompt help in solving their problems." "Lower Party organizations must present periodical reports on their work to the Party organizations above them and ask in good time for instructions on questions which need decision by higher Party organizations."

Secondly, concerning the functions and powers of the central and local organizations and of the higher and lower Party organizations, the following article is added: "The functions and powers of the central Party organizations and those of the local Party organizations shall be appropriately divided. All questions of a national character or questions that require a uniform decision for the whole country shall be handled by the central Party organizations so as to contribute to the centralism and unity of the Party. All questions of a local character or questions that need to be decided locally shall be handled by the local Party organizations so as to find solutions appropriate to the local conditions. The functions and powers of higher local Party organizations and those of lower Party organizations shall be appropriately divided according to the same principle."

Thirdly, with regard to discussions on questions of policy and the carrying out of decisions, the following article is added: "Before decisions on Party policy are made by the leading bodies of the Party, lower Party organizations and members of the Party committees may hold free and practical discussions inside the Party organizations and at Party meetings and submit their proposals to the leading bodies of the Party. However, once a decision is taken by the leading bodies of the Party, it must be accepted. Should a lower Party organization find that a decision made by a higher Party organization does not suit the actual conditions in its locality or in its particular department, it should request the higher Party organization concerned to modify the decision. If the higher Party organization still upholds its decision, then the lower Party organization must carry it out unconditionally."

Another fundamental question with regard to democratic centralism in the Party is the question of collective leadership in Party organizations at all levels. Leninism demands of the Party that all important questions should be decided by an appropriate collective body, and not by any individual. The 20th Congress of the Communist Party of the Soviet Union has thrown a searching light on the profound significance of adhering to the principle of collective leadership and combating the cult of the individual, and this illuminating lesson has produced a tremendous effect not only on the Communist Party of the Soviet Union but also on the Communist Parties of all other countries throughout the world. It is obvious that the making of decisions on important questions by individuals goes counter to the Party-building principles of the political parties dedicated to the cause of communism, and is bound to lead to errors. Only collective leadership, in close touch with the masses, conforms to the Party's principles of democratic centralism and can reduce the possibility of errors to the minimum.

It has become a long-established tradition in our Party to make decisions on important questions by a collective body of the Party, and not by any individual. Although violations of the principle of collective leadership have been frequent in our Party, yet once discovered, they have been criticized and rectified by the Central Committee.

THE SOLIDARITY AND UNITY OF THE PARTY

Our Party has now assumed the leading role in all fields of state affairs and public activities. It is obvious that our Party in its present condition is exercising a more direct and extensive influence on the national life than ever before. It is for the benefit not only of the Party but also of the entire people that we should safeguard the solidarity of the Party and strengthen its unity.

The Party is the highest form of class organization. It is particularly important to point this out today when our Party has assumed the leading role in state affairs. Of course this does not mean that the Party should be directly in command regarding the work of state organs, or discuss at Party meetings questions of a purely administrative nature and overstep the line of demarcation between Party work and the work of state organs. It means, first, that Party members in state organs and particularly the leading Party members' groups formed by those in responsible positions in such departments should follow the unified leadership of the Party. Secondly, the Party must regularly discuss and decide on questions with regard to the guiding principles, policies and important organizational matters in state affairs, and the leading Party members' groups in the state organs must see to it that these decisions are put into effect with the harmonious co-operation of non-Party personalities. Thirdly, the Party must conscientiously and systematically look into the problems and work of the state organs so as to be able to put forward correct, practical and specific proposals or revise them in time in the light of actual practice, and must exercise constant supervision over the work of state organs. Some comrades working in government departments do not respect the leadership of the Party on the pretext that their work is of an exceptional nature, and attempt to turn their own departments into "independent kingdoms." This is a dangerous tendency which must be overcome. At the same time, some Party organizations incorrectly interfere with the administrative work of state organs, while others, without investigation and study, are content to offer a vague, generalized kind of leadership or a leadership based on imagination. This is another tendency which must be overcome.

The points I have mentioned about the relationship between the Party and the state organs in their work also apply in general to the relationship between the Party and the various people's organizations. But as democracy in these organizations is much broader than that in state organs, the Party should take this special feature into consideration when exercising leadership over the leading Party members' groups in these organizations.

In order to strengthen the unity and solidarity within its own ranks, in order to play its role as leader and nucleus to the fullest possible extent, the Party has waged uncompromising struggles against all sorts of deviations in this respect. The long-term existence of the Party in widely-scattered rural areas; the strong influence that feudal, bourgeois and petty-bourgeois ideas and styles of work still have in our society; and the deepening of class struggle at a certain period of the socialist revolution—all these factors cannot but find reflection in the life of the Party. Therefore, the solidarity and unity of the Party are inseparable from inner-Party struggles of varying degrees.

In order to maintain Party solidarity and unity on the basis of Marxism-Leninism, to help comrades overcome their shortcomings and correct mistakes in time, it is necessary to greatly intensify criticism and self-criticism within the Party. To encourage and support criticism from below and to prohibit the suppression of criticism are of decisive importance for the development of criticism in the Party. In the past few years, the Central Committee has several times organized Party-wide campaigns of criticism and self-criticism in the form of "Rectification Campaigns," which have yielded remarkably good results. When calling lower-rank comrades to meetings or in talking to them, leading comrades of the Central Committee have of their own accord asked them to criticize the Central Committee's work, listened patiently to their criticisms, and promptly taken necessary and practical measures to correct the shortcomings and mistakes pointed out, with the result that inner-Party criticism from below has been greatly encouraged. The Central Committee has carried out a sharp struggle against the suppression of criticism and applied disciplinary measures to some leading personnel who arbitrarily stifled criticism from below. But it must be admitted that even now not a few responsible comrades in Party organizations, and not a few Party members who hold responsible positions in government departments and people's organizations still do not encourage and support criticism from below. Some of them even use the shameful method of making personal attacks and carrying out reprisals against their critics. This is also one of the grave signs that the germs of bureaucracy are attacking our Party. Every true Communist must fight to root out this evil.

22. Mao Tse-tung: On the Correct Handling of Contradictions among the People (February, 1957)*

This is the text of a speech made by Mao Tse-tung on February 27, 1957, at the Eleventh Session of the Supreme State Conference. This speech, which was substantially revised at the time of its publication in June, 1957, was regarded as one of Mao's most important theoretical statements since the Communist triumph on the mainland. For almost a year, Mao had been trying to liberate or loosen Communist ideological control, as hinted by the new party slogan (May, 1956): "Let a hundred flowers blossom and a hundred schools of thought contend" (which has been included in his speech).

However, Mao's speech was clearly occasioned in part by the Hungarian Revolution late in 1956. In Mao's eyes, the Hungarian Revolution was largely due to the isolation of the Hungarian Communist bureaucracy from the masses. Mao was aware that such alienation was widespread in China as well, and he tried to allow criticism against Party and government functionaries. Those who took advantage of the offer were later identified as the "culprits" in an anti-rightist campaign. After all, the "blooming and contending" movement was not to encourage "fragrant flowers," but rather to identify "poisonous weeds."

---

* From book so titled, Peking: Foreign Language Press, 1960, pp. 3–27, 48–59. (Extract.)

The significance of this speech lies in its reaffirmation of the importance Mao attaches to the existence of "contradictions" within a post-revolutionary society. Taking Marxist doctrine as a base, Mao insisted that contradictions exist in relations between classes, and must therefore govern politics. According to Mao, there are two types of contradictions: the first, called antagonistic contradictions, exist between hostile classes and hostile social systems. These are contradictions "between the enemy and ourselves," and being essentially violent these contradictions can be resolved only by force. The second is called nonantagonistic contradictions, which exist within the socialist society; being essentially nonviolent these contradictions can be resolved through the process of "uniting, criticizing and educating."

In his speech, Mao stressed on the one hand the universality of these contradictions, and on the other their particularity as determined by the needs of time and place. Anyone who fought an issue at the wrong time or in the wrong place would be a deviationist from the Party line. For every contradiction there can only be a single correct resolution, which springs out of what Mao calls "the basic identity of the interests of the people." The decision as to what this identity is, is left to the Party; the Party acts as the infallible and supreme interpreter. The theoretical authority and infallibility of the Party have been used by Mao to tighten discipline and consolidate his personal leadership. Only in this sense can we understand the emphasis placed by the Communists on the various ideological remolding campaigns and purges.

Two Different Types of Contradictions

Never has our country been as united as it is today. The victories of the bourgeois-democratic revolution and the socialist revolution, coupled with our achievements in socialist construction, have rapidly changed the face of old China. Now we see before us an even brighter future. The days of national disunity and turmoil which the people detested have gone for ever. Led by the working class and the Communist Party, and united as one, our six hundred million people are engaged in the great work of building socialism. Unification of the country, unity of the people and unity among our various nationalities—these are the basic guarantees for the sure triumph of our cause. However, this does not mean that there are no longer any contradictions in our society. It would be naïve to imagine that there are no more contradictions. To do so would be to fly in the face of objective reality. We are confronted by two types of social contradictions—contradictions between ourselves and the enemy and contradictions among the people. These two types of contradictions are totally different in nature.

The contradictions between ourselves and our enemies are antagonistic ones. Within the ranks of the people, contradictions among the working people are non-antagonistic, while those between the exploiters and the exploited classes have, apart from their antagonistic aspect, a non-antagonistic aspect. Contradictions among the people have always existed. But their content differs in each period of the revolution and during the building of socialism. In the conditions existing in China today what we call contradictions among the people include the following: contradictions within the working class, contradictions within the peasantry, contradictions within the intelligentsia, contradictions between the working class and the peasantry, contradictions between the working class and peasantry on the one hand and the intelligentsia on the other, contradictions between the working class and other sections of the working people on the one hand and the national bourgeoisie on the other, contradictions within the national bourgeoisie, and so forth. Our people's government is a government that truly represents the interests of the people and serves the people, yet certain contradictions do exist between the government and the masses. These include contradictions between the interests of the state, collective interests and individual interests; between democracy and centralism; between those in positions of leadership and the led, and contradictions arising from the bureaucratic practices of certain state functionaries in their relations with the masses. All these are contradictions among the people. Generally speaking, underlying the contradictions among the people is the basic identity of the interests of the people.

In our country, the contradiction between the working class and the national bourgeoisie is a contradiction among the people. The class struggle waged between the two is, by and large, a class struggle within the ranks of the people. This is because of the dual character of the national bourgeoisie in our country. In the years of the bourgeois-democratic revolution, there was a revolutionary side to their character; there was also a tendency to compromise with the enemy, this was the other side. In the period of the socialist revolution, exploitation of the working class to make profits is one side, while support of the Constitution and willingness to accept socialist transformation is the other. The national bourgeoisie differs from the imperialists, the landlords and the bureaucrat-capitalists. The contradiction between exploiter and exploited, which exists between the national bourgeoisie and the working class, is an antagonistic one. But, in the concrete conditions existing in China, such an antagonistic contradiction, if properly handled, can be transformed into a non-antagonistic one and resolved in a peaceful way. But if it is not properly handled, if, say, we do not follow a policy of uniting, criticizing and educating the national bourgeoisie, or if the national bourgeoisie does not accept this policy, then the contradiction between the working class and the national bourgeoisie can turn into an antagonistic contradiction as between ourselves and the enemy.

Since the contradictions between ourselves and the enemy and those among the people differ in nature, they must be solved in different ways. To put it briefly, the former is a matter of drawing a line between us and our enemies, while the latter is a matter of distinguishing between right and wrong. It is, of course, true that drawing a line between ourselves and our enemies is also a question of distinguishing between right and wrong. For example, the question as to who is right, we or the reactionaries at home and abroad—that is, the imperialists, the feudalists and bureaucrat-capitalists—is also a question of distinguishing between right and wrong, but it is different in nature from questions of right and wrong among the people.

Ours is a people's democratic dictatorship, led by the working class and based on the worker-peasant alliance. What is this dictatorship for? Its first function is to suppress the reactionary classes and elements and those exploiters in the country who range themselves against the socialist revolution, to suppress all those who try to wreck our socialist construction; that is to say, to solve the contradictions between ourselves and the enemy within the country. For instance, to arrest, try and sentence certain counter-revolutionaries, and for a specified period of time to deprive landlords and bu-reaucrat-capitalists of their right to vote and freedom of speech—all this comes within the scope of our dictatorship. To maintain law and order and safeguard the interests of the people, it is likewise necessary to exercise dictatorship over robbers, swindlers, murderers, arsonists, hooligans and other scoundrels who seriously disrupt social order.

The second function of this dictatorship is to protect our country from subversive activities and possible aggression by the external enemy. Should that happen, it is the task of this dictatorship to solve the external contradiction between our-selves and the enemy. The aim of this dictatorship is to pro-tect all our people so that they can work in peace and build China into a socialist country with a modern industry, agri-culture, science and culture.

Who is to exercise this dictatorship? Naturally it must be the working class and the entire people led by it. Dictatorship does not apply in the ranks of the people. The people cannot possibly exercise dictatorship over themselves; nor should one section of them oppress another section. Law-breaking ele-ments among the people will be dealt with according to law, but this is different in principle from using the dictatorship to suppress enemies of the people. What applies among the people is democratic centralism. Our Constitution lays it down that citizens of the People's Republic of China enjoy freedom of speech, of the press, of assembly, of association, of proces-sion, of demonstration, of religious belief and so on. Our Con-stitution also provides that organs of state must practise demo-cratic centralism and must rely on the masses; that the personnel of organs of state must serve the people. Our social-ist democracy is democracy in the widest sense, such as is not to be found in any capitalist country. Our dictatorship is known as the people's democratic dictatorship, led by the working class and based on the worker-peasant alliance. That is to say, democracy operates within the ranks of the people, while the working class, uniting with all those enjoying civil rights, the peasantry in the first place, enforces dictatorship over the reactionary classes and elements and all those who resist socialist transformation and oppose socialist construc-tion. By civil rights, we mean, politically, freedom and demo-cratic rights.

But this freedom is freedom with leadership and this democracy is democracy under centralized guidance, not anarchy. Anarchy does not conform to the interests or wishes of the people.

Certain people in our country were delighted when the Hungarian events took place. They hoped that something similar would happen in China, that thousands upon thousands of people would demonstrate in the streets against the People's Government. Such hopes ran counter to the interests of the masses and therefore could not possibly get their support. In Hungary, a section of the people, deceived by domestic and foreign counter-revolutionaries, made the mistake of resorting to acts of violence against the people's government, with the result that both the state and the people suffered for it. The damage done to the country's economy in a few weeks of rioting will take a long time to repair. There were other people in our country who took a wavering attitude towards the Hungarian events because they were ignorant about the actual world situation. They felt that there was too little freedom under our people's democracy and that there was more freedom under Western parliamentary democracy. They ask for the adoption of the two-party system of the West, where one party is in office and the other out of office. But this so-called two-party system is nothing but a means of maintaining the dictatorship of the bourgeoisie; under no circumstances can it safeguard the freedom of the working people. As a matter of fact, freedom and democracy cannot exist in the abstract, they only exist in the concrete. In a society where there is class struggle, when the exploiting classes are free to exploit the working people the working people will have no freedom from being exploited; when there is democracy for the bourgeoisie there can be no democracy for the proletariat and other working people. In some capitalist countries the Communist Parties are allowed to exist legally but only to the extent that they do not endanger the fundamental interests of the bourgeoisie; beyond that they are not permitted legal existence. Those who demand freedom and democracy in the abstract regard democracy as an end and not a means. Democracy sometimes seems to be an end, but it is in fact only a means. Marxism teaches us that democracy is part of the superstructure and belongs to the category of politics. That is to say, in the last analysis, it serves the economic base. The same is true of freedom. Both democracy and freedom are relative, not absolute, and they come into being and develop under specific historical circumstances. Within the ranks of our people, democracy stands in relation to centralism, and freedom to discipline. They are two conflicting aspects of a single entity, contradictory as well as united, and we should not one-sidedly emphasize one to the denial of the other. Within the ranks of the people, we cannot do without freedom, nor can we do without discipline; we cannot do without democracy, nor can we do without centralism. Our democratic centralism means the unity of democracy and centralism and the unity of freedom and discipline. Under this system, the people enjoy a wide measure of democracy and freedom, but at the same time they have to keep themselves within the bounds of socialist discipline. All this is well understood by the people.

Marxist philosophy holds that the law of the unity of opposites is a fundamental law of the universe. This law operates everywhere, in the natural world, in human society, and in man's thinking. Opposites in contradiction unite as well as struggle with each other, and thus impel all things to move and change. Contradictions exist everywhere, but as things differ in nature, so do contradictions. In any given phenomenon or thing, the unity of opposites is conditional, temporary and transitory, and hence relative; whereas struggle between opposites is absolute. Lenin gave a very clear exposition of this law. In our country, a growing number of people have come to understand it. For many people, however, acceptance of this law is one thing, and its application in examining and dealing with problems is quite another. Many dare not acknowledge openly that there still exist contradictions among the people, which are the very forces that move our society forward. Many people refuse to admit that contradictions still exist in a socialist society, with the result that when confronted with social contradictions they become timid and helpless. They do not understand that socialist society grows more united and consolidated precisely through the ceaseless process of correctly dealing with and resolving contradictions. For this reason, we need to explain things to our people, our cadres in the first place, to help them understand contradictions in a socialist society and learn how to deal with such contradictions in a correct way.

ON "LETTING A HUNDRED FLOWERS BLOSSOM,"
AND "LETTING A HUNDRED SCHOOLS OF THOUGHT
CONTEND," AND "LONG-TERM CO-EXISTENCE AND
MUTUAL SUPERVISION"

"Let a hundred flowers blossom," and "let a hundred
schools of thought contend," "long-term co-existence and
mutual supervision"—how did these slogans come to be put
forward?

They were put forward in the light of the specific conditions existing in China, on the basis of the recognition that
various kinds of contradictions still exist in a socialist society,
and in response to the country's urgent need to speed up its
economic and cultural development.

The policy of letting a hundred flowers blossom and a
hundred schools of thought contend is designed to promote
the flourishing of the arts and the progress of science; it is
designed to enable a socialist culture to thrive in our land.
Different forms and styles in art can develop freely and different schools in science can contend freely. We think that it is
harmful to the growth of art and science if administrative
measures are used to impose one particular style of art or
school of thought and to ban another. Questions of right and
wrong in the arts and sciences should be settled through free
discussion in artistic and scientific circles and in the course
of practical work in the arts and sciences. They should not be
settled in summary fashion. A period of trial is often needed
to determine whether something is right or wrong. In the past,
new and correct things often failed at the outset to win recognition from the majority of people and had to develop by
twists and turns in struggle. Correct and good things have
often at first been looked upon not as fragrant flowers but as
poisonous weeds. Copernicus' theory of the solar system
and Darwin's theory of evolution were once dismissed as
erroneous and had to win through over bitter opposition.
Chinese history offers many similar examples. In socialist
society, conditions for the growth of new things are radically
different from and far superior to those in the old society.
Nevertheless, it still often happens that new, rising forces are
held back and reasonable suggestions smothered.

The growth of new things can also be hindered, not because of deliberate suppression, but because of lack of dis-

cernment. That is why we should take a cautious attitude in regard to questions of right and wrong in the arts and sciences, encourage free discussion, and avoid hasty conclusions. We believe that this attitude will facilitate the growth of the arts and sciences.

Marxism has also developed through struggle. At the beginning, Marxism was subjected to all kinds of attack and regarded as a poisonous weed. It is still being attacked and regarded as a poisonous weed in many parts of the world. However, it enjoys a different position in the socialist countries. But even in these countries, there are non-Marxist as well as anti-Marxist ideologies. It is true that in China, socialist transformation, in so far as a change in the system of ownership is concerned, has in the main been completed, and the turbulent, large-scale, mass class struggles characteristic of the revolutionary periods have in the main concluded. But remnants of the overthrown landlord and comprador classes still exist, the bourgeoisie still exists, and the petty bourgeoisie has only just begun to remould itself. Class struggle is not yet over. The class struggle between the proletariat and the bourgeoisie, the class struggle between various political forces, and the class struggle in the ideological field between the proletariat and the bourgeoisie will still be long and devious and at times may even become very acute. The proletariat seeks to transform the world according to its own world outlook, so does the bourgeoisie. In this respect, the question whether socialism or capitalism will win is still not really settled. Marxists are still a minority of the entire population as well as of the intellectuals. Marxism therefore must still develop through struggle. Marxism can only develop through struggle—this is true not only in the past and present, it is necessarily true in the future also. What is correct always develops in the course of struggle with what is wrong. The true, the good and the beautiful always exist in comparison with the false, the evil and the ugly, and grow in struggle with the latter. As mankind in general rejects an untruth and accepts a truth, a new truth will begin struggling with new erroneous ideas. Such struggles will never end. This is the law of development of truth and it is certainly also the law of development of Marxism.

It will take a considerable time to decide the issue in the ideological struggle between socialism and capitalism in our country. This is because the influence of the bourgeoisie and of the intellectuals who come from the old society will remain in our country as the ideology of a class for a long time to come. Failure to grasp this, or still worse, failure to understand it at all, can lead to the gravest mistakes—to ignoring the necessity of waging the struggle in the ideological field. Ideological struggle is not like other forms of struggle. Crude, coercive methods should not be used in this struggle, but only the method of painstaking reasoning. Today, socialism enjoys favourable conditions in the ideological struggle. The main power of the state is in the hands of the working people led by the proletariat. The Communist Party is strong and its prestige stands high. Although there are defects and mistakes in our work, every fair-minded person can see that we are loyal to the people, that we are both determined and able to build up our country together with the people, and that we have achieved great successes and will achieve still greater ones. The vast majority of the bourgeoisie and intellectuals who come from the old society are patriotic; they are willing to serve their flourishing socialist motherland, and they know that if they turn away from the socialist cause and the working people led by the Communist Party, they will have no one to rely on and no bright future to look forward to.

People may ask: Since Marxism is accepted by the majority of the people in our country as the guiding ideology, can it be criticized? Certainly it can. As a scientific truth, Marxism fears no criticism. If it did, and could be defeated in argument, it would be worthless. In fact, aren't the idealists criticizing Marxism every day and in all sorts of ways? As for those who harbour bourgeois and petty bourgeois ideas and do not wish to change, aren't they also criticizing Marxism in all sorts of ways? Marxists should not be afraid of criticism from any quarter. Quite the contrary, they need to steel and improve themselves and win new positions in the teeth of criticism and the storm and stress of struggle. Fighting against wrong ideas is like being vaccinated—a man develops greater immunity from disease after the vaccine takes effect. Plants raised in hot-houses are not likely to be robust. Carrying out the policy of letting a hundred flowers blossom and a hundred schools of thought contend will not weaken but strengthen the leading position of Marxism in the ideological field.

What should our policy be towards non-Marxist ideas? As far as unmistakable counter-revolutionaries and wreckers of the socialist cause are concerned, the matter is easy: we simply deprive them of their freedom of speech. But it is quite a different matter when we are faced with incorrect ideas among the people. Will it do to ban such ideas and give them no opportunity to express themselves? Certainly not. It is not only futile but very harmful to use crude and summary methods to deal with ideological questions among the people, with questions relating to the spiritual life of man. You may ban the expression of wrong ideas, but the ideas will still be there. On the other hand, correct ideas, if pampered in hot-houses without being exposed to the elements or immunized from disease, will not win out against wrong ones. That is why it is only by employing methods of discussion, criticism and reasoning that we can really foster correct ideas, overcome wrong ideas, and really settle issues.

The bourgeoisie and petty bourgeoisie are bound to give expression to their ideologies. It is inevitable that they should stubbornly persist in expressing themselves in every way possible on political and ideological questions. You can't expect them not to do so. We should not use methods of suppression to prevent them from expressing themselves, but should allow them to do so and at the same time argue with them and direct well-considered criticism at them.

There can be no doubt that we should criticize all kinds of wrong ideas. It certainly would not do to refrain from criticism and look on while wrong ideas spread unchecked and acquire their market. Mistakes should be criticized and poisonous weeds fought against wherever they crop up. But such criticism should not be doctrinaire. We should not use the metaphysical method, but strive to employ the dialectical method. What is needed is scientific analysis and fully convincing arguments. Doctrinaire criticism settles nothing. We don't want any kind of poisonous weeds, but we should carefully distinguish between what is really a poisonous weed and what is really a fragrant flower. We must learn together with the masses of the people how to make this careful distinction, and use the correct methods to fight poisonous weeds.

While criticizing doctrinairism, we should at the same time direct our attention to criticizing revisionism. Revisionism, or rightist opportunism, is a bourgeois trend of thought which is even more dangerous than doctrinairism. The revisionists, or right opportunists, pay lip-service to Marxism and also attack "doctrinairism." But the real target of their attack is actually the most fundamental elements of Marxism. They oppose or distort materialism and dialectics, oppose or try to weaken the people's democratic dictatorship and the leading role of the Communist Party, oppose or try to weaken socialist transformation and socialist construction. Even after the basic victory of the socialist revolution in our country, there are still a number of people who vainly hope for a restoration of the capitalist system. They wage a struggle against the working class on every front, including the ideological front. In this struggle, their right-hand men are the revisionists.

On the surface, these two slogans—let a hundred flowers blossom and a hundred schools of thought contend—have no class character: the proletariat can turn them to account, so can the bourgeoisie and other people. But different classes, strata and social groups each have their own views on what are fragrant flowers and what are poisonous weeds. So what, from the point of view of the broad masses of the people, should be the criteria today for distinguishing between fragrant flowers and poisonous weeds?

In the political life of our country, how are our people to determine what is right and what is wrong in our words and actions? Basing ourselves on the principles of our Constitution, the will of the overwhelming majority of our people and the political programmes jointly proclaimed on various occasions by our political parties and groups, we believe that, broadly speaking, words and actions can be judged right if they:

(1) Help to unite the people of our various nationalities, and do not divide them;

(2) Are beneficial, not harmful, to socialist transformation and socialist construction;

(3) Help to consolidate, not undermine or weaken, the people's democratic dictatorship;

(4) Help to consolidate, not undermine or weaken, democratic centralism;

(5) Tend to strengthen, not to cast off or weaken, the leadership of the Communist Party;

(6) Are beneficial, not harmful, to international socialist solidarity and the solidarity of the peace-loving peoples of the world.

Of these six criteria, the most important are the socialist path and the leadership of the Party. These criteria are put forward in order to foster, and not hinder, the free discussion of various questions among the people. Those who do not approve of these criteria can still put forward their own views and argue their case. When the majority of the people have clear-cut criteria to go by, criticism and self-criticism can be conducted along proper lines, and these criteria can be applied to people's words and actions to determine whether they are fragrant flowers or poisonous weeds. These are political criteria. Naturally, in judging the truthfulness of scientific theories or assessing the aesthetic value of works of art, other pertinent criteria are needed, but these six political criteria are also applicable to all activities in the arts or sciences. In a socialist country like ours, can there possibly be any useful scientific or artistic activity which runs counter to these political criteria?

All that is set out above stems from the specific historical conditions in our country. Since conditions vary in different socialist countries and with different Communist Parties, we do not think that other countries and Parties must or need to follow the Chinese way.

The slogan "long-term co-existence and mutual supervision" is also a product of specific historical conditions in our country. It wasn't put forward all of a sudden, but had been in the making for several years. The idea of long-term co-existence had been in existence for a long time, but last year when the socialist system was basically established, the slogan was set out in clear terms.

Why should the democratic parties of the bourgeoisie and petty bourgeoisie be allowed to exist side by side with the party of the working class over a long period of time? Because we have no reason not to adopt the policy of long-term co-existence with all other democratic parties which are truly devoted to the task of uniting the people for the cause of socialism and which enjoy the trust of the people.

As early as at the Second Session of the National Committee of the People's Political Consultative Conference in June 1950, I put the matter in this way:

"The people and the People's Government have no reason to reject or deny the opportunity to anyone to make a living and give their services to the country, so long as he is really willing to serve the people, really helped the people when they were still in difficulties, did good things and continues to do them consistently without giving up halfway."

What I defined here was the political basis for the long-term co-existence of the various parties. It is the desire of the Communist Party, also its policy, to exist side by side with the other democratic parties for a long time to come. Whether these democratic parties can long exist depends not merely on what the Communist Party itself desires but also on the part played by these democratic parties themselves and on whether they enjoy the confidence of the people.

Mutual supervision among the various parties has also been a long-established fact, in the sense that they advise and criticize each other. Mutual supervision, which is obviously not a one-sided matter, means that the Communist Party should exercise supervision over the other democratic parties, and the other democratic parties should exercise supervision over the Communist Party. Why should the other democratic parties be allowed to exercise supervision over the Communist Party? This is because for a party as much as for an individual there is great need to hear opinions different from its own. We all know that supervision over the Communist Party is mainly exercised by the working people and Party membership. But we will benefit even more if the other democratic parties do this as well. Of course, advice and criticism exchanged between the Communist Party and the other democratic parties will play a positive role in mutual supervision only when they conform to the six political criteria given above. That is why we hope that the other democratic parties will all pay attention to ideological remoulding, and strive for long-term co-existence and mutual supervision with the Communist Party so as to meet the needs of the new society.

Chapter Six

The Quest for New Ideology and New Strategy

IDEOLOGY HAS consistently been the weapon of the Chinese Communist Party for the consolidation of power as well as a cure-all for China's ills. Under the guidance of Maoism, as we have seen in previous chapters, China has made significant progress. But many of the unresolved problems which confront Chinese leadership today not only date back to the days of the old empire, but are common in all developing nations: rapid population growth, dislocations of rural economy brought about by industrialization, discontent of the impoverished peasant society; and expectations and frustrations of youth and cadres. Thus, the need to maintain a loyal, disciplined bureaucracy dedicated to the cause of building an industrial society has become the prime issue in Communist China today.

Although the Maoists are clearly in the ascendancy in China today as illustrated in Selections 30 and 31, unsolved problems and dilemmas still remain in China.

23. *National Conference of the Chinese Communist Party: Resolution on the Anti-Party Bloc of Kao Kang and Jao Shu-shih (March, 1955)* *

The first important dispute among Chinese leaders was revealed in 1955 when the National Conference of the Chinese Communist Party adopted a resolution "On the Anti-Party Bloc of Kao Kang and Jao Shu-shih," which was a reaffirmation of the 1954 Central Committee's decision to expell Kao Kang and Jao Shu-shih from Party membership. Both Kao and Jao had been Mao Tse-tung's comrades-in-arms since the "Long March" days. When the People's Republic was established in Peking on October 1, 1949, Kao was named a Vice-Chairman of the People's Central Government as well as Chairman of the Northeast People's Government. In fact, he became the undisputed ruler of Manchuria. Jao Shu-shih had also a distinguished career within the Chinese Communist movement. He was Chairman of the East China Military and Administrative Committee until his arrest in February, 1954.

Kao Kang was born in 1891 in Hengshan, Shensi. He became a Communist under the influence of the Russian advisers employed by warlord Feng Yu-hsiang in north Shensi. In 1927 he and Liu Chih-tan, another Communist, established a Soviet area in the northwest and persisted in guerrilla operations in the Shensi-Kansu-Ninghsia areas. These areas became the fountainhead for Mao Tse-tung after the completion of his "Long March" in 1935 when Mao retreated to Paoan, Shensi. During the ensuing years, Kao achieved tremendous success as the protege of Mao.

Jao Shu-shih also had a distinguished career within the Chinese Communist movement. He joined the Chinese Communist Party when a student at Shanghai University in the 1920's. He was named secretary of the Shanghai Municipal Committee in May, 1949, and became Chairman of the East China area.

The open rifts between Kao Kang and Jao Shu-shih and

* From *Documents of the National Conference of the Communist Party of China, March, 1955*, Peking: Foreign Language Press, 1955. (Extract.)

other Chinese Communist leaders, especially Liu Shao-chi,
Teng Hsiao-p'ing and Chou En-lai, began in 1950 over the
question of following Soviet models or a "Maoist" line.
This was at a time when the influence of the Soviet Union
upon China was at its peak. Kao Kang wanted to adopt a
complete Soviet system, especially in the field of industrial
management. However, his proposal would endanger Party
control in industries. As a result, Liu, Teng and Chou suggested the "collective leadership" of the Party Committee
as an alternative for the industrial management by a "single
director" proposed by Kao. (Kao also wanted to be the
single director.)

Under the facade of the ideological debate on the question of applicability of the Soviet model in China, a power
struggle was emerging. Liu, Teng and Chou, by enlisting the
strong support of P'eng Chen, the powerful mayor of Peking, expelled Kao and Jao in the 1954 Party Central Committee meeting. Kao committed suicide and Jao was put into
prison. The resolution adopted by the National Conference was a reaffirmation of the 1954 Central Committee's
decision.

The National Conference of the Communist Party of China
heard a report by Comrade Teng Hsiao-p'ing, on behalf of the
Central Committee, concerning the anti-Party bloc of Kao
Kang and Jao Shu-shih, and unanimously expressed support
for the measures taken by the Political Bureau of the Central
Committee after the fourth plenary session of the Seventh
Central Committee in regard to this question.

Kao Kang's anti-Party activities had a fairly long history.
The facts brought to light before and after the fourth plenary
session of the Seventh Central Committee of the Party held in
February 1954 proved that, from 1949 on, Kao Kang carried
on conspiratorial activities aimed at seizing leadership in the
Party and the state. In Northeast China [the chief industrial
region and the staging area for Chinese "volunteers" in the
1950–1953 Korean War] and other places, he created and
spread many rumors slandering the Central Committee of the
Party and lauding himself, with the aim of sowing discord
and dissension among the comrades and stirring up dissatisfac-
tion with the leading comrades of the Central Committee of
the Party; he thus carried on activities to split the Party and,
in the course of these activities, formed his own anti-Party
faction. In their work in the northeast area, the anti-Party

faction formed by Kao Kang violated the policy of the Central Committee of the Party, tried its utmost to belittle the role of the Party, and to undermine solidarity and unity in the Party, regarding the northeast area as the independent kingdom of Kao Kang. After Kao Kang was transferred to work in the central organs in 1953 [as a vice premier and member of what is now called the Standing Committee of the Political Bureau], his anti-Party activities became even more outrageous. He even tried to instigate Party members in the army to support his conspiracy against the Central Committee of the Party. For this purpose he invented the utterly absurd "theory" that our Party consisted of two parties—one, the so-called "Party of the revolutionary bases and the army," the other, the so-called "Party of the white areas"—and that the Party was created by the army. He himself claimed to be the representative of the so-called "Party of the revolutionary bases and the army" and thus entitled to hold the major authority, and advocated that both the Central Committee of the Party and the government should be reorganized in accordance with his plan, and that he himself should be for the time being general secretary or vice chairman of the Central Committee of the Party and Premier of the State Council. After a serious warning was given to the anti-Party elements by the fourth plenary session of the Seventh Central Committee of the Party, Kao Kang not only did not admit his guilt to the Party, but committed suicide as an ultimate expression of his betrayal of the Party.

Jao Shu-shih was Kao Kang's chief ally in his conspiratorial activities against the Party. It has been fully established that in the ten years between 1943 and 1953 Jao Shu-shih resorted on many occasions to shameless deceit in the Party to seize power. During his tenure of office in East China, he did his utmost to adopt in the cities and countryside a rightist policy of surrender to the capitalists, landlords, and rich peasants. At the same time, he did everything possible to protect counterrevolutionaries in defiance of the Central Committee's policy of suppressing them. After his transfer to the Party Center in 1953, Jao Shu-shih thought that Kao Kang was on the point of success in his activities aimed at seizing power in the Central Committee. Therefore, he formed an anti-Party bloc with Kao Kang and used his office as Director of the Organization Department of the Central Committee to start a struggle with the aim of opposing leading members of the Central Committee, and thus actively carried out activities to split the Party. From the time of the fourth plenary session of the Seventh Central Committee of the Party up to the present, Jao Shu-shih has never shown any signs of repentance, and still persists in an attitude of attacking the Party.

24. Central Committee of the Chinese Communist Party: Resolution on the Establishment of People's Communes in the Rural Areas (August, 1958)*

The success of the First Five Year Plan, which was carried out during the years (1953–1957) of "socialist transformation," led Mao Tse-tung and his comrades to launch the "Great Leap Forward" campaign in 1958, and the commune movement which was a part of the same campaign. In fact, the commune system was not introduced suddenly; it was the culmination of a series of "socialist constructions" from 1957 onward.

The first step toward the communes was taken in September, 1957, at a Party plenum which decided to adopt the policy of "simultaneous development of industry and agriculture." The plenum also concluded that the key to agriculture development was the massive mobilization of labor power. As a result, a peasant labor army of some 100 million was organized to undertake a gigantic program of water conservation and fertilizer accumulation. The commune was designed as a mechanism to co-ordinate and control the labor supply.

The second step toward the communes was the decision in March, 1958, to embark on an expansion of local industry in rural areas for the purpose of greater utilization of the under-employed labor force of co-operatives. Hence it became imperative to have a larger unit in the countryside than the co-operative.

The third step toward the communes was the Communist attempt to create state organs for the "building of Communism." From the writings in 1956–1957 dealing with state structure, it appears that at that time Mao Tse-tung and his

---

* From *Central Committee Resolution on the Establishment of People's Communes in the Rural Areas*, Peking: Foreign Language Press, 1958, pp. 1–8.

comrades indeed believed that the transition to socialism had been largely completed and that they were seeking a new form of state structure. This was the ideological discussion that in 1958 helped to shape the people's communes as the "basic units of Communist society."

The commune system was officially introduced in August, 1958, when the Central Committee of the Party passed a resolution calling for the establishment of communes throughout the country, at the same time enunciating their ideological basis and the principles governing their formation. The experiment had begun in April, 1958, when the Weihsing (Sputnik) People's Commune in Suiping County, Honan Province, was established by the merger of twenty-seven agricultural producers' co-operatives of four townships.

There was more than scattered resistance to communization. The entire structure of Chinese life was altered by the communes. The peasants, who had at first been given land by the Communist regime and then had most of it taken away as they were forced into co-operatives, now found themselves in the midst of still another upheaval, characterized by the establishment of the communes. Even the Central Committee Resolution on Some Questions Concerning the People's Communes (December, 1958), which gave a detailed description of the commune system, in effect stated that the communes had been instituted too quickly, without sufficient preparation.

But by the end of 1958, at the meeting of the Central Committee, it was possible to announce that "over 120 million households, or more than 99 percent of all China's peasant households of various nationalities have joined the people's communes." The people's communes were declared to be a success.

"The primary purpose of establishing people's communes," declared the Commune Resolution, "is to accelerate the speed of socialist construction and the purpose of building socialism is to prepare actively for the transition to Communism." Through Communism, the Chinese Communists hoped that the Chinese society would eventually "enter the era of Communism where the principle of 'from each according to his ability and to each according to his needs' will be practised." This claim for the communes aroused Soviet misgivings, for the commune system could be construed to imply that China would be brought to

Communism before its Russian ally. The Soviets were especially outraged by the Chinese introduction of the free-supply system—"To each according to his needs," for they felt certain that the Chinese steps in this direction would stumble badly.

1. The people's communes are the logical result of the march of events. Large, comprehensive people's communes have made their appearance, and in several places they are already widespread. They have developed very rapidly in some areas. It is highly probable that there will soon be an upsurge in setting up people's communes throughout the country and the development is irresistible. The basis for the development of the people's communes is mainly the all-round, continuous leap forward in China's agricultural production and the ever-rising political consciousness of the 500 million peasants. An unprecedented advance has been made in agricultural capital construction since the advocates of the capitalist road were fundamentally defeated economically, politically and ideologically. This has created a new basis for practically eliminating flood and drought, and for ensuring the comparatively stable advance of agricultural production. Agriculture has leaped forward since Right conservatism has been overcome and the old technical norms in agriculture have been broken down. The output of agricultural products has doubled or increased several-fold, in some cases more than ten times or scores of times. This has further stimulated emancipation of thought among the people. Large-scale agricultural capital construction and the application of more advanced agricultural technique are making their demands on labour power. The growth of rural industry also demands the transfer of some manpower from agriculture. The demand for mechanization and electrification has become increasingly urgent in China's rural areas. Capital construction in agriculture and the struggle for bumper harvests involve large-scale co-operation which cuts across the boundaries between co-operatives, townships and counties. The people have taken to organizing themselves along military lines, working with militancy, and leading a collective life, and this has raised the political consciousness of the 500 million peasants still further. Community dining rooms, kindergartens, nurseries, sewing groups, barber shops, public baths, happy homes for the aged, agricultural middle schools, "red and expert" schools, are

leading the peasants towards a happier collective life and further fostering ideas of collectivism among the peasant masses. What all these things illustrate is that the agricultural co-operative with scores of families or several hundred families can no longer meet the needs of the changing situation. In the present circumstances, the establishment of people's communes with all-round management of agriculture, forestry, animal husbandry, side-occupations and fishery, where industry (the worker), agriculture (the peasant), exchange (the trader), culture and education (the student) and military affairs (the militiaman) merge into one, is the fundamental policy to guide the peasants to accelerate socialist construction, complete the building of socialism ahead of time and carry out the gradual transition to communism.

2. Concerning the organization and size of the communes. Generally speaking, it is at present better to establish one commune to a township with the commune comprising about two thousand peasant households. Where a township embraces a vast area and is sparsely populated, more than one commune may be established, each with less than two thousand households. In some places, several townships may merge and form a single commune comprising about six or seven thousand households, according to topographical conditions and the needs for the development of production. As to the establishment of communes of more than 10,000 or even more than 20,000 households, we need not oppose them, but for the present we should not take the initiative to encourage them.

As the people's communes grow there may be a tendency to form federations with the county as a unit. Plans should be drawn up right now on a county basis to ensure the rational distribution of people's communes.

The size of the communes and the all-round development of agriculture, forestry, animal husbandry, subsidiary production and fishery as well as of industry (the worker), agriculture (the peasant), exchange (the trader), culture and education (the student) and military affairs (the militiaman), demand an appropriate division of labour within the administrative organs of the communes; a number of departments, each responsible for a particular kind of work, should be set up, following the principle of compactness and efficiency in organization and of cadres taking direct part in production. The township governments and the communes should become one, with the township committee of the Party becoming the Party committee of the commune and the township people's council becoming the administrative committee of the commune.

3. Concerning the methods and steps to be adopted to merge small co-operatives into bigger ones and transform them into people's communes. The merger of small co-operatives into bigger ones and their transformation into people's communes is now a common mass demand. The poor and the lower-middle peasants firmly support it; most upper-middle peasants also favour it. We must rely on the poor and the lower-middle peasants and fully encourage the masses to air their views and argue it out, unite the majority of the upper-middle peasants who favour it, overcome vacillation among the remainder, and expose and foil rumour-mongering and sabotage by landlord and rich-peasant elements, so that the mass of the peasants merge the smaller-co-operatives into bigger ones and transform them into communes through ideological emancipation and on a voluntary basis, without any compulsion. As to the steps to be taken, it is of course better to complete the merger into bigger co-ops and their transformation into communes at once; but where this is not feasible, it can be done in two stages, with no compulsory or rash steps. In all counties, experiments should first be made in some selected areas and the experience gained should then be popularized gradually.

The merger of smaller co-operatives into bigger ones and their transformation into communes must be carried out in close co-ordination with current production to ensure that it not only has no adverse effect on current production, but becomes a tremendous force stimulating an even greater leap forward in production. Therefore, in the early period of the merger, the method of "changing the upper structure while keeping the lower structure unchanged" may be adopted. The original, smaller co-operatives may at first jointly elect an administrative committee for the merged co-ops to unify planning and the arrangement of work, and transform themselves into farming zones or production brigades. The original organization of production and system of administration may, for the time being, remain unchanged and continue as before; and then later, step by step, merge, readjust and settle whatever needs merging or readjusting and whatever specific questions demand solution during the merger, so as to make sure there is no adverse effect on production.

The size of the communes, the speed of carrying out the merger of small co-operatives into bigger ones and their transformation into communes, and the methods and steps to be taken in this connection will be decided in accordance with the local conditions by the various provinces, autonomous regions and municipalities directly under the central authorities. But no matter when the merger takes place, whether before or after autumn, in the coming winter or next spring, the small co-operatives which are prepared to merge should be brought together from now on to discuss and jointly work out unified plans for post-autumn capital construction in agriculture and to make unified arrangements of all kinds for preparatory work for an even bigger harvest next year.

4. Concerning some questions of the economic policy involved in the merger of co-operatives. In the course of the merger, education should be strengthened to prevent the growth of departmentalism among a few co-operatives, which might otherwise share out too much or all of their income and leave little or no common funds before the merger. On the other hand, it must be understood that with various agricultural co-operatives established on different foundations, the amount of their public property, their indebtedness inside and outside the co-operatives and so on will not be completely equal when they merge into bigger co-operatives. In the course of the merger, the cadres and the masses should be educated in the spirit of communism so as to recognize these differences and not resort to minute squaring of accounts, insisting on equal shares and bothering with trifles.

When a people's commune is established, it is not necessary to deal with the questions of reserved private plots of land, scattered fruit trees, share funds and so on in a great hurry; nor is it necessary to adopt clear-cut stipulations on these questions. Generally speaking, reserved private plots of land may perhaps be turned over to collective management in the course of the merger of co-operatives; scattered fruit trees, for the time being, may remain privately owned and be dealt with some time later. Share funds etc. can be handled after a year or two, since the funds will automatically become publicly owned with the development of production, the increase of income and the advance in the people's consciousness.

5. Concerning the name, ownership and system of distribution of the communes.

All the big merged co-operatives will be called people's communes. There is no need to change them into state-owned farms, for it is not proper for farms to embrace industry, agriculture, exchange, culture and education and military affairs at the same time.

After the establishment of people's communes, there is no need immediately to transform collective ownership into ownership by the people as a whole. It is better at present to maintain collective ownership to avoid unnecessary complications arising in the course of the transformation of ownership. In fact, collective ownership in people's communes already contains some elements of ownership by the people as a whole. These elements will grow constantly in the course of the continuous development of people's communes and will gradually replace collective ownership. The transition from collective ownership to ownership by the people as a whole is a process, the completion of which may take less time—three or four years—in some places, and longer—five or six years or even longer—elsewhere. Even with the completion of this transition, people's communes, like state-owned industry, are still socialist in character, where the principle of "from each according to his ability and to each according to his work" prevails. After a number of years, as the social product increases greatly, the communist consciousness and morality of the entire people are raised to a much higher degree, and universal education is instituted and developed, the differences between workers and peasants, town and country and mental and manual labour—legacies of the old society that have inevitably been carried over into the socialist period—and the remnants of unequal bourgeois rights which are the reflection of these differences, will gradually vanish, and the function of the state will be limited to protecting the country from external aggression but it will play no role internally. At that time Chinese society will enter the era of communism where the principle of "from each according to his ability and to each according to his needs" will be practised.

After the establishment of people's communes it is not necessary to hurry the change from the original system of distribution, in order to avoid any unfavourable effect on production. The system of distribution should be determined according to specific conditions. Where conditions permit, the shift to a wage system may be made. But where conditions are not yet ripe, the original system of payment according to workdays may be temporarily retained (such as the system of fixed targets for output, workdays and costs, with a part of the extra output as reward; or the system of calculating workdays on the basis of output). This can be changed when conditions permit.

Although ownership in the people's communes is still collective ownership and the system of distribution, either the wage system or payment according to workdays, is "to each according to his work" and not "to each according to his needs," the people's communes are the best form of organization for the attainment of socialism and gradual transition to communism. They will develop into the basic social units in communist society.

6. At the present stage our task is to build socialism. The primary purpose of establishing people's communes is to accelerate the speed of socialist construction and the purpose of building socialism is to prepare actively for the transition to communism. It seems that the attainment of communism in China is no longer a remote future event. We should actively use the form of the people's communes to explore the practical road of transition to communism.

25. Central Committee of the Chinese Communist Party: Resolution Concerning the Anti-Party Clique Headed by P'eng Teh-huai (August, 1959)*

In 1959, political earth-shaking events took place in China with the announcement of the replacement of two key men in the military establishment of China: Marshal P'eng Teh-huai, Minister of Defense and noted revolutionary war hero, and General Huang Ke-ch'eng, Chief of Staff of the Army and P'eng's senior vice-minister. They were replaced by Lin Piao and Lo Jui-ch'ing. Both P'eng and Huang were denounced as "right-wing opportunists"; their crime was anti-Maoism.

The full resolution adopted by the Party to purge P'eng and Huang Ke-ch'eng was not released to the public until 1967 during the Cultural Revolution when the attack upon P'eng Teh-huai continued. This was because disputes in China seldom involve the military, for Mao Tse-tung has always kept the military under his own command.

* From *Peking Review* (No. 34), August 18, 1967, pp. 8–10. (8th Plenary Session of 8th Central Committee; extract.)

According to the official accusations, P'eng Teh-huai and Huang Ke-ch'eng's crime was "a continuation and development of the case of the anti-Party alliance of Kao Kang and Jao Shu-shih." In fact, there was some truth in this because both Kao and P'eng were very pro-Soviet Union. They wanted to adopt Soviet ideology or methods at the expense of Maoist models in China. Kao's field, as we have seen, was industrial management, while P'eng's was military training.

P'eng, despite his loyalty to Mao since the Long March days, had questioned the continuing validity of Mao's theories of "people's wars," as well as Mao's strong support of a professional army as in the Soviet Union. P'eng opposed ideas advanced by Lin Piao and others such as that soldiers should work as part-time auxiliary laborers on roads or in agricultural fields. After his removal, the Party decreed that all members of the People's Liberation Army must work in the villages and communes for a number of months and must study the thought of Mao Tse-tung. In addition, all officers were required to serve for at least a month in the ranks. In 1965, the Chinese Communist Party abolished all the military ranks within the People's Liberation Army.

(1) In the period before the Central Committee of the Party convened an enlarged session of the Political Bureau at Lushan in July 1959 and during the Lushan Meeting, a fierce onslaught on the Party's general line, the great leap forward and the people's communes was made inside our Party by the Right opportunist anti-Party clique which was headed by P'eng Teh-huai and which included a handful of others, such as Huang Ke-ch'eng, Chang Wen-tien and Chou Hsiao-chou. This onslaught came at a time when the reactionary forces at home and abroad were exploiting certain transient and partial shortcomings in our great movements— the great leap forward and the people's communes—to intensify their attack on our Party and people. An attack at such a juncture launched from inside the Party, particularly inside the Central Committee, is clearly more dangerous than an attack from outside the Party. The Eighth Plenary Session of the Eighth Central Committee of the Party holds that to take resolute action and crush the activities of the Right opportunist anti-Party clique headed by P'eng Teh-huai is absolutely necessary not only for safeguarding the Party's general

line, but also for safeguarding the leadership of the Party's Central Committee headed by Comrade Mao Tse-tung, the unity of the Party and the socialist cause of the Party and the people.

(2) The activities of the anti-Party clique headed by P'eng Teh-huai aimed at splitting the Party have been going on for a long time. The letter setting out his views which P'eng Teh-huai wrote to Comrade Mao Tse-tung on July 14, 1959, in the early stage of the Lushan Meeting and his speeches and remarks in the course of the meeting represent the platform of the Right opportunists in their attack on the Party. For all his outward pretensions of support for the general line and for Comrade Mao Tse-tung, in substance his letter, speeches and remarks incited those elements within our Party who have Rightist ideas or bear a grudge against the Party and those political speculators and alien class elements who have sneaked into the Party to rise up and launch a fierce onslaught on the Party's general line and the leadership of the Central Committee and Comrade Mao Tse-tung in response to the slanders of the domestic and foreign reactionaries. P'eng Teh-huai has collected those transient and partial shortcomings, which have either long since been or are rapidly being overcome, exaggerated them out of all proportion and painted a pitch-black picture of the present situation in the country. In essence he negates the victory of the general line and the achievements of the great leap forward, and is opposed to the high-speed development of the national economy, to the movement for high yields on the agricultural front, to the mass movement to make iron and steel, to the people's commune movement, to the mass movements in economic construction, and to Party leadership in socialist construction, that is, to "putting politics in command." In his letter he brazenly slandered as "petty-bourgeois fanaticism" the revolutionary zeal of the Party and of hundreds of millions of people. Time and again in his remarks he went so far as to assert that "if the Chinese workers and peasants were not as good as they are, a Hungarian incident would have occurred in China and it would have been necessary to invite Soviet troops in." It is obvious that the mistakes he has made are not in the nature of isolated mistakes, but are mistakes of a Right opportunist line, which in nature are against the Party, against the people and against socialism.

(3) The mass of facts brought to light at the Eighth Plen-

ary Session of the Eighth Central Committee, including those admitted by P'eng Teh-huai, Huang Ke-ch'eng, Chang Wen-tien, Chou Hsiao-chou and others and those disclosed by their accomplices and followers, prove that the activities of the anti-Party clique headed by P'eng Teh-huai prior to and during the Lushan Meeting were purposive, prepared, planned and organized. They represent a continuation and development of the case of the anti-Party alliance of Kao Kang and Jao Shu-shih. Investigation has now established that P'eng Teh-huai and Huang Ke-ch'eng long ago formed an anti-Party alliance with Kao Kang, of which they were important members. Chang Wen-tien, too, participated in Kao Kang's factional activities. During the struggle against the Kao-Jao anti-Party alliance, the Central Committee of the Party was already in possession of certain facts about P'eng Teh-huai's and Huang Ke-ch'eng's participation in that alliance. The Central Committee seriously criticized them, hoping that they would learn the lesson and repent, and it did not go deeply into the matter. Ostensibly P'eng Teh-huai and Huang Ke-ch'eng made a self-criticism; actually, far from recognizing and rectifying their mistakes, for a long time they concealed from the Party certain important facts concerning their participation in the activities of the Kao-Jao anti-Party alliance and even continued to expand their divisive anti-Party activities. To realize his personal ambitions, P'eng Teh-huai has long been making vicious attacks and spreading slanders inside the Party and the armed forces against Comrade Mao Tse-tung, the leader of the Party, and against other leading comrades of the Central Committee and its Military Commission. In his factional activities which were aimed at splitting the Party, he has resorted to such methods as promising official promotions, trafficking in flattery and favours, first attacking and then cajoling, creating dissension, and spreading rumours, lies and slanders. Since the great leap forward in 1958, the whole Party and people have been united as one and have been working hard. But P'eng Teh-huai painstakingly schemed to undermine the leadership of the Central Committee, carried out anti-Party activities and, together with his accomplices and followers, looked for the opportune moment to launch an attack on the Party and Comrade Mao Tse-tung. He took the Lushan Meeting as the opportune moment. Because of his position in the Central Committee and in the People's Liberation Army, and also because of his tactics of feigning candour and frugality, P'eng Teh-huai's activities could and did mislead a number of people; they are fraught with danger for the future of the Party and the People's Liberation Army. Precisely for this reason, it has necessarily become an important task of the Party and of all who are loyal to the Party, to the People's Liberation Army and the cause of socialism to expose this hypocrite, this careerist and conspirator, in his true colours and to put an end to his divisive anti-Party activities.

(4) P'eng Teh-huai's present mistake is not accidental. It has deep social, historical and ideological roots. He and his accomplices and followers are essentially representatives of the bourgeoisie who joined our Party during the democratic revolution. P'eng Teh-huai joined the Party and the revolutionary army led by the Party with the idea of "investing in a share." He only wants to lead others, to lead the collective, but does not want to be led by others, to be led by the collective. He does not look upon the achievements in the revolutionary work for which he is responsible as achievements in the struggle conducted by the Party and the people, but instead takes all the credit himself. Indeed, his anti-Party activities reflect the kind of class struggle in which the Chinese bourgeoisie opposes the proletarian socialist revolution and attempts to remould the Party, the army and the world in its own bourgeois image. Since his world outlook is incompatible with revolutionary proletarian Marxism-Leninism and runs directly counter to it, inside the Party he is naturally unwilling to accept the Marxist-Leninist leadership represented by Comrade Mao Tse-tung. At several key junctures in the history of the Party, such as the periods of the Li Li-san line, the first Wang Ming line, the second Wang Ming line and the case of the Kao-Jao anti-Party alliance, he invariably sided with the wrong line and opposed the correct line represented by Comrade Mao Tse-tung. After the Party's Tsunyi Meeting established Comrade Mao Tse-tung's position of leadership throughout the Party and the army in January 1935, he still opposed Comrade Mao Tse-tung's leadership and engaged in divisive activities inside the Party and the army. During the War of Resistance Against Japan, he regarded the area under his charge as his independent kingdom and used it as capital to assert his "independence" from the Central Committee. Despite the fact that the Party had resolutely repudiated and corrected the

mistake of the second Wang Ming line, he still stubbornly applied its wrong strategy and repeatedly held down the peasants' anti-feudal struggle in the Shansi-Hopei-Shantung-Honan area. Although in 1945 the Central Committee exposed and criticized the serious political and organizational mistakes he made while working in north China, he never recognized or corrected them. On the contrary, his anti-Party activities became more and more unbridled with the victory of the people's Liberation War and the transformation of the revolution from a bourgeois-democratic one into a proletarian socialist one. As soon as the socialist transformation of agriculture, handicraft and capitalist industry and commerce was begun, he joined Kao Kang in anti-Party activities. The Kao-Jao anti-Party alliance collapsed and the socialist revolution forged rapidly ahead on the economic and the ideological and political fronts. With the victories of the general line of the Party, the great leap forward and the people's commune movement, the capitalist and individual economies were clearly doomed. In these circumstances, the remnants of the Kao Kang clique and the other Right opportunist elements of every variety headed by P'eng Teh-huai could wait no longer, seized on what they considered an opportune moment to stir up trouble and came out in opposition to the general line of the Party, the great leap forward and the people's communes, and to the leadership of the Central Committee and Comrade Mao Tse-tung. The true nature of their attack on the Party, therefore, is that, representing as they do the interests of the bourgeoisie and the upper strata of the petty bourgeoisie, they seek to sabotage the dictatorship of the proletariat and undermine the socialist revolution by splitting and demoralizing the vanguard of the proletariat and organizing opportunist factions.

(5) As stated above, the long-standing anti-Party activities of the Right opportunist anti-Party clique headed by P'eng Teh-huai constitute a grave danger to the socialist cause of the Party and the people. The Eighth Plenary Session of the Eighth Central Committee holds that, in order to carry out its responsibilities with respect to the future of the Party and the People's Liberation Army and to the interests of the socialist cause of the proletariat and the labouring people, the Party must adopt a firm and serious attitude and smash all the activities of the Right opportunist anti-Party clique headed by P'eng Teh-huai. The Party demands that

P'eng Teh-huai, Huang Ke-ch'eng, Chang Wen-tien, Chou Hsiao-chou and others admit and disclose all their mistakes before the Party and rectify them in action. There is no other way out for them. The Eighth Plenary Session of the Eighth Central Committee holds that the Party should continue to Teh-huai and help him recognize and rectify his mistakes. adopt an attitude of great sincerity and warmth towards P'eng Of course, it is essential to transfer P'eng Teh-huai, Huang Ke-ch'eng, Chang Wen-tien, Chou Hsiao-chou and others from their posts in national defence, foreign affairs, provincial Party committee first secretaryship, etc. But they can still keep their membership or alternate membership of the Central Committee or of the Political Bureau, and we shall see how they behave in the future. History has many times proved the complete correctness of the policy regarding inner-Party struggle followed by the great Communist Party of China under the leadership of its Central Committee headed by Comrade Mao Tse-tung. Such inner-Party struggles have not weakened the Party, but on the contrary have strengthened it. The Eighth Plenary Session of the Eighth Central Committee firmly believes that the inner-Party struggle against Right opportunism headed by P'eng Teh-huai waged at this crucial juncture for our country's socialist cause will definitely further strengthen the ranks of the Party and the people and heighten their militancy. The Eighth Plenary Session of the Eighth Central Committee calls on all Party comrades to unite under the banner of defence of the general line and opposition to Right opportunism and to unite under the leadership of the Central Committee of the Party and its great leader Comrade Mao Tse-tung; it calls on them to lead the 650 million brave and industrious Chinese people in advancing boldly and unswervingly and in carrying out the general line of "go all out and aim high to get greater, quicker, better and more economical results in building socialism," so as to battle on to the end for the triumph of socialism and for the sublime communist future.

26. Central Committee of the Chinese Communist Party: A Proposal Concerning the General Line of the International Communist Movement (June, 1963)*

On June 14, 1963, the Chinese Communist Party issued this fundamental statement of the Chinese case in the Sino-Soviet controversy. The proposal was originally offered in the letter of the Central Committee of the Communist Party of China in reply to the letter of the Central Committee of the Communist Party of the Soviet Union of March 30, 1963, calling for "a top-level meeting between representatives of the C.P.S.U. and C.P.C. in Moscow" to discuss "the most urgent problems" concerning "the struggle for peace and peaceful coexistence," "the national-liberation movement," and "the consolidation of the unity and cohesion of the socialist community."

The June 14 proposal by inference corrects the mistakes of Soviet policy concerning these issues. On July 14, the CPSU responded with an "open letter to all Party organizations and Party members," accusing the Chinese Communist Party of deliberately aggravating the dispute since 1960, of interfering in Soviet domestic policy, and of "openly imposing their erroneous views" on bloc parties. Meanwhile, the Soviet Union signed the nuclear test-ban treaty with the United States and Great Britain. In their fury, the Chinese Communists called for a world conference to discuss "the question of complete, thorough, total, and resolute prohibition and destruction of nuclear weapons," and accused the CPSU as a "betrayer of socialism."

From the exchange of letters we note that one of the main disputes between China and the U.S.S.R. is over the global strategy of the "International Communist Movement." Moscow favors the so-called "peaceful expansion" of communism, while Peking resolutely insists on "revolution" and "wars of national liberation."

---

* From book so entitled, Peking: Foreign Language Press, 1963, pp. 1–61. (Appendixes and footnotes omitted.)

Besides the principal issues as discussed in the Chinese statement, there are two main grievances against Soviet domestic policy: the denunciation of Stalin, and the proclaiming of the "state of the whole people." These grievances reflect Mao's concern for his undisputed authority and the absolute unity of his Party, against any attempts by Moscow to influence it. What troubles the Kremlin most is the ambition of Communist China for the leadership of the international Communist movement. Moscow, of course, cannot tolerate any attempts by the Chinese leaders to challenge the leadership of the Soviet Union in the Communist camp. It is very understandable for Moscow to dissociate itself from Peking's militant stance in order to remain aloof from direct involvement in the Sino-American conflict. The doctrinal dispute dividing China and the U.S.S.R. has already had some impact on the external relations of Communist China.

To the Central Committee of the Communist Party of the Soviet Union

Dear Comrades,

The Central Committee of the Communist Party of China has studied the letter of the Central Committee of the Communist Party of the Soviet Union of March 30, 1963.

All who have the unity of the socialist camp and the international communist movement at heart are deeply concerned about the talks between the Chinese and Soviet Parties and hope that our talks will help to eliminate differences, strengthen unity and create favourable conditions for convening a meeting of representatives of all the Communist and Workers' Parties.

It is the common and sacred duty of the Communist and Workers' Parties of all countries to uphold and strengthen the unity of the international communist movement. The Chinese and Soviet Parties bear a heavier responsibility for the unity of the entire socialist camp and international communist movement and should of course make commensurately greater efforts.

A number of major differences of principle now exist in the international communist movement. But however serious these differences, we should exercise sufficient patience and find ways to eliminate them so that we can unite our forces and strengthen the struggle against our common enemy.

It is with this sincere desire that the Central Committee of the Communist Party of China approaches the forthcoming talks between the Chinese and Soviet Parties.

In its letter of March 30, the Central Committee of the C.P.S.U. systematically presents its views on questions that need to be discussed in the talks between the Chinese and Soviet Parties, and in particular raises the question of the general line of the international communist movement. In this letter we too would like to express our views, which constitute our proposal on the general line of the international communist movement and on some related questions of principle.

We hope that this exposition of views will be conducive to mutual understanding by our two Parties and to a detailed, point-by-point discussion in the talks.

We also hope that this will be conducive to the understanding of our views by the fraternal Parties and to a full exchange of ideas at an international meeting of fraternal Parties.

(1) The general line of the international communist movement must take as its guiding principle the Marxist-Leninist revolutionary theory concerning the historical mission of the proletariat and must not depart from it.

The Moscow Meetings of 1957 and 1960 adopted the Declaration and the Statement respectively after a full exchange of views and in accordance with the principle of reaching unanimity through consultation. The two documents point out the characteristics of our epoch and the common laws of socialist revolution and socialist construction, and lay down the common line of all the Communist and Workers' Parties. They are the common programme of the international communist movement.

It is true that for several years there have been differences within the international communist movement in the understanding of, and the attitude towards, the Declaration of 1957 and the Statement of 1960. The central issue here is whether or not to accept the revolutionary principles of the Declaration and the Statement. In the last analysis, it is a question of whether or not to accept the universal truth of Marxism-Leninism, whether or not to recognize the universal significance of the road of the October Revolution, whether or not to accept the fact that the people still living under the imperialist and capitalist system, who comprise two-thirds of the world's population, need to make revolution, and whether or not to accept the fact that the people already on the socialist road, who comprise one-third of the world's population, need to carry their revolution forward to the end.

It has become an urgent and vital task of the international communist movement resolutely to defend the revolutionary principles of the 1957 Declaration and the 1960 Statement.

Only by strictly following the revolutionary teachings of Marxism-Leninism and the general road of the October Revolution is it possible to have a correct understanding of the revolutionary principles of the Declaration and the Statement and a correct attitude towards them.

(2) What are the revolutionary principles of the Declaration and the Statement? They may be summarized as follows:

Workers of all countries, unite; workers of the world, unite with the oppressed peoples and oppressed nations; oppose imperialism and reaction in all countries; strive for world peace, national liberation, people's democracy and socialism; consolidate and expand the socialist camp; bring the proletarian world revolution step by step to complete victory; and establish a new world without imperialism, without capitalism and without the exploitation of man by man.

This, in our view, is the general line of the international communist movement at the present stage.

(3) This general line proceeds from the actual world situation taken as a whole and from a class analysis of the fundamental contradictions in the contemporary world, and is directed against the counter-revolutionary global strategy of U.S. imperialism.

This general line is one of forming a broad united front, with the socialist camp and the international proletariat as its nucleus, to oppose the imperialists and reactionaries headed by the United States; it is a line of boldly arousing the masses, expanding the revolutionary forces, winning over the middle forces and isolating the reactionary forces.

This general line is one of resolute revolutionary struggle by the people of all countries and of carrying the proletarian world revolution forward to the end; it is the line that most effectively combats imperialism and defends world peace.

If the general line of the international communist movement is one-sidedly reduced to "peaceful coexistence", "peaceful competition" and "peaceful transition", this is to violate the revolutionary principles of the 1957 Declaration and the 1960 Statement, to discard the historical mission of proletarian world revolution, and to depart from the revolutionary teachings of Marxism-Leninism.

The general line of the international communist movement should reflect the general law of development of world history. The revolutionary struggles of the proletariat and the people in various countries go through different stages and they all have their own characteristics, but they will not transcend the general law of development of world history. The general line should point out the basic direction for the revolutionary struggles of the proletariat and people of all countries.

While working out its specific line and policies, it is most important for each Communist or Workers' Party to adhere to the principle of integrating the universal truth of Marxism-Leninism with the concrete practice of revolution and construction in its own country.

(4) In defining the general line of the international communist movement, the starting point is the concrete class analysis of world politics and economics as a whole and of actual world conditions, that is to say, of the fundamental contradictions in the contemporary world.

If one avoids a concrete class analysis, seizes at random on certain superficial phenomena, and draws subjective and groundless conclusions, one cannot possibly reach correct conclusions with regard to the general line of the international communist movement but will inevitably slide on to a track entirely different from that of Marxism-Leninism.

What are the fundamental contradictions in the contemporary world? Marxist-Leninists consistently hold that they are:

> the contradiction between the socialist camp and the imperialist camp;
> the contradiction between the proletariat and the bourgeoisie in the capitalist countries;
> the contradiction between the oppressed nations and imperialism; and
> the contradictions among imperialist countries and among monopoly capitalist groups.

The contradiction between the socialist camp and the imperialist camp is a contradiction between two fundamentally different social systems, socialism and capitalism. It is undoubtedly very sharp. But Marxist-Leninists must not regard the contradictions in the world as consisting solely and simply of the contradiction between the socialist camp and the imperialist camp.

The international balance of forces has changed and has become increasingly favourable to socialism and to all the oppressed peoples and nations of the world, and most unfavourable to imperialism and the reactionaries of all countries. Nevertheless, the contradictions enumerated above still objectively exist.

These contradictions and the struggles to which they give rise are interrelated and influence each other. Nobody can obliterate any of these fundamental contradictions or subjectively substitute one for all the rest.

It is inevitable that these contradictions will give rise to popular revolutions, which alone can resolve them.

(5) The following erroneous views should be repudiated on the question of the fundamental contradictions in the contemporary world:

a) the view which blots out the class content of the contradiction between the socialist and the imperialist camps and fails to see this contradiction as one between states under the dictatorship of the proletariat and states under the dictatorship of the monopoly capitalists;

b) the view which recognizes only the contradiction between the socialist and the imperialist camps, while neglecting or underestimating the contradictions between the proletariat and the bourgeoisie in the capitalist world, between the oppressed nations and imperialism, among the imperialist countries and among the monopoly capitalist groups, and the struggles to which these contradictions give rise;

c) the view which maintains with regard to the capitalist world that the contradiction between the proletariat and the bourgeoisie can be resolved without a proletarian revolution in each country and that the contradiction between the oppressed nations and imperialism can be resolved without revolution by the oppressed nations;

d) the view which denies that the development of the inherent contradictions in the contemporary capitalist world inevitably leads to a new situation in which the imperialist countries are locked in an intense struggle, and asserts that the contradictions among the imperialist countries can be reconciled, or even eliminated, by "international agreements among the big monopolies"; and

e) the view which maintains that the contradiction between the two world systems of socialism and capitalism will automatically disappear in the course of "economic competition", that the other fundamental world contradictions will automatically do so with the disappearance of the contradiction between the two systems, and that a "world without wars", a new world of "all-round co-operation", will appear.

It is obvious that these erroneous views inevitably lead to erroneous and harmful policies and hence to setbacks and losses of one kind or another to the cause of the people and of socialism.

(6) The balance of forces between imperialism and socialism has undergone a fundamental change since World War II. The main indication of this change is that the world now has not just one socialist country but a number of socialist countries forming the mighty socialist camp, and that the people who have taken the socialist road now number not two hundred million but a thousand million, or a third of the world's population.

The socialist camp is the outcome of the struggles of the international proletariat and working people. It belongs to the international proletariat and working people as well as to the people of the socialist countries.

The main common demands of the people of the countries in the socialist camp and the international proletariat and working people are that all the Communist and Workers' Parties in the socialist camp should:

Adhere to the Marxist-Leninist line and pursue correct Marxist-Leninist domestic and foreign policies;

Consolidate the dictatorship of the proletariat and the worker-peasant alliance led by the proletariat and carry the socialist revolution forward to the end on the economic, political and ideological fronts;

Promote the initiative and creativeness of the broad masses, carry out socialist construction in a planned way, develop production, improve the people's livelihood and strengthen national defence;

Strengthen the unity of the socialist camp on the basis of Marxism-Leninism, and support other socialist countries on the basis of proletarian internationalism;

Oppose the imperialist policies of aggression and war, and defend world peace;

Oppose the anti-Communist, anti-popular and counter-revolutionary policies of the reactionaries of all countries; and

Help the revolutionary struggles of the oppressed classes and nations of the world.

All Communist and Workers' Parties in the socialist camp owe it to their own people and to the international proletariat and working people to fulfil these demands.

By fulfilling these demands the socialist camp will exert a decisive influence on the course of human history.

For this very reason, the imperialists and reactionaries invariably try in a thousand and one ways to influence the domestic and foreign policies of the countries in the socialist camp, to undermine the camp and break up the unity of the socialist countries and particularly the unity of China and the Soviet Union. They invariably try to infiltrate and subvert the socialist countries and even entertain the extravagant hope of destroying the socialist camp.

The question of what is the correct attitude towards the socialist camp is a most important question of principle confronting all Communist and Workers' Parties.

It is under new historical conditions that the Communist and Workers' Parties are now carrying on the task of proletarian internationalist unity and struggle. When only one socialist country existed and when this country was faced with hostility and jeopardized by all the imperialists and reactionaries because it firmly pursued the correct Marxist-Leninist line and policies, the touchstone of proletarian internationalism for every Communist Party was whether or not it resolutely defended the only socialist country. Now there is a socialist camp consisting of thirteen countries, Albania, Bulgaria, China, Cuba, Czechoslovakia, the German Democratic Republic, Hungary, the Democratic People's Republic of Korea, Mongolia, Poland, Rumania, the Soviet Union and the Democratic Republic of Viet Nam. Under these circumstances, the touchstone of proletarian internationalism for every Communist Party is whether or not it resolutely defends the whole of the socialist camp, whether or not it defends the unity of all the countries in the camp on the basis of Marxism-Leninism and whether or not it defends the Marxist-Leninist line and policies which the socialist countries ought to pursue.

If anybody does not pursue the correct Marxist-Leninist line and policies, does not defend the unity of the socialist camp but on the contrary creates tension and splits within it, or even follows the policies of the Yugoslav revisionists, tries to liquidate the socialist camp or helps capitalist countries to attack fraternal socialist countries, then he is betraying the interests of the entire international proletariat and the people of the world.

If anybody, following in the footsteps of others, defends the erroneous opportunist line and policies pursued by a certain socialist country instead of upholding the correct Marxist-Leninist line and policies which the socialist countries ought to pursue, defends the policy of split instead of upholding the policy of unity, then he is departing from Marxism-Leninism and proletarian internationalism.

(7) Taking advantage of the situation after World War II, the U.S. imperialists stepped into the shoes of the German, Italian and Japanese fascists, and have been trying to erect a huge world empire such as has never been known before. The strategic objectives of U.S. imperialism have been to grab and dominate the intermediate zone lying between the United States and the socialist camp, put down the revolutions of the oppressed peoples and nations, proceed to destroy the socialist countries, and thus to subject all the peoples and countries of the world, including its allies, to domination and enslavement by U.S. monopoly capital.

Ever since World War II, the U.S. imperialists have been conducting propaganda for war against the Soviet Union and the socialist camp. There are two aspects to this propaganda. While the U.S. imperialists are actually preparing such a war, they also use this propaganda as a smokescreen for their oppression of the American people and for the extension of their aggression against the rest of the capitalist world.

The 1960 Statement points out:

"U.S. imperialism has become the biggest international exploiter."

"The United States is the mainstay of colonialism today."

"U.S. imperialism is the main force of aggression and war."

"International developments in recent years have furnished many new proofs of the fact that U.S. imperialism is the chief bulwark of world reaction and an international gendarme, that it has become an enemy of the peoples of the whole world."

U.S. imperialism is pressing its policies of aggression and war all over the world, but the outcome is bound to be the opposite of that intended—it will only be to hasten the awakening of the people in all countries and to hasten their revolutions.

The U.S. imperialists have thus placed themselves in opposition to the people of the whole world and have become encircled by them. The international proletariat must and can unite all the forces that can be united, make use of the internal contradictions in the enemy camp and establish the broadest united front against the U.S. imperialists and their lackeys.

The realistic and correct course is to entrust the fate of the people and of mankind to the unity and struggle of the world proletariat and to the unity and struggle of the people in all countries.

Conversely, to make no distinction between enemies, friends and ourselves and to entrust the fate of the people and of mankind to collaboration with U.S. imperialism is to lead people astray. The events of the last few years have exploded this illusion.

(8) The various types of contradictions in the contemporary world are concentrated in the vast areas of Asia, Africa and Latin America; these are the most vulnerable areas under imperialist rule and the storm-centres of world revolution dealing direct blows at imperialism.

The national democratic revolutionary movement in these areas and the international socialist revolutionary movement are the two great historical currents of our time.

The national democratic revolution in these areas is an important component of the contemporary proletarian world revolution.

The anti-imperialist revolutionary struggles of the people in Asia, Africa and Latin America are pounding and undermining the foundations of the rule of imperialism and colonialism, old and new, and are now a mighty force in defence of world peace.

In a sense, therefore, the whole cause of the international proletarian revolution hinges on the outcome of the revolutionary struggles of the people of these areas, who constitute the overwhelming majority of the world's population.

Therefore, the anti-imperialist revolutionary struggle of the people in Asia, Africa and Latin America is definitely not merely a matter of regional significance but one of overall importance for the whole cause of proletarian world revolution.

Certain persons now go so far as to deny the great international significance of the anti-imperialist revolutionary struggles of the Asian, African and Latin American peoples and, on the pretext of breaking down the barriers of nationality, colour and geographical location, are trying their best to efface the line of demarcation between oppressed and oppressor nations and between oppressed and oppressor countries and to hold down the revolutionary struggles of the peoples in these areas. In fact, they cater to the needs of imperialism and create a new "theory" to justify the rule of imperialism in these areas and the promotion of its policies of old and new colonialism. Actually, this "theory" seeks not to break down the barriers of nationality, colour and geographical location but to maintain the rule of the "superior nations" over the oppressed nations. It is only natural that this fraudulent "theory" is rejected by the people in these areas.

The working class in every socialist country and in every capitalist country must truly put into effect the fighting slogans, "Workers of all countries, unite!" and "Workers and oppressed nations of the world, unite!"; it must study the revolutionary experience of the peoples of Asia, Africa and Latin America, firmly support their revolutionary actions and regard the cause of their liberation as a most dependable support for itself and as directly in accord with its own interests. This is the only effective way to break down the barriers of nationality, colour and geographical location and this is the only genuine proletarian internationalism.

It is impossible for the working class in the European and American capitalist countries to liberate itself unless it unites with the oppressed nations and unless those nations are liberated. Lenin rightly said,

> The revolutionary movement in the advanced countries would actually be a sheer fraud if, in their struggle against capital, the workers of Europe and America were not closely and completely united with the hundreds upon hundreds of millions of "colonial" slaves who are oppressed by capital.

Certain persons in the international communist movement are now taking a passive or scornful or negative attitude towards the struggles of the oppressed nations for liberation. They are in fact protecting the interests of monopoly capital, betraying those of the proletariat, and degenerating into social democrats.

The attitude taken towards the revolutionary struggles of the people in the Asian, African and Latin American countries is an important criterion for differentiating those who want revolution from those who do not and those who are truly defending world peace from those who are abetting the forces of aggression and war.

(9) The oppressed nations and peoples of Asia, Africa and Latin America are faced with the urgent task of fighting imperialism and its lackeys.

History has entrusted to the proletarian parties in these areas the glorious mission of holding high the banner of struggle against imperialism, against old and new colonialism and for national independence and people's democracy, of standing in the forefront of the national democratic revolutionary movement and striving for a socialist future.

In these areas, extremely broad sections of the population refuse to be slaves of imperialism. They include not only the workers, peasants, intellectuals and petty bourgeoisie, but also the patriotic national bourgeoisie and even certain kings, princes and aristocrats, who are patriotic.

The proletariat and its party must have confidence in the strength of the masses and, above all, must unite with the peasants and establish a solid worker-peasant alliance. It is of primary importance for advanced members of the proletariat to work in the rural areas, help the peasants to get organized, and raise their class consciousness and their national self-respect and self-confidence.

On the basis of the worker-peasant alliance the proletariat and its party must unite all the strata that can be united and organize a broad united front against imperialism and its lackeys. In order to consolidate and expand this united front it is necessary that the proletarian party should maintain its ideological, political and organizational independence and insist on the leadership of the revolution.

The proletarian party and the revolutionary people must learn to master all forms of struggle, including armed struggle. They must defeat counter-revolutionary armed force with revolutionary armed force whenever imperialism and its lackeys resort to armed suppression.

The nationalist countries which have recently won political independence are still confronted with the arduous tasks of consolidating it, liquidating the forces of imperialism and domestic reaction, carrying out agrarian and other social reforms and developing their national economy and culture. It is of practical and vital importance for these countries to guard and fight against the neo-colonialist policies which the old colonialists adopt to preserve their interests, and especially against the neo-colonialism of U.S. imperialism.

In some of these countries, the patriotic national bourgeoisie continue to stand with the masses in the struggle against imperialism and colonialism and introduce certain measures of social progress. This requires the proletarian party to make a full appraisal of the progressive role of the patriotic national bourgeoisie and strengthen unity with them.

As the internal social contradictions and the international class struggle sharpen, the bourgeoisie, and particularly the big bourgeoisie, in some newly independent countries increasingly tend to become retainers of imperialism and to pursue anti-popular, anti-Communist and counter-revolutionary policies. It is necessary for the proletarian party resolutely to oppose these reactionary policies.

Generally speaking, the bourgeoisie in these countries have a dual character. When a united front is formed with the bourgeoisie, the policy of the proletarian party should be one of both unity and struggle. The policy should be to unite with the bourgeoisie, in so far as they tend to be progressive, anti-imperialist and anti-feudal, but to struggle against their reactionary tendencies to compromise and collaborate with imperialism and the forces of feudalism.

On the national question the world outlook of the proletarian party is internationalism, and not nationalism. In the revolutionary struggle it supports progressive nationalism and opposes reactionary nationalism. It must always draw a clear line of demarcation between itself and bourgeois nationalism, to which it must never fall captive.

The 1960 Statement says,

> Communists expose attempts by the reactionary section of the bourgeoisie to represent its selfish, narrow class interests as those of the entire nation; they expose the demagogic use by bourgeois politicians of socialist slogans for the same purpose. . . .

If the proletariat becomes the tail of the landlords and bourgeoisie in the revolution, no real or thorough victory in the national democratic revolution is possible, and even if victory of a kind is gained, it will be impossible to consolidate it.

In the course of the revolutionary struggles of the oppressed nations and peoples, the proletarian party must put forward a programme of its own which is thoroughly against imperialism and domestic reaction and for national independence and people's democracy, and it must work independently among the masses, constantly expand the progressive forces, win over the middle forces and isolate the reactionary forces; only thus can it carry the national democratic revolution through to the end and guide the revolution on to the road of socialism.

(10) In the imperialist and the capitalist countries, the proletarian revolution and the dictatorship of the proletariat are essential for the thorough resolution of the contradictions of capitalist society.

In striving to accomplish this task the proletarian party must under the present circumstances actively lead the working class and the working people in struggles to oppose monopoly capital, to defend democratic rights, to oppose the menace of fascism, to improve living conditions, to oppose imperialist arms expansion and war preparations, to defend world peace and actively to support the revolutionary struggles of the oppressed nations.

In the capitalist countries which U.S. imperialism controls or is trying to control, the working class and the people should direct their attacks mainly against U.S. imperialism, but also against their own monopoly capitalists and other reactionary forces who are betraying the national interests.

Large-scale mass struggles in the capitalist countries in recent years have shown that the working class and working people are experiencing a new awakening. Their struggles, which are dealing blows at monopoly capital and reaction, have opened bright prospects for the revolutionary cause in their own countries and are also a powerful support for the revolutionary struggles of the Asian, African and Latin American peoples and for the countries of the socialist camp.

The proletarian parties in imperialist or capitalist countries must maintain their own ideological, political and organizational independence in leading revolutionary struggles. At the same time, they must unite all the forces that can be united and build a broad united front against monopoly capital and against the imperialist policies of aggression and war.

While actively leading immediate struggles, Communists in the capitalist countries should link them with the struggle for long-range and general interests, educate the masses in a Marxist-Leninist revolutionary spirit, ceaselessly raise their political consciousness and undertake the historical task of the proletarian revolution. If they fail to do so, if they regard the immediate movement as everything, determine their conduct from case to case, adapt themselves to the events of the day and sacrifice the basic interests of the proletariat, that is out-and-out social democracy.

Social democracy is a bourgeois ideological trend. Lenin pointed out long ago that the social democratic parties are political detachments of the bourgeoisie, its agents in the working-class movement and its principal social prop. Communists must at all times draw a clear line of demarcation between themselves and social democratic parties on the basic question of the proletarian revolution and the dictatorship of the proletariat and liquidate the ideological influence of social democracy in the international working-class movement and among the working people. Beyond any shadow of doubt, Communists must win over the masses under the influence of the social democratic parties and must win over those left and middle elements in the social democratic parties who are willing to oppose domestic monopoly capital and domination by foreign imperialism, and must unite with them in extensive joint action in the day-to-day struggle of the working-class movement and in the struggle to defend world peace.

In order to lead the proletariat and working people in revolution, Marxist-Leninist Parties must master all forms of struggle and be able to substitute one form for another quickly as the conditions of struggle change. The vanguard of the proletariat will remain unconquerable in all circumstances only if it masters all forms of struggle—peaceful and armed, open and secret, legal and illegal, parliamentary struggle and mass struggle, etc. It is wrong to refuse to use parliamentary and other legal forms of struggle when they can and should be used. However, if a Marxist-Leninist Party falls into legalism or parliamentary cretinism, confining the struggle within the limits permitted by the bourgeoisie, this will inevitably lead to renouncing the proletarian revolution and the dictatorship of the proletariat.

(11) On the question of transition from capitalism to socialism, the proletarian party must proceed from the stand of class struggle and revolution and base itself on the Marxist-Leninist teachings concerning the proletarian revolution and the dictatorship of the proletariat.

Communists would always prefer to bring about the transition to socialism by peaceful means. But can peaceful transition be made into a new world-wide strategic principle for the international communist movement? Absolutely not.

Marxism-Leninism consistently holds that the fundamental question in all revolutions is that of state power. The 1957 Declaration and the 1960 Statement both clearly point out,

"Leninism teaches, and experience confirms, that the ruling classes never relinquish power voluntarily." The old government never topples even in a period of crisis, unless it is pushed. This is a universal law of class struggle.

In specific historical conditions, Marx and Lenin did raise the possibility that revolution may develop peacefully. But, as Lenin pointed out, the peaceful development of revolution is an opportunity "very seldom to be met with in the history of revolutions".

As a matter of fact, there is no historical precedent for peaceful transition from capitalism to socialism.

Certain persons say there was no precedent when Marx foretold that socialism would inevitably replace capitalism. Then why can we not predict a peaceful transition from capitalism to socialism despite the absence of a precedent?

This parallel is absurd. Employing dialectical and historical materialism, Marx analysed the contradictions of capitalism, discovered the objective laws of development of human society and arrived at a scientific conclusion, whereas the prophets who pin all their hopes on "peaceful transition" proceed from historical idealism, ignore the most fundamental contradictions of capitalism, repudiate the Marxist-Leninist teachings on class struggle, and arrive at a subjective and groundless conclusion. How can people who repudiate Marxism get any help from Marx?

It is plain to everyone that the capitalist countries are strengthening their state machinery—and especially their military apparatus—the primary purpose of which is to suppress the people in their own countries.

The proletarian party must never base its thinking, its policies for revolution and its entire work on the assumption that the imperialists and reactionaries will accept peaceful transformation.

The proletarian party must prepare itself for two eventualities—while preparing for a peaceful development of the revolution, it must also fully prepare for a non-peaceful development. It should concentrate on the painstaking work of accumulating revolutionary strength, so that it will be ready to seize victory when the conditions for revolution are ripe or to strike powerful blows at the imperialists and the reactionaries when they launch surprise attacks and armed assaults.

If it fails to make such preparations, the proletarian party will paralyse the revolutionary will of the proletariat, disarm itself ideologically and sink into a totally passive state of unpreparedness both politically and organizationally, and the result will be to bury the proletarian revolutionary cause.

(12) All social revolutions in the various stages of the history of mankind are historically inevitable and are governed by objective laws independent of man's will. Moreover, history shows that there never was a revolution which was able to achieve victory without zigzags and sacrifices.

With Marxist-Leninist theory as the basis, the task of the proletarian party is to analyse the concrete historical conditions, put forward the correct strategy and tactics, and guide the masses in bypassing hidden reefs, avoiding unnecessary sacrifices and reaching the goal step by step. Is it possible to avoid sacrifices altogether? Such is not the case with the slave revolutions, the serf revolutions, the bourgeois revolutions, or the national revolutions; nor is it the case with proletarian revolutions. Even if the guiding line of the revolution is correct, it is impossible to have a sure guarantee against setbacks and sacrifices in the course of the revolution. So long as a correct line is adhered to, the revolution is bound to triumph in the end. To abandon revolution on the pretext of avoiding sacrifices is in reality to demand that the people should forever remain slaves and endure infinite pain and sacrifice.

Elementary knowledge of Marxism-Leninism tells us that the birthpangs of a revolution are far less painful than the chronic agony of the old society. Lenin rightly said that "even with the most peaceful course of events, the present [capitalist] system always and inevitably exacts countless sacrifices from the working class".

Whoever considers a revolution can be made only if everything is plain sailing, only if there is an advance guarantee against sacrifices and failure, is certainly no revolutionary.

However difficult the conditions and whatever sacrifices and defeats the revolution may suffer, proletarian revolutionaries should educate the masses in the spirit of revolution and hold aloft the banner of revolution and not abandon it.

It would be "Left" adventurism if the proletarian party should rashly launch a revolution before the objective conditions are ripe. But it would be Right opportunism if the proletarian party should not dare to lead a revolution and to seize state power when the objective conditions are ripe.

Even in ordinary times, when it is leading the masses in

the day-to-day struggle, the proletarian party should ideologically, politically and organizationally prepare its own ranks and the masses for revolution and promote revolutionary struggles, so that it will not miss the opportunity to overthrow the reactionary regime and establish a new state power when the conditions for revolution are ripe. Otherwise, when the objective conditions are ripe, the proletarian party will simply throw away the opportunity of seizing victory.

The proletarian party must be flexible as well as highly principled, and on occasion it must make such compromises as are necessary in the interests of the revolution. But it must never abandon principled policies and the goal of revolution on the pretext of flexibility and of necessary compromises.

The proletarian party must lead the masses in waging struggles against the enemies, and it must know how to utilize the contradictions among those enemies. But the purpose of using these contradictions is to make it easier to attain the goal of the people's revolutionary struggles and not to liquidate these struggles.

Countless facts have proved that, wherever the dark rule of imperialism and reaction exists, the people who form over ninety per cent of the population will sooner or later rise in revolution.

If Communists isolate themselves from the revolutionary demands of the masses, they are bound to lose the confidence of the masses and will be tossed to the rear by the revolutionary current.

If the leading group in any Party adopt a non-revolutionary line and convert it into a reformist party, then Marxist-Leninists inside and outside the Party will replace them and lead the people in making revolution. In another kind of situation, the bourgeois revolutionaries will come forward to lead the revolution and the party of the proletariat will forfeit its leadership of the revolution. When the reactionary bourgeoisie betray the revolution and suppress the people, an opportunist line will cause tragic and unnecessary losses to the Communists and the revolutionary masses.

If Communists slide down the path of opportunism, they will degenerate into bourgeois nationalists and become appendages of the imperialists and the reactionary bourgeoisie.

There are certain persons who assert that they have made the greatest creative contributions to revolutionary theory since Lenin and that they alone are correct. But it is very dubious whether they have ever really given consideration to the extensive experience of the entire world communist movement, whether they have ever really considered the interests, the goal and tasks of the international proletarian movement as a whole, and whether they really have a general line for the international communist movement which conforms with Marxism-Leninism.

In the last few years the international communist movement and the national liberation movement have had many experiences and many lessons. There are experiences which people should praise and there are experiences which make people grieve. Communists and revolutionaries in all countries should ponder and seriously study these experiences of success and failure, so as to draw correct conclusions and useful lessons from them.

(13) The socialist countries and the revolutionary struggles of the oppressed peoples and nations support and assist each other.

The national liberation movements of Asia, Africa and Latin America and the revolutionary movements of the people in the capitalist countries are a strong support to the socialist countries. It is completely wrong to deny this.

The only attitude for the socialist countries to adopt towards the revolutionary struggles of the oppressed peoples and nations is one of warm sympathy and active support; they must not adopt a perfunctory attitude, or one of national selfishness or of great-power chauvinism.

Lenin said, "Alliance with the revolutionaries of the advanced countries and with all the oppressed peoples against any and all the imperialists—such is the external policy of the proletariat." Whoever fails to understand this point and considers that the support and aid given by the socialist countries to the oppressed peoples and nations are a burden or charity is going counter to Marxism-Leninism and proletarian internationalism.

The superiority of the socialist system and the achievements of the socialist countries in construction play an exemplary role and are an inspiration to the oppressed peoples and the oppressed nations.

But this exemplary role and inspiration can never replace the revolutionary struggles of the oppressed peoples and nations. No oppressed people or nation can win liberation except through its own staunch revolutionary struggle.

Certain persons have one-sidedly exaggerated the role of peaceful competition between socialist and imperialist countries in their attempt to substitute peaceful competition for the revolutionary struggles of the oppressed peoples and nations. According to their preaching, it would seem that imperialism will automatically collapse in the course of this peaceful competition and that the only thing the oppressed peoples and nations have to do is to wait quietly for the advent of this day. What does this have in common with Marxist-Leninist views?

Moreover, certain persons have concocted the strange tale that China and some other socialist countries want "to unleash wars" and to spread socialism by "wars between states". As the Statement of 1960 points out, such tales are nothing but imperialist and reactionary slanders. To put it bluntly, the purpose of those who repeat these slanders is to hide the fact that they are opposed to revolutions by the oppressed peoples and nations of the world and opposed to others supporting such revolutions.

(14) In the last few years much—in fact a great deal— has been said on the question of war and peace. Our views and policies on this question are known to the world, and no one can distort them.

It is a pity that although certain persons in the international communist movement talk about how much they love peace and hate war, they are unwilling to acquire even a faint understanding of the simple truth on war pointed out by Lenin.

Lenin said,

> It seems to me that the main thing that is usually forgotten on the question of war, which receives inadequate attention, the main reason why there is so much controversy, and, I would say, futile, hopeless and aimless controversy, is that people forget the fundamental question of the class character of the war; why the war broke out; the classes that are waging it; the historical and historico-economic conditions that gave rise to it.

As Marxist-Leninists see it, war is the continuation of politics by other means, and every war is inseparable from the political system and the political struggles which give rise to it. If one departs from this scientific Marxist-Leninist proposition which has been confirmed by the entire history of class struggle, one will never be able to understand either the question of war or the question of peace.

There are different types of peace and different types of war. Marxist-Leninists must be clear about what type of peace or what type of war is in question. Lumping just wars and unjust wars together and opposing all of them undiscriminatingly is a bourgeois pacifist and not a Marxist-Leninist approach.

Certain persons say that revolutions are entirely possible without war. Now which type of war are they referring to— is it a war of national liberation or a revolutionary civil war, or is it a world war?

If they are referring to a war of national liberation or a revolutionary civil war, then this formulation is, in effect, opposed to revolutionary wars and to revolution.

If they are referring to a world war, then they are shooting at a non-existent target. Although Marxist-Leninists have pointed out, on the basis of the history of the two world wars, that world wars inevitably lead to revolution, no Marxist-Leninist ever has held or ever will hold that revolution must be made through world war.

Marxist-Leninists take the abolition of war as their ideal and believe that war can be abolished.

But how can war be abolished?

This is how Lenin viewed it:

> . . . our object is to achieve the socialist system of society, which, by abolishing the division of mankind into classes, by abolishing all exploitation of man by man, and of one nation by other nations, will inevitably abolish all possibility of war.

The Statement of 1960 also puts it very clearly, "The victory of socialism all over the world will completely remove the social and national causes of all wars."

However, certain persons now actually hold that it is possible to bring about "a world without weapons, without armed forces and without wars" through "general and complete disarmament" while the system of imperialism and of the exploitation of man by man still exists. This is sheer illusion.

An elementary knowledge of Marxism-Leninism tells us that the armed forces are the principal part of the state machine and that a so-called world without weapons and without armed forces can only be a world without states. Lenin said:

> Only *after* the proletariat has disarmed the bourgeoisie will it be

able, without betraying its world-historical mission, to throw all arma-
ments on the scrap heap; and the proletariat will undoubtedly do this,
but *only when this condition has been fulfilled, certainly not before.*

What are the facts in the world today? Is there a shadow
of evidence that the imperialist countries headed by the
United States are ready to carry out general and complete
disarmament? Are they not each and all engaged in general
and complete arms expansion?

We have always maintained that, in order to expose and
combat the imperialists' arms expansion and war preparations, it is necessary to put forward the proposal for general
disarmament. Furthermore, it is possible to compel imperialism to accept some kind of agreement on disarmament,
through the combined struggle of the socialist countries and
the people of the whole world.

If one regards general and complete disarmament as the
fundamental road to world peace, spreads the illusion that
imperialism will automatically lay down its arms and tries
to liquidate the revolutionary struggles of the oppressed peoples and nations on the pretext of disarmament, then this
is deliberately to deceive the people of the world and help the
imperialists in their policies of aggression and war.

In order to overcome the present ideological confusion in
the international working-class movement on the question
of war and peace, we consider that Lenin's thesis, which
has been discarded by the modern revisionists, must be restored in the interest of combating the imperialist policies
of aggression and war and defending world peace.

The people of the world universally demand the preven-
tion of a new world war. And it is possible to prevent a new
world war.

The question then is, what is the way to secure world peace?
According to the Leninist viewpoint, world peace can be
won only by the struggles of the people in all countries and
not by begging the imperialists for it. World peace can only
be effectively defended by relying on the development of the
forces of the socialist camp, on the revolutionary struggles
of the proletariat and working people of all countries, on
the liberation struggles of the oppressed nations and on the
struggles of all peace-loving people and countries.

Such is the Leninist policy. Any policy to the contrary
definitely will not lead to world peace but will only encourage

the ambitions of the imperialists and increase the danger of world war.

In recent years, certain persons have been spreading the argument that a single spark from a war of national liberation or from a revolutionary people's war will lead to a world conflagration destroying the whole of mankind. What are the facts? Contrary to what these persons say, the wars of national liberation and the revolutionary people's wars that have occurred since World War II have not led to world war. The victory of these revolutionary wars has directly weakened the forces of imperialism and greatly strengthened the forces which prevent the imperialists from launching a world war and which defend world peace. Do not the facts demonstrate the absurdity of this argument?

(15) The complete banning and destruction of nuclear weapons is an important task in the struggle to defend world peace. We must do our utmost to this end.

Nuclear weapons are unprecedentedly destructive, which is why for more than a decade now the U.S. imperialists have been pursuing their policy of nuclear blackmail in order to realize their ambition of enslaving the people of all countries and dominating the world.

But when the imperialists threaten other countries with nuclear weapons, they subject the people in their own country to the same threat, thus arousing them against nuclear weapons and against the imperialist policies of aggression and war. At the same time, in their vain hope of destroying their opponents with nuclear weapons, the imperialists are in fact subjecting themselves to the danger of being destroyed.

The possibility of banning nuclear weapons does indeed exist. However, if the imperialists are forced to accept an agreement to ban nuclear weapons, it decidedly will not be because of their "love for humanity" but because of the pressure of the people of all countries and for the sake of their own vital interests.

In contrast to the imperialists, socialist countries rely upon the righteous strength of the people and on their own correct policies, and have no need whatever to gamble with nuclear weapons in the world arena. Socialist countries have nuclear weapons solely in order to defend themselves and to prevent imperialism from launching a nuclear war.

In the view of Marxist-Leninists, the people are the makers

of history. In the present, as in the past, man is the decisive factor. Marxist-Leninists attach importance to the role of technological change, but it is wrong to belittle the role of man and exaggerate the role of technology.

The emergence of nuclear weapons can neither arrest the progress of human history nor save the imperialist system from its doom, any more than the emergence of new techniques could save the old systems from their doom in the past.

The emergence of nuclear weapons does not and cannot resolve the fundamental contradictions in the contemporary world, does not and cannot alter the law of class struggle, and does not and cannot change the nature of imperialism and reaction.

It cannot, therefore, be said that with the emergence of nuclear weapons the possibility and the necessity of social and national revolutions have disappeared, or the basic principles of Marxism-Leninism, and especially the theories of proletarian revolution and the dictatorship of the proletariat and of war and peace, have become outmoded and changed into stale "dogmas".

(16) It was Lenin who advanced the thesis that it is possible for the socialist countries to practise peaceful coexistence with the capitalist countries. It is well known that after the great Soviet people had repulsed foreign armed intervention the Communist Party of the Soviet Union and the Soviet Government, led first by Lenin and then by Stalin, consistently pursued the policy of peaceful coexistence and that they were forced to wage a war of self-defence only when attacked by the German imperialists.

Since its founding, the People's Republic of China too has consistently pursued the policy of peaceful coexistence with countries having different social systems, and it is China which initiated the Five Principles of Peaceful Coexistence.

However, a few years ago certain persons suddenly claimed Lenin's policy of peaceful coexistence as their own "great discovery". They maintain that they have a monopoly on the interpretation of this policy. They treat "peaceful coexistence" as if it were an all-inclusive, mystical book from heaven and attribute to it every success the people of the world achieve by struggle. What is more, they label all who disagree with their distortions of Lenin's views as opponents of peaceful coexistence, as people completely ignorant of Lenin and Leninism, and as heretics deserving to be burnt at the stake.

How can the Chinese Communists agree with this view and practice? They cannot, it is impossible.

Lenin's principle of peaceful coexistence is very clear and readily comprehensible by ordinary people. Peaceful coexistence designates a relationship between countries with different social systems, and must not be interpreted as one pleases. It should never be extended to apply to the relations between oppressed and oppressor nations, between oppressed and oppressor countries or between oppressed and oppressor classes, and never be described as the main content of the transition from capitalism to socialism, still less should it be asserted that peaceful coexistence is mankind's road to socialism. The reason is that it is one thing to practise peaceful coexistence between countries with different social systems. It is absolutely impermissible and impossible for countries practising peaceful coexistence to touch even a hair of each other's social system. The class struggle, the struggle for national liberation and the transition from capitalism to socialism in various countries are quite another thing. They are all bitter, life-and-death revolutionary struggles which aim at changing the social system. Peaceful coexistence cannot replace the revolutionary struggles of the people. The transition from capitalism to socialism in any country can only be brought about through the proletarian revolution and the dictatorship of the proletariat in that country.

In the application of the policy of peaceful coexistence, struggles between the socialist and imperialist countries are unavoidable in the political, economic and ideological spheres, and it is absolutely impossible to have "all-round co-operation".

It is necessary for the socialist countries to engage in negotiations of one kind or another with the imperialist countries. It is possible to reach certain agreements through negotiation by relying on the correct policies of the socialist countries and on the pressure of the people of all countries. But necessary compromises between the socialist countries and the imperialist countries do not require the oppressed peoples and nations to follow suit and compromise with imperialism and its lackeys. No one should ever demand in the name of peaceful coexistence that the oppressed peoples and nations should give up their revolutionary struggles.

The application of the policy of peaceful coexistence by the socialist countries is advantageous for achieving a peaceful international environment for socialist construction, for exposing the imperialist policies of aggression and war and for isolating the imperialist forces of aggression and war. But if the general line of the foreign policy of the socialist countries is confined to peaceful coexistence, then it is impossible to handle correctly either the relations between socialist countries or those between the socialist countries and the oppressed peoples and nations. Therefore it is wrong to make peaceful coexistence the general line of the foreign policy of the socialist countries.

In our view, the general line of the foreign policy of the socialist countries should have the following content: to develop relations of friendship, mutual assistance and co-operation among the countries in the socialist camp in accordance with the principle of proletarian internationalism; to strive for peaceful coexistence on the basis of the Five Principles with countries having different social systems and oppose the imperialist policies of aggression and war; and to support and assist the revolutionary struggles of all the oppressed peoples and nations. These three aspects are interrelated and indivisible, and not a single one can be omitted.

(17) For a very long historical period after the proletariat takes power, class struggle continues as an objective law independent of man's will, differing only in form from what it was before the taking of power.

After the October Revolution, Lenin pointed out a number of times that:

a) The overthrown exploiters always try in a thousand and one ways to recover the "paradise" they have been deprived of.

b) New elements of capitalism are constantly and spontaneously generated in the petty-bourgeois atmosphere.

c) Political degenerates and new bourgeois elements may emerge in the ranks of the working class and among government functionaries as a result of bourgeois influence and the pervasive, corrupting atmosphere of the petty bourgeoisie.

d) The external conditions for the continuance of class struggle within a socialist country are encirclement by international capitalism, the imperialists' threat of armed intervention and their subversive activities to accomplish peaceful disintegration.

Life has confirmed these conclusions of Lenin's.

For decades or even longer periods after socialist industrialization and agricultural collectivization, it will be impossible to say that any socialist country will be free from those elements which Lenin repeatedly denounced, such as bourgeois hangers-on, parasites, speculators, swindlers, idlers, hooligans and embezzlers of state funds; or to say that a socialist country will no longer need to perform or be able to relinquish the task laid down by Lenin of conquering "this contagion, this plague, this ulcer that socialism has inherited from capitalism".

In a socialist country, it takes a very long historical period gradually to settle the question of who will win—socialism or capitalism. The struggle between the road of socialism and the road of capitalism runs through this whole historical period. This struggle rises and falls in a wave-like manner, at times becoming very fierce, and the forms of the struggle are many and varied.

The 1957 Declaration rightly states that "the conquest of power by the working class is only the beginning of the revolution, not its conclusion".

To deny the existence of class struggle in the period of the dictatorship of the proletariat and the necessity of thoroughly completing the socialist revolution on the economic, political and ideological fronts is wrong, does not correspond to objective reality and violates Marxism-Leninism.

(18) Both Marx and Lenin maintained that the entire period before the advent of the higher stage of communist society is the period of transition from capitalism to communism, the period of the dictatorship of the proletariat. In this transition period, the dictatorship of the proletariat, that is to say, the proletarian state, goes through the dialectical process of establishment, consolidation, strengthening and withering away.

In the *Critique of the Gotha Programme*, Marx posed the question as follows:

> Between capitalist and communist society lies the period of the revolutionary transformation of the one into the other. There corresponds to this also a political transition period in which the state can be nothing but *the revolutionary dictatorship of the proletariat.*

Lenin frequently emphasized Marx's great theory of the dictatorship of the proletariat and analysed the development of this theory, particularly in his outstanding work, *The State and Revolution*, where he wrote:

> ... the transition from capitalist society—which is developing to-

wards communism—to a communist society is impossible without a "political transition period", and the state in this period can only be the revolutionary dictatorship of the proletariat.

He further said:

> The essence of Marx's teaching on the state has been mastered only by those who understand that the dictatorship of a *single* class is necessary not only for every class society in general, not only for the *proletariat* which has overthrown the bourgeoisie, but also for the entire *historical period* which separates capitalism from "classless society", from communism.

As stated above, the fundamental thesis of Marx and Lenin is that the dictatorship of the proletariat will inevitably continue for the entire historical period of the transition from capitalism to communism, that is, for the entire period up to the abolition of all class differences and the entry into a classless society, the higher stage of communist society.

What will happen if it is announced, halfway through, that the dictatorship of the proletariat is no longer necessary?

Does this not fundamentally conflict with the teachings of Marx and Lenin on the state of the dictatorship of the proletariat?

Does this not license the development of "this contagion, this plague, this ulcer that socialism has inherited from capitalism"?

In other words, this would lead to extremely grave consequences and make any transition to communism out of the question.

Can there be a "state of the whole people"? Is it possible to replace the state of the dictatorship of the proletariat by a "state of the whole people"?

This is not a question about the internal affairs of any particular country but a fundamental problem involving the universal truth of Marxism-Leninism.

In the view of Marxist-Leninists, there is no such thing as a non-class or supra-class state. So long as the state remains a state, it must bear a class character; so long as the state exists, it cannot be a state of the "whole people". As soon as society becomes classless, there will no longer be a state.

Then what sort of thing would a "state of the whole people" be?

Anyone with an elementary knowledge of Marxism-Leninism can understand that the so-called "state of the whole people" is nothing new. Representative bourgeois figures have always called the bourgeois state a "state of all the people", or a "state in which power belongs to all the people".

Certain persons may say that their society is already one without classes. We answer: No, there are classes and class struggles in all socialist countries without exception.

Since remnants of the old exploiting classes who are trying to stage a comeback still exist there, since new capitalist elements are constantly being generated there, and since there are still parasites, speculators, idlers, hooligans, embezzlers of state funds, etc, how can it be said that classes or class struggles no longer exist? How can it be said that the dictatorship of the proletariat is no longer necessary?

Marxism-Leninism tells us that in addition to the suppression of the hostile classes, the historical tasks of the dictatorship of the proletariat in the course of building socialism necessarily include the correct handling of relations between the working class and peasantry, the consolidation of their political and economic alliance and the creation of conditions for the gradual elimination of the class difference between worker and peasant.

When we look at the economic base of any socialist society, we find that the difference between ownership by the whole people and collective ownership exists in all socialist countries without exception, and that there is individual ownership too. Ownership by the whole people and collective ownership are two kinds of ownership and two kinds of relations of production in socialist society. The workers in enterprises owned by the whole people and the peasants on farms owned collectively belong to two different categories of labourers in socialist society. Therefore, the class difference between worker and peasant exists in all socialist countries without exception. This difference will not disappear until the transition to the higher stage of communism is achieved. In their present level of economic development all socialist countries are still far, far removed from the higher stage of communism in which "from each according to his ability, to each according to his needs" is put into practice. Therefore, it will take a long, long time to eliminate the class difference between worker and peasant. And until this difference is eliminated, it is impossible to say that society is classless or that there is no longer any need for the dictatorship of the proletariat.

In calling a socialist state the "state of the whole people", is one trying to replace the Marxist-Leninist theory of the state by the bourgeois theory of the state? Is one trying to replace the state of the dictatorship of the proletariat by a state of a different character?

If that is the case, it is nothing but a great historical retrogression. The degeneration of the social system in Yugoslavia is a grave lesson.

(19) Leninism holds that the proletarian party must exist together with the dictatorship of the proletariat in socialist countries. The party of the proletariat is indispensable for the entire historical period of the dictatorship of the proletariat. The reason is that the dictatorship of the proletariat has to struggle against the enemies of the proletariat and of the people, remould the peasants and other small producers, constantly consolidate the proletarian ranks, build socialism and effect the transition to communism; none of these things can be done without the leadership of the party of the proletariat.

Can there be a "party of the entire people"? Is it possible to replace the party which is the vanguard of the proletariat by a "party of the entire people"?

This, too, is not a question about the internal affairs of any particular Party, but a fundamental problem involving the universal truth of Marxism-Leninism.

In the view of Marxist-Leninists, there is no such thing as a non-class or supra-class political party. All political parties have a class character. Party spirit is the concentrated expression of class character.

The party of the proletariat is the only party able to represent the interests of the whole people. It can do so precisely because it represents the interests of the proletariat, whose ideas and will it concentrates. It can lead the whole people because the proletariat can finally emancipate itself only with the emancipation of all mankind, because the very nature of the proletariat enables its party to approach problems in terms of its present and future interests, because the party is boundlessly loyal to the people and has the spirit of self-sacrifice; hence its democratic centralism and iron discipline. Without such a party, it is impossible to maintain the dictatorship of the proletariat and to represent the interests of the whole people.

What will happen if it is annnounced halfway before entering the higher stage of communist society that the party of the proletariat has become a "party of the entire people" and if its proletarian class character is repudiated?

Does this not fundamentally conflict with the teachings of Marx and Lenin on the party of the proletariat?

Does this not disarm the proletariat and all the working people, organizationally and ideologically, and is it not tantamount to helping restore capitalism?

Is it not "going south by driving the chariot north" to talk about any transition to communist society in such circumstances?

(20) Over the past few years, certain persons have violated Lenin's integral teachings about the interrelationship of leaders, party, class and masses, and raised the issue of "combating the cult of the individual"; this is erroneous and harmful.

The theory propounded by Lenin is as follows:

a) The masses are divided into classes;
b) Classes are usually led by political parties;
c) Political parties, as a general rule, are directed by more or less stable groups composed of the most authoritative, influential and experienced members, who are elected to the most responsible positions and are called leaders.

Lenin said, "All this is elementary."

The party of the proletariat is the headquarters of the proletariat in revolution and struggle. Every proletarian party must practise centralism based on democracy and establish a strong Marxist-Leninist leadership before it can become an organized and battle-worthy vanguard. To raise the question of "combating the cult of the individual" is actually to counterpose the leaders to the masses, undermine the party's unified leadership which is based on democratic centralism, dissipate its fighting strength and disintegrate its ranks.

Lenin criticized the erroneous views which counterpose the leaders to the masses. He called them "ridiculously absurd and stupid".

The Communist Party of China has always disapproved of exaggerating the role of the individual, has advocated and persistently practised democratic centralism within the Party and advocated the linking of the leadership with the masses, maintaining that correct leadership must know how to concentrate the views of the masses.

While loudly combating the so-called "cult of the individual", certain persons are in reality doing their best to defame the proletarian party and the dictatorship of the proletariat. At the same time, they are enormously exaggerating the role of certain individuals, shifting all errors onto others and claiming all credit for themselves.

What is more serious is that, under the pretext of "combating the cult of the individual", certain persons are crudely interfering in the internal affairs of other fraternal Parties and fraternal countries and forcing other fraternal Parties to change their leadership in order to impose their own wrong line on these Parties. What is all this if not great-power chauvinism, sectarianism and splittism? What is all this if not subversion?

It is high time to propagate seriously and comprehensively Lenin's integral teachings on the interrelationship of leaders, party, class and masses.

(21) Relations between socialist countries are international relations of a new type. Relations between socialist countries, whether large or small, and whether more developed or less developed economically, must be based on the principles of complete equality, respect for territorial integrity, sovereignty and independence, and non-interference in each other's internal affairs, and must also be based on the principles of mutual support and mutual assistance in accordance with proletarian internationalism.

Every socialist country must rely mainly on itself for its construction.

In accordance with its own concrete conditions, every socialist country must rely first of all on the diligent labour and talents of its own people, utilize all its available resources fully and in a planned way, and bring all its potential into play in socialist construction. Only thus can it build socialism effectively and develop its economy speedily.

This is the only way for each socialist country to strengthen the might of the entire socialist camp and enhance its capacity to assist the revolutionary cause of the international proletariat. Therefore, to observe the principle of mainly relying on oneself in construction is to apply proletarian internationalism concretely.

If, proceeding only from its own partial interests, any socialist country unilaterally demands that other fraternal countries submit to its needs, and uses the pretext of opposing what they call "going it alone" and "nationalism" to prevent other fraternal countries from applying the principle of relying mainly on their own efforts in their construction and from developing their economies on the basis of independence, or even goes to the length of putting economic pressure on other fraternal countries—then these are pure manifestations of national egoism.

It is absolutely necessary for socialist countries to practise mutual economic assistance and co-operation and exchange. Such economic co-operation must be based on the principles of complete equality, mutual benefit and comradely mutual assistance.

It would be great-power chauvinism to deny these basic principles and, in the name of "international division of labour" or "specialization", to impose one's own will on others, infringe on the independence and sovereignty of fraternal countries or harm the interests of their people.

In relations among socialist countries it would be preposterous to follow the practice of gaining profit for oneself at the expense of others, a practice characteristic of relations among capitalist countries, or go so far as to take the "economic integration" and the "common market", which monopoly capitalist groups have instituted for the purpose of seizing markets and grabbing profits, as examples which socialist countries ought to follow in their economic co-operation and mutual assistance.

(22) The 1957 Declaration and the 1960 Statement lay down the principles guiding relations among fraternal Parties. These are the principle of solidarity, the principle of mutual support and mutual assistance, the principle of independence and equality and the principle of reaching unanimity through consultation—all on the basis of Marxism-Leninism and proletarian internationalism.

We note that in its letter of March 30 the Central Committee of the C.P.S.U. says that there are no "superior" and "subordinate" Parties in the communist movement, that all Communist Parties are independent and equal, and that they should all build their relations on the basis of proletarian internationalism and mutual assistance.

It is a fine quality of Communists that their deeds are consistent with their words. The only correct way to safeguard and strengthen unity among the fraternal Parties is genuinely to adhere to, and not to violate, the principle of proletarian internationalism and genuinely to observe, and not to undermine, the principles guiding relations among fraternal Parties —and to do so not only in words but, much more important, in deeds.

If the principle of independence and equality is accepted in relations among fraternal Parties, then it is impermissible for any Party to place itself above others, to interfere in their internal affairs, and to adopt patriarchal ways in relations with them.

If it is accepted that there are no "superiors" and "subordinates" in relations among fraternal Parties, then it is impermissible to impose the programme, resolutions and line of one's own Party on other fraternal Parties as the "common programme" of the international communist movement.

If the principle of reaching unanimity through consultation is accepted in relations among fraternal Parties, then one should not emphasize "who is in the majority" or "who is in the minority" and bank on a so-called majority in order to force through one's own erroneous line and carry out sectarian and splitting policies.

If it is agreed that differences between fraternal Parties should be settled through inter-Party consultation, then other fraternal Parties should not be attacked publicly and by name at one's own congress or at other Party congresses, in speeches by Party leaders, resolutions, statements, etc.; and still less should the ideological differences among fraternal Parties be extended into the sphere of state relations.

We hold that in the present circumstances, when there are differences in the international communist movement, it is particularly important to stress strict adherence to the principles guiding relations among fraternal Parties as laid down in the Declaration and the Statement.

In the sphere of relations among fraternal Parties and countries, the question of Soviet-Albanian relations is an outstanding one at present. Here the question is what is the correct way to treat a fraternal Party and country and whether the principles guiding relations among fraternal Parties and countries stipulated in the Declaration and the Statement are to be adhered to. The correct solution of this question is an important matter of principle in safeguarding the unity of the socialist camp and the international communist movement.

How to treat the Marxist-Leninist fraternal Albanian Party of Labour is one question. How to treat the Yugoslav revisionist clique of traitors to Marxism-Leninism is quite another question. These two essentially different questions must on no account be placed on a par.

Your letter says that you "do not relinquish the hope that the relations between the C.P.S.U. and the Albanian Party of Labour may be improved", but at the same time you continue to attack the Albanian comrades for what you call "splitting activities". Clearly this is self-contradictory and in no way contributes to resolving the problem of Soviet-Albanian relations.

Who is it that has taken splitting actions in Soviet-Albanian relations?

Who is it that has extended the ideological differences between the Soviet and Albanian Parties to state relations?

Who is it that has brought the divergences between the Soviet and Albanian Parties and between the two countries into the open before the enemy?

Who is it that has openly called for a change in the Albanian Party and state leadership?

All this is plain and clear to the whole world.

Is it possible that the leading comrades of the C.P.S.U. do not really feel their responsibility for the fact that Soviet-Albanian relations have so seriously deteriorated?

We once again express our sincere hope that the leading comrades of the C.P.S.U. will observe the principles guiding relations among fraternal Parties and countries and take the initiative in seeking an effective way to improve Soviet-Albanian relations.

In short, the question of how to handle relations with fraternal Parties and countries must be taken seriously. Strict adherence to the principles guiding relations among fraternal Parties and countries is the only way forcefully to rebuff slanders such as those spread by the imperialists and reactionaries about the "hand of Moscow".

Proletarian internationalism is demanded of all Parties without exception, whether large or small, and whether in power or not. However, the larger Parties and the Parties in power bear a particularly heavy responsibility in this respect. The series of distressing developments which have occurred in the socialist camp in the past period have harmed the interests not only of the fraternal Parties concerned but also of the masses of the people in their countries. This convincingly demonstrates that the larger countries and Parties need to keep in mind Lenin's behest never to commit the error of great-power chauvinism.

The comrades of the C.P.S.U. state in their letter that "the Communist Party of the Soviet Union has never taken and will never take a single step that could sow hostility among the peoples of our country towards the fraternal Chinese people or other peoples". Here we do not desire to go back and enumerate the many unpleasant events that have occurred in the past, and we only wish that the comrades of the C.P.S.U. will strictly abide by this statement in their future actions.

During the past few years, our Party members and our people have exercised the greatest restraint in the face of a series of grave incidents which were in violation of the principles guiding relations among fraternal Parties and countries and despite the many difficulties and losses which have been imposed on us. The spirit of proletarian internationalism of the Chinese Communists and the Chinese people has stood a severe test.

The Communist Party of China is unswervingly loyal to proletarian internationalism, upholds and defends the principles of the 1957 Declaration and the 1960 Statement guiding relations among fraternal Parties and countries, and safeguards and strengthens the unity of the socialist camp and the international communist movement.

(23) In order to carry out the common programme of the international communist movement unanimously agreed upon by the fraternal Parties, an uncompromising struggle must be waged against all forms of opportunism, which is a deviation from Marxism-Leninism.

The Declaration and the Statement point out that revisionism, or, in other words, Right opportunism, is the main danger in the international communist movement. Yugoslav revisionism typifies modern revisionism.

The Statement points out particularly:

> The Communist Parties have unanimously condemned the Yugoslav variety of international opportunism, a variety of modern revisionist "theories" in concentrated form.

It goes on to say:

After betraying Marxism-Leninism, which they termed obsolete, the leaders of the League of Communists of Yugoslavia opposed their anti-Leninist revisionist programme to the Declaration of 1957; they set the League of Communists of Yugoslavia against the international communist movement as a whole, severed their country from the socialist camp, made it dependent on so-called "aid" from U.S. and other imperialists. . . .

The Statement says further:

The Yugoslav revisionists carry on subversive work against the socialist camp and the world communist movement. Under the pretext of an extra-bloc policy, they engage in activities which prejudice the unity of all the peace-loving forces and countries.

Therefore, it draws the following conclusion:

Further exposure of the leaders of Yugoslav revisionists and active struggle to safeguard the communist movement and the working-class movement from the anti-Leninist ideas of the Yugoslav revisionists, remains an essential task of the Marxist-Leninist Parties.

The question raised here is an important one of principle for the international communist movement.

Only recently the Tito clique have publicly stated that they are persisting in their revisionist programme and anti-Marxist-Leninist stand in opposition to the Declaration and the Statement.

U.S. imperialism and its NATO partners have spent several thousand millions of U.S. dollars nursing the Tito clique for a long time. Cloaked as "Marxist-Leninists" and flaunting the banner of a "socialist country", the Tito clique have been undermining the international communist movement and the revolutionary cause of the people of the world, serving as a special detachment of U.S. imperialism.

It is completely groundless and out of keeping with the facts to assert that Yugoslavia is showing "definite positive tendencies", that it is a "socialist country", and that the Tito clique is an "anti-imperialist force".

Certain persons are now attempting to introduce the Yugoslav revisionist clique into the socialist community and the international communist ranks. This is openly to tear up the agreement unanimously reached at the 1960 meeting of the fraternal Parties and is absolutely impermissible.

Over the past few years, the revisionist trend flooding the international working-class movement and the many experiences and lessons of the international communist movement have fully confirmed the correctness of the conclusion in the Declaration and the Statement that revisionism is the main danger in the international communist movement at present.

However, certain persons are openly saying that dogmatism and not revisionism is the main danger, or that dogmatism is no less dangerous than revisionism, etc. What sort of principle underlies all this?

Firm Marxist-Leninists and genuine Marxist-Leninist Parties must put principles first. They must not barter away principles, approving one thing today and another tomorrow, advocating one thing today and another tomorrow.

Together with all Marxist-Leninists, the Chinese Communists will continue to wage an uncompromising struggle against modern revisionism in order to defend the purity of Marxism-Leninism and the principled stand of the Declaration and the Statement.

While combating revisionism, which is the main danger in the international communist movement, Communists must also combat dogmatism.

As stated in the 1957 Declaration, proletarian parties "should firmly adhere to the principle of combining . . . universal Marxist-Leninist truth with the specific practice of revolution and construction in their countries".

That is to say:

On the one hand, it is necessary at all times to adhere to the universal truth of Marxism-Leninism. Failure to do so will lead to Right opportunist or revisionist errors.

On the other hand, it is always necessary to proceed from reality, maintain close contact with the masses, constantly sum up the experience of mass struggles, and independently work out and apply policies and tactics suited to the conditions of one's own country. Errors of dogmatism will be committed if one fails to do so, if one mechanically copies the policies and tactics of another Communist Party, submits blindly to the will of others or accepts without analysis the programme and resolutions of another Communist Party as one's own line.

Some people are now violating this basic principle, which was long ago affirmed in the Declaration. On the pretext of "creatively developing Marxism-Leninism", they cast aside the universal truth of Marxism-Leninism. Moreover, they describe as "universal Marxist-Leninist truths" their own pre-

scriptions which are based on nothing but subjective con-
jecture and are divorced from reality and from the masses,
and they force others to accept these prescriptions unconditionally.

That is why many grave phenomena have come to pass in
the international communist movement.

(24) A most important lesson from the experience of the
international communist movement is that the development
and victory of a revolution depend on the existence of a
revolutionary proletarian party.

There must be a revolutionary party.

There must be a revolutionary party built according to the
revolutionary theory and revolutionary style of Marxism-Leninism.

There must be a revolutionary party able to integrate the
universal truth of Marxism-Leninism with the concrete practice of the revolution in its own country.

There must be a revolutionary party able to link the leadership closely with the broad masses of the people.

There must be a revolutionary party that perseveres in the
truth, corrects its errors and knows how to conduct criticism and self-criticism.

Only such a revolutionary party can lead the proletariat
and the broad masses of the people in defeating imperialism
and its lackeys, winning a thorough victory in the national
democratic revolution and winning the socialist revolution.

If a party is not a proletarian revolutionary party but a
bourgeois reformist party;

If it is not a Marxist-Leninist party but a revisionist party;

If it is not a vanguard party of the proletariat but a party
tailing after the bourgeoisie;

If it is not a party representing the interests of the proletariat and all the working people but a party representing the
interests of the labour aristocracy;

If it is not an internationalist party but a nationalist party;

If it is not a party that can use its brains to think for itself
and acquire an accurate knowledge of the trends of the different classes in its own country through serious investigation and study, and knows how to apply the universal truth
of Marxism-Leninism and integrate it with the concrete
practice of its own country, but instead is a party that parrots
the words of others, copies foreign experience without
analysis, runs hither and thither in response to the baton of

certain persons abroad, and has become a hodgepodge of revisionism, dogmatism and everything but Marxist-Leninist principle;

Then such a party is absolutely incapable of leading the proletariat and the masses in revolutionary struggle, absolutely incapable of winning the revolution and absolutely incapable of fulfilling the great historical mission of the proletariat.

This is a question all Marxist-Leninists, all class-conscious workers and all progressive people everywhere need to ponder deeply.

(25) It is the duty of Marxist-Leninists to distinguish between truth and falsehood with respect to the differences that have arisen in the international communist movement. In the common interest of the unity for struggle against the enemy, we have always advocated solving problems through inter-Party consultations and opposed bringing differences into the open before the enemy.

As the comrades of the C.P.S.U. know, the public polemics in the international communist movement have been provoked by certain fraternal Party leaders and forced on us.

Since a public debate has been provoked, it ought to be conducted on the basis of equality among fraternal Parties and of democracy, and by presenting the facts and reasoning things out.

Since certain Party leaders have publicly attacked other fraternal Parties and provoked a public debate, it is our opinion that they have no reason or right to forbid the fraternal Parties attacked to make public replies.

Since certain Party leaders have published innumerable articles attacking other fraternal Parties, why do they not publish in their own press the articles those Parties have written in reply?

Latterly, the Communist Party of China has been subjected to preposterous attacks. The attackers have raised a great hue and cry and, disregarding the facts, have fabricated many charges against us. We have published these articles and speeches attacking us in our own press.

We have also published in full in our press the Soviet leader's report at the meeting of the Supreme Soviet on December 12, 1962, the *Pravda* Editorial Board's article of January 7, 1963, the speech of the head of the C.P.S.U. delegation at the Sixth Congress of the Socialist Unity Party of Germany on January 16, 1963 and the *Pravda* Editorial Board's article of February 10, 1963.

We have also published the full text of the two letters from the Central Committee of the C.P.S.U. dated February 21 and March 30, 1963.

We have replied to some of the articles and speeches in which fraternal Parties have attacked us, but have not yet replied to others. For example, we have not directly replied to the many articles and speeches of the comrades of the C.P.S.U.

Between December 15, 1962 and March 8, 1963, we wrote seven articles in reply to our attackers. These articles are entitled:

"Workers of All Countries, Unite, Oppose Our Common Enemy!",

"The Differences Between Comrade Togliatti and Us",

"Leninism and Modern Revisionism",

"Let Us Unite on the Basis of the Moscow Declaration and the Moscow Statement",

"Whence the Differences?—A Reply to Thorez and Other Comrades",

"More on the Differences Between Comrade Togliatti and Us—Some Important Problems of Leninism in the Contemporary World",

"A Comment on the Statement of the Communist Party of the U.S.A.".

Presumably, you are referring to these articles when towards the end of your letter of March 30 you accuse the Chinese press of making "groundless attacks" on the C.P.S.U. It is turning things upside down to describe articles replying to our attackers as "attacks".

Since you described our articles as "groundless" and as so very bad, why do you not publish all seven of these "groundless attacks", in the same way as we have published your articles, and let all the Soviet comrades and Soviet people think for themselves and judge who is right and who wrong? You are of course entitled to make a point-by-point refutation of these articles you consider "groundless attacks".

Although you call our articles "groundless" and our arguments wrong, you do not tell the Soviet people what our arguments actually are. This practice can hardly be described as showing a serious attitude towards the discussion of problems by fraternal Parties, towards the truth or towards the masses.

We hope that the public debate among fraternal Parties can be stopped. This is a problem that has to be dealt with in accordance with the principles of independence, of equality and of reaching unanimity through consultation among fraternal Parties. In the international communist movement, no one has the right to launch attacks whenever he wants, or to order the "ending of open polemics" whenever he wants to prevent the other side from replying.

It is known to the comrades of the C.P.S.U. that, in order to create a favourable atmosphere for convening the meeting of the fraternal Parties, we have decided temporarily to suspend, as from March 9, 1963, public replies to the public attacks directed by name against us by comrades of fraternal Parties. We reserve the right of public reply.

In our letter of March 9, we said that on the question of suspending public debate "it is necessary that our two Parties and the fraternal Parties concerned should have some discussion and reach an agreement that is fair and acceptable to all".

The foregoing are our views regarding the general line of the international communist movement and some related questions of principle. We hope, as we indicated at the beginning of this letter, that the frank presentation of our views will be conducive to mutual understanding. Of course, comrades may agree or disagree with these views. But in our opinion, the questions we discuss here are the crucial questions calling for attention and solution by the international communist movement. We hope that all these questions and also those raised in your letter will be fully discussed in the talks between our two Parties and at the meeting of representatives of all the fraternal Parties.

In addition, there are other questions of common concern, such as the criticism of Stalin and some important matters of principle regarding the international communist movement which were raised at the 20th and 22nd Congresses of the C.P.S.U., and we hope that on these questions, too, there will be a frank exchange of opinion in the talks.

With regard to the talks between our two Parties, in our letter of March 9 we proposed that Comrade Khrushchev come to Peking; if this was not convenient, we proposed that another responsible comrade of the Central Committee of the C.P.S.U. lead a delegation to Peking or that we send a delegation to Moscow.

Since you have stated in your letter of March 30 that Comrade Khrushchev cannot come to China, and since you have not expressed a desire to send a delegation to China, the Central Committee of the Communist Party of China has decided to send a delegation to Moscow.

In your letter of March 30, you invited Comrade Mao Tse-tung to visit the Soviet Union. As early as February 23, Comrade Mao Tse-tung in his conversation with the Soviet Ambassador to China clearly stated the reason why he was not prepared to visit the Soviet Union at the present time. You were well aware of this.

When a responsible comrade of the Central Committee of the Communist Party of China received the Soviet Ambassador to China on May 9, he informed you that we would send a delegation to Moscow in the middle of June. Later, in compliance with the request of the Central Committee of the C.P.S.U., we agreed to postpone the talks between our two Parties to July 5.

We sincerely hope that the talks between the Chinese and Soviet Parties will yield positive results and contribute to the preparations for convening the meeting of all Communist and Workers' Parties.

It is now more than ever necessary for all Communists to unite on the basis of Marxism-Leninism and proletarian internationalism and of the Declaration and the Statement unanimously agreed upon by the fraternal Parties.

Together with Marxist-Leninist Parties and revolutionary people the world over, the Communist Party of China will continue its unremitting efforts to uphold the interests of the socialist camp and the international communist movement, the cause of the emancipation of the oppressed peoples and nations, and the struggle against imperialism and for world peace.

We hope that events which grieve those near and dear to us and only gladden the enemy will not recur in the international communist movement in the future.

The Chinese Communists firmly believe that the Marxist-Leninists, the proletariat and the revolutionary people everywhere will unite more closely, overcome all difficulties and obstacles and win still greater victories in the struggle

against imperialism and for world peace, and in the fight for
the revolutionary cause of the people of the world and the
cause of international communism.

Workers of all countries, unite! Workers and oppressed
peoples and nations of the world, unite! Oppose our common enemy!

With communist greetings,

The Central Committee of
the Communist Party of China

27. P'eng Chen: Talk at the Festival of Peking Opera on Contemporary Themes (July, 1964)*

P'eng Chen was not only a devoted Communist from his
youth, he was also a Party theoretician. He was President of
the Party's Central Party School from 1938 to 1942; he
worked closely with both Mao Tse-tung and Lin Piao during the war years. In 1948 he was a deputy director of the
Organizational Department of the Party Central Committee.
Then, in 1951, he was appointed Mayor of Peking, the capital of Communist China. And later he also served as Vice-
Chairman of the Chinese People's Congress. He had also
represented China at many international congresses and
participated in the important but unsuccessful negotiations
with the Soviet Communist Party on Sino-Soviet ideological
differences. He was one of the few members of the Chinese
Communist Party entrusted with the responsibility of inter-
preting Maoism to Communists in other countries.

When Mao began his "socialist education campaign" in
1962, the purposes were (1) to purify ideology and to rectify revisionist tendencies; and (2) to re-establish socialist,
collective controls over the economy, especially in the rural
areas. However, in the intellectual community this movement encountered stiff and stubborn resistance. As a result,
a new rectification campaign had started in 1964 to push
the "socialist-education" movement into a new stage. Mao
selected P'eng to take charge of this task. Ironically, two

---

* From *A Great Revolution on the Cultural Front*, Peking: Foreign Language
Press, 1965, pp. 1–20.

years later, P'eng himself was purged for his own "revisionist" tendency when he defended a revisionist play, *The Dismissal of Hai Jui*, written by his closest associate, Wu Han, the Vice-Mayor of Peking.

First of all let me congratulate you on the successes achieved in the reform of Peking opera and on the successful staging of Peking operas on contemporary revolutionary themes.

There are many types of plays on contemporary themes. Hollywood is also producing "plays on contemporary themes"; the rubbish the modern revisionists are staging also goes under the name of "plays with contemporary themes". But what we are staging are plays on contemporary revolutionary themes serving the workers, peasants and soldiers and the socialist revolution and socialist construction.

Many Peking operas of the past portrayed emperors and kings, generals, ministers, scholars, beauties, lords and dowagers, young gentlemen and ladies; they prettified the exploiting classes and denigrated the working people. Very few plays were staged on contemporary revolutionary themes. Over a long period in the past Peking opera in the main served feudalism and capitalism. Many attempts were made to reform Peking opera, and a number of plays were successfully revised, but at the current Festival of Peking Opera on Contemporary Themes we are witnessing for the first time reforms that are so comprehensive and systematic, so rich in content and well received by the broad masses of the people. This is indeed a revolution in Peking opera.

Today, we should study Peking opera from two aspects. So far as their contents are concerned, many plays in the past served feudalism or capitalism. These plays dominated the stage and they must be reformed. There are also a small number of historical plays and plays on contemporary themes whose content is fairly good; these should be further improved. So far as artistic form is concerned, Peking opera has a relatively long history and has attained a relatively high artistic level; it is a type of opera with relatively strict conventions. For these reasons it is rather difficult to reform. But once successfully reformed, it will have a bright future. Now that so many comrades and friends are determined to reform it, to revolutionize it, and great successes have been achieved in this revolution, we can say that this revolution has been successful. The reform of Peking opera—its transformation from an art that in the main served feudalism and capitalism into one serving the workers, peasants, soldiers and socialism —is a great event in literary and artistic circles; it is a great revolution. Initial success has been gained in this revolution. We congratulate you on the success of this reform; and extend our deepest thanks.

The question now is: How to carry the revolution in Peking opera through to the end; and how to reform Peking opera successfully.

There are still quite a number of differing opinions on whether Peking opera should be reformed at all and how to reform it systematically and comprehensively. The vast majority of these opinions are well-intentioned and constructive. There are also a small number of persons who are fundamentally opposed to reform. Their cry is: "What sort of Peking opera is this without the long sleeves or the long beards? This is sheer nonsense!" So there are still a lot of problems to solve. Comrades should not imagine that this festival has solved everything and that the revolution has been accomplished. That is not so. Certain questions, therefore, still have to be dealt with, and they must be brought up for discussion.

I

The first question: Is it necessary to reform Peking opera? How should we reform it?

It must be reformed and reformed successfully. I shall deal with five aspects of this question.

1. Should Peking opera serve socialism, or should it serve feudalism or capitalism? Literature and art should serve politics and the development of the productive forces. Now that we are living in a socialist society, whom should our Peking opera serve? What kind of plays should we stage? Should we serve socialism by staging plays that advance the socialist revolution and socialist construction, or should we stage plays that benefit feudalism or capitalism? This is a fundamental question. It is quite clear that if one does not want to see feudalism or capitalism restored, if one does not hanker after these systems, then in a socialist society one cannot be always staging plays about such representatives of the exploiting classes as emperors, kings, generals, ministers, scholars and beauties. What is an emperor? He is the representative of the landlord class, the chieftain of the landlords. What is an empress? She is the chief of the landlords' wives. To be sure, some working people were portrayed in Peking operas in the past, but most of them were shown in a distorted and unfavourable light. How can we in our socialist society tolerate such a state of affairs with Peking opera—so important a stage art, a stage art with a relatively high artistic level and an important artistic heritage—continuing to portray emperors, kings, generals and ministers, and continuing to stage operas which are detrimental to the socialist revolution and socialist construction? That can't be! That would mean in actual fact helping the attempts of the feudal forces to restore feudalism or of the capitalist forces to restore capitalism. Therefore, Peking opera must be reformed. Either Peking opera will die out or it must mainly portray workers, peasants and soldiers and serve them and socialism; either one way or the other. There is no third way.

2. *Should Peking opera serve the majority or the minority?* Should it serve the workers, peasants and soldiers (including the revolutionary intellectuals), or should it serve those old and young "remnants" of the old society, and the landlords, rich peasants, counter-revolutionaries, undesirable elements and bourgeois Rightists? Should it serve more than 90 per cent of the population, or should it serve only a few per cent of the population? Should it serve six hundred and many tens of millions, or should it serve a few millions or a few tens of millions who make up only a few per cent of the population? In the past, it was always those few per cent of the population who dominated the stage. Our country today is the People's Republic of China led by the proletariat and based on the worker-peasant alliance. In such a country, a socialist country, where do our workers in literature and art, our fighters on the front of the art of Peking opera, stand? Should they stand with more than 90 per cent of the population, with the workers, peasants and soldiers, that is, on the side of socialism, or on the side of our enemies, the landlords, rich peasants, counter-revolutionaries, undesirable elements and bourgeois Rightists? I can't say that absolutely none of you would wish to stand with the landlords, rich peasants, counter-revolutionaries, undesirable elements and bourgeois Rightists, but I am confident the overwhelming majority of you are not willing to stand on their side.

The mass of workers, peasants and soldiers, and especially the young people, are dissatisfied with Peking opera always staging plays about emperors, kings, generals and ministers and not staging plays on contemporary revolutionary themes. They expressed their attitude long ago. They did this very simply—by refusing to buy tickets. Old Peking operas have been less heavily booked up than several kinds of local opera precisely because these latter staged plays on contemporary revolutionary themes. Theatres in which old Peking operas about emperors, kings, generals, ministers, scholars and beauties are staged are always poorly attended. Is it not true that the artistic level of Peking opera is rather high? Is it not true that there are some nationally famous actors with very high artistic attainments? But their box-office draws less people compared with some of the local operas. What does this mean? It means that the masses are telling us by their acts: "Peking opera must be reformed. If there is no reform, we'll stay away!" If things go on like this, with so many of the masses, so many of the young people, not attending, and with audiences of just a few in their fifties and sixties and a handful of ardent Peking opera fans, then Peking opera will have faded away in 20 or 40 years, and if it hasn't pretty well died out in 40 years then it certainly will have in 60. The mass of workers and peasants and young people have shown where they stand. If you still do not reform, but go on putting on operas about emperors, kings, generals, ministers, scholars and beauties, doesn't this mean that you will be letting Peking opera sit passively waiting for its end? Then again: our theatre is there to serve the masses of the people, but when the masses do not attend the theatre, and you do not reform it, what else then are you waiting for? As I see it, there must be reforms, inevitably, otherwise there is no future for Peking opera.

3. To present the dead or the living? There are few characters on the Peking opera stage who are living people. Besides there is a theory that "characters of living people on the Peking opera stage cannot be lifelike, or that it is very difficult to make them resemble living people, whereas in regard to the dead, the further they are from us in time the more lifelike they appear." Strange indeed! There is the opera, *King Pa Bids Farewell to Lady Yu*, but have you ever seen King Pa, or his Lady Yu? How do you know they resemble the stage types? How can you say such stage characters are like the people of old, when neither you nor I have ever seen the originals to know? Well, that's what you say and who's to contradict you? And why insist that workers, peasants and soldiers in Peking opera can't be lifelike? At least there are models to follow when portraying contemporary people; our workers, peasants, and soldiers are all models, and where the stage characters are not lifelike, then go and see and study them for yourself and you will find that you will be able to create lifelike characters. To argue as a reason for opposing the reform of Peking opera that the characters of living people on the Peking opera stage are not lifelike and only people of the past are, just won't stand scrutiny.

Something like six hundred million and more workers and peasants (including revolutionary soldiers, i.e., workers and peasants in arms) are engaged in a great revolutionary struggle; they are engaged in a revolutionary movement of unprecedented greatness and construction of heroic proportions; isn't it well worth putting all this on the stage? Is it really only those few ancients who are worthy of being portrayed on the stage? There are so many inspiring heroic deeds; there are so many heroes, yet you do not portray them on the stage; you keep on staging feudal characters long since dead. Aren't our revolutionary heroes and heroic revolutionary masses worth depicting? Isn't it worth describing them—putting all this down on paper, on the stage, into music or on canvas? Our great socialist revolution and socialist construction arouse no interest, but those few whom no one has ever set eyes on and who are long since dead—landlord chieftains and chiefs of landlords' wives, or feudal or bourgeois "scholars and beauties"—arouse great interest. Isn't this strange? But it is not so strange really. This concerns the question of serving the more than 90 per cent of the people, or of serving that few remaining percentage, that is, it is a question of serving socialism or serving capitalism or feudalism. At the moment there are still people who do actually want to restore capitalism or feudalism, but these are after all a small minority. To advocate serving feudalism or capitalism openly in the People's Republic of China is very difficult because they would be immediately given a telling rebuff by the masses of the people, and few dare court that. So those with ulterior motives take another line: They fill the stage exclusively with the ancients. A few working in modern drama say, "Though what I put on is bourgeois, it is of the dead bourgeoisie of the 18th and 19th centuries; and I do indeed portray feudal people but they are people who have long since passed away." A handful of persons would like to use this sort of feudalism and capitalism to corrode and poison the minds of our people and our youth. Objectively, that is what they do. Of course, the great majority of those who stage such plays do so unconsciously, because when they were in old-style opera classes, or when apprenticed to their masters, these were the plays they were taught, and though in their hearts they do not wish to put them on, there is nothing else they can put on. As for a handful of people, I doubt very much whether they do so completely unconsciously. If they are doing so unconsciously, then why do they hate the reform of Peking opera so much? We have a song that says: "Socialism is good." But they say: it isn't. They say "feudalism is good", or "capitalism is good" and they say this through the forms of art. "See how good feudalism or capitalism is on the stage!" This is the song they want to sing. So you see, presenting people of the past and people of the present on the stage is not simply a question of the dead and the living. This is a question of a political nature, a question reflecting class character, political orientation, the path to take. Isn't it so? Some people prefer to stage foreign people and people of past times. Well, Lenin is a foreigner, and a man of times past, but how comes it then that so few plays are staged about Lenin leading the October Revolution; why are there so few good foreign dramas about the proletarian revolution on our stage?

We are historical materialists. We are not indiscriminately opposed to staging historical plays. When we oppose putting on plays about people of the past, we are opposing those plays about people of the past which laud feudalism or capitalism, which prettify the exploiting classes. As for those historical plays which fortify the will of the people and destroy the arrogance of the exploiting classes, and which benefit the cause of the people, help social development and the revolution, and further socialism—historical plays which tell of the fine traditions of the Chinese people—of course these can be staged. But the emphasis must be on staging contemporary revolutionary plays, plays about the living masses of people fighting their struggles, about the living proletariat in the midst of its struggles. A couple of years ago I took this matter up with comrades of the Peking People's Art Theatre:

How about devoting just a few per cent of your time to staging plays about people of the past and about foreigners, and more than 90 per cent of your time to staging contemporary revolutionary Chinese plays? I said, and I proposed that they think it over. I am not saying that no historical plays should be staged, but I am saying that the emphasis should be on staging plays about the living, about our workers, peasants, and soldiers, contemporary plays which further socialism and help the struggle against the enemy.

Some people in Peking opera circles said that the staging of contemporary revolutionary plays is just a gust of wind. We must tell them that this wind is mighty strong and it won't stop blowing. This wind would stop blowing only if capitalism were restored and modern revisionists got into power in China. Comrades and friends in Peking opera circles, I think that for the time being it is better for you to put aside those plays about the ancients while concentrating your energies on making a break-through in contemporary drama. You have been performing the old plays for so long and have become so accustomed to them that you feel quite at home in them, while you feel awkward and up against many difficulties when you take up contemporary plays. The question is that you haven't got enough experience, and you haven't quite got the hang of things yet; when you do, everything will be all right. Put everything else aside and give it a trial for a time; get the hang of staging contemporary revolutionary plays and then put on some plays about people of olden days at the same time. I think that unless this is done for a period of time, contemporary revolutionary drama cannot be consolidated.

4. The question of content and form. As I've just said, the ideological content of Peking opera should be revolutionary. But this revolutionary ideological content must be integrated with the special artistic characteristics of Peking opera. It is here that the difficulty of reform lies. Set forms already exist in the special characteristic features of the art of performing Peking operas on ancient themes but there are no set forms as yet for portraying workers, peasants and soldiers in operas on contemporary themes. Some new forms were created in the course of this festival, but the experience gained is of an initial nature so it is necessary to continue to create, to sum up our experience and improve on it.

Two questions arise in integrating a revolutionary content

with the special characteristics of Peking opera art. The first is: Must Peking opera conventions change? The conventions of Peking opera were originally developed to portray the ancients. Today the task is mainly to portray people of the present day—workers, peasants and soldiers—therefore, certain changes are imperative. Changes will have to be made in the music, singing, recitative, acting and acrobatic routines. Refusal to make changes will mean that the portrayal of workers, peasants and soldiers will not be convincing.

The other question is: Should the good features of other art forms be adapted to the uses of Peking opera? Peking opera was originally created and developed by assimilating the good features of other operatic forms. As it originated that way, why then should it not today learn and adapt to itself good features from other art forms? It should make such adaptations. Of course, the result after adaptation must still be wholly in the character of Peking opera. That is to say, Peking opera must still be Peking opera. It should not be turned into a hodge-podge of something that resembles nothing. It is like eating, for example. Whatever a man eats—so long as it is nutritious—will become his own blood, flesh, bones, and so on, after he has digested it. If the result of reforming Peking opera even makes those people who love it dislike it, then it cannot possibly be said that our reforms have been successful.

5. The question of strategically despising and tactically taking into full account. By strategically despising, we mean that we are confident that Peking opera can be successfully reformed, and we will despise those people who oppose the reform of Peking opera. There are some people who oppose the reform of Peking opera, aren't there? Yes, but these sort of people who turn their backs on socialism and turn towards capitalism or feudalism are bound to come to grief. It is absolutely right that the masses look down upon them. While we are working for socialism, they are working for feudalism or capitalism. Today the more than 600 million theatre-goers want to see plays on living people but they only like to perform plays about the dead. They have cut themselves off from 95 per cent of the people. What is so grand about that?

Tactically, however, comrades must not treat this problem off-handedly but must take full account of it. Full account must be taken of the script, directing, acting and singing; every act, every scene, every character, in fact, every sentence sung or spoken and every movement must be carefully considered. Workers must be like workers, peasants must be like peasants, soldiers must be like soldiers, whomever is being portrayed must be like the "real thing". To be in the style of Peking opera and at the same time to be like what is being portrayed is difficult and if full account is not taken of everything, things won't come out right. In this great cultural revolutionary struggle to reform Peking opera, care must be taken to maintain a high quality and not to turn out rough and slipshod work. Reforming Peking opera is not like roasting chestnuts—tipping them into the pan to roast and then selling them while you are still roasting them. Nor is it like eating tripe when you can toss some sheep's stomach into boiling water and take it out in an instant ready for eating. This matter is not as simple as all that. It cannot be done at one stroke, nor can it be perfected in an instant. Take some of the surviving traditional operas, for example. Do you realize how many hands they have passed through; how much they were reformed; how much polishing they went through? What we are doing today is something completely new. It is to portray our workers, peasants and soldiers on the stage. Previously the Peking opera stage did not portray these people but today we are going to do it and do it well. But it isn't going to be all that easy, is it? Therefore, it is necessary to take full account of this task. Do not think that in one attempt all will be changed satisfactorily. That is impossible. If it is reformed basically well, then that will be very good. So long as it is revolutionary it will be good. There may be some defects in the content and artistic technique, but that will be corrected with more and constant polishing.

In the course of the reform, it is impossible not to have various opinions and disputes. It is quite logical that there should be differing views and disputes. Before, all we had were portrayals of ancients—emperors, kings, generals, ministers, scholars and beauties; with the reform people are suddenly performing operas on contemporary revolutionary themes. If there were no differences of opinion at all about this, that indeed would be surprising.

What is to be done when there are different opinions and disputes? We should discuss and look into things in a comradely way so as to help each other and put things right. Because some opera on a contemporary revolutionary theme has some slight defects, we should not trample it to death or kill it with one blow. Every one of us should cherish this fresh, newly blossoming flower of Peking opera on contemporary themes. Don't worry if there is a dispute, so long as it really is for reform. Everyone should listen to all kinds of constructive criticisms and discuss them together. If there are criticisms they should be made face to face and not behind someone's back. This should become a habit. In the past among Peking opera circles it was a matter of "you form your group, I form mine"; bickering between this and that company, and between this and that guild was quite serious. This bad habit was a left-over from the old society. Has it all been swept away at one stroke? It is not likely. "You put on an opera and I pull away a prop from behind. I put on an opera and you pull away one of my props from behind." That was how things were. Each held together his own group but they did not want to form the big group of the People's Republic of China, not to speak of the big group of proletarian internationalism. The People's Republic of China will soon number 700 million, and under the Central Committee of the Chinese Communist Party and Comrade Mao Tse-tung we all work for a great unity, isn't that better? Some people are not content with such a great unity but want to set up their own little unity before they are content. I urge these comrades and friends to enlarge their circle of unity.

This is the question of whether or not to reform Peking opera and how to reform it. I ask everyone to consider the few ideas I have put forward. That is the first question.

II

The second question: What must be done to ensure the successful reform of Peking opera; what are the prerequisites?
There are two prerequisites.
1. Script writers, directors and actors of Peking opera must go deep among the workers, peasants and soldiers, become one with them and establish ties of flesh-and-blood with them. That is to say, in reforming Peking opera, the line of "from the masses, to the masses" put forward by Comrade Mao Tse-tung must also be followed. Only in this way can good plays be written and Peking operas on contemporary revolutionary themes be successfully performed. How can you recreate the heroic images of workers, peasants and soldiers on the stage if you have never lived among them and

are not acquainted with them? Living together with the workers, peasants and soldiers alone will not suffice, you must also distil the essential merits of the heroes among them and create typical images of them on the stage. Therefore, workers in Peking opera must go deep among the workers, peasants and soldiers, go to their factories, production teams and companies and become one with them. Some comrades and friends have found they have gained much after spending even only a short time in the factories, production teams or army companies. Wouldn't you gain even more if you stayed there for a year or two, or several years? There are many writers and playwrights in the capital, but they have produced few plays. Why? Mainly because they are divorced from the masses and from reality. They stay in their offices and do not go out to the factories, production teams or army companies. Under such conditions how can they produce good works? How can they turn out many good works? Of course, it is impossible. Some plays have been acted rather unconvincingly and they have been rather unconvincingly directed. This is chiefly due to the fact that their directors and actors have not yet lived with the workers, peasants and soldiers or that they have lived with them only for a very short time.

The fact is that to go deep among the workers, peasants and soldiers is not so simple. It is comparatively easy to go for a few days, like a guest, but it is not so easy to be at one with the workers, peasants and soldiers, to establish flesh-and-blood relations with them. To attain this, one must, first of all, have the standpoint of the proletariat; be of one mind with the workers, peasants and soldiers, with the proletariat, with the poor and lower-middle peasants, and serve them wholeheartedly. We should all of us make ourselves willing pupils of the masses. This refers not only to you but also to us Party workers, Members of the Party's Central Committee. If we go out just to criticize and point things out right away instead of first learning from the masses like pupils, then the peasants and workers won't open their hearts to us. Although many Party workers have established regular contacts with the mass of workers and peasants, they still need to choose some place for gaining experience at the grass-roots, where they eat, live and work together with the masses, as the willing pupils of the masses. So is it possible for Peking opera workers not to be willing pupils of the masses when they go to the countryside, the factories, or army companies? Of course they should. Naturally, we should not insist that those who are aged and physically weak eat, live and work with the masses, but it is good too to give them a chance to visit. Those artists and writers who are young and in the prime of life should, like our Party workers and the workers in other fields, live among the workers, peasants and soldiers.

This is a prerequisite for the success of the reform of Peking opera.

2. *Peking opera workers must revolutionize their ideology, that is to say, they must become revolutionized and proletarianized.* "Ize" means thorough change, from top to bottom and inside out. One must be revolutionized within, revolutionized not in part, but from head to foot. This is not so easy! You work on plays on contemporary revolutionary themes, but if your ideology is not revolutionized and proletarianized, how can you write, direct or act a play on these themes well? If your ideology is not revolutionized you cannot be at one with the workers, peasants and soldiers, you cannot establish flesh-and-blood relations with them. If your head is full of the ideology of the feudal landlord class or bourgeoisie, how can you identify yourselves with the proletariat and the working masses? Under such circumstances how can you establish flesh-and-blood ties with them? So, if you want to perform a play on a contemporary revolutionary theme you need, in the first place, to have a revolutionized ideology. You should be determined to remould yourself and raise your political level. Once you are determined to be revolutionary, things will go well. Change a little bit today and a little bit tomorrow, and you'll build up a revolutionary ideology bit by bit. In time you'll achieve a fundamental change. In his *Talks at the Yenan Forum on Literature and Art* Comrade Mao Tse-tung very clearly dealt with the fundamental questions involved here. I suggest you comrades read over those talks carefully once again.

To speak frankly, there are some people who are in an acute contradiction. Physically speaking, they have already entered socialist society, yet their heads are still in feudal or capitalist society. Surely it's not very comfortable to have one's body at one place and one's neck stretched out to one's head somewhere else? Such a person eats socialist rice and wears socialist clothes. All his amenities of life are supplied by socialism, by the workers, peasants and soldiers, yet he does not act plays to serve them, to serve socialism. His ideology is still feudalistic or capitalistic. This is an acute contradiction. If a person is like this, that's his business. But if, in accordance with his own outlook, he attempts to use Peking opera to transform the world, to oppose our staging of plays on contemporary revolutionary themes, that's very bad. Then, what is to be done? I suggest that these people had better make a big effort to remould their ideology so that they can bring their heads into socialist society too.

During the current movement for socialist education in the rural areas, Comrade Mao Tse-tung has called on us to "re-educate people, reorganize the ranks of revolution". Why re-educate people? It is for the cause of socialist revolution and socialist construction. What kind of revolutionary ranks are to be reorganized?—The revolutionary ranks of socialism. In the past, many people were mentally prepared for the democratic revolution, but not very well prepared for the socialist revolution, and some were not in the least prepared for it. In the past, we did not undertake any systematic, all-round socialist education in every way throughout the country. Now a movement for socialist education is going ahead in the urban as well as rural areas. So long as we go on taking care of things like this, not only will we be able to carry on our socialist revolution successfully and day by day improve our socialist construction, but we will also be able to dig out thoroughly the root cause of revisionism.

Comrades! Please don't think that there can be no revisionism in China. If we don't grasp the tasks of class struggle well and of socialist education too, then, it is also possible for revisionism to appear. Speaking frankly, there are quite a few problems in literary and artistic circles, surely no less than in other fields of work. Therefore, it is necessary to launch a rectification campaign and a movement for socialist education and wage the struggle between the two roads of socialism and capitalism on the front of literature and art. We must study Comrade Mao Tse-tung's works carefully, learn Marxism-Leninism, and maintain a firm proletarian stand. I suggest that all of you examine and sift through the works you have written, the plays you have performed, the films you have acted in, the songs you have sung, the music you have performed and the pictures you have drawn in the past few years. See what is bourgeois in them or what has been influenced by the remnants of bourgeois ideas, or what is feudalistic. If you find mistakes or shortcomings, correct them and things will go well! This must be done in all spheres of literature and art, and Peking opera circles are no exception. Let everyone work for socialism and communism and thoroughly wipe out the influence of feudal and bourgeois ideology! If we act in this way, I am positive that the reform of Peking opera can certainly be done successfully, and that Peking opera certainly has a bright and great future.

28. Lin Piao: The International Significance of Comrade Mao Tse-tung's Theory of People's War (September, 1965)*

Lin Piao, a native of Hupei, Vice-Chairman of the Central Committee of the Chinese Communist Party and Minister of National Defense of Communist China, has been a soldier throughout his career—fighting against the Japanese, the Nationalists, and the UN in Korea. He joined the Communist Party in 1925 and graduated from the Whampoa Military Academy in 1926. He took part in the Nanchang uprising and retreated with Chu Teh to join Mao Tse-tung in the Kiangsi hinterland. Since then he has become one of the outstanding field commanders of the Red Army. In 1932 he became Commander-in-Chief of the First Army group of the Red Army, which acted as the vanguard in the historic "Long March" of 1934–1935. During the Sino-Japanese War, he headed both the Chinese Worker-Peasant Red Army University and the Anti-Japanese Military and Political University, the highest institutions in the Communist-controlled area. Cadres trained at these two institutions staffed the Party and the military apparatus throughout the final stages of the war with Japan and then during the post-1945 campaign against the Nationalists. And it was these cadres who took the major posts when, in 1949, the Communists conquered the mainland. In 1937 he led the Red Army in a major victory over the Japanese, but was critically wounded in the battle. He was sent to the USSR for

---

* From Lin Piao, *Long Live the Victory of People's War*, Peking: Foreign Language Press, 1965, pp. 42–52. (Footnotes omitted.)

medical treatment; in 1941 he returned to China and became Vice-President of the Party School with Mao Tse-tung as President. After the Japanese surrender in 1945, Lin was ordered to Manchuria, where he equipped his guerrilla forces with Japanese arms and built them into the Fourth Field Army. It was the Fourth Field Army which defeated the Nationalists and occupied North China in 1948. His forces then swept southward across China and paved the way for Communist domination of the mainland in 1949.

Lin Piao was totally out of the public eye during the early 1950's because of his "bad health." He re-emerged in 1956 when he was re-elected to the Central Committee and the Politburo in the Eighth Party Congress. In 1959, Lin replaced Marshal P'eng Teh-huai as Minister of National Defense. He is now the youngest of the "Big Seven" of Chinese Communist leadership. Lin gained international prominence in the autumn of 1965 when he published his essay "Long Live the Victory of People's War!" in commemoration of the twentieth anniversary of victory in the Chinese People's War of Resistance Against Japan. The recent political maneuvering in China that has resulted in the downfall or demotion of a number of senior members of the Politburo underlines Lin's new role as heir-apparent to Mao Tse-tung.

Lin's essay "Long Live the Victory of People's War!" has been widely publicized as "a comprehensive, systematic and profound analysis of Comrade Mao Tse-tung's theory and strategic concept of people's war and provides the revolutionary people of the whole world with a powerful ideological weapon in the fight against imperialism and modern revisionism." The following selection, which is a part of this essay, outlines Mao's "village-encircle-city" strategy for carrying out the world-wide Communist revolution. Lin, following the current "anti-imperialist," "anti-revisionist" doctrine, feels strongly a sense of mission to spread Communism in the world. He considers the Chinese Revolution, based on "the theory of countering war against the people by people's war," "a successful lesson for making a thoroughgoing national-democratic revolution," as well as "for the timely transition from national-democratic revolution to the socialist revolution," "under the leadership of the proletariat."

On the other hand, there are competent scholars in the United States who consider this document "defensive" in nature.[1] This is because Lin Piao speaks of "the policy of self-reliance" in a people's war. For example, Lin wrote: "In order to make a revolution and to fight a people's war and be victorious, it is imperative to adhere to the policy of self-reliance, rely on the strength of the masses in one's own country and prepare to carry on the fight independently even when all material aid from outside is cut off. If one does not operate by one's own efforts, does not independently ponder and solve the problems of the revolution in one's own country and does not rely on the strength of the masses, but leans wholly on foreign aid—even though this be aid from socialist countries which persist in revolution— no victory can be won, or be consolidated even if it is won."[2]

The Chinese revolution is a continuation of the great October Revolution. The road of the October Revolution is the common road for all people's revolutions. The Chinese revolution and the October Revolution have in common the following basic characteristics: (1) Both were led by the working class with a Marxist-Leninist party as its nucleus. (2) Both were based on the worker-peasant alliance. (3) In both cases state power was seized through violent revolution and the dictatorship of the proletariat was established. (4) In both cases the socialist system was built after victory in the revolution. (5) Both were component parts of the proletarian world revolution.

Naturally, the Chinese revolution had its own peculiar characteristics. The October Revolution took place in imperialist Russia, but the Chinese revolution broke out in a semi-colonial and semi-feudal country. The former was a proletarian socialist revolution, while the latter developed into a socialist revolution after the complete victory of the new-democratic revolution. The October Revolution began with armed uprisings in the cities and then spread to the country-side, while the Chinese revolution won nation-wide victory through the encirclement of the cities from the rural areas and the final capture of the cities.

Comrade Mao Tse-tung's great merit lies in the fact that he

---

[1] Uri Ra'Anan, Professor of World Politics at the Fletcher School of Law and Diplomacy, Tufts University, considers for example Lin Piao an "isola-tionist," as he expressed it during the University of Chicago's Center for Policy Study's China Year in March, 1966.

[2] Lin Piao, *Long Live the Victory of People's War*, Peking: Foreign Language Press, 1965, pp. 41–42.

has succeeded in integrating the universal truth of Marxism-Leninism with the concrete practice of the Chinese revolution and has enriched and developed Marxism-Leninism by his masterly generalization and summation of the experience gained during the Chinese people's protracted revolutionary struggle.

Comrade Mao Tse-tung's theory of people's war has been proved by the long practice of the Chinese revolution to be in accord with the objective laws of such wars and to be invincible. It has not only been valid for China, it is a great contribution to the revolutionary struggles of the oppressed nations and peoples throughout the world.

The people's war led by the Chinese Communist Party, comprising the War of Resistance and the Revolutionary Civil Wars, lasted for twenty-two years. It constitutes the most drawn-out and most complex people's war led by the proletariat in modern history, and it has been the richest in experience.

In the last analysis, the Marxist-Leninist theory of proletarian revolution is the theory of the seizure of state power by revolutionary violence, the theory of countering war against the people by people's war. As Marx so aptly put it, "Force is the midwife of every old society pregnant with a new one."

It was on the basis of the lessons derived from the people's wars in China that Comrade Mao Tse-tung, using the simplest and the most vivid language, advanced the famous thesis that "political power grows out of the barrel of a gun".

He clearly pointed out:

> The seizure of power by armed force, the settlement of the issue by war, is the central task and the highest form of revolution. This Marxist-Leninist principle of revolution holds good universally, for China and for all other countries.

War is the product of imperialism and the system of exploitation of man by man. Lenin said that "war is always and everywhere begun by the exploiters themselves, by the ruling and oppressing classes". So long as imperialism and the system of exploitation of man by man exist, the imperialists and reactionaries will invariably rely on armed force to maintain their reactionary rule and impose war on the oppressed nations and peoples. This is an objective law independent of man's will.

In the world today, all the imperialists headed by the

United States and their lackeys, without exception, are strengthening their state machinery, and especially their armed forces. U.S. imperialism, in particular, is carrying out armed aggression and suppression everywhere.

What should the oppressed nations and the oppressed people do in the face of wars of aggression and armed suppression by the imperialists and their lackeys? Should they submit and remain slaves in perpetuity? Or should they rise in resistance and fight for their liberation?

Comrade Mao Tse-tung answered this question in vivid terms. He said that after long investigation and study the Chinese people discovered that all the imperialists and their lackeys "have swords in their hands and are out to kill. The people have come to understand this and so act after the same fashion." This is called doing unto them what they do unto us.

In the last analysis, whether one dares to wage a tit-for-tat struggle against armed aggression and suppression by the imperialists and their lackeys, whether one dares to fight a people's war against them, means whether one dares to embark on revolution. This is the most effective touchstone for distinguishing genuine from fake revolutionaries and Marxist-Leninists.

In view of the fact that some people were afflicted with the fear of the imperialists and reactionaries, Comrade Mao Tse-tung put forward his famous thesis that "the imperialists and all reactionaries are paper tigers". He said,

> All reactionaries are paper tigers. In appearance, the reactionaries are terrifying, but in reality they are not so powerful. From a long-term point of view, it is not the reactionaries but the people who are really powerful.

The history of people's war in China and other countries provides conclusive evidence that the growth of the people's revolutionary forces from weak and small beginnings into strong and large forces is a universal law of development of class struggle, a universal law of development of people's war. A people's war inevitably meets with many difficulties, with ups and downs and setbacks in the course of its development, but no force can alter its general trend towards inevitable triumph.

Comrade Mao Tse-tung points out that we must despise the enemy strategically and take full account of him tactically.

To despise the enemy strategically is an elementary requirement for a revolutionary. Without the courage to despise the
enemy and without daring to win, it will be simply impossible
to make revolution and wage a people's war, let alone to
achieve victory.

It is also very important for revolutionaries to take full
account of the enemy tactically. It is likewise impossible to
win victory in a people's war without taking full account of
the enemy tactically, and without examining the concrete conditions, without being prudent and giving great attention to
the study of the art of struggle, and without adopting appropriate forms of struggle in the concrete practice of the revolution in each country and with regard to each concrete problem of struggle.

Dialectical and historical materialism teaches us that what
is important primarily is not that which at the given moment
seems to be durable and yet is already beginning to die away,
but that which is arising and developing, even though at the
given moment it may not appear to be durable, for only that
which is arising and developing is invincible.

Why can the apparently weak new-born forces always triumph over the decadent forces which appear so powerful?
The reason is that truth is on their side and that the masses
are on their side, while the reactionary classes are always
divorced from the masses and set themselves against the
masses.

This has been borne out by the victory of the Chinese
revolution, by the history of all revolutions, the whole history
of class struggle and the entire history of mankind.

The imperialists are extremely afraid of Comrade Mao
Tse-tung's thesis that "imperialism and all reactionaries are
paper tigers", and the revisionists are extremely hostile to it.
They all oppose and attack this thesis and the philistines
follow suit by ridiculing it. But all this cannot in the least
diminish its importance. The light of truth cannot be dimmed
by anybody.

Comrade Mao Tse-tung's theory of people's war solves not
only the problem of daring to fight a people's war, but also
that of how to wage it.

Comrade Mao Tse-tung is a great statesman and military
scientist, proficient at directing war in accordance with its
laws. By the line and policies, the strategy and tactics he formulated for the people's war, he led the Chinese people in

steering the ship of the people's war past all hidden reefs to the shores of victory in most complicated and difficult conditions.

It must be emphasized that Comrade Mao Tse-tung's theory of the establishment of rural revolutionary base areas and the encirclement of the cities from the countryside is of outstanding and universal practical importance for the present revolutionary struggles of all the oppressed nations and peoples, and particularly for the revolutionary struggles of the oppressed nations and peoples in Asia, Africa and Latin America against imperialism and its lackeys.

Many countries and peoples in Asia, Africa and Latin America are now being subjected to aggression and enslavement on a serious scale by the imperialists headed by the United States and their lackeys. The basic political and economic conditions in many of these countries have many similarities to those that prevailed in old China. As in China, the peasant question is extremely important in these regions. The peasants constitute the main force of the national-democratic revolution against the imperialists and their lackeys. In committing aggression against these countries, the imperialists usually begin by seizing the big cities and the main lines of communication, but they are unable to bring the vast countryside completely under their control. The countryside, and the countryside alone, can provide the broad areas in which the revolutionaries can manoeuvre freely. The countryside, and the countryside alone, can provide the revolutionary bases from which the revolutionaries can go forward to final victory. Precisely for this reason, Comrade Mao Tse-tung's theory of establishing revolutionary base areas in the rural districts and encircling the cities from the countryside is attracting more and more attention among the people in these regions.

Taking the entire globe, if North America and Western Europe can be called "the cities of the world", then Asia, Africa and Latin America constitute "the rural areas of the world". Since World War II, the proletarian revolutionary movement has for various reasons been temporarily held back in the North American and West European capitalist countries, while the people's revolutionary movement in Asia, Africa and Latin America has been growing vigorously. In a sense, the contemporary world revolution also presents a picture of the encirclement of cities by the rural areas. In the final analysis, the whole cause of world revolution hinges on the revolutionary struggles of the Asian, African and Latin American peoples who make up the overwhelming majority of the world's population. The socialist countries should regard it as their internationalist duty to support the people's revolutionary struggles in Asia, Africa and Latin America.

The October Revolution opened up a new era in the revolution of the oppressed nations. The victory of the October Revolution built a bridge between the socialist revolution of the proletariat of the West and the national-democratic revolution of the colonial and semi-colonial countries of the East. The Chinese revolution has successfully solved the problem of how to link up the national-democratic with the socialist revolution in the colonial and semi-colonial countries.

Comrade Mao Tse-tung has pointed out that, in the epoch since the October Revolution, anti-imperialist revolution in any colonial or semi-colonial country is no longer part of the old bourgeois, or capitalist world revolution, but is part of the new world revolution, the proletarian-socialist world revolution.

Comrade Mao Tse-tung has formulated a complete theory of the new-democratic revolution. He indicated that this revolution, which is different from all others, can only be, nay must be, a revolution against imperialism, feudalism and bureaucrat-capitalism waged by the broad masses of the people under the leadership of the proletariat.

This means that the revolution can only be, nay must be, led by the proletariat and the genuinely revolutionary party armed with Marxism-Leninism, and by no other class or party.

This means that the revolution embraces in its ranks not only the workers, peasants and the urban petty bourgeoisie, but also the national bourgeoisie and other patriotic and anti-imperialist democrats.

This means, finally, that the revolution is directed against imperialism, feudalism and bureaucrat-capitalism.

The new-democratic revolution leads to socialism, and not to capitalism.

Comrade Mao Tse-tung's theory of the new-democratic revolution is the Marxist-Leninist theory of revolution by stages as well as the Marxist-Leninist theory of uninterrupted revolution.

Comrade Mao Tse-tung made a correct distinction between the two revolutionary stages, *i.e.*, the national-democratic and the socialist revolutions; at the same time he correctly and closely linked the two. The national-democratic revolution is the necessary preparation for the socialist revolution, and the socialist revolution is the inevitable sequel to the national-democratic revolution. There is no Great Wall between the two revolutionary stages. But the socialist revolution is only possible after the completion of the national-democratic revolution. The more thorough the national-democratic revolution, the better the conditions for the socialist revolution.

The experience of the Chinese revolution shows that the tasks of the national-democratic revolution can be fulfilled only through long and tortuous struggles. In this stage of revolution, imperialism and its lackeys are the principal enemy. In the struggle against imperialism and its lackeys, it is necessary to rally all anti-imperialist patriotic forces, including the national bourgeoisie and all patriotic personages. All those patriotic personages from among the bourgeoisie and other exploiting classes who join the anti-imperialist struggle play a progressive historical role; they are not tolerated by imperialism but welcomed by the proletariat.

It is very harmful to confuse the two stages, that is, the national-democratic and the socialist revolutions. Comrade Mao Tse-tung criticized the wrong idea of "accomplishing both at one stroke", and pointed out that this utopian idea could only weaken the struggle against imperialism and its lackeys, the most urgent task at that time. The Kuomintang reactionaries and the Trotskyites they hired during the War of Resistance deliberately confused these two stages of the Chinese revolution, proclaiming the "theory of a single revolution" and preaching so-called "socialism" without any Communist Party. With this preposterous theory they attempted to swallow up the Communist Party, wipe out any revolution and prevent the advance of the national-democratic revolution, and they used it as a pretext for their non-resistance and capitulation to imperialism. This reactionary theory was buried long ago by the history of the Chinese revolution.

The Khrushchev revisionists are now actively preaching that socialism can be built without the proletariat and without a genuinely revolutionary party armed with the advanced proletarian ideology, and they have cast the fundamental tenets of Marxism-Leninism to the four winds. The revisionists' purpose is solely to divert the oppressed nations from their struggle against imperialism and sabotage their national-democratic revolution, all in the service of imperialism.

The Chinese revolution provides a successful lesson for making a thoroughgoing national-democratic revolution under the leadership of the proletariat; it likewise provides a successful lesson for the timely transition from the national-democratic revolution to the socialist revolution under the leadership of the proletariat.

Mao Tse-tung's thought has been the guide to the victory of the Chinese revolution. It has integrated the universal truth of Marxism-Leninism with the concrete practice of the Chinese revolution and creatively developed Marxism-Leninism, thus adding new weapons to the arsenal of Marxism-Leninism.

Ours is the epoch in which world capitalism and imperialism are heading for their doom and socialism and communism are marching to victory. Comrade Mao Tse-tung's theory of people's war is not only a product of the Chinese revolution, but has also the characteristics of our epoch. The new experience gained in the people's revolutionary struggles in various countries since World War II has provided continuous evidence that Mao Tse-tung's thought is a common asset of the revolutionary people of the whole world. This is the great international significance of the thought of Mao Tse-tung.

29. Central Committee of the Chinese Communist Party: Decision Concerning the Great Proletarian Cultural Revolution (August, 1966)*

Tens of thousands of young students from universities and secondary schools in Peking, calling themselves *Hung Wei Ping* or Red Guards, appeared at Tien-An-Men Square on August 18, 1966, to celebrate the beginning of the "Great Proletarian Cultural Revolution." During the first

* From book so titled, Peking: Foreign Language Press, 1966, pp. 1–13.

year, some 30 million youthful Red Guards marched and counter-marched across the face of Communist China, repeating with religious fervor quotations from Mao Tse-tung. Thus, we saw a new stage of Chinese Revolution under the full banner of Maoism.

The gravity and seriousness of the problem exploded because Mao Tse-tung himself used the youthful and fanatic Red Guards to attack the entire power structure of the Chinese Communist Party. He personally enlarged the Standing Committee from seven to eleven members adding such individuals as his personal secretary, Chen Po-ta, and Chief of Secret Police, Kang Sheng. In addition, he reorganized Party bureaucracy from the Central Committee at the top to various municipal and provincial committees.

This revolutionary campaign soon spread throughout the country and many changes were made. "Revolutionary committees" with the aid of the military took over many municipal and provincial authorities from established Party and government administrations. The Central Committee which issued the call for the Cultural Revolution had ceased to function because of power struggles between pro-Mao and anti-Mao forces within the Committee.[1] The Party became paralyzed. In some areas, actual armed clashes occurred.

No one outside of China can be certain of the exact reason or cause for this radical change by Mao. According to a Japanese reporter who was on the scene in Peking between November 9, 1965, and January 9, 1966, the Cultural Revolution was some sort of a "counter-coup" by Mao Tse-tung after his "successful escape from imprisonment" by the "anti-Mao forces" headed by Liu Shao-chi in the winter of 1965.[2] Other more responsible observers, such as Robert S. Elegant, attribute the present disorder in China to Mao's "attempt to impose complete centralization and total conformity upon a nation and a race which feel themselves one but cherish their differences above their similarities in times of crisis like the present."[3]

---

[1] Fang Chun-kuei, "Current Situation of the Eighth Central Committee of the Chinese Communist Party," *Studies on Chinese Communism*, Vol. I (No. 5), May 31, 1967.

[2] Mineo Nakajima, "Why Mao Escaped and Fled Peking," *The East* (Tokyo), May–June, 1967.

[3] Robert S. Elegant, "China's Next Phase," *Foreign Affairs*, October, 1967, p. 149.

In the field of economics, foreign trade suffered as a result of extreme anti-foreign attitudes of the Red Guards. For instance, in the first six months of 1967, Chinese exports to Japan decreased 7.1 percent compared with the same six-month period the year before. Statistics also show that Chinese exports suffered even more with such important trading partners as West Germany (−14.8 percent) and Great Britain (−9.9 percent).[4]

There are still others describing these conditions as a "titanic power struggle," or a "struggle for succession."[5] This writer believes that what is happening in China today involves more than the obvious power struggle or a struggle for succession. In fact, it is a form of mass revolt with Mao himself as the catalyst.[6] From the purge of Kao Kang and Jao Shu-shih to the Socialist Education campaign in 1962 and finally the Cultural Revolution in 1966, step by step the revolt is progressing toward a goal established by Mao Tse-tung—to "catch up with and surpass the advanced world levels in the not too distant future."[7]

1. A New Stage in the Socialist Revolution

The great proletarian cultural revolution now unfolding is a great revolution that touches people to their very souls and constitutes a new stage in the development of the socialist revolution in our country, a stage which is both broader and deeper.

At the Tenth Plenary Session of the Eighth Central Committee of the Party, Comrade Mao Tse-tung said: To overthrow a political power, it is always necessary first of all to create public opinion, to do work in the ideological sphere. This is true for the revolutionary class as well as for the counter-revolutionary class. This thesis of Comrade Mao Tse-tung's has been proved entirely correct in practice.

---

[4] Chien Yuan-heng, "Current Economic Problems of the Chinese Communist Regime," *Studies on Chinese Communism*, September 30, 1967, p. 78.

[5] *U.S. News and World Report*, January 30, 1967.

[6] For a detailed study of the Great Proletarian Culture Revolution in Communist China, see Winberg Chai, *Mass Revolt in Communist China*, New York: Oxford University Press, 1968–1969.

[7] *Peking Review*, November 3, 1967, p. 15.

Although the bourgeoisie has been overthrown, it is still trying to use the old ideas, culture, customs and habits of the exploiting classes to corrupt the masses, capture their minds and endeavour to stage a come-back. The proletariat must do the exact opposite: it must meet head-on every challenge of the bourgeoisie in the ideological field and use the new ideas, culture, customs and habits of the proletariat to change the mental outlook of the whole of society. At present, our objective is to struggle against and overthrow those persons in authority who are taking the capitalist road, to criticize and repudiate the reactionary bourgeois academic "authorities" and the ideology of the bourgeoisie and all other exploiting classes and to transform education, literature and art and all other parts of the superstructure not in correspondence with the socialist economic base, so as to facilitate the consolidation and development of the socialist system.

2. THE MAIN CURRENT AND THE TWISTS AND TURNS

The masses of the workers, peasants, soldiers, revolutionary intellectuals and revolutionary cadres form the main force in this great cultural revolution. Large numbers of revolutionary young people, previously unknown, have become courageous and daring pathbreakers. They are vigorous in action and intelligent. Through the media of big-character posters and great debates, they argue things out, expose and criticize thoroughly, and launch resolute attacks on the open and hidden representatives of the bourgeoisie. In such a great revolutionary movement, it is hardly avoidable that they should show shortcomings of one kind or another; however, their general revolutionary orientation has been correct from the beginning. This is the main current in the great proletarian cultural revolution. It is the general direction along which this revolution continues to advance.

Since the cultural revolution is a revolution, it inevitably meets with resistance. This resistance comes chiefly from those in authority who have wormed their way into the Party and are taking the capitalist road. It also comes from the force of habits from the old society. At present, this resistance is still fairly strong and stubborn. But after all, the great proletarian cultural revolution is an irresistible general trend. There is abundant evidence that such resistance will be quickly broken down once the masses become fully aroused.

Because the resistance is fairly strong, there will be reversals and even repeated reversals in this struggle. There is no harm in this. It tempers the proletariat and other working people, and especially the younger generation, teaches them lessons and gives them experience, and helps them to understand that the revolutionary road zigzags and does not run smoothly.

3. Put Daring Above Everything Else and Boldly Arouse the Masses

The outcome of this great cultural revolution will be determined by whether or not the Party leadership dares boldly to arouse the masses.

Currently, there are four different situations with regard to the leadership being given to the movement of cultural revolution by Party organizations at various levels:

(1) There is the situation in which the persons in charge of Party organizations stand in the van of the movement and dare to arouse the masses boldly. They put daring above everything else, they are dauntless communist fighters and good pupils of Chairman Mao. They advocate the big-character posters and great debates. They encourage the masses to expose every kind of ghost and monster and also to criticize the shortcomings and errors in the work of the persons in charge. This correct kind of leadership is the result of putting proletarian politics in the forefront and Mao Tse-tung's thought in the lead.

(2) In many units, the persons in charge have a very poor understanding of the task of leadership in this great struggle, their leadership is far from being conscientious and effective, and they accordingly find themselves incompetent and in a weak position. They put fear above everything else, stick to outmoded ways and regulations, and are unwilling to break away from conventional practices and move ahead. They have been taken unawares by the new order of things, the revolutionary order of the masses, with the result that their leadership lags behind the situation, lags behind the masses.

(3) In some units, the persons in charge, who made mistakes of one kind or another in the past, are even more prone to put fear above everything else, being afraid that the masses will catch them out. Actually, if they make serious self-criticism and accept the criticism of the masses, the Party and the masses will make allowances for their mistakes. But if the persons in charge don't, they will continue to make mistakes and become obstacles to the mass movement.

(4) Some units are controlled by those who have wormed their way into the Party and are taking the capitalist road. Such persons in authority are extremely afraid of being exposed by the masses and therefore seek every possible pretext to suppress the mass movement. They resort to such tactics as shifting the targets for attack and turning black into white in an attempt to lead the movement astray. When they find themselves very isolated and no longer able to carry on as before, they resort still more to intrigues, stabbing people in the back, spreading rumours, and blurring the distinction between revolution and counter-revolution as much as they can, all for the purpose of attacking the revolutionaries.

What the Central Committee of the Party demands of the Party committees at all levels is that they persevere in giving correct leadership, put daring above everything else, boldly arouse the masses, change the state of weakness and incompetence where it exists, encourage those comrades who have made mistakes but are willing to correct them to cast off their mental burdens and join in the struggle, and dismiss from their leading posts all those in authority who are taking the capitalist road and so make possible the recapture of the leadership for the proletarian revolutionaries.

4. Let the Masses Educate Themselves in the Movement

In the great proletarian cultural revolution, the only method is for the masses to liberate themselves, and any method of doing things in their stead must not be used.

Trust the masses, rely on them and respect their initiative. Cast out fear. Don't be afraid of disturbances. Chairman Mao has often told us that revolution cannot be so very refined, so gentle, so temperate, kind, courteous, restrained and magnanimous. Let the masses educate themselves in this great revolutionary movement and learn to distinguish between right and wrong and between correct and incorrect ways of doing things.

Make the fullest use of big-character posters and great debates to argue matters out, so that the masses can clarify the correct views, criticize the wrong views and expose all the ghosts and monsters. In this way the masses will be able to raise their political consciousness in the course of the struggle, enhance their abilities and talents, distinguish right from wrong and draw a clear line between ourselves and the enemy.

5. Firmly Apply the Class Line of the Party

Who are our enemies? Who are our friends? This is a question of the first importance for the revolution and it is likewise a question of the first importance for the great cultural revolution.

Party leadership should be good at discovering the Left and developing and strengthening the ranks of the Left; it should firmly rely on the revolutionary Left. During the movement this is the only way to isolate the most reactionary Rightists thoroughly, win over the middle and unite with the great majority so that by the end of the movement we shall achieve the unity of more than 95 per cent of the cadres and more than 95 per cent of the masses.

Concentrate all forces to strike at the handful of ultra-reactionary bourgeois Rightists and counter-revolutionary revisionists, and expose and criticize to the full their crimes against the Party, against socialism and against Mao Tse-tung's thought so as to isolate them to the maximum.

The main target of the present movement is those within the Party who are in authority and are taking the capitalist road.

The strictest care should be taken to distinguish between the anti-Party, anti-socialist Rightists and those who support the Party and socialism but have said or done something wrong or have written some bad articles or other works.

The strictest care should be taken to distinguish between

the reactionary bourgeois scholar despots and "authorities" on the one hand and people who have the ordinary bourgeois academic ideas on the other.

6. Correctly Handle Contradictions Among the People

A strict distinction must be made between the two different types of contradictions: those among the people and those between ourselves and the enemy. Contradictions among the people must not be made into contradictions between ourselves and the enemy; nor must contradictions between ourselves and the enemy be regarded as contradictions among the people.

It is normal for the masses to hold different views. Contention between different views is unavoidable, necessary and beneficial. In the course of normal and full debate, the masses will affirm what is right, correct what is wrong and gradually reach unanimity.

The method to be used in debates is to present the facts, reason things out, and persuade through reasoning. Any method of forcing a minority holding different views to submit is impermissible. The minority should be protected, because sometimes the truth is with the minority. Even if the minority is wrong, they should still be allowed to argue their case and reserve their views.

When there is a debate, it should be conducted by reasoning, not by coercion or force.

In the course of debate, every revolutionary should be good at thinking things out for himself and should develop the communist spirit of daring to think, daring to speak and daring to act. On the premise that they have the same general orientation, revolutionary comrades should, for the sake of strengthening unity, avoid endless debate over side issues.

7. Be on Guard Against Those Who Brand the Revolutionary Masses as "Counter-Revolutionaries"

In certain schools, units, and work teams of the cultural revolution, some of the persons in charge have organized counter-attacks against the masses who put up big-character posters criticizing them. These people have even advanced such slogans as: opposition to the leaders of a unit or a work team means opposition to the Central Committee of the Party, means opposition to the Party and socialism, means counter-revolution. In this way it is inevitable that their blows will fall on some really revolutionary activists. This is an error on matters of orientation, an error of line, and is absolutely impermissible.

A number of persons who suffer from serious ideological errors, and particularly some of the anti-Party and anti-socialist Rightists, are taking advantage of certain shortcomings and mistakes in the mass movement to spread rumours and gossip, and engage in agitation, deliberately branding some of the masses as "counter-revolutionaries". It is necessary to beware of such "pick-pockets" and expose their tricks in good time.

In the course of the movement, with the exception of cases of active counter-revolutionaries where there is clear evidence of crimes such as murder, arson, poisoning, sabotage or theft of state secrets, which should be handled in accordance with the law, no measures should be taken against students at universities, colleges, middle schools and primary schools because of problems that arise in the movement. To prevent the struggle from being diverted from its main target, it is not allowed, under whatever pretext, to incite the masses or the students to struggle against each other. Even proven Rightists should be dealt with on the merits of each case at a later stage of the movement.

8. THE QUESTION OF CADRES

The cadres fall roughly into the following four categories:
(1) good;
(2) comparatively good;
(3) those who have made serious mistakes but have not become anti-Party, anti-socialist Rightists;
(4) the small number of anti-Party, anti-socialist Rightists.

In ordinary situations, the first two categories (good and comparatively good) are the great majority.

The anti-Party, anti-socialist Rightists must be fully exposed, refuted, overthrown and completely discredited and their influence eliminated. At the same time, they should be given a chance to turn over a new leaf.

9. CULTURAL REVOLUTIONARY GROUPS, COMMITTEES AND CONGRESSES

Many new things have begun to emerge in the great proletarian cultural revolution. The cultural revolutionary groups, committees and other organizational forms created by the masses in many schools and units are something new and of great historic importance.

These cultural revolutionary groups, committees and congresses are excellent new forms of organization whereby the masses educate themselves under the leadership of the Communist Party. They are an excellent bridge to keep our Party in close contact with the masses. They are organs of power of the proletarian cultural revolution.

The struggle of the proletariat against the old ideas, culture, customs and habits left over by all the exploiting classes over thousands of years will necessarily take a very, very long time. Therefore, the cultural revolutionary groups, committees and congresses should not be temporary organizations but permanent, standing mass organizations. They are suitable not only for colleges, schools and government and other organizations, but generally also for factories, mines, other enterprises, urban districts and villages.

It is necessary to institute a system of general elections, like that of the Paris Commune, for electing members to the cultural revolutionary groups and committees and delegates to the cultural revolutionary congresses. The lists of candidates should be put forward by the revolutionary masses after full discussion, and the elections should be held after the masses have discussed the lists over and over again.

The masses are entitled at any time to criticize members of the cultural revolutionary groups and committees and delegates elected to the cultural revolutionary congresses. If these members or delegates prove. incompetent, they can be replaced through election or recalled by the masses after discussion.

The cultural revolutionary groups, committees and congresses in colleges and schools should consist mainly of representatives of the revolutionary students. At the same time, they should have a certain number of representatives of the revolutionary teaching and administrative staff and workers.

10. EDUCATIONAL REFORM

In the great proletarian cultural revolution a most important task is to transform the old educational system and the old principles and methods of teaching.

In this great cultural revolution, the phenomenon of our schools being dominated by bourgeois intellectuals must be completely changed.

In every kind of school we must apply thoroughly the policy advanced by Comrade Mao Tse-tung of education serving proletarian politics and education being combined with productive labour, so as to enable those receiving an education to develop morally, intellectually and physically and to become labourers with socialist consciousness and culture.

The period of schooling should be shortened. Courses should be fewer and better. The teaching material should be thoroughly transformed, in some cases beginning with simplifying complicated material. While their main task is to study, students should also learn other things. That is to say, in addition to their studies they should also learn industrial work, farming and military affairs, and take part in the struggles of the cultural revolution to criticize the bourgeoisie as these struggles occur.

11. THE QUESTION OF CRITICIZING BY NAME IN THE PRESS

In the course of the mass movement of the cultural revolution, the criticism of bourgeois and feudal ideology should be well combined with the dissemination of the proletarian world outlook and of Marxism-Leninism, Mao Tse-tung's thought.

Criticism should be organized of typical bourgeois representatives who have wormed their way into the Party and typical reactionary bourgeois academic "authorities", and this should include criticism of various kinds of reactionary views in philosophy, history, political economy and education, in works and theories of literature and art, in theories of natural science, and in other fields.

Criticism of anyone by name in the press should be decided after discussion by the Party committee at the same level, and in some cases submitted to the Party committee at a higher level for approval.

12. Policy Towards Scientists, Technicians and Ordinary Members of Working Staffs

As regards scientists, technicians and ordinary members of working staffs, as long as they are patriotic, work energetically, are not against the Party and socialism, and maintain no illicit relations with any foreign country, we should in the present movement continue to apply the policy of "unity, criticism, unity". Special care should be taken of those scientists and scientific and technical personnel who have made contributions. Efforts should be made to help them gradually transform their world outlook and their style of work.

13. The Question of Arrangements for Integration with the Socialist Education Movement in City and Countryside

The cultural and educational units and leading organs of the Party and government in the large and medium cities are the points of concentration of the present proletarian cultural revolution.

The great cultural revolution has enriched the socialist education movement in both city and countryside and raised it to a higher level. Efforts should be made to conduct these two movements in close combination. Arrangements to this effect may be made by various regions and departments in the light of the specific conditions.

The socialist education movement now going on in the countryside and in enterprises in the cities should not be upset where the original arrangements are appropriate and the movement is going well, but should continue in accordance with the original arrangements. However, the questions that are arising in the present great proletarian cultural revolution should be put to the masses for discussion at the proper time, so as to further foster vigorously proletarian ideology and eradicate bourgeois ideology.

In some places, the great proletarian cultural revolution is being used as the focus in order to add momentum to the socialist education movement and clean things up in the fields of politics, ideology, organization and economy. This may be done where the local Party committee thinks it appropriate.

14. TAKE FIRM HOLD OF THE REVOLUTION AND STIMULATE PRODUCTION

The aim of the great proletarian cultural revolution is to revolutionize people's ideology and as a consequence to achieve greater, faster, better and more economical results in all fields of work. If the masses are fully aroused and proper arrangements are made, it is possible to carry on both the cultural revolution and production without one hampering the other, while guaranteeing high quality in all our work.

The great proletarian cultural revolution is a powerful motive force for the development of the social productive forces in our country. Any idea of counterposing the great cultural revolution to the development of production is incorrect.

15. THE ARMED FORCES

In the armed forces, the cultural revolution and the socialist education movement should be carried out in accordance with the instructions of the Military Commission of the Central Committee of the Party and the General Political Department of the People's Liberation Army.

16. MAO TSE-TUNG'S THOUGHT IS THE GUIDE TO ACTION IN THE GREAT PROLETARIAN CULTURAL REVOLUTION

In the great proletarian cultural revolution, it is imperative to hold aloft the great red banner of Mao Tse-tung's thought and put proletarian politics in command. The movement for the creative study and application of Chairman Mao Tse-tung's works should be carried forward among the masses of the workers, peasants and soldiers, the cadres and the intellectuals, and Mao Tse-tung's thought should be taken as the guide to action in the cultural revolution.

In this complex great cultural revolution, Party committees at all levels must study and apply Chairman Mao's works all the more conscientiously and in a creative way. In particular, they must study over and over again Chairman Mao's writings on the cultural revolution and on the Party's methods of leadership, such as *On New Democracy, Talks at the Yenan Forum on Literature and Art, On the Correct Handling of Contradictions Among the People, Speech at the Chinese Communist Party's National Conference on Propaganda Work, Some Questions Concerning Methods of Leadership* and *Methods of Work of Party Committees*.

Party committees at all levels must abide by the directions given by Chairman Mao over the years, namely that they should thoroughly apply the mass line of "from the masses, to the masses" and that they should be pupils before they become teachers. They should try to avoid being one-sided or narrow. They should foster materialist dialectics and oppose metaphysics and scholasticism.

The great proletarian cultural revolution is bound to achieve brilliant victory under the leadership of the Central Committee of the Party headed by Comrade Mao Tse-tung.

30. Hung Ping: The Traitor's Philosophy of China's Khrushchev (April, 1967)*

The current Cultural Revolution in China can be considered as a desperate attempt on the part of Mao to bring about an "ideological rejuvenation" in Communist China. Soon after the beginning of the movement a number of high Party officials fell from power, such as P'eng Chen, member of the Politburo and Mayor of Peking; Lo Jui-ch'ing, the Army's Chief of Staff; Lu Ting-yi, Party propa-

---

* From *Guangming Ribao*, April 7, 1967. (Extract.)

ganda director; P'eng Teh-huai, China's one-time Defense Minister who was replaced by Lin Piao in 1959. These are all Mao's close comrades for thirty, forty years and more. In fact, of a total of 172 full and alternate members of the powerful Party Central Committee, some 106 were either purged or fell into disgrace.[1]

The greatest tragedy during the Cultural Revolution was the humiliating attack by the Red Guards upon China's chief of state, Liu Shao-chi. Liu, as we have seen from his early works, was Communist China's leading party theoretician and Mao's closest comrade-in-arm's for some forty years. His works, such as "How to Be a Good Communist" (Selection 11), "On the Intra-Party Struggle" (Selection 13) and "On the Party" (Selection 17), were required reading for millions in China before the present purge. He was once considered with certainty the political heir of Mao Tse-tung.

"The Traitor's Philosophy of China's Khrushchev" is one of the prime examples of the works of Red Guards to discredit Mao's opposition, in this case, Liu Shao-chi. Calling Liu the "Khrushchev of China" would be delivering the ultimate insult, by Chinese standards.

In sharp and intense class struggles, real Marxist-Leninists and proletarian revolutionary fighters must show their proletarian revolutionary integrity. In all circumstances, they must draw a clear-cut line of distinction between the enemy and themselves and be determined with fearless heroism to overwhelm the enemy and never yield.

Chairman Mao teaches us: "No matter what the difficulties and hardships, so long as a single man remains, he will fight on." He also says: "Wherever there is struggle there is sacrifice, and death is a common occurrence. But we have the interests of the people and the sufferings of the great majority at heart, and when we die for the people it is a worthy death."

Proletarian revolutionaries are wholeheartedly devoted to the public interest; devoid of selfish aims, they work solely for the interests of the proletariat and the people; that is why they are unyielding and undaunted in the face of the enemy. To defend the revolutionary principles of Marxism-Leninism, Mao Tse-tung's thought, and the proletarian, revolutionary

---

[1] Staff report, *Studies on Chinese Communism*, September 30, 1967, p. 20.

interests of socialism and communism, they stand ready to give up their all, even their lives.

China's Khrushchev, however, has consistently peddled the reactionary bourgeois philosophy of survival, the philosophy of traitors. In his book on "self-cultivation" of Communists, he argues that a Communist "has the greatest self-respect and self-esteem. For the sake of the Party and the revolution he can be most forbearing and tolerant towards comrades and can suffer wrong in the general interest, . . . He knows how to take good care of himself in the interests of the Party and the revolution and how to strengthen both his grasp of theory and his practical effectiveness." As for the Party organization, he says, "As far as possible, the Party will attend to and safeguard its members' essential interests; . . . and, when necessary, it will even give up some of its work in order to preserve comrades."

As used in the reactionary, preposterous theory of this Khrushchev of China, the phrase "in the interests of the Party and the revolution" is just a subterfuge to deceive people. In reality what he advocates is putting oneself, one's personal interests and one's own life in the first place. He sings the very same tune as Khrushchev and Co. who preach that survival is everything, and assert that "everyone wants to live," "everyone wants to live better" and that the policy of the Communist Party "is a policy of the highest humanity."

Steeped to the very depths of his being in the idea of putting survival ahead of everything, this No. 1 Party person in authority taking the capitalist road gave currency to a policy of making "false confessions" and euphemistically termed it a method of "preserving strength" and "striving for legal existence." This is purely and simply a shameless traitor's philosophy. It is precisely the theory of survival advocated by Khrushchev and Co., the theory that principles are irrelevant when one's head has been chopped off.

In defending this philosophy, the top Party person in authority taking the capitalist road says that he is only speaking about "false confessions" while his real purpose is to "preserve strength"; when he says "taking good care of oneself," he means he is taking into consideration "the interests of the Party and the revolution." He thinks that making such confessions is only a "shortcoming," and that in evaluating a man with this "shortcoming," people should take into account his contributions and merits and not simply write them off at one stroke. In line with this view, he thinks that those who betray the revolution and surrender to the enemy can become "revolutionary heroes." This is the traitor's sophistry which he used in his manoeuvres to recruit deserters and form cliques to pursue selfish interests, and engage in insidious activities to usurp the leadership of the Party and government and restore capitalism.

This traitor's philosophy is sophistry justifying self-confessions, betrayal of the revolution and surrender to the enemy; it is a reactionary, preposterous theory which obliterates the dividing line between the enemy and ourselves and protects traitors. We must rebel and make revolution against the No. 1 Party person in authority taking the capitalist road and the handful of counter-revolutionary revisionists under him—the publicists for this sophistry of traitors; we must resolutely overthrow them and pin them down so that they never rise again. In accordance with the longstanding teachings in our great, most respected and beloved leader Chairman Mao, proletarian revolutionaries must preserve their integrity on matters of principle, preserve it to the end of their days. They must value their proletarian revolutionary integrity more than their own lives. If a man, no matter who, ultimately commits such a monstrous evil as to betray the revolution, even if he has done nine and ninety good deeds, he is a traitor, and that crosses out everything else.

31. Chinese Editorial: Revolutionary Committees Are Fine (March, 1968)*

The Chinese Cultural Revolution became, in 1968, a movement against the entire Party apparatus. All of China's twenty-two provinces and autonomous regions are systematically being taken over by the newly organized "Revolutionary Committees."

The "Revolutionary Committees" are organized by the so-called representatives of "revolutionary cadres," "armed forces" and "revolutionary masses." However, the backbone

---

* From a joint editorial of *Renmin Ribao, Hongqi* and *Jiefangjun Bao,* March 30, 1968.

of the Committee is the Chinese Army. The increasing role
of the military in the internal affairs of China can be realized in Mao Tse-tung's March 7, 1967, directive:

> Comrades Lin Piao, Chou En-lai and the Comrades of the Cultural
> Revolution Group:
> This document could be distributed to the whole country to be acted
> upon accordingly. The army should give military and political train-
> ing in the universities, middle schools and the higher classes of pri-
> mary schools, stage by stage and group by group. It should help in re-
> opening school classes, strengthening organization, setting up the
> leading bodies on the principle of the "three-in-one" combination and
> carrying out the task of "struggle-criticism-transformation." It should
> first make experiments at selected points and acquire experience and
> then popularize it step by step. . . .
>
>   Mao Tse-tung

This special emphasis on the military's role is also evident
in this joint editorial by China's three most influential official newspapers.

The spring breeze of Mao Tse-tung's thought has reached
every corner of our motherland. The revolutionary committees which have come into being one after another stand like
red flags flying in the wind. To date, revolutionary committees have been established in 17 provinces and municipalities
and in one autonomous region. More are in the preparatory
stage in other areas. Vast numbers of units at the grassroot
levels have set up their own revolutionary committees. This
is a significant indication of the fact that the situation in the
great proletarian cultural revolution is excellent and is getting
even better. This is a magnificent act in the struggle for all-
round victory in this revolution.

When the new-born revolutionary committees appeared on
the eastern horizon a year ago, our revered and beloved
leader Chairman Mao, with his great proletarian revolutionary genius, pointed out with foresight: "In every place or
unit where power must be seized, it is necessary to carry out
the policy of the revolutionary 'three-in-one' combination in
establishing a provisional organ of power which is revolutionary and representative and enjoys proletarian authority. This
organ of power should preferably be called the Revolutionary
Committee."

Our great leader Chairman Mao again recently pointed
out: "The basic experience of revolutionary committees is this

—they are three-fold: they have representatives of revolutionary cadres, representatives of the armed forces and representatives of the revolutionary masses. This forms a revolutionary 'three-in-one' combination. The revolutionary committee should exercise unified leadership, do away with redundant or overlapping administrative structures, have 'better troops and simpler administration' and organize a revolutionized leading group which is linked with the masses." Chairman Mao's brilliant directive sums up the experience of revolutionary committees at all levels and gives the basic orientation for building revolutionary committees.

The "three-in-one" revolutionary committee is a creation of the working class and the masses in the current great cultural revolution. Chairman Mao teaches: "We must have faith in and rely on the masses, the People's Liberation Army and the majority of the cadres." The "three-in-one" revolutionary committee is the organ which organizationally knits closely together the three sides pointed out by Chairman Mao after having summed up the experience of the masses, so as more effectively to meet the needs of the socialist economic base and the needs of consolidating the dictatorship of the proletariat and preventing the restoration of capitalism.

The "three-in-one" revolutionary committee is a great creation of the hundreds of millions of the revolutionary masses that appeared in the course of their struggle to seize power from the handful of Party people in authority taking the capitalist road. It has shown enormous vitality in leading the proletariat and the revolutionary masses in the fight against the class enemy over the past year and more.

This "three-in-one" organ of power enables our proletarian political power to strike deep roots among the masses. Chairman Mao points out: "The most fundamental principle in the reform of state organs is that they must keep in contact with the masses." The representatives of the revolutionary masses, particularly the representatives of the working people—the workers and peasants—who have come forward en masse in the course of the great proletarian cultural revolution are revolutionary fighters with practical experience. Representing the interests of the revolutionary masses, they participate in the leading groups at various levels. This provides the revolutionary committees at these levels with a broad mass foundation. Direct participation by the revolutionary masses in the running of the country and the enforcement of revolutionary supervision from below over the organs of political power at various levels play a very important role in ensuring that our leading groups at all levels always adhere to the mass line, maintain the closest relations with the masses, represent their interests at all times and serve the people heart and soul.

This "three-in-one" organ of power strengthens the dictatorship of the proletariat. "If the army and the people are united as one, who in the world can match them?" The great Chinese People's Liberation Army is the main pillar of the dictatorship of the proletariat and a Great Wall of steel defending the socialist motherland. The revolutionary "three-in-one" combination carries our army-civilian unity to a completely new stage. In its work of helping the Left, helping industry and agriculture, exercising military control and giving military and political training, the People's Liberation Army has made big contributions over the past year and more and has been well steeled in the process. As a result of the direct participation of P.L.A. representatives in the work of the provisional organs of power at all levels, our dictatorship of the proletariat is better able to withstand storm and stress, better able to smash the intrigues by any enemy, whether domestic or foreign, and play a more powerful role in the cause of socialist revolution and socialist construction.

Revolutionary leading cadres are the backbone of the "three-in-one" organs of power. They have rich experience in class struggle and are a valuable asset to the Party and people. By going through the severe test of the great proletarian cultural revolution and receiving education and help from the masses, they were touched to the soul and remoulded their world outlook further. The combination of the revolutionary leading cadres and representatives of the P.L.A. and of the revolutionary masses in the revolutionary committees makes them better able to carry out Chairman Mao's proletarian revolutionary line, grasp and implement the Party's policies, and correctly organize and lead the masses forward. At the same time, veteran cadres and young new cadres work together in the revolutionary committees, learn from each other and help each other so that, as Chairman Mao teaches, the veterans are not divorced from the masses and the young people are tempered. Organizationally, this guarantees the work of training successors to the proletarian revolutionary cause.

This "three-in-one" organ of power has absolutely nothing in common with the over-staffed bureaucratic apparatus of the exploiting classes in the old days. It has an entirely new and revolutionary style of work of its own and it functions in a way which is beneficial to the people. The "three-in-one" revolutionary leading body brings together the P.L.A. "three-eight" working style (The Chinese People's Liberation Army, under the leadership of Chairman Mao, has fostered a fine tradition. This fine tradition is summed up by Chairman Mao in three phrases and eight additional characters, meaning firm, correct political orientation; a plain, hard-working style; flexibility in strategy and tactics; and unity, alertness, earnestness and liveliness.), the labouring people's hard-working spirit and our Party's fine tradition of maintaining close contact with the masses. "Remain one of the common people while serving as an official." Maintain "better troops and simpler administration," and drastically reform old methods of office and administrative work. Have a small leading body and a small staff, as certain revolutionary committees have begun doing, so that there is no overlapping or redundancy in the organization and no over-staffing, so that bureaucracy can be prevented. In this way, the style of hard work, plain living and economy is fostered, corrosion by bourgeois ideology is precluded; and the revolutionary committee becomes a compact and powerful fighting headquarters which puts proletarian politics to the fore and is full of revolutionary enthusiasm and capable of taking prompt and resolute action.

In order to become genuinely revolutionary headquarters with proletarian revolutionary authority, the revolutionary committees should hold fast to the general orientation for the struggle, consistently direct the spearhead of attack against China's Khrushchev and the handful of other top Party persons in authority taking the capitalist road and their agents, distinguish the contradictions between ourselves and the enemy from contradictions among the people, carry on revolutionary mass criticism and repudiation, continue to consolidate and develop the revolutionary great alliance and the revolutionary "three-in-one" combination and constantly sum up experience and draw lessons. It is precisely in the storm of class struggle that the revolutionary committees in many places are being consolidated.

Of all the good things characterizing the revolutionary

committees, the most fundamental is the creative study and application of the thought of Mao Tse-tung and the doing of this well. Revolutionary committee members are outstanding P.L.A. commanders and fighters, revolutionary leading cadres and representatives of the revolutionary masses who have been assessed and selected by the broad masses in the course of the struggle. The highest demand which they put upon themselves is to be loyal to Chairman Mao, to the thought of Mao Tse-tung and to Chairman Mao's proletarian revolutionary line. We hope that all the leading members of the revolutionary committees will continue to regard studying, carrying out, spreading and defending Chairman Mao's instructions as their most sacred duty. The revolutionary committees should see to it that Chairman Mao's instructions are transmitted most promptly and accurately so that the masses of workers, peasants and soldiers are imbued with the thought of Mao Tse-tung, and so that it is translated into the conscious action of the masses and becomes an inexhaustible source of strength in transforming the world.

The revolutionary committee is something new which has emerged in the course of the revolutionary mass movement and it is continuing to develop. It should be cherished and supported by all revolutionary comrades. As for the shortcomings and mistakes which are inevitable in the course of its growth, we should make well-intentioned criticism so as to help it keep on making progress and improving. It is necessary to be on guard against and expose plots by the class enemy to shake and subvert the revolutionary committees either from the Right or the extreme "Left." All personnel of the revolutionary committees should resolutely implement Chairman Mao's proletarian revolutionary line, carry out his latest instructions in an exemplary way, make strict demands on themselves, have a correct attitude to themselves and to the masses, conduct constant criticism and self-criticism and pay the closest attention to wiping out any vestige of being divorced from the masses.

The revolutionary "three-in-one" provisional organs of power which have sprung up all over the country will lead the proletariat and the revolutionary masses in establishing proletarian authority and in playing a vital revolutionary role in the momentous struggle to win all-round victory in the great proletarian cultural revolution.

32. Chinese Editorial: "Develop the Party's Working Style of Forging Close Links with the Masses" (July, 1968)*

On July 1, 1968, Peking published an important policy statement in commemoration of the 47th anniversary of the founding of the Communist Party of China. Unlike previous policy papers, this is in the form of a joint editorial by China's three leading newspapers: *Jenmin Jih Pao* (People's Daily), *Hongqi* (Red Flag), and *Jiefangjun Pao* (Liberation Army Daily). The reason for this highly irregular behavior is that the Party, after 47 years, no longer exists as a cohesive political body in China. The Cultural Revolution turned against the entire Party apparatus—as the Maoists put—"to rectify the Party organization and strengthen the Party building."†

This editorial seems uncertain about the accomplishments of the Cultural Revolution, stating in one section that "now, the great proletarian cultural revolution has won decisive victory" and in another that "the time is now not far off when all-round victory will be won in the great proletarian cultural revolution." This statement warns of further complicated and difficult struggles against anti-Maoists and calls for unity "in the fight against the enemy" on the part of the different revolutionary organizations.

Full of vigour, the great, glorious and correct Chinese Communist Party with Comrade Mao Tse-tung as its leader, ushers in the glorious day of its 47th anniversary during the great march towards all-round victory in the great proletarian cultural revolution.

Chairman Mao teaches us: "Armed with Marxist-Leninist theory and ideology, the Communist Party of China has

---

* From *Peking Review*, July 5, 1968, pp. 11–13.
† For a detailed study of the reorganization of Chinese Communist Party see Winberg Chai, "The Reorganization of the Chinese Communist Party (1966–68)," *Asian Survey*, November, 1968.

brought a new style of work to the Chinese people, a style of work which essentially entails integrating theory with practice, forging close links with the masses and practising self-criticism." Our Party's excellent style of work of forging close links with the masses, which Chairman Mao has fostered personally, has been greatly developed and has aroused the masses to the full and displayed unprecedentedly great revolutionary power in transforming the world in the course of the tempestuous mass movement of the great proletarian cultural revolution and in the fierce struggle against the counter-revolutionary revisionist line of China's Khrushchev.

Now, the great proletarian cultural revolution has won decisive victory. The bourgeois reactionary forces, which have China's Khrushchev and company as their representatives, have failed ignominiously in their scheme to restore capitalism in China. Mao Tse-tung's thought and Chairman Mao's proletarian revolutionary line are being grasped by the revolutionary masses. Revolutionary committees have been established at all levels in the overwhelming majority of areas of the country. The socialist motherland is thriving. The situation in the country is better than ever. However, the class struggle remains acute and complicated. The handful of class enemies who have been defeated and are at their last gasp will still put up a death-bed struggle. In these circumstances, the continued development of our Party's working style of forging close links with the masses is of extremely great significance for the consolidation and development of the victories of the great proletarian cultural revolution, for the consolidation and growth of the newly established revolutionary committees, for strengthening the dictatorship of the proletariat and for carrying the great proletarian cultural revolution through to the end.

Chairman Mao recently made this penetrating statement: "To protect the masses or to repress them—here is the basic distinction between the Communist Party and the Kuomintang, between the proletariat and the bourgeoisie, and between the dictatorship of the proletariat and the dictatorship of the bourgeoisie."

Since the great proletarian cultural revolution is a great political revolution carried out by the proletariat against the bourgeoisie and all other exploiting classes, it has to advance through repeated and extremely fierce class struggles. The struggle between the bourgeoisie which attempts to stage a come-back and the proletariat which opposes its come-back will be a very protracted one. The gradual consolidation and growth of the revolutionary committees will be a process of serious class struggle. At the same time, it will be a process of learning from the masses and of constantly summing up experience. We must soberly recognize this. At present, the enemy is using every means to sow dissension between the new-born revolutionary committees and the masses and to destroy the ties which have been forged between them. He is going all-out to stir up an evil Right deviationist wind to reverse correct decisions in a vain effort to blur the distinction between classes and turn the struggle away from its general orientation; or he is sugar-coating his bullets to deceive and corrupt our comrades and alienate certain members of revolutionary committees from the masses. Taking these characteristics into account, the revolutionary committees must at all times direct the spearhead of struggle against the handful of diehard capitalist roaders, renegades, enemy agents, and the landlords, rich peasants, counter-revolutionaries, bad elements and Rightists who have not reformed themselves. The revolutionary committees must take the initiative and lead the revolutionary masses in dealing steady, accurate and relentless blows at the enemy. And, at the same time, the revolutionary committees must, at all times and in all circumstances, firmly protect the masses. Reliance on the masses and the strengthening of the dictatorship of the proletariat are two aspects of the same question. Repudiation of Right opportunism, Right splittism and Right capitulationism, and taking stock of the class ranks have the same class content; both are aimed at protecting the masses and hitting at the small handful of class enemies. Revolutionary mass criticism and repudiation should be carried on vigorously in close combination with taking stock of the class ranks and with struggle-criticism-transformation in each unit. We must be good at seeing through and courageously exposing the attempts of the small handful of counter-revolutionaries to undermine and distort the strategic tasks put forward by the proletarian headquarters, and all the other dirty intrigues of the enemy. The revolutionary masses of various groupings must pay attention to building unity in the fight against the enemy and make a strict distinction between the two different types of contradictions in the complicated class struggle; they should be good both at dealing with contradictions among the people and at discerning contradictions between ourselves and the enemy.

Chairman Mao points out in his work *On the Correct Handling of Contradictions Among the People* that the first function of the dictatorship of the proletariat "is to suppress the reactionary classes and elements and those exploiters in our country who resist the socialist revolution, to suppress those who try to wreck our socialist construction, or in other words, to resolve the internal contradictions between ourselves and the enemy." Chairman Mao also says: "Who is to exercise this dictatorship? Naturally the working class and the people under its leadership. Dictatorship does not apply within the ranks of the people. The people cannot exercise dictatorship over themselves, nor must one section of the people oppress another." What great significance there is in this extremely penetrating Marxist analysis by Chairman Mao in guiding us at the present time in handling the contradictions between ourselves and the enemy and those among the people (for instance, contradictions between revolutionary organizations)!

Chairman Mao points out: "Having close ties with the masses is most fundamental in reforming state organs." The masses are the source of strength for the political power of the proletariat. Resolute reliance on the masses of the people and having close ties with them is the fundamental hallmark distinguishing the political party of the proletariat and the political power of the proletariat from all forms of political parties and political power of the bourgeoisie. The rich experience of revolutionary committees in many places has shown that the "three-in-one" revolutionary committee, born in the storm of the mass movement of the great proletarian cultural revolution and embracing representatives of the revolutionary masses, representatives of the armed forces and representatives of the revolutionary cadres, has a solid mass basis and inherently good conditions for linking itself with the masses. We must bring this advantage into full play and develop it, resolutely oppose the corrosion by bureaucracy, firmly reform old regulations and customs which divorce us from the masses, and constantly maintain the most extensive and close ties with the working people, so that the revolutionary committee is able to take deep root among the masses and become a vigorous, militant command post which is revolutionary and enjoys proletarian authority.

The members of the revolutionary committee are ordinary workers. They should go deep among the masses and not take special privileges. They should consult the masses extensively whenever there are problems and take an active part in socialist productive labour. Chairman Mao teaches us: "Take the ideas of the masses and concentrate them, then go to the masses, persevere in the ideas and carry them through, so as to form correct ideas of leadership—such is the basic method of leadership." Both the veteran revolutionary cadres and the new cadres who emerge in the mass movement of the great cultural revolution, must carry out this instruction of Chairman Mao's and always maintain flesh-and-blood ties with the masses. Their posts may change but they must not alter their working style of linking themselves with the masses.

The members of the revolutionary committee, no matter where they come from, should serve as representatives of the revolutionary masses and act in accordance with Mao Tse-tung's thought and proletarian Party spirit. They must not just represent certain small "mountain-strongholds" and fail to represent the vast revolutionary masses; they must not just unite a minority and ignore the overwhelming majority of people. Individualism, the "mountain-stronghold" mentality, "small group" mentality, sectarianism and anarchism are not proletarian ideology but bourgeois. Within the revolutionary committee, we must constantly use Mao Tse-tung's thought, that is, the world outlook of the proletariat, to criticize and repudiate all the influences of bourgeois ideology. Only in this way can the revolutionary great alliance and revolutionary committee be continuously consolidated.

The revolutionary masses should cherish the new-born revolutionary committees. The revolutionary committees should take the initiative in accepting criticism and supervision by the revolutionary masses. Wherever the masses constantly and enthusiastically and with an attitude of cherishing the committees, are able to offer criticism and make suggestions for improving the work, this will be an indication that there are a good democratic atmosphere, vigour in work and close links between the revolutionary committees and the masses. Chairman Mao points out: "The Communist Party does not fear criticism because we are Marxists, the truth is on our side, and the basic masses, the workers and peasants, are on our side." As for the plots of the handful of enemies who, under the pretence of "criticism," stir up trouble and make vicious attacks in an attempt to shake the revolutionary committees, they must resolutely be exposed and dealt blows.

"The people, and the people alone, are the motive force in the making of world history." When we read this brilliant axiom of Chairman Mao, we feel how profound it is. The rich experience of the great proletarian cultural revolution has taught us that to carry out a thoroughgoing revolution against the bourgeoisie and all other exploiting classes, we must have the great guidance of Mao Tse-tung's thought, must arouse the broad masses of revolutionary people and rely on them, must rely on the People's Liberation Army and on the great majority of the cadres. China's Khrushchev and company, the handful of agents in our Party—agents of the remnants of the Kuomintang and the landlords, rich peasants, counter-revolutionaries, bad elements and Rightists, for a long time pushed an all-embracing counter-revolutionary, revisionist line and adopted the working style of the Kuomintang. In doing so, they were trying to divorce the Party and proletarian political power from the masses so as to achieve their criminal aim of concealing their reactionary features and restoring capitalism. The great proletarian cultural revolution initiated and being led by Chairman Mao has gone further in fundamentally solving the question of the links between the Party and political power and the masses, thus guaranteeing that our country will never change its political colour.

Mao Tse-tung's thought and Chairman Mao's revolutionary line represent the basic interests of the masses and embody the will and demands of the proletariat and the masses in the most concentrated way. The basic task of the revolutionary committee is this—to persist in the creative study and application of Mao Tse-tung's thought, unswervingly carry out Chairman Mao's revolutionary line, and ensure that the fighting tasks, principles and policies of the proletarian headquarters with Chairman Mao as the leader and Vice-Chairman Lin Piao as the deputy leader are grasped by the masses promptly, accurately and comprehensively and turned into their conscious action. Only in the process of striving to fulfil this task can the revolutionary committee have close ties with the masses and be one with them. In order to carry out this task on a still wider scale and in a penetrating way, further big efforts must be made to run Mao Tse-tung's thought study classes of all types well; with the development of the revolutionary mass movement, new content must be added and the political consciousness of the revolutionary masses must be raised continuously so that Mao Tse-tung's thought study classes are turned into a tremendous force promoting the success of work of all kinds.

At historic turning points in winning great victories, such as on the eve of the victory of the War of Resistance Against Japan and at the approach of nationwide victory in the Liberation War, when Chairman Mao put forward the revolutionary tasks, line, principles and policies, he always warned the whole Party and called on it to pay great attention to the question of working style and to look upon the maintenance and development of the Party's traditional style of work as an important guarantee for uniting the whole Party and the revolutionary masses, overcoming difficulties, defeating the enemy and consolidating victory and carrying it forward.

The time is now not far off when all-round victory will be won in the great proletarian cultural revolution, yet it will take a very long time and require tremendous efforts to consolidate and develop this victory. As long as we rely on the people, believe firmly in the inexhaustible creative power of the masses and hence trust and identify ourselves with them, we can overcome every difficulty, and no enemy can crush us while we can crush any enemy.

The great proletarian cultural revolution is a great movement in which the revolutionary masses in their hundreds of millions are mobilized to rectify Party organizations. Under the guidance of Chairman Mao's proletarian line on Party building, the whole Party and the people throughout the country have undertaken revolutionary mass criticism and repudiation on an unprecedented scale against China's Khrushchev's counter-revolutionary revisionist line on Party building. Cleansed, tempered and tested by the storm of this mass movement, our Party has greatly strengthened its ties with the masses and it is becoming purer, stronger and more vigorous. In the great proletarian cultural revolution, we Party members in our vast numbers must be able to stand up to every harsh test of the class struggle, make further efforts to use Mao Tse-tung's thought to remould our world outlook and strive truly to be vanguards of the proletariat. Assuredly we will be able to fulfil the great historic mission of continuing to make revolution under the dictatorship of the proletariat and make still greater contributions to the communist movement.

Long live the great, glorious and correct Communist Party of China!

Long live the invincible thought of Mao Tse-tung!

Long live our great leader Chairman Mao!

Who's Who in Communist China Today

Mao's search for a reintegrated political community has suffered a serious setback because of the opposition he created within the Party organizations. It has been estimated that he could not count more than 30 percent support from the membership of the ruling Central Committee (52 out of 172 full and alternate members in 1967). The extent of opposition to Mao can also be seen from the purges of Party officials during the current Cultural Revolution (1966–1968). The publication of a list of 127 prominent Party officials and intellectuals as "Monsters and Demons" or "Black Gangsters" in November, 1966, reveals the vindictiveness of the purge. During 1967, an additional 326 high Party officials were removed from office. The latest publication by Peking lists a group of 26 prominent Party officials who stood on the Tien An Men rostrum on May 1, 1968, with Mao Tse-tung and are probably Mao's most loyal supporters in China and thus perhaps the most influential officials.

Mao Tse-tung: Party Chairman; Chairman, Military Affairs Commission; Communist Party's "great teacher, great leader, great supreme commander and great helmsman." Born December 26, 1893, in Hsiangtan, Hunan.

Lin Piao: Vice-Chairman of the Party; Vice-Chairman, Military Affairs Commission; Defense Minister. Born in 1907 in Huangkang, Hupei.

Chou En-lai: Premier of State Council. Born in 1899 in Shaohsing, Chekiang.

Chen Po-ta: Chairman, Central Cultural Revolutionary Committee; a leading Party theoretician, editor-in-chief of *Red Flag* as well as personal secretary to Mao. Born in 1904 in Huian, Fukien.

Kang Sheng: Vice-Chairman, Standing Committee of National People's Congress; also head of secret police. Born in 1903 in Chu-cheng, Shantung.

Chu Teh: Chairman, Standing Committee of National People's Congress; a senior statesman within the CCP. Born in 1886 in Ma-an village, Szechuan.

Li Fu-chun: Vice-Premier, State Council; Chairman of National Planning Commission. Born 1900 in Changsha, Hunan.

Chen Yun: Vice-Premier, State Council; Minister of Commerce. Born 1905 in Chingpu, Kiangsu.

Chiang Ching: Mao's wife and Vice-Chairman, Central Cultural Revolutionary Committee. A former actress, she has always worked with the Ministry of Culture. Born in 1913 in Chiu-cheng, Shantung.

Chang Chun-chiao: Vice-Chairman, Central Cultural Revolutionary Committee. He has been secretary of the East China Bureau of the CCP Central Committee and concurrently secretary of the CCP Shanghai Municipal Committee. Personal data unknown.

Yao Wen-yuan: Member of the Central Cultural Revolutionary Committee. He has been director of the propaganda department of the CCP Shanghai Municipal Committee and chief editor of *Chieh-fang Jih-pao* of Shanghai. It was Yao Wen-yuan's early articles in 1965–1966 that sounded the trumpet calls for the Cultural Revolution. Personal data unknown.

Tung Pi-wu: Vice-Chairman of People's Republic of China who has replaced Liu Shao-chi in state functions during the Cultural Revolution. He was President of the Supreme People's Court (1954–1959). Born in 1886 in Huangan, Hupei.

Chen Yi: Vice-Premier, State Council; Minister of Foreign Affairs. He is also a powerful member of the Military Affairs Commission. Born in 1901 in Loshan, Szechuan.

Liu Po-cheng: Vice-Chairman, Standing Committee of National People's Congress; member of the Military Affairs Commission. Born in 1892 in Szechuan.

Li Hsien-nien: Director of Finance and Trade Office, State Council; China's leading economic expert. Born in 1900 in Changsha, Hunan.

Hsu Hsiang-chien: Vice-President, National Defense Council; member, Military Affairs Commission. Born in 1902 in Wutai, Shensi.

Nieh Jung-chen: Vice-Premier, State Council; Vice-Chairman, National Defense Council; member of the Military Affairs Commission. Born in 1899, Chiangchien, Szechuan.

Yeh Chien-ying: Vice-Chairman, National Defense Council; Political Commissar, Institute of Military Sciences; member, Military Affairs Commission. Born in 1897, Mei-hsien, Kwangtung.

Li Hsueh-feng: Vice-Chairman, Standing Committee of the National People's Congress; First Secretary of North China Bureau of CCP Central Committee. Born in 1907 in Yungchi, Shansi.

Hsieh Fu-chih: Chairman, Peking Revolutionary Committee; Vice-Premier of State Council; Political Commissar, Public Security Forces. Born in 1898 in Hunan.

Huang Yung-shen: Recently appointed chief of staff of China's armed forces; formerly commander of Canton garrison force. Was born in 1906 in Yungfeng, Kiangsi.

Wu Fa-hsien: Commander of Chinese Air Force. Personal data unknown.

Yeh Chun: Wife of Lin Piao and member of the Cultural Revolution Central Committee of the People's Liberation Army.

Li Tso-peng: Commander, Chinese Navy. Personal data unknown.

Chiu Hui-tso: Director, General Rear Service Department of People's Liberation Army. Personal data unknown.

Liu Hsien-chuan: Vice-Minister of Foreign Affairs. Personal data unknown.

Wang Tung-hsing: Vice-Minister of Public Security. Personal data unknown.

Resource Information Guide on Communist China

Today it is possible to study Chinese Communism without knowing the Chinese language or going to China. Major centers of Chinese studies, established in numerous American universities, have published important studies on Communist China. These centers include the Hoover Institution at Stanford University, Harvard University, Columbia University, University of Washington (Seattle), University of California (Berkeley), University of Southern California (Los Angeles), University of Michigan (Ann Arbor) and the East West Center at the University of Hawaii.

In addition, a number of scholarly magazines which have been published in recent years supply useful information on Communist China. They include *Asian Survey*, (2234 Piedmont Ave., Berkeley, California 94720); *China Quarterly* (Contemporary China Institute, 36 Howland Street, London, W. 1, England); *Issues and Studies* (Institute of International Relations, P.O. Box 1189, Taipei, Taiwan, China); and *Far Eastern Economic Review* (Hong Kong).

The U.S. government is also a main source of information on Communist China. The U.S. Consulate-General, Hong Kong, publishes *Current Background: Extracts from China Mainland Press* (weekly) and *Survey of China Mainland Press* (daily). The U.S. Information Agency publishes *Problems of Communism* (monthly) and the U.S. Department of Commerce sponsors the U.S. Joint Publications Research Service which publishes research translations from Communist China and other areas. Unclassified materials can also be obtained from the Research and Reference Service of the U.S. Department of State and U.S.I.A. The U.S. government also publishes the foreign broadcasting translations which can be obtained at major university libraries.

Hundreds of books have been published since 1960 on Communist China, and the single most comprehensive bibliography is issued by the Association for Asian Studies, Ann Arbor, Michigan in September each year entitled: *Bibliography of Asian Studies.*

Last but not least, the Peking Foreign Language Press also publishes an abundance of materials, always representing their own point of view. They are available for American readers through China Books and Periodicals, (2929–24th Street, San Francisco, California, 94110) under a license issued by the Department of Justice, Washington, D.C.

Appendix: The New Constitution of the Communist Party of China, October 31, 1968

The "enlarged" 12th Plenary Session of the 8th Central Committee of CCP met in October, 1968. In addition to expelling President Liu Shao-chi from the Party and calling for a meeting of the 9th Party Congress in 1969, the Committee adopted a new draft Constitution to replace the 1956 Constitution. It is to be ratified by the 9th Party Congress.

The new Constitution consists of only 2,700 words as compared with 15,000 words in the 1956 Constitution. In addition, there are several substantive changes:

1. "The Thought of Mao Tse-tung" is now added as part of the official Party ideology; Lin Piao is named as "the closest comrade-in-arms and successor of Comrade Mao Tse-tung;" both the U.S. and the U.S.S.R. are called "imperialists" and thus the enemies of China.

2. Only "workers, poor peasants, lower-middle peasants, revolutionary soldiers and other revolutionaries" may be admitted to Party membership.

3. Party members may report "directly" to the Party chairman "without formal procedure;" the various "front" organizations and youth groups are "all subject to the Party's leadership."

4. Party organization is essentially the same except the Central Control Commission is abolished; the new Constitution allows more flexibility of the central leadership; there is no mention of Party organizations in provinces and autonomous regions.

5. Stress is placed on "close association with the masses" rather than "cementing the ties of the workers, peasants, intellectuals and other patriotic people" (See Article 50, 1956 Constitution).

Index